# Epitaph for an Era

Wala, abbot of Corbie, played a major role in the rebellions against Emperor Louis the Pious, especially in 830, for which he was exiled. Radbert defended his beloved abbot, known to his monks as Arsenius, against accusations of infidelity in an 'epitaph' (funeral oration), composed as a two-book conversation between himself and other monks of Corbie. Whereas the restrained first book of Radbert's *Epitaphium Arsenii* was written not long after Wala's death in 836, the polemical second book was added some twenty years later. This outspoken sequel covers the events of the early 830s, but it mostly addresses the political issues of the 850s, as well as Radbert's own contemporary predicament. In *Epitaph for an Era*, an absorbing study of this fascinating text, Mayke de Jong examines the context of the *Epitaphium*'s two books, the use of hindsight as a rhetorical strategy, and the articulation of notions of the public good in the mid-ninth century.

Mayke de Jong taught Medieval History at the Universities of Nijmegen and Utrecht from 1987 until her retirement in 2016. She has been a Fellow of the Netherlands Institute for Advanced Study, Visiting Fellow Commoner at Trinity College, Cambridge, and a Member of the Princeton Institute for Advanced Study. Since 1999, she has been a Corresponding Fellow of the Royal Historical Society. Publishing widely on the interface between religion and politics in the early Middle Ages, her works include *In Samuel's Image* (1995), *Topographies of Power,* edited with Frans Theuws and Carine van Rhijn (2001), and *The Penitential State* (2009), also published by Cambridge University Press.

# Epitaph for an Era

*Politics and Rhetoric in the Carolingian World*

Mayke de Jong

*Utrecht University, The Netherlands*

CAMBRIDGE
UNIVERSITY PRESS

CAMBRIDGE
UNIVERSITY PRESS

University Printing House, Cambridge CB2 8BS, United Kingdom

One Liberty Plaza, 20th Floor, New York, NY 10006, USA

477 Williamstown Road, Port Melbourne, VIC 3207, Australia

314-321, 3rd Floor, Plot 3, Splendor Forum, Jasola District Centre, New Delhi - 110025, India

79 Anson Road, #06-04/06, Singapore 079906

Cambridge University Press is part of the University of Cambridge.

It furthers the University's mission by disseminating knowledge in the pursuit of education, learning and research at the highest international levels of excellence.

www.cambridge.org
Information on this title: www.cambridge.org/9781108813884
DOI: 10.1017/9781139013710

© Mayke de Jong 2019

First published 2019
First paperback edition 2020

*A catalogue record for this publication is available from the British Library*

ISBN 978-1-107-01431-2 Hardback
ISBN 978-1-108-81388-4 Paperback

Cambridge University Press has no responsibility for the persistence or accuracy of URLs for external or third-party internet websites referred to in this publication, and does not guarantee that any content on such websites is, or will remain, accurate or appropriate.

To the participants of 'Texts and Identities in the Early Middle Ages'

1997–2017

# Contents

# Maps and Tables

## Maps

## Tables

# Preface and Acknowledgements

This book grew out of a translation. Once my *The Penitential State* had appeared in 2009, I realised that I had barely scratched the surface of the most intriguing of the ninth-century narratives discussed there: Paschasius Radbertus' *Epitaphium Arsenii*. There was a widely used English translation, published in 1967 by Allen Cabaniss, who had clearly struggled with Radbert's idiosyncratic Latin. Could I do any better? It was a challenge, but one that would allow me to engage with one particular text, its author and its context, as I had done, with gusto, at the beginning of my career. Once I began to work on the *Epitaphium Arsenii*, I was hooked. In the years thereafter, my addiction yielded a series of exploratory articles and, finally, this monograph entitled *Epitaph for an Era*. The translation itself, now in its final phase, has become a joint venture with Justin Lake, and will appear in the Manchester Medieval Sources series. It is a real bonus to work with Justin, who is a Latinist by training and an experienced translator.

Since I committed myself to these projects, I had some much-needed extra research time. In 2012, I spent an intensive semester of reading and writing at the Princeton Institute for Advanced Study. It was an honour and pleasure to be there, under Patrick Geary's stimulating guidance, and with a small but lively band of congenial medievalists. In 2015, I received an Alexander von Humboldt Research Award, which enabled me to live in Berlin for half a year, as part of Stefan Esders' inspiring group of late antique and early medieval historians at the Freie Universität. I am grateful to the institutions and individuals that made these two sabbaticals possible, and my gratitude certainly includes my colleagues in Utrecht.

When, in May 2016, I retired from the Utrecht Chair of Medieval History, 'the book' was not yet finished, yet my CUP editor, Liz Friend-Smith, remained a model of patience and encouragement. The final spurt to the finish started only in January 2017, when I was able to retire fully to my own study at home. I cherish the solitude of this 'room of my own', but also the continued dynamics of collaborating with close colleagues, who in many cases have long been firm friends. Our

generation of early medievalists has managed (and still manages) to mix
the business of research and its management with the pleasure of each
other's company, and this is a real privilege. I am indebted to many of
them, but above all to Rosamond McKitterick. Without her constant
support and advice, writing *Epitaph for an Era* would have been a much
lonelier affair, and it certainly would have taken me much longer.
Rosamond read and commented on all of this book, from my very first
drafts of tentative chapters in 2012 to its final version in 2018, improving
its contents, structure and style. She was a sparring partner in the true
sense of the word, who gave me quick and effective feedback whenever I
needed it. This has been a real act of friendship, and one I hope to be able
to reciprocate.

Once this book began to take a more definitive shape, benevolent
readers gave me welcome feedback on individual chapters: David Ganz
commented on chapters 1–2, Charles West on chapter 3, Robin Whelan
and Justin Lake on chapters 4–5, and Jinty Nelson and Warren Pezé on
chapters 7–9. Invariably, their comments were helpful, yet it will come as
no surprise to anyone that Jinty's general approval of my third section on
Carolingian politics was a real boost for my morale. The same held true
for CUP's 'clearance reader' Tom Noble, who not only gave me the
clearance I needed, but also went over my entire manuscript with track
changes, and made me stick my neck out on one important point: audience. There were also other helpers to whom I am grateful. Gaëlle Calvet-
Marcadé and Frédéric Gross kindly sent me their unpublished doctoral
theses. In Berlin, in our shared office, Gerda Heydemann and I had many
conversations about 'our' Paschasius Radbertus, and then, throughout
both our book projects, there was the constant exchange of information
and ideas with my Utrecht sparring partner, Irene van Renswoude. Erik
Goosmann created my map of the Carolingian world.

It may sound as if *Epitaph for an Era* is the result of a collective effort,
and this is true, yet I remain responsible for the final result, and for any
errors. I dedicate this book to 'the participants of "Texts and Identities in
the Early Middle Ages", 1997–2017'. This enterprise, known among
insiders as 'T&I', began as a scheme to continue some of the fruitful
discussions in the ESF project on the Transformation of the Roman
World (1992–1997), especially about the ways in which texts helped to
shape different kinds of collective or individual identities. We wanted to
share what we had learned with a younger generation, and to create a
manageable forum which would give research students from different
academic cultures the chance to try out their ideas on a receptive audience. For two decades, five supervisors (Walter Pohl, Rosamond
McKitterick, Régine Le Jan, Ian Wood and myself) would meet in the

autumn or winter for a long weekend with about twenty to twenty-five budding scholars, who would then, in the summer, present a more developed version of their papers at the International Medieval Congress in Leeds. Over the years, all participants, be they junior, senior or anything in between, have greatly benefited from our discussions; these helped us write the books we really wanted to write. In my case, there would not have been any *Epitaph for an Era* without 'T&I'. Hence, I dedicate this book to all its participants, with a special star for the seniors, my fellow organisers and friends, who are almost all retired now, but still going strong.

# A Note on Annotation, Citation, Translation and Names

Throughout the footnotes, short titles have been used. The full titles are listed in the bibliography. The most frequently used titles, particularly of primary sources, have been abbreviated, and can be found in the list of abbreviations. The footnotes have been kept as succinct as possible, and I have emphasised more recent literature. The bibliography, however, also contains some scholarly works that have inspired me, even though these have not been cited explicitly.

Unless indicated otherwise, biblical citations come from Robert Weber's standard edition of the Vulgate, and translations of biblical texts from the Douay-Rheims Bible, in the version revised by Richard Challoner. I have gratefully made use of the translation of the *Epitaphium Arsenii* I am presently preparing together with Justin Lake, but this is still a work in progress, so eventually there may be some discrepancies with the final version of our translation, to be published by Manchester University Press.

In modern scholarship, Paschasius Radbertus is referred to either as 'Paschasius' (his monastic byname) or as 'Radbert(us)' (his birth name). I call him 'Radbert', in order to distinguish the author and historical figure from the persona he adopts in his *Epitaphium Arsenii*: that of the narrator 'Pascasius', as the name is spelled in the *Epitaphium*'s one manuscript. Throughout, I refer to this narrator and literary persona as Pascasius. In more general discussions of Radbert's monastic byname, I revert to the modern spelling, Paschasius.

# Abbreviations

| | |
|---|---|
| *AASS* | *Acta Sanctorum quotquot tot orbe coluntur,* ed. J. Bollandus et al. (Antwerp/Brussels, 1643–) |
| Ansegis | Ansegisus, *Collectio Capitularium* (ed. G. Schmitz), *Die Kapitulariensammlung des Ansegis*, MGH Capit. n.s. I (Hanover,1996). |
| *Annales q.d. Einhardi* | *Annales qui dicuntur Einhardi*, ed. F. Kurze, *MGH SRG* 6 (Hanover, 1895). |
| *ARF* | *Annales regni Francorum,* ed. F.Kurze, *MGH SRG* 6 (Hanover, 1895). |
| *ASOB* | *Acta Santorum Ordinis Sancti Benedicti,* ed. J. Mabillon, 9 vols., Paris 1668–1701. |
| Astronomer | Astronomus, *Vita Hludowici imperatoris,* ed. E. Tremp, *MGH SRG* 64 (Hanover, 1995). |
| Augustine, *DDC* | *Augustine of Hippo, De doctrina christiana,* ed. and transl. R.P.H. Green. *Oxford Early Christian Texts* (Oxford, 1995). |
| BAV | Biblioteca apostolica Vaticana, Rome |
| BHF | Bibliotheca hagiographica Latina antiquae et mediae aetatis |
| BnF | Bibliothèque nationale de France |
| CCCM | Corpus Christianorum, Continuatio Mediavalis |
| CCM | Corpus consuetudium monasticarum, ed. K. Hallinger (Siegburg, 1963–). |
| CCSL | Corpus Christianorum, Series Latina |
| CSEL | Corpus Scriptorum Ecclesiasticorum Latinorum |

| | |
|---|---|
| *DA* | *Deutsches Archiv für Erforschung des Mittelalters* |
| *EA* | Paschasius Radbertus, *Epitaphium Arsenii*, ed. E. Dümmler, in *Abhandlungen der Königlichen Akademie der Wissenschaften zu Berlin*, Phil.-Historische Abhandlungen 2 (Berlin,1900), 1–98. |
| *EME* | *Early Medieval Europe* |
| *FmSt* | *Frühmittelalterliche Studien* |
| *HZ* | *Historische Zeitschrift* |
| *In Matthaeum* | Paschasius Radbertus, *Expositio in Matheo libri XII*, ed. B. Paulus, 3 vols., CCCM 56-56A-56B (Turnhout, 1984). |
| LCL | Loeb Classical Library |
| Lewis & Short | Lewis, C.L. and C. Short, *A Latin Dictionary* (Oxford, 1975). |
| *Manuscrits datés* | *Catalogue des manuscrits en écriture latine portant des indications de date, de lieu ou de copiste,* publ. sous la direction de C. Samaran et R. Marichal, T. III: Bibliothèque nationale, fonds latin (Nos 8001 à 18613), sous la direction de M.-T. d'Alverny. Notices établies par M. Mabille, M.-C. Garand et D. Escudier. Paris, 1964. 2 vols. |
| *MGH* | *Monumenta Germaniae Historica* |
| *Auct. Ant.* | *Auctores antiquissimi* |
| *Capit.* | *Capitularia regum francorum* |
| *Conc.* | *Concilia Karolini Aevi* |
| *DD LdF* | *Die Urkunden Ludwig des Frommen*, 3 vols., ed. T. Kölzer et al., *MGH Diplomata Karolinorum II, 1–3* (Wiesbaden, 2016). |
| *DD Merov.* | *Die Urkunden der Merowinger*, 2 vols., ed. T. Kölzer, *MGH Diplomata regum Francorum e stirpe Merovingica* (Hanover, 2001). |
| *Epp.* | *Epistulae Karolini aevi* |
| *Epp. sel.* | *Epistulae selectae* |
| *Fontes* | *Fontes iuris germanici antiqui* |
| *Poet. lat.* | *Poetae Latini aevi Carolini* |
| *SRG* | *Scriptores rerum Germanicarum* |

| | |
|---|---|
| *SRL* | *Scriptores rerum Langobardicarum* |
| *SRM* | *Scriptores rerum Merovingicarum* |
| *SS* | *Scriptores* |
| *NCMH II* | *The New Cambridge Medieval History II c. 700–c. 900*, ed. R. McKitterick (Cambridge, 1995). |
| Niermeyer, *Lexicon Minus* | Niermeyer, J.F., with C. van de Kieft, *Mediae Latinitatis Lexikon Minus* (Leiden/New York/Cologne, 1993). |
| Nithard | Nithard, *Historiarum libri IV*, ed. and transl. P. Lauer, revised by S. Glansdorff, *Nithard: Histoire des fils de Louis le Pieux* (Paris, 2012). |
| Notker | Notker, *Gesta Karoli magni imperatoris*, ed. H.F. Haefele, *MGH SRG*, n.s. 12 (Berlin, 1959). |
| *PL* | *Patrologiae cursus completus, series latina*, ed. J.-P. Migne, 221 vols., Paris (1841–64). |
| *Regesta imperii* | J.F. Böhmer and E. Mühlbacher, *Regesta Imperii*, vol. 1: *Die Regesten des Kaiserreichs unter den Karolingern, 751–918*, 2nd ed. (Innsbruck, 1908); http://www.regesta-imperii.de. |
| *Relatio episcoporum* (833) | *Episcoporum de poenitentia, quam Hludowicus imperator professus est, relatio Compendiensis, MGH Capit.* II/2, 51–5. |
| Settimane | Settimane di studio del Centro italiano di studi sull'alto medioevo (Spoleto, 1954–). |
| SC | Sources Chrétiennes |
| Thegan | Thegan, *Gesta Hludowici imperatoris*, ed. E. Tremp, *MGH SRG* 64 (Hanover, 1995). |
| *VA* | Paschasius Radbertus, *Vita Adalhardi*, *PL* 120, cols. 1507–82. |

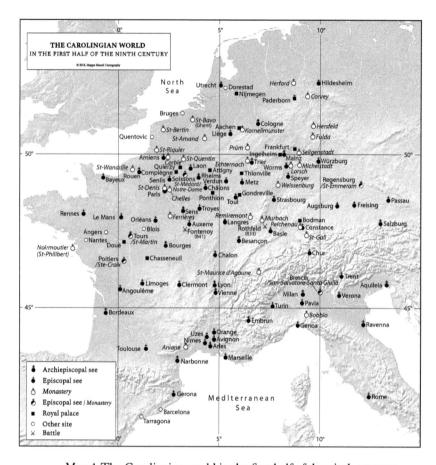

**THE CAROLINGIAN WORLD**
IN THE FIRST HALF OF THE NINTH CENTURY

© 2018, Mappa Mundi Cartography

North Sea

Utrecht · ○ Dorestad · Herford ○ · ● Hildesheim

■ Nijmegen · ○ Corvey

Paderborn ■

Bruges ○

○ St-Bavo (Ghent) · Aachen · ● Cologne · ○ Hersfeld

○ St-Bertin · Liège ○ · ○ Kornelimünster

Quentovic ○ · St-Amand ○ · ○ Fulda

○ St-Riquier · Prüm ○ · Frankfurt ○ · ○ Seligenstadt

Amiens ● · St-Quentin ○ · Ingelheim ■ · Mainz ○ · ● Würzburg

St-Wandrille ○ · Corbie ● · Echternach ○ · ● Trier · ○ Michelstadt

Quierzy ■ · Laon ● · Attigny ■ · Worms ● · Lorsch

Rouen ● · Compiègne ■ · Rheims ● · Thionville ■ · Speyer ● · Regensburg

Bayeux ● · Soissons ● · Verdun ● · Metz ● · Weissenburg ○ /St-Emmeram ○

Senlis ● · St-Médard/ · Châlons ● · Gondreville ■ · Strasbourg ●

St-Denis ○ · Notre-Dame ● · Ponthion ■ · Toul ● · Augsburg ● · Freising ● · Passau ●

Paris ○ · Chelles ○

Rennes ● · Le Mans ● · Sens ● · Troyes ● · Remiremont ○ · Murbach ○ · ■ Bodman

Orléans ● · Ferrières ○ · Langres ● · Reichenau ○ · Constance ○ · Salzburg ●

Angers ○ · Blois ○ · Auxerre ● · Fontenoy · Rothfeld × · Basle ● · St-Gall ○

Nantes ○ · Tours ○ · (841) · (833)

Noirmoutier ○ · Doué ■ · /St-Martin · Bourges ● · Besançon ●

(St-Philibert)

Poitiers ● · Chasseneuil ■ · Chalon ● · Chur ●

/Ste-Croix

Limoges ● · Clermont ● · Lyon ● · St-Maurice d'Agaune ○ · Brescia

Angoulême ● · Vienne ● · /San-Salvatore-Santo Giulia ○ · Trent ●

Milan ● · Verona ● · Aquileia ●

Bordeaux ● · Turin ● · Pavia ●

Embrun ● · ○ Bobbio · Ravenna ●

Genoa ●

Uzès ● · ○ Orange

Nîmes ● · Avignon ●

Toulouse ● · Aniane ○ · Arles ●

Narbonne ● · Marseille ●

Gerona ● · Mediterranean Sea · Rome ●

Barcelona ○

Tarragona ○

| | |
|---|---|
| ● | Archiepiscopal see |
| ● | Episcopal see |
| ○ | Monastery |
| ○ | Episcopal see / Monastery |
| ■ | Royal palace |
| ○ | Other site |
| × | Battle |

Map 1 The Carolingian world in the first half of the ninth century

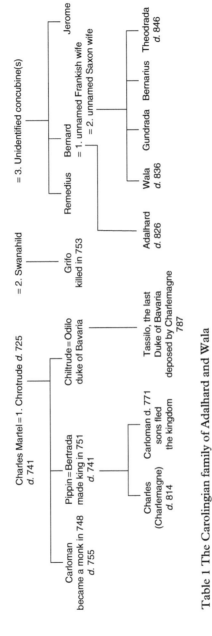

Table 1 The Carolingian family of Adalhard and Wala

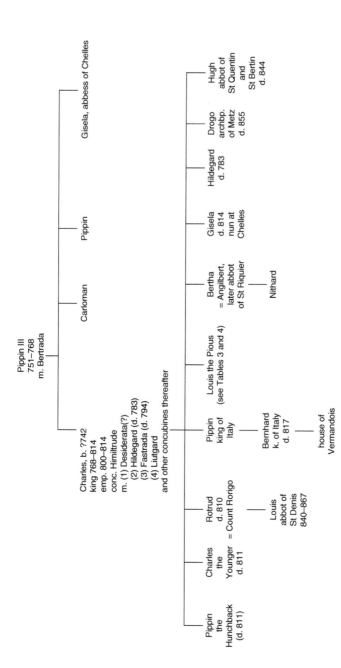

Table 2 Pippin and Charlemagne

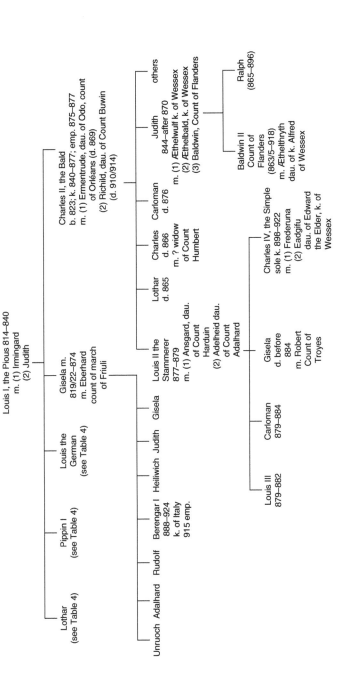

Table 3 The descendants of Louis the Pious, part I

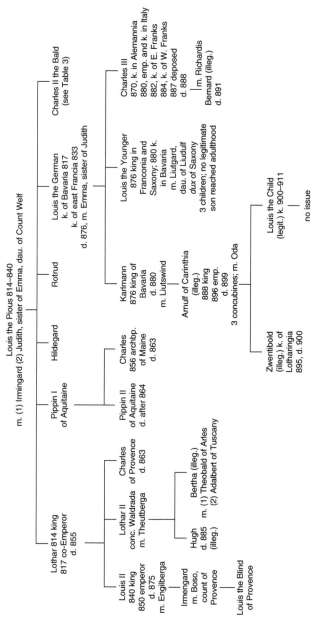

Table 4 The descendants of Louis the Pious, part II

# 1    Introduction: Epitaph for an Era

## 1    *Epitaphium Arsenii*

This is a book about one text: the *Epitaphium Arsenii*, a dialogue written by Paschasius Radbertus, monk of Corbie and well-known biblical commentator, who lived from c. 790 until c. 860.[1] He wrote this funeral oration ('epitaph') for his deceased abbot Wala, who went by the name of Arsenius. The *Epitaphium*'s first book was written not long after Wala's death in 836, the second roughly two decades later. The two books were structured as a conversation between three monks of Corbie, with the author in the role of a narrator called Pascasius. This was the author's monastic byname which, together with his birth name Radbert, he used in the dedications of his many works of exegesis. There were other instances when he identified himself simply as *Radbertus levita*, or *Radbertus abbas*.[2] For practical purposes, and to distinguish the historical figure and author from the dialogue's narrator, I shall refer to him as Radbert, even though a conflation was clearly intended. Through the narrator Pascasius, the author Radbert portrayed himself as an actor in his own narrative.

That the *Epitaphium Arsenii* was planned as one work from the outset becomes clear from the systematic manner in which Radbert used his main model, the funeral oration composed by Bishop Ambrose of Milan in 378 for his brother Satyrus. Furthermore, there is the presence throughout of the Prophet Jeremiah, which holds the two books together, as well the persistent theme of the nature of loyalty (*fides*) to God and to the earthly ruler. Nevertheless, the two books are very different in tenor and approach, and this difference is deliberately emphasised, because the second is presented as having been added considerably later. Pascasius and his fellow monks perceived Wala's contested participation in the rebellions from the distance of a dismal present. Yet this 'nowadays' (*hodie*) continued to be shaped by the recent past of the 830s, when a totally confused leadership

---

[1] The years of his birth and death are tentative; see Ganz, '*Epitaphium*', pp. 539–40.
[2] See below, pp. 57, 134–5.

failed to heed Wala's salutary advice. As Pascasius expressed it: 'This is why, up to the present day, none of the rulers can show the *respublica* the ways towards justice'.[3]

These are the bare outlines of Radbert's *Epitaphium Arsenii*, the topic of a book that I embarked on in 2009, when I had finished *The Penitential State*, a study of the ninth-century narratives about Louis the Pious and the two rebellions of the early 830s.[4] It all started with the process of making my own working translation of this text, for by then, I was well aware that much more could have been said about this remarkable 'Epitaph for Arsenius'. What better way to get to know it properly than translating it from beginning to end? Getting to know the *Epitaphium* and its author better made me realise that this was first and foremost a source for a wider debate about Louis that followed the emperor's death in 840, rather than a eyewitness report on the rebellions of the early 830s. Radbert's second book, written at the earliest in the mid-850s, tells us a lot about his concerns when he had only recently been deposed as abbot of Corbie, and rather less about Wala's thought and motives two decades before. This does not detract from the value of the *Epitaphium* as a source for Carolingian political history and discourse. On the contrary, treating Radbert's second book consistently as a text of the 850s turns it into an even more valuable source of information, albeit for the reign of Charles the Bald, rather than for that of his father Louis.

Radbert's productive hindsight inspired this book's main title: *Epitaph for an Era*. Its subtitle, *Politics and Rhetoric in the Carolingian World,* reflects my aim to show that political and literary history not only go well together, but are in fact mutually indispensable in the analysis of a text like the *Epitaphium Arsenii*. There is a fruitful middle ground between the traditional extremes: a text like this has served as a convenient yet disjointed source of information concerning Carolingian politics, on the one hand, but might also become a disembodied subject of literary analysis and theorising on the other. Political and literary historians need to join forces, and here I use the expression 'political history' in the widest possible sense. Ninth-century issues of authority and power are by definition also religious, social, cultural, economic and institutional, to name but a few modern categories. I have tried to include all these aspects, and often felt like an amateur, which is as it should be.

---

[3] *EA* II, c. 6, p. 66: 'Inde est quod adhuc hodie nemo principum explicare potest reipublicę vias ad iustitiam.'

[4] The translation, which I completed in collaboration with Justin Lake, is forthcoming at Manchester University Press, as *Confronting Crisis in the Carolingian Empire: Paschasius Radbertus' Lament for Wala.*

What I present here is a focused exploration of one particular text, as a route towards a better understanding of its author and the world he lived in. Least of all is this book a comprehensive study of Radbert as an author. There is no way I can do justice to the massive oeuvre of this prolific and original biblical commentator, even though some of his other works will now and then enter upon the scene. These include in particular his *Vita Adalhardi*, written not long after Wala's brother Adalhard's death in January 826, and, to a lesser extent, the commentaries on Lamentations and St Matthew's Gospel. Throughout the subsequent chapters of the book, however, I keep the *Epitaphium* centre stage.

In what follows, I intend to confront the difficulties of this text head-on, and to make the most of them. To name just one contentious question: how can one distinguish between the author and his subject, and get at the historical Wala? The answer is, only to a limited extent, yet Radbert's identification with Wala/Arsenius and his one-time mentor's ideals gets us closer to any historical reality than the traditional use of the *Epitaphium*'s second book as a repository of facts about the rebellions against Louis does. It has also been treated as a star witness to Carolingian clerical misogyny, and as proof that Radbert was behind the Pseudo-Isidorian forgeries. Until recently, the *Epitaphium* was seen as an expression of the typically clerical reform ideals that precipitated the reign of Louis into the crisis of the 830s: the so-called *Reichseinheitspartei* (the party for a united empire), as it was called in twentieth-century German historiography.[5] Apart from the anachronism inherent in this particular notion, there is the more general problem that a text that should be situated in the context of the 850s has been used as a straightforward source for the rebellions of the 830s.[6] This has also meant an almost exclusive focus on the second book, because of its polemics and politics, while the first book was deemed too monastic and inward-looking for consideration. This is a mistake, for the Wala/Arsenius of the first book is equally principled and uncompromising, and his ideals are as radical.[7] The difference between the two books is that the first is holding back in an emphatic way, with regular references to the need to remain silent, while the second appears to be written by an author with no holds barred. In fact, there were definite limits, also for Radbert. As I shall argue, he

[5] For a fundamental critique and overview of the discussion hitherto, see Patzold, 'Eine "loyale Palastrebellion"' and '"Einheit" versus "Fraktionierung"'; also De Jong, 'The Two Republics'. But old habits die hard: Hindrichs, 'Zwischen Reichseinheit und adeligen Machtegoismen'. The title sums up the old paradigm of Carolingian decline.

[6] Especially in recent discussions about Radbert as Pseudo-Isidore; see below, pp. 199–205. But see Ganz, '*Epitaphium*', p. 539, who dates the second book 'to 856, or even later', and Krüger, *Studien*, p. 65, who opts for 'etwa 852'.

[7] As argued rightly by Ganz, '*Epitaphium*'.

seems to have left his reticent earlier book largely intact, using it as a foil for its much more explicit and polemical successor. In other words, both parts of the *Epitaphium* should be taken into account, for they are complementary, and their different literary approaches were designed to make them work in tandem.

The *Epitaphium* has been transmitted in only one manuscript, from Corbie (Paris, BnF lat. 13909), produced not long after the mid-850s, when the work was completed. It has therefore been taken as a text for internal consumption, intended for an audience that was limited to Radbert's own monastic community. This impression is reinforced by the fact that, as far as I can see now, the *Epitaphium* left no traces in later texts.[8] All this raises questions about the audience Radbert had in mind. Was this really an idiosyncratic and private work, primarily written for the author's own satisfaction, and at best for the benefit of his own monastic community?[9] There is much about its content that points in a different direction. In my view, Radbert aimed his sharp literary arrows at a wider constituency, namely his peers, whose unfavourable opinion of Wala was worth changing, and who, once persuaded, could be expected to extend their support and patronage to Radbert himself. This court-connected elite included prelates as well as lay magnates active in the 850s, who had good reason to be affected by Radbert's arguments. After all, these revolved around the dilemmas of fidelity to God and to one's ruler, which some had already experienced during the rebellions against Louis the Pious, while others were confronted with them in a turbulent present.

In the course of this book I shall address the question of Radbert's audience from various perspectives, without being able to answer it in any watertight way. At this point, I shall simply state my view of the matter in brief, for future reference. There is of course a difference between an intended audience and an actual one: Radbert may have wanted to reach a larger group, without ever succeeding. I am also aware of the time-honoured tendency to view Carolingian moralising as 'merely' the business of clerics; that I hold another view should be known from my previous book, and I am surely not alone in this.[10] More recently, I have argued that the *Epitaphium* is part of what one might call a Carolingian culture of public debate, and it certainly addresses the concerns of those members of the elite who defined their own worth, as

---

[8] Ganz, *Corbie*, p. 113, with reference to the 'obscurity and allusiveness of the style'.

[9] Ganz, '*Epitaphium*' is inclined to this view; also Kempshall, *Rhetoric*, p. 204.

[10] De Jong, *Penitential State*. The interdependency of the clerical and lay spheres is also a persistent theme in the work of McKitterick, Nelson and Patzold; for a clear and concise discussion, see Noble, 'Secular Sanctity'.

well as their standing in the eyes of their peers, in terms of public service.[11] The men and women whose lives were bound up with this 'ministry' (*ministerium*) to God and to their ruler were Radbert's intended audience, especially the great and good, who, because of their own standing, would be capable of making and breaking the reputations of their peers. This restricted group might include some monks and nuns, but it was not just them that Radbert sought to impress with his moral fervour and literary fireworks. He wrote a work aimed at those 'in the know', insiders who wielded political clout, deliberately excluding a wider readership by his demanding style and use of aliases. Of course, such exclusiveness did not facilitate a wide manuscript dissemination.

Once one accepts these premises, the *Epitaphium* becomes much more than a narrative of the two rebellions, or a sharp critique of the Emperor Louis and Judith, his second spouse.[12] It not only addresses the dilemmas concerning faith and loyalty (*fides*) that had been posed by the revolts of 830 and 833, but also, albeit indirectly, the conflicts between Louis's successors in the early 840s, in which Radbert had become involved as abbot of Corbie. Furthermore, it reflects a new awareness among members of the elite of the complex nature of political order, and a sharper articulation of the public domain (*respublica*) and its office-holders, be they ecclesiastical or lay magnates. This becomes especially visible in the second book, and is one of the reasons why it should clearly be dated to a later phase of the author's life. His hindsight should be of intrinsic interest to historians, rather than be stripped off in the name of historical accuracy. This also goes for the first book, which does its own share of looking back to a different age. It dates from the late 830s, after the major monastic reforms of Louis's reign, and looks back at an earlier age when the mighty Adalhard and Wala had ruled their monks like kings. This world had disappeared by then, and so had the tight personal union between Corbie and Corvey, the monastery the two brothers had founded in Saxony in 822. Together with Wala's death in faraway Italy, this was another reason for grief and lament when Radbert began to write his commemoration and defence of Arsenius.

Inevitably, my previous research interests and experience have shaped my perspective on the *Epitaphium,* and the questions I have asked of this text. Having started as an historian of monasticism, I then concentrated on the interface between religion and politics, mainly with a focus on historical narratives and biblical commentary. Although not a literary

---

[11] See the themed issue of *Early Medieval Europe* (25/1, 2017) on Carolingian cultures of dialogue, debate and disputation, edited by Irene van Renswoude and myself.

[12] For a pioneering article on this topic, see Ward, 'Agobard of Lyons and Paschasius Radbertus'; recently, Dohmen, *Die Ursache*, pp. 125–80.

historian by training, over the past years I have grown increasingly intrigued by the ninth-century use of authoritative literary models and rhetorical strategies, be they classical or late antique and patristic. My own discovery of this field began when I was researching the book that would become *The Penitential State*, which is about the discursive fallout of one particular event, namely the public penance of Louis the Pious in 833. Jinty Nelson's exemplary studies of Nithard and Dhuoda made me think of my next book, in which I could once more concentrate on one author and his world, as I had so much enjoyed doing in the early 1980s.[13] I was not the only one to see the wider social and political vistas that opened when one engages closely with one early medieval author and his world. Stuart Airlie explored Nithard and Agobard, and Simon MacLean published a translation of Regino of Prüm's *Chronicle* that doubles as an indepth study of history and politics in late Carolingian Europe.[14] A conference in Vienna in 2008 under the heading 'Ego Trouble' discussed the self-referential nature of early medieval Christian discourses, and the wider implications thereof for the use of such texts by historians.[15] In this context I wrote my first article on the *Epitaphium Arsenii*, which turned out to be a pilot study for this book.[16] Meanwhile, working shoulder to shoulder with senior and junior colleagues in the network 'Texts and Identities in the Early Middle Ages' taught me a lot. This holds true especially of Irene van Renswoude and her PhD research on frank speech,[17] but also for other one-time members of 'T&I', such as the authors of a recent themed issue of *Early Medieval Europe* on Carolingian cultures of dialogue, debate and disputation.[18]

In the course of writing *Epitaph for an Era*, I have profited from a recent upsurge of interest in Radbert's tribute to Wala as a text to be considered in its entirety. This ranged from Chiara Verri's investigation of its first book as a highly idiosyncratic instance of hagiography, to Courtney Booker's analysis of the work as evidence for a new authorial sensibility stimulated by the Carolingian reception of ancient drama.[19] My own approach is a different one, however. It is the political and religious

---

[13] De Jong, 'Growing Up in a Carolingian Monastery', on Hildemar of Corbie, and 'Internal Cloisters', on Ekkehard IV of St Gall. Both are based on articles published in Dutch in 1980–3.
[14] MacLean, *History and Politics*.    [15] Corradini et al., *Ego Trouble*.
[16] De Jong, 'Becoming Jeremiah'.
[17] Van Renswoude, 'Licence to Speak', forthcoming at Cambridge University Press as *The Rhetoric of Free Speech in Late Antiquity and the Early Middle Ages*.
[18] *Early Medieval Europe* 25/1 (2017), ed. De Jong and Van Renswoude, with contributions by Robin Whelan, Irene van Renswoude, Janneke Raaijmakers, Rutger Kramer, Warren Pezé and myself.
[19] Verri, 'Il libro primo'; Booker, *Past Convictions*, pp. 42–50; Booker, 'Hypocrisy'; Kempshall, *Rhetoric*, pp. 196–208.

world in which this work's two books originated that has captivated me most, together with the self-referential narrative of an author who evoked a turbulent past that he himself had helped to shape. My interest in this rich text was first kindled by David Ganz's seminal 1990 article on the *Epitaphium Arsenii* and the rebellions against Louis the Pious, with its even-handed discussion of Radbert's religious and political ideals, and its firm refusal to neglect the first book, as historians had tended to do.[20] Ganz's pioneering exploration of Carolingian Corbie and its library has been tremendously helpful,[21] as has Peter von Moos' multi-volume study of the late antique and medieval literature of consolation. Both provided me with an essential framework of information when I began to work on the *Epitaphium* in its wider Carolingian context.[22]

## 2      Two Books, One Creation

The main model for Radbert's epitaph for Arsenius was the funeral oration written by Ambrose of Milan (d. 397) for his brother Satyrus.[23] This poignant two-book meditation on grief in the face of overwhelming loss resonated with Radbert and the other monks who had recently lost their beloved Arsenius. Ambrose's work is especially present in the *Epitaphium*'s beginning, and towards the very end of its second book. It furnished Radbert with an overall framework for his own epitaph, as well as with a two-book structure. This structure seems to have been planned from the outset, which means we are dealing with one work. I have already signalled the presence of Jeremiah in both books. Arsenius is likened to this prophet at the very beginning of the first book, where the narrator, Pascasius, reminds his fellow monks that 'our most unhappy times made another Jeremiah of him'.[24] In the second book, this latter-day Jeremiah comes into his own as a prophet of doom, warning his contemporaries about the impending disaster caused by their disobedience to God.

As mentioned above, there is only one Carolingian manuscript, from Corbie, in which the *Epitaphium* survives (Paris, BnF lat. 13909). It is thought to be from the third quarter of the ninth century and was certainly copied after the mid-850s. By the beginning of the thirteenth century, BnF lat. 13909 was in the library of the abbey of Saint-Arnoul de Crépy-

---

[20] Ganz, '*Epitaphium*'.    [21] Ganz, *Corbie*.    [22] Von Moos, *Consolatio*.

[23] Ambrose, *De excessu fratris*, pp. 209–325; Von Moos, *Consolatio*, I, pp. 137–46 and II, pp. 97–106; Biermann, *Leichenreden*, pp. 24–43, 57–81, 122–33; McLynn, *Ambrose*, pp. 69–78.

[24] *EA* I, prologue, p. 19: 'An ignoras, Severe, quod nostrae hunc infelicissimae vitae saecula Jeremiam alterum tulerunt ab illo?'

en-Valois, in Picardy; it ended up in the Bibliothèque nationale de France via the Maurist library of St Germain des Prés. It is small book of 111 folia (17.4 x 15.3 cm), prepared to the highest standards of book production in Corbie, with coloured uncial initials in red and green. Missing words have been added regularly, either in the margin or between the lines, by a contemporary but different hand.[25] This implies the existence of an exemplar against which it was corrected, possibly the autograph or Radbert's working copy. The other possibility is that these were authorial revisions, but this remains to be established by a palaeographer able to identify the correcting hand. The *Manuscrits datés des bibliothèques de France* calls it 'an original copy', which seems to allow for all these possibilities.[26]

Radbert is identified as its author only in a thirteenth-century hand; the same is true of the ninth-century copy of Radbert's *Vita Adalhardi*. The absence of the author's name is not unusual, but may also indicate an early circulation among insiders, as in the case of Einhard's *Life of Charlemagne*, which was initially transmitted without the preface that identifies its author; this was added only at a later stage.[27] The transition to the second book (fol. 62r) is clearly marked in uncial script ('here ends the first book; the second one begins') as well as by a large initial, yet it is the same hand that continues the text, in the middle of the page, so there is no significant codicological break.[28] The text runs continuously, without chapter headings; these have been added by Jean Mabillon and are noted in the margin in Dümmler's edition, which I use here.[29]

The manuscript of the *Epitaphium* contains no other texts. The discussion between Pascasius and his fellow monks, usually as a threesome, is not visually structured in any way. In the running text, only the capital initials of the discussants' names, usually preceded by a space, indicate that another speaker is taking over. In Corbie, it was produced as a free-standing publication, as we would call it today: carefully prepared and corrected, and ready to be sent off to a third party as a single work, and a substantial one, given the c. 60,000 words it occupies in modern editions. At least three different scribes were

---

[25] Ganz, *Corbie*, pp. 56, 145; *Manuscrits datés* III, p. 345; Bischoff & Ebersperger, *Katalog* III, nr 4945, p. 213.

[26] 'Un exemplaire original de l'oeuvre', *Manuscrits datés* III, p. 344.

[27] On the *Vita Karoli* and its three stages and strands of transmission, see Ganz, 'Einhard's Charlemagne', p. 51, n. 19.

[28] BnF lat. 13909, fol. 62r; see https://gallica.bnf.fr/ark:/12148/btv1b9076783s/f2.image.r =latin%2013909, last consulted on 28 October 2018.

[29] See Weinrich, *Wala*, pp. 93–8, for some helpful corrections and additions to Dümmler's edition.

involved in its production: fols. 1–32v, 33r–49r, 49r–103r have been written by the first scribe, fols. 103r–110r by a second, and fols. 110r–112 by a third. It is significant for our understanding of the unity of intention in the production of the text that there is no change of hands at the transition from the first to the second book.[30] In other words, the earlier date of the first book can only be surmised from its contents, for it has been transmitted as an integral part of the completed *Epitaphium*. Towards the very end of BnF lat. 13909 (on fols. 110v and 111r) the parchment is damaged, and here the text becomes increasingly illegible. As far as I can make out, it is a final reflection on God's grace and eternal life, following Wala's death, so it could indeed be the end of the second book.[31] Somewhat puzzling is the change of scribes, twice, towards the very end of the manuscript. The very last hand (in the middle of 110r) starts with the passage about the Empress Ermengard's reporting on Wala's death; in this case, there is not just a change of hands, but also a clear break in the narrative.[32]

It has been suggested that the script of whomever copied fols. 49–103r, which includes the transition from the first to the second book, resembles that of the Corbie scribe Warembert, who signed his name to the end of a quire in Paris, BnF lat. 12296, the Corbie copy of the first four books of Radbert's commentary on Matthew. Furthermore, a similarity between the *Epitaphium*'s uncial rubrics and those of the Corbie copy of his commentary on Lamentations (Paris, BnF lat. 12994) has been noted.[33] This does not necessarily mean that these two works were composed at the same time, but does imply that a clean copy of each was produced in Corbie's scriptorium, together with other works by Radbert. The manuscripts can be set out in summary as follows:

> *Epitaphium Arsenii*, BnF lat. 13909. Fols 49–103 possibly by the scribe Warembert, with uncial rubrics resembling those of BnF lat. 12274.
>
> *In Matthaeum*, BnF lat. 12296, with scribe Warembert (also extant in Laon BM 67).
>
> *Expositio in Lamentationes*, BnF lat. 12994, with uncial rubrics resembling those of BnF lat. 13909.

---

[30] Ganz, *Corbie*, p. 145; Bischoff, *Katalog* III, nr 4945, p. 213.

[31] In an email communication of 2 October 2011, David Ganz kindly shared his view that the manuscript has not lost much text: 'It now has 111 folia; 14 regular quires of 8 leaves would make a volume of 112 folia … '.

[32] *EA* II, c. 24, p. 96: 'Quod autem ad aeternae vitae gaudia angelicis sit ipse deportatus manibus, venerabili referente Ermengardi regina omnino cognovimus.'

[33] *Manuscrits datés* III, p. 345; on both manuscripts, see Ganz, *Corbie*, p. 145.

>*Vita Adalhardi* and other Corbie saints' *vitae*, BnF lat. 18296,
>with the *Vita Adahardi* (fols. 36–67) as a distinct codicological
>unit.[34]

>*De corpore et sanguine*, Arras BM 775.

To this list, the Rouen copy of the *Expositio in Matheo* (Ms. 141,
formerly A 22) should also be added.[35] The similarities between these
manuscripts merit further investigation. For the time being, I suggest that
after having stepped down as abbot, Radbert not only intended to get his
intellectual legacy copied, but also aimed to spread it judiciously in order
to justify himself. The precision with which the manuscript has been
produced and corrected does indicate an audience that was not in any
sense 'private', however restricted it may have been. When it comes to
private use, Walahfrid Strabo's personal compilation, a *vademecum*
recently studied by Richard Corradini, springs to mind sooner than this
carefully prepared copy of Radbert's tribute to Wala.[36]

Yet there is more to the *Epitaphium*'s one manuscript than meets the
eye at first glance, for it is part of a batch of five so-called original manuscripts of Radbert's works: carefully corrected copies that were made
either under the supervision of the author himself, or by someone who
was correcting this particular copy against a master copy on his desk. Not
only was it part of the batch of five manuscripts already noted, but these
are part of a larger group from Corbie with a distinctive version of
Caroline minuscule script that David Ganz has called 'the Corbie calli-
graphic minuscule of the ninth century'.[37] This group includes an
impressive series of manuscripts of classical authors, also written in this
distinctive script.[38] Although in Bischoff's view this script probably originated earlier in the ninth century, it emerged as fully formed in the early
850s, and soon became dominant. This was 'a distinctive and elegant
scriptorium at the height of its powers';[39] Bischoff thought this increase in
'cultural labour', as he called it, was so systematic and marked that he
wondered who the moving force behind it was. He opted for the librarian
Hadoardus, but noted that this upsurge had already started during the last
years of Radbert's abbacy.[40] If we are to follow Bischoff (and why should
we not?), the earliest inception of this 'cultural labour' roughly coincides
with our author's tenure as schoolmaster and abbot. In a recent

---

[34] Ganz, *Corbie*, p. 145; Bischoff, *Katalog* III, nr 5047, p. 231; *Manuscrits datés* III, p. 345.
[35] As David Ganz pointed out to me in an email communication of 26 June 2018; see also
Ganz, *Corbie*, pp. 56 and 158. See also Bishop, 'The Script of Corbie'.
[36] Corradini, 'Pieces of a Puzzle'.   [37] Ganz, *Corbie*, p. 58.
[38] Bischoff, 'Hadoardus and the Manuscripts of Classical Authors from Corbie', especially
pp. 52–4.
[39] Ganz, *Corbie*, p. 56   [40] Bischoff, 'Hadoardus', p. 53.

palaeographical study of the manuscripts of Corbie, Bart Huelsenbeck situates BnF lat. 13909 among the two earliest of the five categories of scripts that developed between ca. 850 and 880, which at least seems not to contradict Bischoff's chronology.[41]

## 3    A Very Short Summary of the *Epitaphium Arsenii*

Here I offer a succinct overview of the subject matter dealt with in the *Epitaphium*. It is meant for quick guidance and reference, and has no pretension to relay more than the barest outlines of this complex text. For convenience's sake, I have followed the modern chapter division that can be found in Migne's PL 120, as well as in Dümmler's edition.

### *Book I*

**Prologue** The monks Pascasius, Severus and Adeodatus, grieving for their deceased abbot Arsenius, embark on a conversation that will lament and commemorate him. These unhappy times had made a Jeremiah of him, unlike the Arsenius of yore, who was more like Benedict. What the monks want to offer in their dialogue is history, not fables. From boyhood onwards, like the ancient Arsenius, this new Arsenius was one of the greatest and most virtuous men of his age, the cousin of the greatest of emperors.

***cc. 2–3*** Although, like Jeremiah, he was a 'man of strife and discord', and torn by many vexations, Arsenius was loved by all. Like Jeremiah, who ceaselessly prayed to God and composed Lamentations, Arsenius will look after his own in prayer, and they should feel consoled. His enemies should stop their slander and scandalous accusations. They say that Arsenius was faithless towards his emperor, but they do not understand the true nature of faith, which works only through love. We live in miserable times, in which men act like wilful and giddy children. But we cannot speak of this openly, even though we know that Arsenius truly kept his fidelity, and always asked himself whether he was acting in the name of truth.

***cc. 4–5*** Arsenius was a magnate who was a monk inside, always a more severe judge of himself than of others. We grieve for him, deeply, but we also rejoice, for the death awaiting us is a happy departure. What is death

---

[41] Huelsenbeck, 'A Nexus of Manuscripts', with plate 9, with my thanks to David Ganz for this reference.

except for sleep? (An extensive meditation inspired by Ambrose's *De excessu*).

*cc. 6–7* On Arsenius' education as a youth at Charlemagne's court, which was like the trials and tribulations undergone by a monastic novice, like gold in a furnace. The young man was duly humiliated, but then rose to the highest position in the palace, second only to Caesar, and led armies against barbarians. Once he had become a monk, they (the barbarians) still knew him for the magnate he had once been, as he was one of those who had learned virtue in military practice before joining the *militia* of Christ. Arsenius' virtues are discussed, amidst banter about the slanderous tales about him: had the monks themselves become corrupted by these? No, this vessel of honour would be promoted from the pinnacle of secular might to that of monastic life.

*cc. 8–10* Two new interlocutors enter the confabulation: Cremes, who was with Arsenius in Italy, and the illiterate Allabigus, who defends Arsenius vociferously, spouting Terence in an inspired manner. Pascasius then remembers how he first heard about his abbot's exile, when he was in Cologne 'on the emperor's business'. The monks are tempted to speak out, but return to grief and lament instead, and decide (with Severus protesting loudly) to remain silent. A meditation on Arsenius' many virtues follows, and on his perfection as a novice, despite harsh rebuke from his seniors. But for our man, the hard way was easy: he was a monk. The confabulators discuss true and false monks, and praise Arsenius and his fasting, weeping and keeping of his vigils.

*cc. 11–19* Adalhard dies and Arsenius is to succeed: Radbert visits the palace with this request. Then there is much ado about the need for silence, followed by a return to lament and praise. Then follows the long section (cc. 12–18) on the collaboration between Antony/Adalhard and Arsenius/Wala, and their joint foundation of Corvey, which ends (c. 19) in a brief altercation about Corbie's loss of property due to its enforced separation from Corvey (833).

*cc. 20–25* Back to lament and praise, interspersed with veiled attacks on Arsenius' enemies. More on the great man as the ideal abbot, a master of thoughtful and effective discipline. He conformed insufficiently to the general norms, but he was inspired by Job: this was the one he imitated, even though he was Job's inferior.

*cc. 26–28* On perfidious Italy (*Ausonia*) and Arsenius' attempts to impose justice on this kingdom, as Lothar's second in command. The monk Cremes, a witness, waxes eloquent about a Frankish widow who was first robbed and then killed, and about a fraud involving a donation charter. Arsenius saw through it all, withstood corrupt magnates, and got the culprits to confess. He himself was different, and never accepted gifts in Italy unless he had to. Rather abruptly, there then follows: 'Now that this has been said and we are finally turning our pen back to Gaul, let us bring this book to an end', and Pascasius expresses his dread of having to write about the horrible events that were to follow. This reads as if it was a later attempt to create a transition between the first book and the second.

### Book II

**Prologue** Adeodatus urges Pascasius to complete his *Epitaphium*, and to 'recall what we formerly omitted'. Much has changed since their earlier confabulation: Severus has died and Cremes disappeared. They therefore need a third witness to testify to the truth, and Teofrastus is recruited.

**cc. 1–6** Before returning to the main duty at hand, lamenting Arsenius, Adeodatus wants Pascasius to explain about how this crisis began, by which God was so much offended. The narrator then relates how Arsenius composed a list (*schedula*) of all the vices committed in the realm. In a winter assembly at the court, Arsenius held forth at length how these sins might be identified and remedied. Most of the evils had been caused by a lack of distinction between the various orders (*ordines*), and by misuse of monastic property for military purposes. Whereas Arsenius spoke boldly and fearlessly, like Jeremiah (c. 5), the royal counsellors behaved like robbers, so up to the present day, none of the rulers have been able guide the *respublica* to justice. Pascasius bewails the dismal confusion of their own day and age, caused by a refusal to heed Aresenius' advice (c. 6).

**cc. 7–10** This section is on the rebellion of 830, its justification and its aftermath. It opens with Bernard of Septimania's rise to power as chamberlain, his stranglehold on the court, Louis, and Judith, and his evil designs: killing the emperor and his sons, marrying the empress. Arsenius, as a member of the family, tries to reason with the tyrant but has no choice but to join those, including the royal sons, who wish to prevent Louis's downfall. They acted against the emperor, but in fact they fought for his survival as a ruler. Initially, Louis was grateful and publicly declared that he would do all the loyal rebels had demanded, but soon he reneged on promises. Judith returned to the palace, and Arsenius was expelled, allowed to return only if he compromised his principles, which he refused to do. For his efforts to save the emperor and the realm, he was rewarded with exile.

*cc. 11–13* By no means was his name and reputation blemished by his exile. It was those who banished him who were the truly exiled. Because Arsenius was still much in demand as an adviser to the royal sons, he was dispatched ever further, ending up in Noirmoutier. But he was venerated everywhere, and by everyone.

*cc. 14–16* The narrative moves on to the rebellion of 833. Having spent his exile in many different places, culminating in Noirmoutier, Arsenius returns to Corbie, deprived of his abbacy, but acting as abbot all the same. After much resistance on his part, a delegation from the royal sons and the pope manages to persuade him to offer his services to those intent on reconciliation. Together with Pascasius, Arsenius makes the dangerous journey to Lothar's camp. There he encounters the Roman pontiff, the shocked victim of a bad reception by Louis, Judith and their bishops, who are encamped in the vicinity. Arsenius and Pascasius furnish Gregory IV with documents that remind the pope of his true authority, but Judith dominates Louis, so the pontifical mediation is rejected.

*cc. 17–21* On the Field of Lies, Louis and his sons conduct a public judicial debate, (*altercatio, querela*), with the sons elaborately answering their father's blunt and boorish complaints. The emperor's refusal to heed the pontiff's advice and establish a reconciliation leads to a divine judgement, and all his faithful men desert him overnight. Lothar's instant succession to sole rule (*monarchia*) is criticised by Arsenius and Pascasius: neither father nor son 'walked before God sincerely', and cupidity drove the victors. Louis and Lothar did not acknowledge the one and only Almighty King, as Pascasius explains in words borrowed from the Book of Job. Arsenius then departed to Italy, 'with winged step'. Many blamed him for leaving his own community and becoming the abbot of another, but this had been his only option: to flee from persecution by a woman, as Columbanus once had fled to Italy and founded Bobbio (in 614). The monks of Bobbio invited Arsenius to take charge; it had nothing to do with Lothar.

*cc. 22–24* After 'bewailing so many catastrophes and their consequences' and setting out their case for the defence, Pascasius and his two fellow monks now return to their original purpose: lamenting their abbot's death and consoling themselves for this loss. This prompts another meditation on death and resurrection, inspired by Ambrose's *De bono mortis*. The details of Arsenius' illness and death in Italy became known in Corbie thanks to the Empress Ermengard, Lothar's wife, who acted as go-between. She relayed reliable reports, confirmed by angels, of Arsenius' ascent to Heaven. 'There may be incredulous backbiters who believe that a man exposed to temptations and disturbed by oppressions of such magnitude did not deserve this, but … '. Radbert ends with another attack on those who doubt Arsenius and himself, but then, towards the very end, the text becomes too damaged to make much sense of it.

## 4    History, Rhetoric, Politics: The Structure of This Book

*Epitaph for an Era* is divided into three parts. The first section comprises two chapters and is an exploration of the historical context of the *Epitaphium*'s two books. 'Interconnected Lives' (chapter 2) provides some basic information on the lives of Adalhard, Wala and their 'third man' Radbert. For clarity's sake, I shall adhere to the chronology of their lives, but at the same time, in this chapter I raise some questions about the use of Radbert's *Vita Adalhardi* and his *Epitaphium Arsenii* for modern political biography. Radbert's prose dominates what we now know about Adalhard, and particularly about Wala, which poses problems that need to be faced. 'Between the Cloister and the Court' (chapter 3) concentrates on the tension between these two domains, which can be felt throughout the entire text, but which is most in evidence in the first book. Here, I try to determine the underlying factors for changes brought by monastic reform in Corbie after Adalhard and Wala, and Radbert's reactions to these changes in the first book. Furthermore, this chapter is about Radbert's efforts as abbot to protect the integrity of his community's landed wealth. Did these contribute to his deposition? Even if no certainty is possible, it is a question worth discussing.

The second part, 'Rhetoric', highlights the formidable literary skills displayed in the *Epitaphium Arsenii*. Radbert was a biblical commentator, first and foremost, but also an eclectic author who managed to combine various models and genres, such as the dialogue and the funeral oration (chapter 4). Having studied classical rhetorical works, above all Cicero's, he was sufficiently well versed in the rules of eloquence to use them confidently for his own purposes. Yet, in the authoritative late antique literature in which he immersed himself, he encountered eclecticism, especially in Augustine and Jerome, who had effortlessly harnessed Virgil and Terence to their own Christian purposes. These were the resources of the past that Radbert had already drawn upon in his *Vita Adalhardi,* and which he deployed even more brilliantly in the *Epitaphium Arsenii.* The aim of this operation was telling the truth about Arsenius, first by embedding Terence's witty language in a text full of biblical citations, and then, in the second book, by assuming the thunderous voice of Jeremiah or Job, according to Augustine's definitions of grand speech. These strategies are investigated in chapter 5, together with the marked differences between the *Epitaphium*'s two parts. As I noted earlier, the deliberately reticent first book serves as a foil for the outspoken second. As we shall see, however, outspoken did not mean uncontrolled, for speaking truth to power followed specific rules as well. The sixth chapter, and the last of this section ('What's in a Name?') discusses Radbert's famous 'pseudonyms', the aliases he used in his second book for the political protagonists involved in his narrative. These were not in any way pseudonyms hiding identities, and they occur only in the second book, which requires explanation.

My exploration of Radbert's naming strategy forms a bridge to the third and last part, on 'Politics', which revolves mostly around the second book as an articulation of ideals and concepts typical of the reign of Charles the Bald. It opens with a close reading of Radbert's narrative of the two rebellions against Louis (chapter 7), and is followed by an analysis of some of the central concepts of his Latin political discourse, such as *fides, respublica, honestas* and *utilitas*, which were partly inspired by his reading of Cicero. Against this background, there is a brief discussion of Radbert's much vaunted yet tenuous connections with Pseudo-Isidore. Finally, in chapter 9, I offer some comparisons with Nithard's *Histories* and Dhuoda's *Liber manualis*, two other texts by authors who, in the new world that emerged after Louis's death, expressed their personal ideals concerning the public domain. Like Radbert, they did so for a restricted audience of peers, and all the more articulately at a time when the pressures of conflicting loyalties had become ever greater than before.

*Part I*

# History

## 2    Interconnected Lives: Adalhard, Wala and Radbert

In the *Epitaphium*'s first book, the narrator Pascasius recalls how much joy it had given him to be so often in the company of his two patrons, Antony and Arsenius. Although unworthy, he had been 'the third member of their fellowship.'[1] The context is the foundation of the monasteries of Corvey and Herford in Saxony in 822, a joint venture of the two half-brothers Adalhard and Wala, when both were back in the emperor's good graces. It is a bold gesture on the part of two men who had formally left the world years before; founding two monasteries, one for men and one for women, was nothing short of a resounding comeback, and the start of a second phase of political prominence. That this would end with Adalhard's death on 2 January 826, and, in Wala's case, with the rebellions against Louis in the early 830s, was not something anyone in 821 could have foreseen. Charlemagne's powerful cousins were back on the scene, the one as abbot of Corbie and the other as something resembling an informal vice-abbot of this monastery. And then there was Radbert, the remarkably self-referential 'third man'. Not only was he recognisable as the narrator who told the story from his own experience, constantly correcting the perspective of his fellow monks and interlocutors, but he also moved himself onto the scene, first as the constant companion of his two heroes, and then, in the second book, as Wala's trusted emissary, and a go-between connecting Corbie and Louis's court.

In the course of the twentieth century, book-length and still valuable scholarly studies have been devoted to Adalhard, Wala and Radbert himself.[2] Whereas, in 1938, the theologian Henri Peltier concentrated on his subject's work and thought, the historians Lorenz Weinrich, in 1963, and Brigitte Kasten, in 1986, produced political biographies of Wala and Adalhard, respectively. The problem here is not, as in Radbert's case, a lack of biographical data, but that the evidence is dominated by Radbert's two portraits of his illustrious abbots. Inevitably, the *Vita Adalhardi* and the *Epitaphium* have shaped later

---

[1] *EA* I, c. 15, p. 43 (Pascasius): ' . . . quorum in consortio, etsi indignus, tertius eram'.
[2] Peltier, *Pascase*; Weinrich, *Wala*; Kasten, *Adalhard*.

perspectives on the biography of these two men, but the kind of truth
Radbert was after in these works does not conform to modern standards
of factual and chronological precision. This chapter is largely about the
difficulties of using these two texts for biography. In the course of this, and
against the grain, I shall also provide some additional basic information
on the lives of Adalhard and Wala, and finally on Radbert himself.


## 1    Adalhard

As Radbert expressed it, Adalhard stemmed from a royal lineage (*regalis
prosapia*). He was 'the nephew of the great King Pippin, first cousin of
Charles Augustus, educated among the young recruits of the palace in all
the prudence of the world, entrusted to masters together with the ruler of
the earth'.[3] His father Bernard was a son of Charles Martel and the half-
brother of Pippin III. Bernard was born from an illegitimate union,[4]
although this qualification may well have been bestowed mostly with
hindsight. The distinction between more or less official marriages only
became clearer in the course of the ninth century, and besides, a spouse
who once was perfectly legitimate might on second consideration be
relegated to a lower status.[5] Adalhard and Wala had different mothers,
said Radbert, who is the only source for this information: Adalhard's
mother was of Frankish origin,[6] whereas Wala's was of Saxon descent.[7]
After giving birth to Wala, this unnamed woman produced three younger
siblings: Gundrada, Bernarius and Theodrada.[8] It is not certain when
either of the two elder half-brothers was born. While estimates of
Wala's year of birth range from 772 to 780,[9] Adalhard's is usually thought
to be 750/1, because of Radbert's contention that he entered Corbie at the
age of twenty.[10] This is also the biblical number that signified a perfect
time span for waiting and preparation prior to achievement, however.[11]

---

[3] *VA*, c. 7, col. 1511: 'Qui cum esset regali prosapia, Pippini magni regis nepos, Caroli
consobrinus Augusti, inter palatii tirocinia omni mundi prudentia eruditus, una cum
terrarum principe magistris adhibitus ... '.

[4] *VA*, c. 61, col. 1539; Weinrich, *Wala*, pp. 90–1; Hlawitschka, 'Vorfahren', p. 81; Kasten,
*Adalhard*, pp. 13–15.

[5] For an overview, see Konecny, *Frauen*, pp. 65–117; see also the discussion of the notion
of *concubina* in Dohmen, *Ursache*, pp. 54–63.

[6] *VA*, c. 56, col. 1537.    [7] *EA* I, c. 12, p. 40; also *EA* I, c. 13, p. 42.

[8] Weinrich, *Wala*, pp. 11–14; Hlawitschka, 'Vorfahren', p. 81.

[9] Weinrich, *Wala*, p. 13; Depreux, *Prosopographie*, p. 390.

[10] Kasten, *Adalhard*, pp. 24–35; on Adalhard's biography, see also Ganz, *Corbie*, pp. 23–8;
Depreux, *Prosopographie*, pp. 76–9.

[11] Jacob waited this long to get possession of his wives and property (Gen. 31:38–41); Israel
had to wait at least twenty years before the Ark would be moved again (1 Kgs (1 Sam.)
5:7). Solomon spent seven years building the house of God in Jerusalem and another
thirteen building his own home, for a grand total of twenty years (3 Kgs (1 Kgs) 9:10–11).

Twenty as an age for Adalhard to enter Corbie as a monk may have been chosen more for symbolic than for literal reasons.

Similarly, the story about Adalhard's conversion may be less of a factual narrative than it has been taken to be. According to Radbert, and to him alone, Adalhard embraced monastic life in protest against Charlemagne's repudiation of the daughter of Desiderius, the king of Lombard Italy. Charles had asked for her hand in marriage, a commitment that was confirmed by the oaths of some of his followers, but then the king chose another wife, exposing his loyal Franks to the sin of perjury. As Radbert maintained, there was no way that Adalhard, then still a youngster at the palace, would serve the new queen while her legitimate predecessor was still alive. Like John the Baptist, he was unafraid to speak out against Charlemagne's unwarranted audacity and his unlawful marriage. Rather than being accepted as a potential ruler, as if he were a king's son, Adalhard wanted to share Christ's ignominy at the cross. Despising the riches of Pharaoh, he went like Moses into the desert, and became a monk in Corbie.[12]

This version of events should be put next to Einhard's succinct statement that Charlemagne, at his mother Bertrada's behest, married Desiderius' daughter, 'but for some unknown reason he sent her away after a year and took Hildegard, a very noble woman from the Swabian people'.[13] Notker of St Gall elaborated on this text in his Gesta Karoli, claiming that Desiderius' daughter was sickly and could not conceive, so 'according to the judgement of the holiest bishops' Charles put her aside, to the fury of the woman's father, who went to Pavia to fight the invincible emperor.[14] Notker's tale is usually seen as the product of monastic fancy, but Einhard's and Radbert's versions carry the weight of much modern historiography, even though their accounts were also written with considerable hindsight, and with a specific agenda that related to their time of composition.[15] It goes too far to dispute the very existence of this temporary Lombard alliance simply because it is not mentioned in contemporary sources, but one should keep in mind that Einhard and Radbert, at a later stage, had diametrically opposed reasons for mentioning

[12] VA, c. 8, col. 1512A–D.
[13] Einhard, Vita Karoli, c. 18, p. 22: 'Deinde cum matris hortatu filiam Desiderii regis Langobardorum duxisset uxorem, incertum qua de causa, post annum eam repudiavit et Hildigardam de gente Suaborum praecipuae nobilitatis feminam in matrimonium accepit.'
[14] Notker, Gesta Karoli II, c. 17, p. 82: ' ... iudicio sanctissimorum sacerdotum ... '; pace Ganz, Einhard and Notker the Stammerer, p. 107, who has 'by the counsel of the holiest of the clergy'.
[15] Kasten, Adalhard, pp. 24–35; for an in-depth discussion of the marriage, see Nelson, 'Making a Difference'.

Desiderius' daughter. Whereas, in Einhard's eyes, Hildegard was the legitimate queen, for Radbert she was an impostor, whose appearance upon the scene had turned Charlemagne into a bigamist and the Franks into perjurers. The point here, of course, is that Hildegard was the mother of Louis the Pious, so Radbert may have wished to cast doubt on the legitimacy of the reigning emperor.

Perhaps a well-informed Radbert indeed broke the silence about Adalhard's conversion, after well over half a century, and was accurate in all that he reported. It seems more likely, however, that Desiderius' daughter and her repudiation served as a suitable context to explain the one-time entry into monastic life of Adalhard, whose political career had been so closely connected with Italy.[16] Radbert even came up with a name for the repudiated Italian wife: Desiderata. It is improbable that Desiderius ever had a daughter of this name; his youngest may have been called Gerperga.[17] Yet the impact of literary traditions should also be taken into account. In early medieval hagiography, saintly men and women did not leave the world as a matter of course; they did so as a result of resistance to the powers of the world that pulled them in the other direction, such as parents wishing them to marry, or kings demanding their continued service. This theme of conflict helped to underline the suddenness, magnitude and voluntariness of the conversion, and this is precisely what it does in Radbert's depiction of Adalhard's entry into monastic life.[18] Furthermore, the comparison with John the Baptist evokes the spectre of a latter-day Herod and Salome, whose depravity was countered by Adalhard's intransigent moral courage. Given Adalhard's exile upon Louis's accession in 814, and his relatively recent reconciliation with this emperor in 821/2, Louis was the Herod whom Radbert had in mind.

Again, this is not to say that his story about Adalhard's heroic resistance to Charlemagne's marriage politics should be entirely discredited, but his sudden and politically motivated entry into monastic life is reminiscent of other narratives about the conversion of Frankish magnates, usually in the context of some kind of political conflict involving royal disfavour. Often this was a matter of lying low, temporarily, until they were accepted at the court once more. An essential prerequisite for salvaging their reputation was that their 'opting out' was portrayed and understood as a voluntary gesture.[19] In hagiographical terms, this meant that the more traditional and general theme of the radical break with one's family could be turned

---

[16] For some reasonable doubt, see McKitterick, *Charlemagne*, pp. 84–8.
[17] Nelson, 'Making a Difference', p. 183.
[18] De Jong, *In Samuel's Image*, pp. 47–8, 196, 202–5.     [19] De Jong, 'Monastic Prisoners'.

into something more specific, namely the saint's courageous resistance against the ruler's wishes.[20] As we shall see, this also played an important role in Radbert's depiction of Wala.

With regard to Adalhard, the conversion of Carloman may have been on Radbert's mind, especially when he related how Adalhard first became gardener in Corbie, and then fled this monastery because of his many visitors, *cognati et amici*.[21] Carloman, brother to the future King Pippin III, had converted to monastic life in 747, and went first to Monte Soracte and then to Monte Cassino, an episode deftly portrayed and glossed over by Einhard. The latter claimed that this was 'for some unknown reason, although it seems he was inflamed by a desire for the contemplative life'.[22] Like Adalhard in Corbie, Carloman had so many noble Frankish visitors in Monte Soracte that he withdrew to Monte Cassino to regain real monastic tranquillity.[23] Adalhard's chief byname, at the court and in Corbie, was 'Antony', after the renowned desert father who retreated from the world, only to attract a multitude of visitors and pupils. This was how Alcuin addressed him in his letters.[24] But, as Radbert noted, others had compared Adalhard to Aurelius Augustinus, and the great man also had qualities reminiscent of Gregory the Great, as well as of Pope Sylvester.[25] All the same, 'Antony' was an apt byname for a prominent political player who entered a monastery, but continued to act as a magnet for followers from the world outside. As the influential *Life of Antony* the desert father has it, the further the saint retreated into the desert, the more people sought his advice.

For all we know, Adalhard's retreat to Corbie was a judicious political move. King Carloman died on 4 December 771, and Charles became the sole ruler. A general reshuffle followed. There is the distinct possibility that Adalhard, as one of Carloman's leading men, thought it prudent to withdraw from the political arena, but Radbert's story about Adalhard's heroic resistance to the Italian marriage is the only indication that he had any conflict with Charlemagne at all. According to Radbert, Charles could not do without him, and Adalhard was recalled to royal service by the king's envoys, who accompanied him back to Francia from Monte Cassino.[26] Although the 'unofficial' members of the ruling family, such as

---

[20] On the topos of the young saint's conflict with his parents and other relatives, see Illmer, *Erziehung*, pp. 119–20, 151–2; on the biblical key texts, Angenendt, *Monachi peregrini*, pp. 130–2. For examples of saints entering clerical or monastic life against the wishes of their parents *and* their king: De Jong, *In Samuel's Image*, pp. 202–3.

[21] Goosmann, 'Politics and Penance'.      [22] Einhard, *Vita Karoli*, c. 2, pp. 4–5.

[23] *VA*, c. 11, col. 1514B–D.

[24] Bullough, *Alcuin*, pp. 76–7; Ganz, *Corbie*, p. 137 (on BnF lat. 13373).

[25] *VA*, c. 21, col. 1519B–C; the same theme of the subject's composite character can be found in *EA* I, prologue, p. 20; see below, p. 33.

[26] *VA*, c. 12, col. 1515A–B.

Adalhard and Wala, remained a source of potentially dangerous political competition, they could also be useful. If kinsmen were loyal, they were the most trustworthy allies a monarch could wish for, especially if they had become high-ranking clerics. Louis's half-brother Drogo, archbishop of Metz, was a case in point.[27]

This also seems to have been Charlemagne's purpose with Adalhard, yet the modern debate about the precise date of their reconciliation leaves one wondering whether there was any conflict at all. By 780/1 at the very latest, Adalhard was rewarded for his services, which had apparently been going on for some while, with an important office, the abbacy of Corbie.[28] Abbots tend to be ignored when public offices in the Carolingian world are discussed. After an almost complete focus on counts, one generation ago, bishops have now been recognised as the pillars of the Frankish states that they were, but the importance of abbots (and, up to a point, of abbesses) of royal monasteries and their participation in the public arena is still underestimated. This is because discourse about the abbots' proper distance from 'the world' tends to obscure the fact that they attended assemblies, raised royal troops and commanded vast landed wealth which enjoyed royal protection, and therefore could be harnessed to the needs of the *respublica*.[29] Adalhard was a case in point: as abbot of Corbie, he enjoyed a long and distinguished career in the service of Charlemagne, as a trusted member of the king's inner circle who was active as a *missus* and royal envoy.[30] Whether in 781 he became the mentor and regent of Charles' young son, King Pippin, to Italy, is a moot point; this is attested only in the *Vita Adalhardi*, and may well be an instance of Radbert projecting the abbot's later connections with Italy onto an earlier period.[31]

Whatever the case, in due course Italy did become Adalhard's principal sphere of official political action, and the same would be true of Wala in the 820s.[32] Upon the death of King Pippin in July 810, Abbot Adalhard was sent south to take charge of the *regnum Italiae* on Charles's behalf, while towards the end of 812 Wala accompanied Pippin's son Bernard from Aachen back to his Italian kingdom.[33] Especially during the last decade of Charlemagne's reign, his two cousins rose to great prominence at the imperial court. When the emperor died in January 814, Adalhard

[27] On Drogo's central role after 833, see De Jong, *Penitential State*, pp. 52–8.
[28] Kasten, *Adalhard*, pp. 42–43.
[29] De Jong, 'The Power of Prayer', pp. 623–36; see below, pp. 93–7.
[30] Kasten, *Adalhard*, pp. 47–78; Depreux, *Prosopographie*, pp. 76–9.
[31] Kasten, *Adalhard*, pp. 42–43.
[32] Kasten, *Adalhard*, pp. 42–72; Weinrich, *Wala*, pp. 43–52.
[33] Kasten, *Adalhard*, p. 68; Werner, 'Gouverner l'empire chrétien', pp. 30–7.

rushed back from Italy to his much-neglected monastery of Corbie, while Wala remained at the palace in Aachen. They were the new emperor's kinsmen, but they also, more than anybody else, embodied the *ancien regime*. This surely was not the first royal succession that put the fear of God in an entrenched palace clique: what would happen to them, under the new incumbent of the throne? In this sense, there was nothing novel about the transition of 814, but it was exceptional that there was an account of the takeover written by Louis's most influential biographer, the so-called Astronomer, in which Wala played a central and sinister role.[34]

## 2    Wala

Wala was the eldest of the children born from Bernard's second marriage. Radbert makes much of the fact that their mother hailed from Saxony. Whenever Wala went there, according to Radbert, he was truly at home, wearing native dress and being alternately admired and feared by the locals. Wala's habit of wearing Saxon attire surfaces several times in the *Epitaphium*'s first book.[35] This may have been for the benefit of the younger monks of Corvey, whom Radbert wished to provide with a portrait of Arsenius, yet these passages also exude a sense of Carolingian imperialism: many different peoples were now united within one empire/ *ecclesia*. Wala was probably born in the early 770s, around the time when Adalhard became a monk in Corbie. Their considerable age gap was underlined by Radbert's frequent references to Adalhard as 'the old man' (*senex*), and the occasional one to Wala as 'the youth' (*iuvenis*).[36] The younger brother pursued a secular career. According to Radbert, Wala had once been married to the sister of William of Gellone, which accounted for his almost paternal care for William's son Bernard of Septimania, who would later become Wala's nemesis.[37]

This snippet of information, provided as part of vicious diatribe against Bernard, adds more to Wala's biography than the highly stylised chapters on his youth and secular career in the *Epitaphium*'s first book. From the outset, Radbert cast Wala as an epitome of virtue who had remained

---

[34] Nelson, 'Women at the Court of Charlemagne', pp. 239–42; De Jong, 'Einhard'.

[35] *EA* I, c. 16, p. 46, on Wala's Saxon attire; c. 15, p. 45, on Wala's connections with Saxony, his *patria*.

[36] Depreux, *Prosopographie*, p. 390, has between 772 and 780, based on Weinrich, *Wala*, p. 13. *EA* I, c. 12, p. 40: 'Licet enim unus eorum esset aetate senior, et alter admodum iuvenis ... siquidem iste acutior sensu, sed senex noster in consilio et caritate latior'; *EA* I, c. 12, p. 41: ' ... ille senex senior ... '; *EA* I, c. 13, p. 42: '. ... senex Antonius ab exilio regressus ... '; *EA* I, c. 14, p. 43: ' ... sanctus senex noster ... '.

[37] *EA* II, c. 8, p. 69; see below, p. 155.

unchanged throughout his turbulent life, and this included his conversion to monasticism. As the youngest interlocutor in the dialogue marvelled, how had it been possible that, amidst his innumerable activities, Wala had always found the inner tranquillity to devote himself to God?[38] This is not to say that Radbert turned the youthful Arsenius entirely into a monk *avant la lettre*, for the setting of Wala's early formation is clearly the royal court, but his *apprentissage* is presented as if it were a noviciate, with the ruler apparently acting the part of the abbot: 'Augustus' tested the young Wala like gold in a furnace (Wisd. 3:6), a biblical turn of phrase cited in the Rule of Benedict: this characterised the right kind of monk.[39] The ensuing confrontation with the unnamed emperor is reminiscent of that of Adalhard, who stood up to Charlemagne, but in this case there was no conversion. Wala remained in the world, but nonetheless, there are clear echoes of the hagiographical conflict topos just discussed. In an intriguing passage, the emperor decides to humiliate Wala and depose him from his rank, 'even though this was his cousin, the son of his paternal uncle'.[40] Radbert, in his turn, takes the ruler down a peg by depicting Wala as a youngster who out-humbled everyone else: encountering a peasant driving his oxen, the young courtier offered to exchange his armour for the yokel's farming equipment, claiming that this suited him better, 'because at present I do not devote myself to the business of worldly service, but to that of the monastic life'.[41] Only shortly thereafter, the outcast was restored to imperial favour, and eventually he was appointed 'steward of the entire palace'. He became second only to Caesar, holding sway like another Joseph in Pharaoh's palace.[42]

On the basis of this episode, Wala's precocious rise to power in Charlemagne's entourage and its concomitant conflicts have been turned into a 'first exile', which was supposedly connected with the rebellion of the king's son Pippin the Hunchback in 792.[43] What Radbert wanted to get across was something entirely different, however: namely that Wala had always, from boyhood onwards, oscillated between formidable secular power and monastic virtue, and was eminently capable of making this

---

[38] *EA* I, c. 4, pp. 25–6 (Adeodatus).

[39] *Regula Benedicti.* c. 1.6, p. 16. On Wala (or rather Radbert) as a Benedictine abbot, see Mayr-Harting, 'Two Abbots in Politics'. On Charlemagne's court: Nelson, 'Was Charlemagne's Court a Courtly Society?'.

[40] *EA* I, c. 6, p. 28: ' ... licet consobrinus ipius esset, patrui filius ... '.

[41] *EA* I, c. 6, p. 29; Leyser, 'Early Medieval Canon Law', p. 57; Innes, 'A Place of Discipline', pp. 70–1.

[42] *EA* I, c. 6, p. 29: ' ... constituitur ab augusto echonomus totius domus, et venerabatur passim secundus a cesare, quasi putares alium Ioseph sceptra regni movere'. On the Pharaoh in monastic narratives, see Kramer, 'Pharaoh'.

[43] Weinrich, *Wala*, pp. 14–18.

transition, time and again.[44] Effortlessly changing from charismatic magnate into ascetic monk and back again, Wala represented an ideal of monastic leadership that was to remain typical for writings connected to Carolingian and Ottonian royal abbeys.[45] A good abbot was capable of wielding authority in the cloister as well as at the court. In this respect, the ideal Wala as depicted by Radbert had never changed, and all that befell him at a later stage, including great glory as well as terrible humiliation, was already fully present in his youth. The story of his demotion by Charlemagne did not so much refer to a first instance of exile, as to Wala's ability to cope with royal disfavour, and to remain supremely unaffected by such trials and tribulations.

In sources other than the *Epitaphium*, references to Wala before 814 are scant. He probably figures in a list of Saxon hostages and their Frankish guardians of 805/6,[46] but the first certain mention dates only from 811, when *Walach filius Bernhardi* figures in the Royal Frankish Annals as the first of a group of Frankish counts negotiating peace with the Danish king Henning.[47] What Wala was up to before this time remains guesswork, except that it seems likely that Radbert's narrative of his abbot's rise to power at the court of 'Augustus' or 'Caesar' drew mostly upon what he knew about the last, and imperial, phase of Charlemagne's reign. By then, Wala's sister Gundrada, the recipient of letters and work by Alcuin, also formed part of Charlemagne's entourage. In 801, Wala's brother Bernarius, a monk at Lérins, had been ordered to come to the palace together with his abbot: a visit that, in Alcuin's view, would cause serious moral damage if prolonged. Consequently, Alcuin wrote to Adalhard, urging him to send Bernarius back to his monastery in Lérins, so he might escape the moral peril of the court.[48] One is reminded of Radbert's typically monastic comment in Adalhard's *Life* about Gundrada, who was allegedly the only woman who managed to hang on to her chastity in a palace full of delights and passions.[49] All the same, Bernard's children

---

[44] An aspect rightly stressed by Verri, 'Il libro primo'.
[45] De Jong, 'Internal Cloisters', pp. 212–6; Raaijmakers, *Making of the Monastic Community*, pp. 122–5, 244–9.
[46] Weinrich, *Wala*, p. 18. Innes, 'Practices of Property', pp. 226–88; McKitterick, *Charlemagne*, pp. 106–7; Kosto, *Hostages*, pp. 66–7; Nelson, 'Charlemagne and Empire', pp. 223–8; Rembold, *Conquest*, pp. 54–61.
[47] *ARF* s.a. 811, p. 134; Weinrich, *Wala*, p. 23.
[48] Alcuin, *Epistolae*, no. 220, p. 364, to Adalhard; Alcuin, *Epistolae* no. 24, pp. 386–7, to Gundrada/Eulalia, pp. 386–7, praising her chastity and asking her to make his excuses to Charlemagne because of illness. See also Alcuin, *Epistolae*, no. 279, p. 435–6 and no. 309, pp. 473–78 (801–4), with an extensive dedication to Gundrada of *De ratione animae* (incomplete in Dümmler's edition in the *MGH*). On the latter, see Nelson, 'Women at the Court of Charlemagne', pp. 37, 40; Van Renswoude, 'Art of Disputation', pp. 50–1.
[49] *VA*, c. 33, col. 1526C.

were at home in these circles; the youngest, Theodrada, became abbess of Nôtre-Dame of Soissons in 810.[50]

By this time, Wala indeed had become 'second only to Caesar', for he headed the list of fourteen counts who, together with eleven bishops and four abbots, witnessed Charlemagne's will. Wala was the highest-ranking secular magnate, a position he surely did not gain overnight.[51] Wala's leading position in the palace is vividly depicted by the Astronomer, in a tense narrative about Louis's take-over of Aachen in the early spring of 814: ' ... Wala, who held the highest place with Emperor Charles, was especially feared in case he might be organising something sinister against the new emperor.' But Wala commended himself to the new emperor, submitting to the latter's will, and then all the Franks followed suit.[52]

The implication is that, without Wala's cooperation, Louis could not have taken charge of the palace in Aachen and, *mutatis mutandis*, of his father's inheritance. This also transpires from the Astronomer's contention that Louis put Wala in charge of the purification of Aachen. At the head of a small posse of strongmen, he had to seize the courtiers who were 'particularly debauched or whose scornful arrogance was treasonous', until Louis could deal with them upon arrival.[53] As we have seen, according to the Astronomer, Wala was suspected of plotting 'something sinister' (*aliquid sinistri*). Did this mean he had his own designs on the throne? Possibly, for both Adalhard and Wala were members of the ruling dynasty.[54] Still, it should be kept in mind that the Astronomer wrote in the early 840s, fully aware of Wala's chequered career: in 821, Charlemagne's old courtier once more rose to prominence at Louis's palace, but then years later he was banished from the court for a second time. Moreover, it is clear from his *Life of Louis* that the Astronomer lost no opportunity to put Wala in an unfavourable light. The long and the short of it was, I suspect, that Wala was instrumental in Louis's takeover: so much so, that the new emperor could not afford to retain his older kinsman in his powerful position. Unlike Charlemagne, who kept his two formidable cousins close to him, Louis decided to exclude these members of the older generation from his entourage.

All Bernard's offspring were barred from Louis's court, and insofar as they had a public office, they were removed from it. Adalhard was exiled to Noirmoutier, a monastery on an island in the Atlantic Ocean, south of the mouth of the Loire. Probably it was not all that hard to get to, but for

[50] See below, p. 35.
[51] Einhard, *Vita Karoli*, c. 33, pp. 37–41. Innes, 'Charlemagne's Will'.
[52] Astronomer, c. 20, p. 346; transl. Noble, *Charlemagne and Louis the Pious*, p. 246.
[53] Astronomer, c. 21, p. 348; transl. Noble, *Charlemagne and Louis the Pious*, p. 247.
[54] Nelson, 'Women at the Court of Charlemagne', pp. 239–41.

Radbert this was as far as one could possibly be banished; eventually, Wala would end up here as well. When Adalhard was exiled to Noirmoutier, it was without a verdict, and as Radbert put it, without any accuser or proper hearing. The old abbot was sent off, defiled by public opinion, for the sake of the *respublica*.[55] Gundrada was dispatched to Poitiers, to the prestigious nunnery of Ste-Croix, founded in the mid-sixth century by Queen Radegund. Bernarius, who was in Corbie at the time, was sent back to Lérins, the community where he had made his monastic profession. Only Theodrada, abbess of Nôtre-Dame of Soissons, could remain where she was, but no doubt she was also excluded from the new emperor's inner circle.[56] Wala, finally, had no choice but to withdraw from the political arena. That he did so entirely of his own accord is crucial in Radbert's narrative, and in other early medieval depictions of so-called 'political tonsure': through emphasis on the voluntariness of this act, the honour and reputation of those banished from the political arena was left intact.[57]

Radbert's portrayal of Wala's new status, once he entered Corbie, is equally circumspect. Having discarded the highly symbolic 'belt' that signified secular office (*cingulum militiae*), the great man joined the School of Paradise (*tirocinium paradisi*), which is nothing more nor less than the monastic community.[58] But did this imply a monastic conversion in the full sense of the word? A marginal notice in the so-called *Annales Iuvavenses* says that Wala was tonsured in 814 (*Wahl tonsus est*), but this is not a contemporary reference. It was added in the years after 828 when this computistical manuscript was brought to Salzburg.[59] By this time, Wala had become famous throughout the realm, so his tonsure had become noteworthy. That Wala became a monk in 814 is a mere assumption. It is more likely that he received only a clerical tonsure, from which it transpired that he had left the world, but that he might return to it, if the ruler so decided; many of the so-called monastic exiles who were compelled to 'opt out' did not make a formal monastic profession, but remained clerics for the duration of their exile, thus keeping their options open.[60] Yet even though there is no sign that Wala ever made a formal profession, there was no doubt about his ascetic virtues, nor about his dominant position in his

---

[55] *VA*, c. 30, col. 1524B: ' ... ob beneficium reipublicae exsilium tulit.'
[56] *VA*, c. 35, col. 1528A–C.    [57] De Jong, 'Monastic Prisoners'.
[58] *VA*, c. 35, col. 1528A: 'Wala vero tuus Corbeia, ut dixi, tiro recipitur. Qui deponens militiae cingulum, ut te totum velle sanctitatis indueret, arripuit primum tirocinia paradisi, ut consummaret in se mensuram Christi.'
[59] *Annales Iuvavenses maiores MGH SS* XXX/2, p. 738; Würzburg, Univ.bibl., theol. fol. 46 *saec. ix in.*, fol. 15v–16r. The marginal entry 'Wahl tonsus est' was made by the scribe and teacher Baldo once the manuscript had come to Salzburg in 828. I am grateful to Rosamond McKitterick, who called my attention to this manuscript.
[60] De Jong, 'Monastic Prisoners'.

new community. In Radbert's representation of the years of Adalhard's absence, 'Arsenius' clearly was the most influential figure in Corbie.[61]

According to friend and foe, Louis himself came to realise the far-reaching implications for his own conscience of what he had done to Adalhard and Wala. What rankled most was that the two illustrious half-brothers were the emperor's kinsmen, whom he had promised his father to protect. By mid-October 821 they had been recalled to the court. In August 822, they were emphatically included in the imperial atonement at the public assembly in Attigny, even though the focus of this penitential gesture was the unfortunate Bernard of Italy, whose death by blinding had aroused such indignation that the emperor felt compelled to make amends four years later.[62] Whether he did so at Adalhard's behest is doubtful, for Radbert's portrayal of Louis's penance is nothing less than scathing, which suggests at least some initiative on the emperor's part.[63] According to Charlemagne's succession arrangement of 806, his sons should have refrained from blinding those with whom they were in competition or dispatching them to monasteries, yet this is precisely what Louis had done. In the *Royal Frankish Annals*, the emperor's public confession and penance at the assembly of Attigny (822) is emphatically presented as an atonement for the injustice committed against his kinsmen, that is, members of the dynasty. Louis atoned for the involuntary tonsure he had imposed on his half-brothers Drogo and Hugh, and 'for what had been done against Bernard the son of his brother Pippin, as well as with regard to Abbot Adalhard and his brother Wala ... '.[64]

Adalhard and Wala's comeback was a fact when Louis allowed them to found the monastery of Corvey and the nunnery of Herford, both in Saxony. Already during the assembly of Attigny in August 822, Adalhard and Wala, together with Helisachar, abbot of St-Riquier, controlled the access to the ruler, for this was the formidable trio with whom Archbishop Agobard of Lyon had to contend when he sought the emperor's ear. In the event, he was unsuccessful.[65] Later in the same year, Wala accompanied Lothar to Italy, as mentor and deputy to the co-emperor. At the time, Lothar was twenty-seven years old. He had married in 821 and could now set up his own royal household in Italy, with Ermengard at his side, the daughter of Count Hugh of Tours, another former member

---

[61] See below, pp. 52–6.

[62] De Jong, *Penitential State*, pp. 122–7; Depreux, 'The Penance of Attigny'.

[63] *VA*, c. 51, cols. 1534D–1535A.

[64] *ARF* s.a. 822, p. 158 ' ... et de his, quae erga Bernhardum filium fratris sui Pippini necnon et his, quae circa Adalhardi abbatem et fratrem eius Walahum gesta sunt, publicam confessionem et paenitentiam egit.'

[65] Agobard, *De dispensatione*, c. 4, p. 123; De Jong, *Penitential State*, pp. 142–3; Airlie, 'I, Agobard', pp. 176–7.

of Charlemagne's entourage. Definitely, a new leaf had been turned. For
the three years to come, running the kingdom of Italy as Lothar's deputy
was Wala's main business; he was deeply involved in quashing political
violence in Rome, and presumably also in the creation of the *Constitutio
Romana* that further tightened the bonds between St Peter's Republic and
its Frankish protectors. In 823, Pope Paschal I crowned Lothar, whose
formal co-emperorship since 817 now became more prominent and
effective.[66]

This close cooperation with Lothar, combined with his having left the
world in 814, must have earned Wala the nickname 'Arsenius'. Whereas
the Astronomer had likened Louis's public atonement in 822 to
Theodosius' penance in 392,[67] Radbert pointedly omitted this reference
in the second book of his *Epitaphium*. This was all the more meaningful
given his use of the bynames 'Arsenius' (Wala) and 'Honorius' (Lothar),
which were both connected to Theodosius. Wala had gained his byname
'Arsenius' well before it appeared in the *Epitaphium Arsenii*. When in 831/
2 Radbert dedicated the first version of his treatise on the Eucharist to
Warin, then *magister* in Corvey, he referred to 'our Arsenius, whom these
times of ours have turned into another Jeremiah'.[68] There is no doubt that
the byname Arsenius came from the rich and varied tradition of the Latin
*Vitae/Vitas patrum*. Originating in the sixth century, its three main versions drew upon an older Greek corpus of *Apophthegmata patrum*.[69]
As Irene van Renswoude noted, a full narrative about Arsenius' role at
Theodosius' court, notably as the tutor of Theodosius' sons Honorius
and Arcadius, is first found in the *Life of Arsenius* by Theodore the Studite
(759–826). Given Radbert's portrait of Wala/Arsenius as Lothar/
Honorius' educator, how did he know of this legend if, in the ninth
century, it was only transmitted in Greek? It has been suggested that
there existed an older Latin version of Arsenius' *Life*, now lost, which
was used by Theodore the Studite.[70] This may well be the case, yet
Radbert's knowledge of Arsenius is best explained by his familiarity
with the so-called *Vitas patrum*. He was after all a monk who, in

---

[66] Noble, *Republic*, pp. 310–3; Weinrich, *Wala*, pp. 48–51.     [67] Astronomer, c. 35, p. 406.
[68] Paschasius Radbertus, *De corpore*, prologue to Warin, ed. Paulus, p. 3: '... quod Arsenius
noster quem nostra nunc nobis saecula Hieremiam alterum tulerunt ab illo, in fidei te
mihi commiserat ratione.'
[69] The best access to the Latin reception of the *Apophthegmata* and the manuscripts involved
is provided by Batlle, *Adhortationes sanctorum patrum*, pp. 1–15, 299–305; see also
Berschin, *Biographie* I, pp. 128–33, and Freire, 'Traductions latines'.
[70] Van Renswoude, 'Licence to Speak', p. 120, nn. 121–2, with reference to Theodore the
Studite, *Life of Arsenius*, cc. 3–6, 13 and 20–1, where Arsenius is called 'the father of
emperors' (c. 21); she also cites a publication in Russian by D. Afinogenov, 'To the
Origins of the Legend about St Arsenius'.

accordance with the Rule of Benedict, regularly listened to the
'Conferences and Lives of the Fathers' (*Collationes vel Vitas patrum*);[71]
to these texts he referred readers wishing to know more about the monasticism that once flourished in Egypt.[72] By Radbert's time, the expression 'Lives of the Fathers' could refer to a multitude of Latin monastic
histories, which only roughly corresponded with any Greek 'original'.

Although much substantial work has been done on the manuscript
tradition of their main strands,[73] there is still only the quite misleading
edition by Heribert Rosweyde (1569–1627), which is reprinted in
Migne's *Patrologia Latina*. Manuscript research would be required for
any in-depth investigation of how precisely Radbert came by his information about Arsenius. Yet, for what it is worth, in his *De corpore et sanguine
domini* of 831 Radbert combined two stories about Arsenius derived from
the Latin translation (*Verba seniorum*) ascribed to the deacon and future
pope Pelagius (556–61) and his successor John (561–73).[74] Abbas
Arsenius is depicted as dwelling in the Scythian desert, so full of penitential compunction that he could never be without a cloth to wipe off his
tears; he also proved himself a staunch defender of the real presence of the
Christ's body and blood in the bread and wine of the Eucharist.
Admittedly, the material gathered by Rosweyde does not mention
Arsenius as the tutor of Theodosius' two sons, but a chapter on humility
from the *Verba seniorum*, associated with Pelagius, relates that Arsenius
lived in the palace of Theodosius, who was the father of Arcadius and
Honorius, and that he fled to the silence of the desert.[75] The so-called
collection of Pseudo-Rufinus is more specific, and ventures the information that Arsenius had been the godfather of Theodosius' sons.[76] These
texts still await further study and reliable dating;[77] for our present purpose, it is relevant that Arsenius' conversion from the palace to the desert
was well known, as was his connection with Theodosius' son Honorius.

[71] *Regula Benedicti*, c. 41, p. 144.    [72] *In Matthaeum* II, p. 170, ll. 171–2.
[73] Batlle, *Adhortationes sanctorum patrum* concentrates on the *Verba seniorum* ascribed to the
Romans Pelagius and John; on the version transmitted by Paschasius of Dumio, see
Freire, *A versão latino*. Philippart, 'Vitae patrum' (an illuminating review of the two
previously cited publications). I have also profited from the third chapter of Bertrand's
PhD thesis, Die Evagriusübersetzung der *Vita Antonii*.
[74] Batlle, *Adhortationes sanctorum patrum*, pp. 11–12, 216–7: Radbert, *De corpore*, c. 14.4,
pp. 88–9.
[75] *De Vitis patrum sive Verba seniorum* V (BHL 6527), c. 15, 10, PL 73 col 955C.
[76] *De Vitis patrum sive Verba seniorum* III (BHL 6565), c. 37, PL 73, cols. 762D–763A: 'Fuit
quidam vir in palatio sublimis, sub Theodosio imperatore, nomine Arsenius, cuius filios,
id est Arcadium et Honorium Augustus de baptismo suscepit.' The manuscript tradition
of this Pseudo-Rufinus version allegedly starts only in the tenth century, but according to
Batlle, *Adhortationes sanctorum patrum*, p. 10. This is almost certainly a reworking of the
translation produced in the mid-sixth century by Paschasius of Dumium.
[77] Philippart & Trigalet, 'Latin hagiography', p. 128.

As Radbert explained, Wala was a multi-faceted figure, to whom it was difficult to do justice in any written memorial. Not only did he possess the same character traits as the 'earlier Arsenius', but he sometimes appeared in the guise of St Benedict, and occasionally he 'took on the role of Jeremiah, with his steely visage and fierce determination, though in truth he was gentle in spirit and the mildest of men'.[78] This reveals the full range of a repertoire of identification that included both biblical and monastic tradition, as well as the different functions of the names in question.[79] As an abbot, Wala reminded his monks of the venerated author of their Rule, while his outspokenness in the political arena, followed by his exile from the court in 831, made him seem like another Jeremiah. Although he bore the imprint (*typus*) of this prophet of doom,[80] and was closely identified with him throughout the *Epitaphium*, the byname that characterised him most completely was Arsenius.

Radbert rendered a vivid portrait of Wala/Arsenius in Italy as an uncompromising pillar of justice, in order to refute accusations of corruption.[81] This serious denunciation was countered in a long digression, related by the monk Cremes, allegedly an eyewitness, about Wala's staunch defence of a widow who had been done out of her rightful property by greedy local officials. For Franks north of the Alps, Italy equalled corruption. Was this why Wala was faced with stiff disapproval in Corbie, when he returned from Italy in the autumn of 825, laden with gifts? The monks accused him of having kept for himself what should have been handed over to his community. Radbert's strenuous efforts to counter these accusations indicate that Wala's Italian riches had become the topic of gossip and scandal. A snide remark of Amalarius of Metz points in the same direction. Sent by Louis as an envoy to Gregory IV, Amalarius claimed to have been told by the pope: 'I have no antiphonaries which I might send my son and lord emperor, because when he was engaged here in some mission, Wala carried off those that we used to have with him, from here to Francia.'[82] Amalarius had indeed found 'plenty of antiphonaries' to work with in the library of Corbie,[83] which

---

[78] *EA* I, prologue, p. 20.

[79] On repertoires of identification, see Pohl, 'Introduction: Strategies of Identification', pp. 32–8; De Jong, 'Carolingian Political Discourse', pp. 89–90.

[80] *EA* I, c. 2, p. 23.

[81] Weinrich, *Wala*, pp. 51–2; McKitterick, 'Perceptions of Justice', pp. 1087–9.

[82] Amalarius, *Prologus antiphonarii*, c. 2, p. 361: 'Nam quando fui missus Romam a sancto et christianissimo imperatore Hludovico ad sanctum et reverendissimum papam Gregorium, de memoratis voluminibus retulit mihi ita idem papa: Antiphonarium non habeo quam possim mittere filio domino imperatori, quoniam hos quos habuimus, Wala, quando functus est huc legatione, abduxit eos ab hinc secum in Franciam.'

[83] Amalarius, *Prologus antiphonarii*, c. 1, p. 361: 'Inventa copia antiphonarium in monasterio Corbeiensis … '.

made him happy, but he could not resist a crack at Wala, intimating he had taken all the liturgical books in Rome to Corbie.

When Adalhard died on 2 January 826, Wala was his obvious successor. With intense pride, Radbert let it be known that he, and nobody else, was sent to Louis's court to secure Wala's succession, while the abbot designate himself awaited the emperor's verdict in Corvey. Clearly, there was resistance in Corbie that needed to be overcome; one reason for writing a *Life of Adalhard*, shortly after the old abbot's death, was to convince the monks of Corbie that Adalhard's half-brother was the most suitable candidate to lead both the mother and the daughter, as Corbie and Corvey were usually designated. This was what happened eventually, but at the time of writing it was not a foregone conclusion. Addressing the 'mother of religious life', Corbie, Radbert urges her to be comforted and act strongly when the Amalekites would march against them: she already has another Joshua with her, namely Wala.[84] All this suggests that Wala's transition from informal to formal leadership had not yet been completed, at least not in Corbie. In this monastery, there remained a vociferous group of monks who were highly critical of Wala's prominent position at Louis's court.

One of the reasons for this was that monastic norms had evolved since the days of Charlemagne. The councils of Aachen (816–17) had bound monks and nuns to a stricter interpretation of the Rule of Benedict, and decided that abbots were expected to live a monastic life, at least when they resided in their community. Moreover, their often liberal use of monastic landed resources was regulated by a separation of the resources of the community and those at the disposal of the abbot. There is no sign that Corbie's property was ordered accordingly. In many ways, Adalhard and Wala were old-style abbots who treated monastic property as if it was their own to dispense of, and to divert from Corbie to their new foundation, the 'daughter' Corvey. When Wala was exiled in 831, and the connection between mother and daughter was finally and formally severed by Louis in 833, when he appointed Radbert's pupil Warin abbot of Corvey, this created huge difficulties and conflicting property claims. Yet, before getting to Wala's exile after the first rebellion against Louis, I must now turn to Radbert, the main source of information for this tumultuous episode, who was himself so much part of these events.

---

[84] *VA*, c. 86, cols. 1551D–1552A.

## 3    Paschasius Radbertus

Of Radbert's own social background, nothing is known. There is a short *Life* transmitted in a late twelfth-century manuscript from Corbie (Paris, BnF lat. 12607). Henri Peltier, Radbert's most recent biographer, thought it a faithful rendition of an older *vita*, now lost, produced in 1058 on the occasion of the translation of Radbert's remains to the abbey church of St Peter in Corbie.[85] This text reads like that of a critical author who put together whatever information he could find, weighing different traditions in the process, rather than as a typical mid-eleventh-century document written for the festive translation of a saint. It was apparently rewritten by Dom Antoine de Coulaincourt (d. 1536/40) and integrated into his still unedited chronicle of Corbie;[86] both the *vita* and the chronicle were used, along with other Corbie traditions, by Dom Jean Mabillon for his outline of Radbert's life of 1680.[87] Reprinted in J.-P. Migne's *Patrologia Latina* of 1854, this became the authoritative short biography, although it must be said that Mabillon as well as Peltier were more cautious than later historians. Radbert is said to have been born around 790,[88] yet this remains a tentative date, as is the alleged year of his profession in Corbie, namely 812. David Ganz rightly questioned the diverse estimates of Radbert's death, ranging from 856 to 865.[89] Together with Peltier's monograph, Ludwig Traube's introduction to Radbert's poems offers a good overview of our author's life and work, as does Ganz's study of Corbie's Carolingian library.[90]

The mostly implicit references scattered through his exegetical works reveal that he was raised by the nuns of Nôtre-Dame in Soissons. Wala's youngest sister Theodrada became abbess there only in 810,[91] so Radbert must have arrived before this time, as a motherless child. His pupil Engelmodus, bishop of Soissons (862–5) wrote an elaborate and

---

[85] The *Vita Paschasii* was edited by Jean Mabillon in *ASOB* IV, 2, cols. 122–34; also by Holder-Egger in *MGH SS* XV/1, pp. 452–4; Peltier, *Pascase*, pp. 13–14.

[86] Denoel, 'Antoine de Caulaincourt (1482–1536/40?)'; on Radbert's early biographers, see Peltier, *Pascase*, pp. 12–25.

[87] Mabillon, *Eulogium historicum* of Paschasius Radbertus, in *ASOB* IV, 2, t. 6, cols. 122–34; reprinted in *PL* 120, cols. 9–24.

[88] Aris, 'Paschasius Radbertus': around 790; Weinrich, *Wala*, pp. 7–10, followed by De Jong, *Penitential State*, p. 103, n. 218: between 785 and 795; Brunhölzl, *Histoire de la literature latine*, I/2, p. 125: towards the end of the eighth century.

[89] Ganz, '*Epitaphium*', pp. 539–40; The year 860 is not a *terminus ante quem* for Radbert's death, as Breternitz, 'Ludwig der Fromme', pp. 193–4 points out, contra De Jong, 'Becoming Jeremiah', p. 189. Breternitz is right.

[90] Traube, *Prooemium*, and Ganz, *Corbie*, especially pp. 30–3, 103–20.

[91] Kasten, *Adalhard*, pp. 103–4. For a specious argument that Theodrada was the widow of Pippin of I of Italy who died in 824, rather than in 846, see Fried, 'Elite und Ideologie', pp. 93–4, 107–9.

affectionate praise poem for his one-time master, in which he intimated that Radbert's mother died in childbirth, and it was God's providence that saved the newborn child: 'As indeed the provident author [...] appointed your tender self to be given life, when the black shroud of the mother who gave birth to you was wrapped around your first rattle, and the ravenous likeness of death stalked you, the abandoned child.'[92] The orphan Radbert became one of those very young children taken in by religious communities, formally as oblates or more informally destined for monastic training. Some were deemed too young for the demands of a male community, and entrusted to nuns for their earliest upbringing.[93] Throughout his entire life, Radbert felt closely connected with the nuns of Nôtre-Dame, calling himself 'your foster child from my boyhood',[94] dedicating exegesis to them, and referring to Soissons as 'our place' (apud nos).[95] What Radbert wrote to them must also have pertained to himself: 'Nothing else are you but a sacrifice to God, the vowed gift of your parents, the possession of the Holy Spirit by whose infusion you have been sanctified and nourished.'[96] For his beloved nuns in Soissons he also composed a sermon on the Assumption of the Virgin, in which he adopts the authorial persona of his much-admired Jerome, who addresses his patroness Paula and her daughter Eustochium.[97]

Among Radbert's very last exegetical works was the commentary on Psalm 44 that he had promised to Theodrada and her nuns. Unable to present his gift in her lifetime, he dedicated it to Theodrada's daughter and successor, Abbess Imma, but she also died before he managed to finish it.[98] In this work, completed in ripe old age, he again called himself the foster child of his beloved nuns of Soissons.[99] He also recalled that, before becoming a monk in Corbie, he had been 'exiled for a long time in

---

[92] Engelmodus, *Carmina* no. 3, *Ad Radbertum abbatem*, p. 64 ll. 66, 69–70: 'etenim ... providus auctor/.../Legavit tenerum, cum prima crepundia matris,/Quae genuit, nigri fascirent tegmina panni/Expositumque vorax ambiret mortis imago'. See Peltier, *Pascase*, pp. 28–9. I am grateful to Robert Smith for helping me with the English translation of this passage, and informing me that the verb 'fascire' is used in Ezek. 30:20.

[93] Paschasius Radbertus, *Carmina*, p. 38, n. 1; Peltier, *Pascase*, pp. 28–32; De Jong, *In Samuel's Image*, pp. 126–7, 180; De Jong, 'Becoming Jeremiah', pp. 187–8.

[94] Paschasius Radbertus, *De partu virginis*, p. 47: ' ... A puero vestro alumnus ... '; Peltier, *Pascase*, p. 30.

[95] *EA* I, c. 1, p. 22 (Pascasius), with regard to the arrival of the relics of St Sebastian in St-Médard in 826.

[96] Paschasius Radbertus, *Expositio in psalmum XLIV* 3, p. 104: 'Nihil enim aliud estis quam sacrificium Deo, vota parentum, possessio sancti Spiritus cuius infusione sanctificatae estis et nutritae.'

[97] Ripberger, *Der Pseudo-Hieronymus-Brief IX "Cogitis me"*. On ninth-century Marian devotion, see Leyser, 'From Maternal Kin'.

[98] Paschasius Radbertus, *Expositio in Psalmum XLIV*, Introduction, pp. v–vi.

[99] Paschasius Radbertus, *Expositio in Psalmum XLIV* 1, p. 6, ll. 170–5.

the world' (*exulatus longdiu in saeculo*). Contaminated by many wordly acts, Radbert said, he had lost the crown – that is, his tonsure – which he had received as a little boy (*puerulus*) at one of the altars of Nôtre-Dame, in a rite accompanied by the nuns' praying and singing.[100] In adolescence or young adulthood, Radbert apparently interrupted his monastic career and led a different life, but regardless of where he was or what he did during these mysterious years of exile, as he called them, they did not stop him from becoming very learned indeed, for he ended up as one of Corbie's foremost teachers and intellectuals. Given that Radbert's monastic profession in Corbie took place when Adalhard was still active as Corbie's abbot, the period between 810 and 814 seems a likely timeframe for this return to monastic life. Perhaps Theodrada chose her half-brother Adalhard as a suitable abbot and patron for her precocious alumnus? Or were Radbert's unknown parents connected with this 'royal lineage' in some way? This remains a tantalising mystery.

To a large extent, Theodrada, Adalhard and their siblings became Radbert's adoptive family, but he was well aware of the difference between having royal blood and merely being associated with it. First and foremost, he was a monk, as he underlined by calling himself, from his earliest work onwards, 'Paschasius Radbertus the Deacon, scum of all the monks' (*Paschasius Radbertus levita, monachorum omnium peripsema*).[101] This exceptional expression of humility was derived from St Paul's first letter to the Corinthians: 'We are made as the refuse of this world, the scum of everything, even until now'.[102] As for his byname Paschasius, one likely model for identification from Christian literature was the deacon Paschasius about whom Gregory the Great wrote in his *Dialogues*. Reference to him in this work meant that this saintly man, who wrote 'illuminating and orthodox books' about the Holy Spirit, was widely known. During the Laurentian Schism (498–506), this Paschasius chose Laurentius' side, and he tenaciously stuck to this position, which earned him the punishment after death of having to become a servant in a bathhouse. Prayer released him, however. Because he had not sinned with evil intent, but through misunderstanding and error, he could be

---

[100] Paschasius Radbertus, *Expositio in Psalmum XLIV* 3, p. 74, ll. 51–7: 'Quas cum in dextris benignissimi Dei et Salvatoris nostri Christi contueor multiplici varietate decoratas ingemisco valde eo quod coronam quam susceperam puerulus coram sancto altare Genitricis Dei vestris cum precibus et officio laudis quo vestra spons<o> Deo regi immortali corda consecrantur et capita, longe diu exsulatus in saeculo perdidi eam, coinquinatus multis mundanis actibus.'
[101] Paschasius Radbertus, *De corpore*, Prologus ad Karolum Calvum, p. 8.
[102] 1 Cor. 4:13: ' ... tamquam purgamenta huius mundi facti sumus omnium peripsima usque adhuc ... '.

purified from sin after death.[103] On the other hand, 'Paschasius' was also a prominent name in the wide-ranging tradition of the *Vitas Patrum* discussed earlier in this chapter. According to modern scholarship, one influential version of these Latin renderings of Greek monastic tradition should be ascribed to Paschasius of Dumium, who dedicated this work to Abbot Martin of Braga.[104] Yet, traditionally, a Roman deacon named Paschasius was seen as the author of this particular translation – an identification still followed by Rosweyde.[105] Possibly this Roman Paschasius, translator of influential Lives of the Fathers, was identified with the deacon Paschasius discussed in Gregory's *Dialogues*, but even if not, the name 'Paschasius' was connected with authoritative Roman traditions, which explains why this became Radbert's monastic name.

Radbert remained a deacon all his life, possibly because during his years outside the monastery he had committed sins which barred him from the priesthood. In two acrostic dedicatory poems he identified himself, through the first letters of each line, as *Radbertus levita*.[106] If this were indeed the case, one can see why he would have identified himself with the Paschasius of the *Dialogues*, who had also been a deacon, and a sinner who was ultimately granted mercy. On the other hand, the celebrated Alcuin of York never became a priest either, without any damage to his reputation. Both he and Radbert were influential *magistri*, and for this reason may not have aspired to the priesthood.

Once in Corbie, Radbert cannot have seen much of Adalhard, for his abbot was often absent on imperial business, in Italy and elsewhere. In 814, he was banished from the court as well as his monastery while Wala was confined there, and the latter assumed the informal yet effective leadership of Corbie. As far as Radbert was concerned, Wala was the one who ruled Corbie until the rightful abbot's return. It was during these years between 814 and 821 that Radbert must have become Wala's protégé, even though he wrote with equal affection of Adalhard: both were his fathers. He became one of Corbie's brightest intellectual stars, a *magister* who trained the monastery's great and good, such as Warin, who in 833 became abbot of Corvey. In his praise poem, Engelmodus, another former pupil, likened his one-time master to a bee who flew through the glade of sacred speech (*eloquii sacri*), waking up the flowers;

---

[103] Gregory the Great, *Dialogi* IV, 42, p. 150; Leyser, *Authority and Asceticism*, p. 108. According to the late twelfth-century *Vita Paschasii*, p. 453, ll. 34–5, there were those who had confused Paschasius Radbertus with this Roman deacon Paschasius – but wrongly (*sed frustra*), as the author commented.

[104] Freire, *A versão latino*.

[105] *De Vitas patrum sive Verba Seniorum* VII (BHL 6531), *PL* 73, col. 1025.

[106] Paschasius Radbertus, *Carmina* no. 2 ('Ad Warinum') and no. 3 ('Ad Placidium'), *MGH Poet. lat.* III, pp. 51–2.

having gleaned the nectar from documents, he created honeycombs of books.[107] Like Hraban Maur, his slightly older contemporary, Radbert was a schoolmaster who eventually became his monastery's abbot.[108] Both men also wrote important commentaries on Lamentations.[109] Due to the influence of the twelfth-century author of the *Vita Paschasii*, one still finds this mentioned as Radbert's very last work.[110] I agree with those who think it more likely that he embarked on this venture not long after 845, when 'Vikings' captured Paris and he was still abbot of Corbie.[111] Beda Paulus, the modern editor of most of Radbert's exegetical work, points out that the Lamentations commentary is referred to in the tenth book of the commentary on Matthew, which was written after Radbert had stepped down as abbot in 849–53.[112] There is yet another reason to think of his exegesis of Lamentations as a work of the second half of the 840s: he dedicated all of its five books to his friend Odilman, the monk of Corbie who participated as 'Severus' in the discussions of the *Epitaphium*'s first book, but 'had gone the way of all flesh' by the time Radbert had lost his abbacy and started on the second book.[113]

The question is whether Radbert, for all the praise he lavished on Wala's many virtues in the first book, still needed to put some careful distance between himself and this abbot who, according to some, had been more at home at the imperial court than in Corbie's cloister. If he wrote the first part of his *Epitaphium Arsenii* in the late 830s, which is most likely, depicting himself as Adalhard and Wala's 'third man' and constant companion also meant that Radbert presented himself as the obvious successor of his two illustrious abbots. Defending their reputation, and especially Wala's utterly contentious renown, went a long way towards clearing his own. Was this why Radbert told the elaborate anecdote about his visit to Louis's court, underlining that it had been he himself who had been sent to negotiate the emperor's acceptance of Wala as the new abbot in 826?[114] He also made it clear that when the shocking news of Wala's exile reached him in Cologne in 831, he was there on important business on behalf of 'Augustus', that is, Louis. Apart from nervous pride inspired

---

[107] Engelmodus, *Carmina* no. 3, *Ad Radbertum abbatem*, p. 65, ll. 110–17.

[108] For a comprehensive account of Hraban's career and abbacy, and its impact on Fulda, with references to older literature, see Raaijmakers, *The Making of the Monastic Community*, pp. 175–264.

[109] Matter, 'Lamentations Commentaries'.      [110] Aris, 'Paschasius Radbertus'.

[111] This particular siege is referred to in Paschasius Radbertus, *Expositio in Lamentationes* IV, c. 12, p. 282, ll. 1218–21; Traube, introduction to Paschasius Radbertus, *Carmina*, *MGH Poet. lat. III*, p. 39, n. 5, and Ganz, *Epitaphium Arsenii*, p. 540. Both think this is the siege Radbert refers to, and so do I.

[112] See Beda Paulus (ed.), *Expositio in Lamentationes*, p. v, who situates the commentary between 845 and 857, the years in which Paris was taken by Northmen.

[113] *EA* II, prologue, p. 60.      [114] See below, pp. 55–6.

by any proximity to the court, this may also have been an effort to show his own loyalty to the emperor, who, for all we know, was still alive when the first book was written. I do not wish to suggest that Radbert embarked on the *Epitaphium* only to further his own ambitions, but clearing his own reputation, along with Wala's, was certainly one of the aims of the enterprise. After Wala left for Italy in 834, Radbert was left high and dry in Corbie, and even more so when the news of Wala's death in Italy reached him, along with that of others of Lothar's bishops and magnates who had followed him there. All had succumbed to an epidemic in the autumn of 836.[115] By then it was clear that Radbert's formidable patron, still formally the abbot of Corbie, would not return. Meanwhile, if Radbert was indeed a candidate for Wala's succession, as I suspect, this prospect had become problematic, to say the least. The *Epitaphium*'s first book was created at a time when not only Wala's name needed to be cleared, but also Radbert's. As Wala's close associate, his reputation was at stake.

Shortly after Lent 830, the first rebellion against Louis broke out, initiated by his son Pippin I of Aquitaine, who in May was joined by his eldest brother, Lothar. The latter had been sent off to Italy by his father in August of 829, and had been replaced as the second man at Louis's court by Bernard of Septimania, the emperor's godson.[116] This was a palace rebellion, primarily aimed against Bernard's sudden dominance over the imperial court, and his influence over the Empress Judith, which allegedly included an adulterous and even incestuous liaison. Prominent courtiers who had been squeezed out by Bernard backed the rebellion; the Astronomer singled out Hilduin and Wala as the two central figures. Of these two, Wala was clearly Lothar's man, and worked towards a reinstatement of the elder son as the co-emperor, ruling together with his father. This had been Lothar's title and position in the years before the summer of 829, when Bernard of Septimania was installed in the palace as chamberlain and as a 'bastion' against the forces of opposition. Initially, the rebellion seemed to succeed, for during an assembly in Compiègne in May 830, the clock was turned back and Louis duly reinstated Lothar, but by the autumn, the old emperor, backed by loyal *Germani* from the Eastern parts of his realm, managed to turn the tables on the rebels.[117]

Wala was banished from the court, first to Corbie, to live there as a proper monk (finally!), as the Astronomer expressed it,[118] and then, in

[115] Astronomer, c. 56; see *EA*, c. 24 on the Empress Ermengard (d. 20 March 851), who had informed the monks of Corbie of this news. I suspect this passage was written after her death.
[116] See below, pp. 151–8.    [117] De Jong, *Penitential State*, pp. 41–44.
[118] Astronomer, c. 45, p. 464.

831, to a series of other monasteries, ending up in Noirmoutier, where his brother Adalhard had been sent in 814. At least, this is what Radbert claimed, in a part of his narrative that was emphatically meant to convey that Wala the lofty exile was so much sought out by potential followers, including the emperor's sons, that he had to be sent ever further, to the most distant parts of the realm. Whether this was indeed the case, remains a question.[119] Radbert emphatically claimed that he was sent to his master by Louis as a mediator, offering Wala a reconciliation if the latter would only also admit to some responsibility of his own, but all to no avail. He regularly visited Wala in exile, and apparently enjoyed a liberty of movement denied to his abbot. During the second rebellion against Louis in 833, the two men were briefly reunited, as part of Lothar's retinue. Both were present in July in Alsace on the 'Field of Lies', but, as far as I can see, not in October in Soissons, when Louis submitted to the imposition of a public penance.[120] This would explain why this momentous event is referred to only obliquely in the *Epitaphium*'s second book; it is also evident that for Radbert, the failed restoration of Lothar in 830, followed by Wala's disgrace, was far more important than the revolt of 833, in which Wala played only a marginal role.

Once the rebellious eldest son Lothar was defeated, in the summer of 834, Wala followed him to Italy, where he was made abbot of Bobbio, Columbanus' illustrious foundation. Surely this was a suitable position for this grand old man, but Radbert immediately thought of the evil Queen Brunhild, who had persecuted Columbanus until he had to leave for Italy. Like Columbanus, Wala had been exiled from Corbie 'by the zealous vengeance of some woman'. He was widely criticised for having deserted his monks and taken up another abbacy, most of all in Corbie.[121]

About Wala's last years, Radbert was curiously silent, possibly because the communication between Corbie and its departed abbot was infrequent. According to the Astronomer, Louis and Judith were eager to reconcile themselves with Wala, and did so at the assembly of Thionville in May 836, having used him earlier as an intermediary between Lothar and themselves.[122] Was Radbert unaware of his master's rapprochement with the emperor, or did he gloss it over, choosing to emphasise Wala's intransigence in exile?[123] There may be another possibility: namely, that Radbert compressed the last part of his chronological narrative, and situated Wala's activity as a mediator between Louis and his eldest son right after the dramatic events on the Field of Lies. It was important for him to show

---

[119] See below, pp. 154–9.
[120] *EA* II, cc. 17–18, pp. 85–9; De Jong, *Penitential State*, pp. 224–8.
[121] *EA* II, c. 21, p. 92.     [122] Astronomer, c. 55, p. 506.
[123] The two possibilities are suggested by Ganz, *Corbie*, p. 30.

that Wala still was in command of the situation, and that his departure for Italy was in no way involuntary. The *Epitaphium* conveys exactly this impression. While Louis and Lothar were still vying for his loyalty and services, Wala went south of his own accord, 'with winged step'.[124]

Radbert did not follow his abbot to Italy. He remained in Corbie, which was by then a community in considerable disarray. At least part of this could be, and was, blamed on Abbot Wala and his having got on the wrong side of the emperor. This explains why Radbert's turn as abbot of Corbie came only in late 843, after the short-lived and undocumented abbacies of one Heddo and the equally obscure Isaac.[125] Radbert had to wait. But, in January 843, the new monarch, Charles the Bald, recently married to his first wife Ermentrude,[126] took a clear interest in Corbie, for he visited this monastery to pray.[127] This was a young king who needed all the support he could get: he was about to enter the negotiations that would lead to the partition of the empire in Verdun.[128] It was probably on this occasion that Charles, displaying typically royal behaviour, set the best minds of the monastery to work on pressing questions with regard to the nature of the Eucharist. He not only got Ratramnus of Corbie to express his views, but also ordered Radbert to present him with a copy of his *De corpore et sanguine domini*, the first version of which was completed in the early 830s, during Wala's exile.[129] Charles received this work either at Christmas 843 or at Easter 844.[130] Such gifts of biblical commentary implied a public recognition of the legitimacy of the ruler in question[131], but in this case Charles' request may well have amounted to an equally public rehabilitation of Radbert, which cleared his way to the abbacy.

Radbert's subscription to the acts of the synod of Quierzy in the spring of 849, where Gottschalk of Orbais was publicly flogged and silenced, is the last secure evidence for him as abbot of Corbie.[132] Four years later, in April 853, his successor Odo attended the synod of Soissons.[133] Sometime in between, Radbert ceased to be abbot. This 'shipwreck'

---

[124] *EA* II, c. 20, p. 92.
[125] *Ganz*, Corbie, p. 30; Heddo died in June 837. According to Traube, *Prooemium*, 39, n. 4, this information is not reliable; it comes from Mabillon's *Prolegomena*, col. 12. The source for Heddo and Isaac, a brief mention, is the *Vita Paschasii*, p. 453. See also Levillain, *Examen des chartes*, p. 319.
[126] Nelson, *Charles the Bald*, p. 127; the marriage took place on 12 December 842. Ermentrude was the niece of Adalhard, the Seneschal; see below, pp. 206–7.
[127] *Regesta imperii*, nos. 355 and 406 (Karl der Kahle, 840–8).
[128] Nelson, *Charles the Bald*, pp. 126–30.
[129] Paschasius Radbertus, *De corpore*, prologue, p. 8.
[130] *Regesta imperii*, no. 406 (Karl der Kahle, 840–8).
[131] Hrabanus Maurus, *Epistolae*, no. 28, p. 444; De Jong, 'Empire as *ecclesia*', pp. 207–8.
[132] Gillis, *Heresy and Dissent*, pp. 134–45; Pezé, *Le virus de l'erreur*, pp. 164–74.
[133] *MGH Conc.* III, no. 27, p. 265; Grierson, 'Eudes', p. 16.

(*naufragium*), as he called it later on,[134] was not something he had
wanted, but he seems to have bowed out with good grace all the same.
He retired to the nearby community of St-Riquier, where Charles's
maternal uncle Rudolf had succeeded Nithard as lay abbot in 844.[135]
Radbert's biographer, Henri Peltier, thought that Radbert returned to
Corbie, after having initially sought refuge in St-Riquier. However, the
relevant passage about brothers from this monastery who visited Radbert,
asking for his commentary on Matthew, may well have referred to an ex-
abbot who lived in a *cella* near St-Riquier.[136] As an ex-abbot, Radbert
seems to have been at home in both monasteries, and in both libraries.[137]
Of his successor Odo, a young man 'hardly out of school', who would
become bishop of Beauvais in the early 860s, he wrote with great
affection.[138]

It is possible that after his deposition, Radbert still did not envisage his
role in public life as entirely finished, even though the only sign of this is
his prolific writing. Like Hraban, another abbot who bowed out under
political pressure,[139] Radbert already had a great reputation as a biblical
commentator when he had to give up the abbacy. During those last years
of his life, he produced nine of the twelve books of the big commentary on
Matthew, the first four of which he had already completed in 831 and
dedicated to his fellow monk Gundland of St-Riquier; then there were the
exposition on Psalm 44 for the nuns of Nôtre-Dame of Soissons,
the second book of the *Epitaphium Arsenii*, and a treatise for Fredegard,
a monk of St-Riquier, on the nature of the Eucharist.[140] His last work was
an exegetical exposition on the Benedictions of the patriarchs Jacob and
Moses, which confirms that he was still active as an author well into the
850s, for this work was dedicated to Abbot Eigil of Prüm (853–60).[141]
After these Benedictions, the trail of Radbert's authorial activity goes
cold.

---

[134] *In Matthaeum* V, prologue, p. 463 ; see below, pp. 64–5.
[135] Nelson, *Charles the Bald*, p. 177.
[136] Peltier, *Pascase*, pp. 81–2, with reference to *In Matthaeum* V, prologue, p. 463.
[137] On Radbert and St-Riquier, see Ganz, *Corbie*, p. 32, with n. 147, who lists all the
references to St-Riquier in Radbert's *In Matthaeum*. Radbert dedicated the books
V–XII of this to the monks of St-Riquier.
[138] *In Matthaeum* IX, prologue, p. 932, ll. 44–5. Ganz, *Corbie*, pp. 31–2; Grierson, 'Eudes'.
[139] De Jong, 'Empire as *ecclesia*'.
[140] Paschasius Radbertus, *Epistula ad Fredegardum*, *PL* 120, col. 1351; Radbert also called
himself a *senex* in his prologue to Book v of *In Matthaeum*, p. 469, ll. 213–5.
[141] Paschasius Radbertus, *De benedictionibus patriarcharum*, pp. 3–11; Ganz, *Corbie*, p. 32;
Breternitz, 'Ludwig der Fromme', pp. 193–4.

# 3    Between the Cloister and the Court

In this chapter, I explore, first of all, the respective contemporary contexts in which the two books of Radbert's *Epitaphium Arsenii* originated, but also the way in which the author presents himself as an actor in a narrative full of tension between the cloister and the court. As we have seen, Radbert's childhood was spent in a nunnery, and most of his adolescent and adult life in Corbie, a community that prided itself on its Merovingian royal founders and its close connections with the palace. Abbots Adalhard and Wala were of royal descent, and major political players throughout their lives, despite periods of exile. In the first book, Radbert portrays himself as their favourite and most trusted disciple, a constant companion during the foundation of Corvey in 822, and the obvious emissary to Louis's court when Adalhard has died in 826, sent to Aachen to secure Wala's succession as abbot of Corbie and Corvey. He was deeply conscious of his monastic status, but also took great pride in being dispatched on 'imperial business'.

The push and pull of these two closely connected yet opposite worlds comes especially to the fore in an extensive and idealised double portrait of Adalhard and Wala at the time of their joint foundation of Corvey. Yet, by the time this was written, the 'mother' Corbie and the 'daughter' Corvey were no longer a single institutional entity. As will become clear, this connection had formally come to an end in June 833, and so had Corbie's control of its estates in Saxony. Although some of the frustration about this loss can already be felt in the first book, Radbert's primary reaction here is to idealise a lost world of harmony and unity. Corbie's objections only fully surface in the second book, and especially in the narrative about Wala's retreat to Italy in 834. Some monks clearly blamed their one-time abbot for first incurring Louis's disfavour and then leaving his own community and becoming abbot of Bobbio; his subsequent death in 836 must have left Corbie in even more disarray. This background, and especially the painful loss of Corvey, will be discussed at some length in this chapter, as will the later and different context that left its mark on the second book: Radbert's experiences as abbot of Corbie, fighting for the integrity of his monastery's property and at loggerheads with court-connected enemies who finally, sometime between 849 and 853, forced him to resign.

Thus, the focus in this chapter is not on Wala or the rebellions, but on Radbert, as author and abbot. For this, the *Epitaphium*, with its dual perspective on the recent and more distant past, is a precious source. Of course, these memories were perceived through the prism of later experiences and contemporary predicaments; in what follows, this will be central to my concerns. Both in the late 830s and the mid- to late 850s, when Radbert wrote the two books of his *Epitaphium*, he needed all the political and institutional support he could get, within and outside Corbie. I suspect that at both stages, defending 'his' Arsenius also meant that he was defending himself by proxy, and attempting to improve his precarious position.

## 1     After Wala

It is not easy to get an idea of Radbert's position in Corbie after August 834, when Wala followed Lothar to Italy. Wala became abbot of Columbanus' foundation of Bobbio, clearly as the reward for his loyalty to Lothar, but Radbert presents Wala's retreat to Italy entirely as his own initiative. 'With winged step' (*pennigero gressu*) he went south, where he gained the abbacy of Bobbio merely because of its monks, who begged him to protect their abbey against robbers.[1] This lame justification, offered by the narrator Pascasius towards the end of the second book, is countered by the outspoken Teofrastus: would it not have been more monastic (*religiosus*) for Arsenius to remain in his own community, where he had been professed and elected abbot, or more humble to retreat to Bobbio without assuming the burden of the abbacy?[2] This is the voice of the monks of Corbie who felt deserted by Wala, but Pascasius then tries to counter this grievance by comparing Arsenius' escape from Judith's wrath to the flight of Bobbio's founder Columbanus, who had also gone to Italy because of the evil designs of a woman, Queen Brunhild. Both men, he argues, had faced real and mortal danger:

I do not know whether he could have saved himself together with us amidst so many upheavals, in a place where fidelity can no longer to be found, or only rarely, especially among those who desired to be the greatest or to appear as such: among them, to spurn the honours of the world because of religious life was considered faintheartedness.[3]

---

[1] *EA* II, c. 20, pp. 91–2; Weinrich, *Wala*, pp. 85–7.    [2] *EA* II, c. 20, p. 92.

[3] *EA* II, c. 21, p. 92: ' ... qui nescio si se salvare posset nobiscum inter tot discrimina, ubi iam nulla fides vel vix rara invenitur, maximę inter eos, qui summi esse cupiunt, vel videntur: inter quos, honores contempnere seculi pro religione, ignavia putatur.'

Otherwise, the *Epitaphium* is remarkably silent on the years between Wala's departure in August 834 and his death two years later, on 31 August 836. This is not just because its author was left behind in Corbie and lost contact with his Arsenius, who was in hiding in Italy. Wala's position in Bobbio may have been not entirely that of the fugitive and exile that Radbert made him out to be. According to the Astronomer, Louis's biographer, Wala headed a delegation from Lothar to his father in May 836. With some misgiving, the Astronomer remarks that by this time, the imperial couple was ready to be reconciled with Wala, as a preparation for making their peace with Lothar. Louis and Judith, 'with hearts full of kindness', forgave their elder kinsman all the offences he had committed; in the Astronomer's view, Wala was indeed in need of much forgiveness.[4] This perception of the matter is entirely in keeping with the Astronomer's overall portrait of his emperor, namely as a Christian ruler who was always prepared to forgive his enemies, but it also suggests that even though based in Italy, Wala still had access to Louis's court and functioned as an intermediary between father and son.

As in other cases, the Astronomer presents a mirror image of the *Epitaphium*'s version of events.[5] In the latter, we find an intransigent Wala, who flatly rejected any attempt at compromise, even when in 831 his disciple Radbert was the one bearing a message of appeasement from the court to Arsenius in his 'very high and narrow cave' in the mountains, to which only angels had access.[6] But Arsenius preferred exile over any unwarranted admission of guilt,[7] and when the second rebellion had run its course, he refused both Louis's and Lothar's attempts to turn him into their ally. Radbert claimed that he had witnessed how Louis 'most insistently wanted to keep him at his side, with all honour and reverence due to the highest rank,' while Lothar urged him to swear an oath of fidelity and wished to take him to Italy.[8] This image of a principled Arsenius, for whose favour rulers continued to compete, fits a more general pattern in the *Epitaphium*. Wala's shameful rejection and exile were turned into their opposite, a memory that was easier to cherish than the reminiscence of an abbot who had been ready to compromise, and then deserted his own community. In the words of Teofrastus: 'Hence, this is what many try to blame him for, that he left his own [monastery] in which he had been

---

[4] Astronomer, c. 55, p. 506; transl. Noble, *Charlemagne and Louis*, p. 289.
[5] See, for example, their very different treatment of the presence of Pope Gregory IV in Francia in May and June 833; De Jong, *Penitential State*, pp. 214–21.
[6] *EA* II, c. 10, p. 74.    [7] *EA* II, c. 10, p. 75.
[8] *EA* II, c. 20, p. 92: 'Nam pater voluit eum, me teste, multum instanter secum tunc cum omni honestate et reverentia summae honoris retinere, etiam si vellet iuramentum a suis fidemque facere, deinde augustus filius secum abducere.'

professed and elected, and snatched up another one, as if driven by cupidity, by some kind of deal (*pactum*)'.[9]

There is no indication that a new abbot of Corbie was appointed during the few years that remained of Wala's lifetime. Apparently, Louis kept his options open, including the possibility of his kinsman's return to Corbie. This lends substance to the Astronomer's remark about a rapprochement in May 836. A formal reconciliation of Louis and Lothar was impending, but was prevented by an epidemic in Italy.[10] While Lothar survived, Wala and a host of other Frankish leaders perished towards the end of August of that year.[11] In Corbie, Radbert was left to cope with the fallout of his abbot's choices. He may well have exercised some kind of informal leadership, but if he was indeed Wala's earmarked successor to the abbacy, as I suspect, these expectations had to be shelved for the time being. Radbert's own turn to become abbot came only after the short-lived tenures of a certain Heddo and the equally obscure Isaac, who, according to a later and possibly unreliable Corbie tradition, died in September 843.[12] Sometime later in this year, or at the beginning of 844, Radbert was entrusted with the leadership of his beloved Corbie.

Within this community and perhaps also outside it, the *Epitaphium*'s first book may have helped to restore both Wala's reputation and his own, paving the way to high office. There is no way to prove this, but there is some circumstantial evidence. A concerted effort was made to be discreet, and to refrain from offending Louis. The first book touches upon the rebellion era only incidentally and obliquely, without giving any indica-tion that the emperor had already died at the time of writing. Louis is referred to as *Augustus* or *Caesar* as a matter of course, without any of the disparagement that characterises the second book, or any of its revealing aliases for the political protagonists.[13] With considerable pride, Radbert presents himself as the emperor's envoy, and as the one who successfully petitioned Louis concerning Wala's succession in 826.[14] In spite of his obvious dismay about his abbot's disgrace and exile, and the intense grief over Wala's death in Italy, far from his community, the overall impression given by the first book is that when Radbert started on his *Epitaphium*, he was careful not to offend an emperor whose support he still very much needed. By contrast, in the *Vita Adalhardi*, written shortly after Adalhard's death in January 826, he had criticised Louis's spontaneous

---

[9] *EA* II, c. 21, p. 92: 'Hinc est quod multi eum reprehendere conantur, quia suum in quo professus et electus est, reliquit; et aliud, quasi cupiditate ductus, quolibet pacto praeripuit.'
[10] Astronomer, c. 55, p. 50.    [11] Astronomer, c. 56, pp. 510–14.
[12] Cf. Ganz, *Corbie*, p. 30; *Vita Paschasii*, p. 452.
[13] On these aliases, see below, pp. 136–46.    [14] *EA* I, c. 7, p. 33; *EA* I, c. 11, p. 39.

penance at Attigny as an empty and even hypocritical gesture, and compared it to Adalhard's clear-headed vision of the truth. Whereas the latter was a 'truth-teller', Louis was blind to what was really the trouble, and merely went through the motions of atonement.[15] One explanation for this striking lack of restraint may be the fact that, in the years after Adalhard's demise, Radbert was still under Wala's powerful wing. A decade later, however, Wala's death had left him without a protector, and he could ill afford outright criticism of the recently restored emperor. This is one explanation for his circumspect treatment of Louis in the first book, as well as his eager depiction of himself as someone who was regularly and honourably sent on imperial business; another is that, at the time of writing, Radbert yearned to return to the emperor's service, and reminded his audience that he had proven his merits in this respect.

## 2     Gaining and Losing a Daughter

The foundation of Corvey is the centrepiece of the first book. In the context of this narrative, Radbert portrays himself as the constant companion of Adalhard and Wala, the founders of 'new Corbie' (*Nova Corbeia*), or 'the daughter', as Radbert called Corbie's Saxon dependency, praising the glorious renown of 'the mother's daughter's fertility'.[16] From other sources, one learns that this was actually a re-foundation of an earlier monastic settlement, a *cella* called Hethis, established during Adalhard's exile by the abbot of the same name who took his place under Louis's orders.[17] I shall say more about this other Adalhard below, but at this point I simply note that the *Epitaphium* largely ignores this temporary replacement, and certainly his role in the foundation of the first phase of Corvey. Here, the two illustrious half-brothers are the true initiators of the Saxon monastic dependence, with Radbert as the third man in their *consortium*.[18]

The other main player in this enterprise who is emphatically written out of Corvey's foundation story is Louis the Pious. Radbert treats Höxter, the estate on which the fledgling community was re-established in 822,[19]

---

[15] *VA*, c. 51, cols. 1534D–1535A; De Jong, *Penitential State*, pp. 126–8.

[16] *EA* I, c. 20, p. 49: ' ... de fecunditate filiae matris ubique fama adnuntietur valde gloriosa ... '.

[17] *Translatio S. Viti*, c. 3, p. 40: Semmler, 'Corvey und Hereford'; Krüger, *Studien*, pp. 74–6, 101–15; Flierman, *Saxon Identities*, pp. 137–46; Rembold, *Conquest*, pp. 175–6.

[18] *EA* I, c. 15, p. 43.

[19] The chronology: mid-October, Adalhard and his brother Bernarius were recalled from exile (Bernarius was then in Fleury) and allowed to return to Corbie. Cf. *ARF* s.a. 821, p. 826; Astronomer, c. 34, p. 404–6. Semmler, 'Corvey und Hereford', pp. 296–8.

as the property of an anonymous Saxon aristocrat who had been persuaded to donate the land, urged to do so by Wala. Nobody but Arsenius
would have managed to persuade him, Radbert claims, 'not even, if I may
say so, the king'.[20] In a twelfth-century *Notitia* about Corvey's foundation, the Saxon donor has acquired a name: this Count Bernard, 'a most
noble man among the Saxons and a pre-eminent leader among his people', voluntarily handed over the *villa* of Höxter and its entire territory
(*marca*) to Louis the Pious.[21] Yet two royal charters for Corvey, issued on
27 July 823 in Ingelheim, suggest that the *villa* of Höxter was in fact
a royal fisc. In the first document, the emperor donated not only this *villa*,
but also, with the consent of the abbot and monks of Corbie, all the estates
of this monastery situated in Saxony. Furthermore, he granted Corvey the
right to elect its own abbot.[22] The second charter was a grant of immunity
and royal protection (*tuitio*) of the kind enjoyed by all religious communities in Francia, issued at the request of Abbot Adalhard.[23]

There is no sign that either Corbie or Corvey had a separate *mensa
fratrum* – that is, estates of which the revenues were reserved for the
monks, as distinct from those destined for the abbot.[24] On the contrary,
Adalhard's *Statuta vel Brevia* of 822 indicates an undivided monastic
economy administered by a hands-on abbot who was once more firmly
in charge after his exile.[25] Likewise, the unity of Corbie and Corvey
depended on being governed by one and the same abbot who also controlled all the monastic property, regardless of whether it was destined for
the upkeep of either community.

From these two charters for Corvey, it transpires that Louis the Pious
was actively involved in getting the new foundation off to a flying start.
Hard on the heels of the reconciliation in Thionville came the emperor's
public atonement, in Attigny in August 822, for the ill treatment of his
kinsmen, in which not only Louis's half-brothers and Bernard of Italy
were included, but also, quite explicitly, Adalhard and Wala.[26] Less than
a year later, the emperor showered Corvey with privileges and property.

---

[20] *EA* I, c. 16, p. 45: '... cum nulli alteri omnino cessisset in vita, etiam (ut ita fatear) nec
regi ...'.

[21] *Notitia fundationis monasterii Corbeiensis*, p. 1044; my thanks to Justin Lake for alerting me
to this. See Krüger, *Studien*, pp. 203–19.

[22] *MGH DD LdF* no. 226, pp. 559–62. On Corbie and the privilege of free abbatial election,
see below, pp. 57–9.

[23] *MGH DD LdF* no. 227, pp. 563–5: '... qualem omnes ecclesiae in Frantia habent'.

[24] Kasten, *Adalhard*, p. 113; differently, Calvet-Marcadé, 'Les clercs', p. 418. For a detailed
and excellent discussion of the 'mense conventuelle' in the kingdom of Charles the Bald,
see Gross, 'Abbés', pp. 631–58. Corbie does not figure in Gross's documentation.

[25] See Adalhard, *Statuta seu Brevia*, and the enlightening discussion in Kasten, *Adalhard*,
pp. 110–37.

[26] De Jong, *Penitential State*, pp. 122–31; *ARF* s.a. 822, p. 128.

This very much looks like the third and final stage of a successful rapprochement between Louis and his two illustrious older relatives, but this was not the impression Radbert wished to convey. One of the reasons must have been that in the late 830s, when he wrote the *Epitaphium*'s first book, Corbie had lost her daughter: in early June 833, Louis made Warin abbot of Corvey. He thereby not only put an end to the one abbacy that had held the two monasteries together, but also to any claims on Corbie's part to their Saxon estates. When, in 823, Adalhard and his monks had destined these lands exclusively for Corvey's use, the later total loss of control was surely not what they had had in mind.

Karl Heinz Krüger argues convincingly that Warin became abbot in his own right only in 833, as a reward for his loyalty to Louis on the eve of the second rebellion. Before, he had already exercised an informal type of leadership in Corvey, under Abbot Wala's aegis.[27] According to a twelfth-century tradition of Corvey, however, Warin had already succeeded Adalhard after the latter's death in January 826, and this is implicitly supported by the *Translatio S. Viti*, written in the late 840s or early 850s by a monk from Corvey.[28] Here, Wala's role in the foundation of Corvey is downplayed, while Adalhard, the real founder, is said to have named the young and aristocratic monk Warin as his successor in the Saxon foundation.[29] The *Translatio* claims that once Adalhard died, the monks of Corvey acted upon his wishes and duly elected Warin as their abbot, even though those in Corbie supported Wala.

This tradition situated the separation of Corbie and Corvey in the year 826, but Radbert took a different view of the matter: Wala was his brother's undisputed successor who, after Adalhard's death, assumed the formal leadership, until he was forced to relinquish the governance of both abbeys in the course of the two rebellions. By the time he wrote the *Epitaphium*'s first book, however, the separation was a fact, and it rankled. Warin had been a favourite pupil of Radbert's, and was therefore nicknamed Placidius, after one of the favourite child oblates in Gregory's *Life of Benedict*. Radbert dedicated two of his more important works to Warin, a first version of *De corpore*, his famous treatise on the Eucharist, and the equally ambitious *De fide*. From the former, composed during Wala's exile from 831 to 833, it transpires that Warin was not yet Corvey's abbot, but when *De fide* followed, sometime in 833, Radbert headed his dedication with a ponderous and perhaps ironical address referring to his former pupil's new dignity.[30] Further evidence from charters shows that Warin's

---

[27] Krüger, 'Nachfolgeregelung', especially pp. 189–95.
[28] *Translatio S. Viti*, c. 3, p. 42; Flierman, *Saxon Identities*, pp. 139–4.
[29] *Translatio S. Viti*, c. 4, p. 44; Depreux, *Prosopographie*, pp. 394–6.
[30] Krüger, 'Nachfolgeregelung', pp. 190–3.

formal appointment as abbot must have taken place during the first week of June 833, when he was with the emperor in Worms. This was on the eve of the confrontation between Louis and his sons on the Field of Lies, at the very time when Wala and Radbert had joined Lothar's camp.[31]

Radbert's exasperation about Warin's siding with Louis, and being richly rewarded for it, transpires from the comments made by the young monk Adeodatus on the ensuing alienation of Corbie's Saxon property. As noted above, these estates had been destined for Corvey's use since 823, but as of June 833, the newly independent community and its abbot Warin were fully in charge of these estates. Wistfully, Radbert imagined how different things might have been if Arsenius had still been in their midst. Quite apart from preserving the unity of the two communities, he would have been a far better leader of Corvey than 'that prelate', that is, Warin. Had Wala not been forced to return so quickly to Italy in 834, he would have turned the monks of Corvey into true citizens of heaven, rather than allowing them to move away from monastic discipline and towards the outside world. Above all, he would have revealed that the man whom the monks of Corvey had preferred as their leader was in fact a puffed-up worldling.[32] Warin had risen above himself and contaminated the purity of Corbie's daughter, a grievous accusation to level at one's former disciple and favourite.

The many differences between the *Epitaphium*'s perspective and that of the *Translatio S. Viti* suggest that Adalhard's succession did not proceed without problems, and so does Radbert's *Vita Adalhardi*, from which it transpires that Wala's succession in 826 was no foregone conclusion: Corbie was called upon to support the new Joshua that was already in its midst, and apparently needed to be convinced.[33] That Wala did become abbot of both Corbie and Corvey, eventually, is confirmed by all the evidence mustered by Krüger, yet in the late 830s this was still something that needed to be argued strenuously in the *Epitaphium*'s first book, as was Wala's prominent role in Corvey's foundation. In the first book, Radbert explicitly mentions the younger monks of Corvey as part of his intended audience: they, most of all, had much to learn about their illustrious founder and former abbot, whom they had not known personally.[34] But they also got their unpleasant share of the truth as

---

[31] *MGH DD LdF* no. 328 and 329, pp. 810–15: 'Warinus, quem in eodem monasterio abbatem praeficimus,' – (present tense!) – 'suggerendo petiit celsitudine nostrae ... '. The charter concerns a share for Corvey in a salt mine. Krüger, 'Nachfolgereglung', pp. 191–3.

[32] *EA* I, c. 20, p. 49. It was the younger monk Adeodatus who pronounced this severe verdict: was he perhaps a monk of Corvey?

[33] *VA*, c. 86, col. 1552A; Krüger, 'Nachfolgereglung', pp. 185–6.     [34] *EA* I, c. 16, p. 45.

Radbert saw it. Warin's blatant ambition had led to the separation of mother and daughter, and, moreover, his fame would soon eclipse the memory of the great Arsenius. This fear was by no means unfounded, for, in the late 840s or early 850s, the author of the *Translatio S. Viti* produced a 'Wala light' version of Corvey's foundation story, perhaps also in response to Radbert's version, in which Wala played a major role.

## 3     Two Brothers

The *Epitaphium*'s narrative about the Saxon foundation is embedded in a long digression on the unbreakable bond between Adalhard/Antony and Wala/Arsenius. However different their nature and history, the two half-brothers always acted in perfect harmony, and founding Corvey together was the zenith of their close collaboration. One gets the impression that Radbert protests a bit too much, and indeed, he himself identifies the problem. During the years 814–21, when Adalhard was in exile, Wala became Corbie's *de facto* leader and, at least from Radbert's perspective, entirely dominated the temporary 'younger' Abbot Adalhard, elected at Louis the Pious' behest. When, in the autumn of 821, the senior Adalhard returned from Noirmoutier, however, Wala had to step back. This situation was resolved when he joined Lothar in Italy as the latter's deputy, later in 822. Subsequently, Wala went on to become one of the dominant figures at Louis's court, but the potential controversy must have loomed large earlier in 822, when the brothers travelled to Saxony to found what would become one of its major monasteries.

There is no doubt that they did so together, but the question debated at some length in the *Epitaphium* is which of the brothers had been more important to Corvey's foundation. After Wala's disgrace in the wake of the two rebellions, this was surely an issue in Corbie as well as Corvey, with some monks trying to distance themselves from this controversial former abbot. Severus, the outspoken interlocutor of the first book, articulates some of the strains that may have ensued when Adalhard came back and took charge of Corbie once more, where his half-brother had held sway for the past seven years. In spite of his actual dominance, Arsenius had never been the monastery's abbot; the one formally in office had been the 'younger Adalhard', elected at Louis's behest, who gets quite a stellar role in the *Translatio S. Viti*, but hardly any mention in the *Epitaphium*. Given that he bore the same name as 'the' Adalhard of Corbie, it is likely that he was a relative, but this remains uncertain. Radbert mentions the abbacy of this other Adalhard just once, and then makes it clear that although he worked together with this 'father' (*cum patre*), Arsenius in fact supervised him and had the ultimate authority, albeit informally: ' ... he governed the house of his brother[35] and already charged himself with the office of abbot ... '. Arsenius was ultimately responsible for the community's salvation, and he ensured that nothing occurred by which 'our saintly old man', his brother, would displease God.[36] At the time, Arsenius had no *potestas* whatsoever, that is, power of the abbatial office, for this rested with his elder brother, Adalhard.[37]

Radbert's emphasis on this problem indicates that the old abbot's return from exile created some tension, and the same is true of his long digression on the two brothers' unshakable harmony and unity of purpose, and in the way in which, however different, they complemented each other. On the one hand, there was the elderly (*senex*) Adalhard/Antony, the rigorously ascetic abbot; on the other, Wala/Arsenius, a monastic leader who, for all his fasting and vigils, still radiated all the formidable charisma of a secular magnate, and a truly Saxon one, for that matter. This double portrait of two loving but very different brothers also reveals how elite monks like Radbert could be torn between their belonging to cloister and their admiration for the court. As members of a royal monastery, they were fascinated with the court, to the extent that it was the epicentre of their lives outside their community. This fascination with the world of kings, queens and palaces is a remarkable feature of Carolingian monastic historiography. It inspired Notker's *Gesta Karoli*, the Annals of Metz, and countless minor annals that duly took note of significant events, both locally and within the wider context of the kingdom or empire. Yet, much as the royal court was an integral part of their world, even high-born monks and nuns were keenly aware that they had become life-long insiders who belonged to the secluded domain of the *claustrum* and should not stray far from it, lest they be damned.[38] The royal court was close, but it was also a dangerous place that needed to be kept at a mental distance. This identity conflict is writ large in Radbert's narrative of his experiences at Adalhard and Wala's side when they jointly founded Corvey.

Although Antony and Arsenius both held high and equal secular rank, 'they nonetheless competed with one another to see who could be found

---

[35] *EA* I, c. 14, p. 43 (Severus): 'Gubernabat autem fratris domum, et commendabat iam in se officium abbatis.' Cf. Ambrose, *De excessu* I, c. 20, p. 221: ' ... et gubernasti fratris domum et commendasti sacerdotium.'

[36] *EA* I, c. 14, p. 43 (Severus): 'Porro, ut dixi, iam tunc cum patre curam monasterii gerens, quasi arbiter in consilio erat, atque ordinator rerum, curam habens de omnibus. Provisor quoque sollicitus animarum, ne displiceret sanctus senex noster in aliquo Deo, sicque ut placeret in omnibus laborabat.'

[37] *EA* I, c. 16, pp. 44–5 (Severus and Pascasius).

[38] De Jong, '*Imitatio morum*', 'Internal cloisters'.

most humble'.[39] As Radbert makes clear, this was a contest easily won by
Antony. During an assembly in Saxony in 821, the local members of the
elite knew real authority when they saw it. All those present crowded
around Arsenius, unable to take their eyes off the great man, while none
of them paid any attention to Antony, 'though he held the office of abbot
and we were all propping him up ... and thronging around him as our lord
as best we could'.[40] Arsenius, for his part, acknowledged the allegiance he
received in Saxony due to his descent, but not to the point of actually
wearing the felt slippers (*ruhilingos*) he had made for himself, for by this he
would have stretched the limits of his abbot's discretion.[41] Radbert's
admiration for the ease with which the former magnate commanded an
assembly full of potentially unruly Saxons is palpable, but he is very clear
about his abbot's position as well as his own. Adalhard decided to leave the
assembly, taking Radbert with him: since they had made no impression
whatsoever, as two mere monks, they might as well return to their cloister.
The delightful story of their voyage home reveals how our author posi-
tioned himself within this spectrum, as well as his occasional ambivalence:

But I wonder why he [Adalhard] wanted to be so punctilious in this particular
matter, when in his own behaviour he could be deemed excessively scrupulous (if
it is permissible to say so). For at that time when he was travelling, he refused to
allow any contraption to be made for himself at night, such as travellers are
accustomed to make, so that we could be sheltered from the rain. Nor did he
permit any kind of tent to be erected for himself by day or night, but we rested
spread out upon the ground, and according to what a certain person sings, 'the
grass itself provided us with refreshing sleep'.[42] At the same time, in an admirable
manner the blessed abbot provided deep and wide furrows in the fields (such as
are typically found in that country) for himself and me, where he ordered me to
spread out our bedding. On both sides their flanks surrounded us and kept us
warm with their lovely bedposts. The saddle of a horse was placed in the middle,
one peak of which supported my head and the other his. And we had nothing else
there save what was above and below us from day to day. This had all the softness
of a bed, and was quite a respectable arrangement.[43]

---

[39] *EA* I, c. 16, p. 45–6: 'Nam cum esset uterque secundum saeculi dignitatem eximius,
vicissim tamen decertabant ut inveniretur quilibet eorum humilior.'

[40] *EA* I, c. 16, p. 45 (Pascasius): ' ... quia nullus eorum Antonium, cuius erat potestas,
respiciebat, quem omnes fulciebamus hinc inde et venerabamur pro viribus constipati ut
dominum ... '.

[41] *EA* I, c. 16, p. 46.

[42] Boethius, *De consolatione philosophiae* II, metrum 5, p. 206, l. 10.

[43] *EA* I, c. 16, p. 46 (Pascasius): 'Sed miror cur ille in hoc facto tam discretus esse voluit, qui
in suo (si dici fas est) superstitiosus potest iudicari. Nam eo in tempore in itinere positus,
nullum in noctibus apparatum sibi sinebat fieri, sicut solent viantes facere, quo tegeremur
imbribus; neque tentorium aliquod sibi permittebat exigere die et nocte; sed fusi super
terram quiescebamus, et iuxta illud quod quidam canit, salubres nobis herba dabat
somnos, nisi quod beatus pater sibi ac mihi providebat egregie satis profundos atque

Although Radbert felt a special kinship with the monkish Adalhard, his admiration for the charismatic Wala knew no bounds. Whether this double portrait does justice to Adalhard is a moot point. After all, he was raised at the courts of Pippin and Charlemagne, before he withdrew from the political arena to Corbie in 774. Since then, he had been a monk of Corbie, and from 780/1 its abbot, but during this entire period his political clout remained formidable. Adalhard served as Charlemagne's *missus*, and as the adviser and deputy of Pippin of Italy.[44] Contemporaries were impressed with his eloquence and *gravitas* on public occasions,[45] so surely he could hold his own during an assembly in Saxony.

These differences between the brothers may have genuinely existed, yet Radbert is also sketching the outlines of two types of legitimate monastic leadership, both well within the range of ninth-century experience. Some abbots were recruited from the longstanding membership of the community itself, but more often they were parachuted into a monastery by a ruler exercising his right of protection. From the 840s onwards, resistance against lay magnates, palatine clerics and bishops receiving multiple abbacies grew.[46] Adalhard and Wala came from an older world, however, in which a retreat into the monastery meant a visible departure from the court, and hence from the public arena, but by no means the end of political activity. Such men took all their palace-connected charisma into the monastery, as well as their political networks. This was how Adalhard had entered Corbie, according to Radbert's *Vita Adalhardi*, yet in the *Epitaphium* he cast him in the role of the elderly and other-worldly abbot, content with leaving the limelight to his powerful younger half-brother.

Radbert, who defined himself as a man of the cloister, probably visited the palace with some regularity, but this familiarity had definite limits. If not fear, the court at least inspired trepidation, as becomes clear from a tight little narrative about his presence there. Radbert, dispatched to the palace to make sure of Louis's approval of Wala's succession in 826, was

---

amplissimos (ut assolent fieri illa in terra) agri sulcos, ubi iubebat mihi nostrum sternere lectum, quorum latera hinc inde pulchris nos ambiendo fovebant fulcris, dum equi sella in medio posita, quae unam mihi alpem ad caput prebebat, alteram illi. Nec aliud quid habentes in eo, nisi quod in die supra et deorsum habuimus. Haec tota mollities lecti erat, et ambitio satis honesta.'

[44] Kasten, *Adalhard*, pp. 47–72.   [45] See below, pp. 57–8.

[46] Felten, 'Laienäbte'; *Äbte und Laienäbte*, pp. 280–304 ; Gross, 'Abbés', pp. 591–630. But see the Council of Paris (829) II, c. 6, *MGH Conc.* II/2, p. 656 on clerics and laymen adorned with *honores palatini*, and the *Relatio episcoporum* (829), c. 12, *MGH Capit.* II/2, p. 39 on palace priests and chapels without proper ecclesiastical authority or discipline. This was already a problem in Wala's lifetime.

challenged by some magnates about this candidate's suitability as an abbot: would he not be far too strict?

At that time some of the chief men (at the behest of the emperor, as I understood it) asked me about the austerity of his life and the rigour of his discipline, suggesting that we would not be able to endure him or follow in the footsteps of his conduct. To this I responded, with a smile, as it were: 'See here, don't you know who we are? Do you really think that, contrary to nature, we want to elect a tail instead of a head, as some are wont to do?[47] And if he were equal in virtue to one of the saints, what of it? Because we cannot keep up with him, are we really supposed to set over ourselves one who follows behind rather than leads from the front?' He smiled briefly at this, and reported it back, I believe, to the emperor. Following these discussions, I obtained absolutely everything that I wanted, just as I wanted it, and under compulsion from the emperor he [Wala] who had for some time now avoided preferment yielded to our wishes, albeit unwillingly.[48]

Two contested points are driven home: that Wala was the choice of his own monks, both in Corbie and Corvey, and that he was a strict disciplinarian. Furthermore, Radbert portrays himself as able to hold his own with Louis's courtiers, by means of a clever joke that they may even have passed on to the emperor himself. This anecdote conveys the mixture of pride and awe with which Radbert looked back at the mission he accomplished, but it is also another dig at the high-born Warin, who would have been much more at home at the court than Radbert himself. It is Warin who is targeted in the witty allusion to Deuteronomy about the head that should lead, rather than the tail. Whether the ambitious young monk and *magister* already aimed for the leadership of Corvey in 826 remains doubtful. By the time this was written, he had already been its abbot for well over three years, and the separation of the two communities was an irreversible fact. Radbert's ardent praise for their unity, both in the *Ecloga* he added to the *Vita Adalhardi*[49] and in the second book of his *Epitaphium*, reveals how much this breakup must have grieved him.

---

[47] Deut. 28:13: '... constituet te Dominus in caput et non in caudam et eris semper supra et non subter si audieris mandata Domini Dei tui quae ego praecipio tibi hodie et custodieris et feceris ... '.

[48] *EA* I, c. 11, p. 39 (Pascasius): 'De cuius nimirum vitae abstinentia et rigore castigationis tunc mihi a quibusdam optimatum, ut persensi, augusto iubente, suasum est, quod non eum ferre possemus, neque vitae vestigia imitari. Ad quod ego quasi arridens: An nescis, heus tu, nos qui sumus? numquid caudam pro capite, ut quidam assolent, monstruose volumus eligere? quid putas si tantus esset, quantus excellentior aliquis sanctorum? numquid quia commeare nequimus, eum preferre oportet, qui postergum eat, et non potius eum qui precedat? Tum ille pauliser subridens, augusto haec, ut credo, retulit. Quibus ita dictis, cuncta quae volui, et ut volui, penitus impetravi; atque cogente illo, nostris, licet invitus, paruit votis, qui dudum subterfugerat quantisper prelatus.'

[49] *VA*, cols. 1552D–1556C; Paschasius Radbertus, *Carmina*, no. 1, pp. 45–51.

## 4    *Radbertus abbas*

Twenty bishops and two abbots, gathered at a synod in Paris in the winter of 846/7, issued a lengthy *privilegium* for Corbie, of which Radbert almost certainly was the intellectual author. The document is dated to the autumn of 846 and subscribed by *Radbertus abbas*, who declared that he had read and verified it.[50] Together with the *Epitaphium*, this synodal privilege provides a mine of information about our author's aims and ideals during his brief tenure as abbot of Corbie, and on his devotion to this royal monastery with its long and illustrious history. His abbacy lasted only seven years at most, but clearly Radbert worked hard to guarantee Corbie's rights and integrity, making the most of the royal privileges that he had at his disposal. The relatively recent right to elect one's abbot freely especially needed to be guaranteed and upheld, and this is what the synodal privilege was meant to do, first and foremost.

In 823, Louis the Pious had granted Corvey a free abbatial election,[51] but Corbie only received this two years later, in a charter issued jointly by Louis and his eldest son, Lothar, in August 825. This is not to say that Corbie lacked royal privileges of immunity, both Merovingian and Carolingian.[52] In 815, Louis had confirmed his father's grant, with a reference to the many earlier Frankish kings that had extended their most complete *defensio et immunitas* to this monastery.[53] There is no mention of the right to elect one's abbot, however. Even in the imperial privilege of 825, this is added almost as an afterthought, at the very end of the charter: 'We also want the monks of the aforesaid monastery to have the licence to elect themselves an abbot according to the precept of regular life, as long as royal might will flourish.'[54] Still, this addition was why Adalhard petitioned the two emperors for yet another grant of *defensio tuitionis et immunitatis*, on top of Louis's confirmation of his father's privilege, issued ten years before. It cannot have been a coincidence that the privilege of 825 for Corbie was the first of the

---

[50] *Privilege* (846/7), *MGH Conc.* III, no. 13, pp. 140–9. For a more extensive discussion of this text, including a translation, see De Jong, 'Our Sons and Lords'; I have profited from the discussion in Gross, 'Abbés', pp. 578–80. As Wilfrid Hartmann explains in his introduction to the edition in *MGH Conc.* III, pp. 140–1, the privilege is dated to 846, and the tenth indiction, which puts it between 1 September and 31 December of this year, but the synod in Paris at which it was issued took place either in the autumn of 846 or early in 847.

[51] *MGH DD LdF* no. 226, pp. 559–62.

[52] Most are lost, or survive only in later copies. See Brühl, *Studien*, pp. 226–59; further, Barbier & Morelle, 'Le diplôme de fondation'.

[53] *MGH DD LdF* no. 243 (825), pp. 606–10; no. 52 (815), pp. 135–6.

[54] *MGH DD LdF* no. 243 (825), pp. 609–10: 'Vol[umus quoque, ut predicti mo]nasterii monachi habeant secundum regularis vite inst[itutionem] eligendi sibi abbatem, quam-diu regalis [cels]itudo viguerit.'

charters Louis issued together with Lothar as co-emperor; in 826–7 at least five other privileges of free abbatial election were granted jointly by father and son. As Franz Felten has pointed out, until then Louis had been cautious in this respect, especially when it came to older monastic establishments in the centre of the realm. Before the mid-820s, immunities that included the right to elect one's abbot were mostly reserved for more recent foundations on the periphery of the realm, such as Corvey.[55] Were the new grants in more central regions due to Lothar's influence? Possibly, but there is no doubt that the close connection that Adalhard and Wala had forged with Louis's eldest son helped to create this extraordinary imperial privilege of August 825, issued only half a year before Adalhard's death on 2 January 826.[56] It looks as if the old abbot was eager to ensure a smooth succession for his half-brother, even though a 'free' election still required the emperor's approval. Still, this formal right gave the community more influence over the outcome.

Radbert presented this privilege of August 825 to the synod gathered in Paris in the autumn of 846, together with Charles the Bald's subsequent confirmation charter of 840/1. The latter is no longer extant. The synodal privilege says that these were only two documents 'among others', but clearly these were the ones that mattered most. Then 'he [Radbert] asked from us that what had been confirmed in the sacred charters of the most pious rulers would also be confirmed by our charter (auctoritas), at the behest of the ruler'.[57] Radbert was the one who had petitioned the synod for it, and it seems likely that it was also Radbert or someone working under his supervision who produced a draft of the privilegium agreed upon and subscribed by the synod. It is also worth noting from the outset that the emphasis in this document is on the confirmation of royal charters, issued by past rulers (principes), and also on the voluntas, the wish and active cooperation, of the ruling monarch, Charles the Bald.[58]

The privilege is transmitted in a later version, which includes the subscriptions of churchmen not yet in office at the time of the synod of Paris in 846/7: these include Odo, Radbert's successor as abbot of Corbie, who subscribed when he had become bishop of Beauvais (862–81), and Hincmar of Laon (858–79). Interestingly, the synodal privilege remained a legally valid document to which subsequent bishops also committed

---

[55] Felten, Äbte und Laienäbte, pp. 259–64.

[56] Aachen, 2–13 August; on this date, see MGH DD LdF no. 243, p. 607–8; this would make it the first joint charter issued by Louis and Lothar, until their break in the summer of 829.

[57] Privilege (846/7), p. 144: 'Petiit itaque a nobis, quo ea, quae sacris litteris piissimorum principum confirmata fuerant, nostra quoque auctoritate ex voluntate principis confirmarentur.'

[58] As rightly noted by Gross, 'Abbés', p. 578.

themselves. It also became the jumping board for the papal privileges obtained by Odo, from Benedict III in 855, when he was still abbot of Corbie, and in 863 as bishop of Beauvais from Nicholas I.[59] Odo's approach was no different from that of his predecessor, for he continued Radbert's policy of bolstering Corbie's rights in every possible way. It is only in the privilege of Nicholas I that Corbie gets the right to appeal directly to the pope in order to defend its free election of an abbot and other liberties.[60]

All this gets us as close as possible to Radbert as the leader of his community, fighting for its rights every inch of the way. It is also one of the very first ecclesiastical confirmations of royal grants of immunity. Against a historical background that goes all the way back to the founders, Queen Balthild and her son King Chlotar II, the synod issued an eloquent warning to their 'sons and lords, most pious rulers' to preserve and guarantee Corbie's immunity and the integrity of its property. This community had an unbroken tradition of staunch monastic regularity, as well as constant proximity to the royal court. Both were a matter of intense religious and aristocratic pride:

This is why also the noblest of men converged upon this monastery (*locus*)[61]to serve God freely, and also adorned this community by their nobility as well as by the merit of their life. Hence it happened that this monastery became more familiar with the affairs of the lords of the land, to such an extent that kings and queens received it under their protection (*tuitio*).[62]

This was the monastic identity Radbert shared and chose to project, yet he had a more pressing and concrete goal as well, for which he wished to enlist the synod's help. First and foremost, this was about safeguarding Corbie's right of freely electing its abbot.

Charles' confirmation charter of 840/1 is lost, so we do not know what was confirmed, precisely: was it Louis's general grant of immunity of 815, or the more specific one of 825, issued together with Lothar? The wording of the synodal *privilegium* seems vague to the point of deliberately obfuscating the issue: 'In addition, he handed over the confirmation charter of the most excellent and illustrious

---

[59] Levillain, *Examen des chartes*, no. 29, pp. 266–77; no. 32, pp. 282–8. Both papal *bullae* were requested by Radbert's successor, Abbot Odo. See Boshof, 'Traditio Romana', pp. 8–11, and the informative discussion in Gross, 'Abbés', pp. 580–4.

[60] Gross, 'Abbés', pp. 580–3.

[61] As in Radbert's *Epitaphium*, *locus* is used consistently to refer to Corbie.

[62] *Privilege* (846/7), p. 145: 'Qua de causa et nobilissimi viri in eodem loco ad dei servitium sponte confluxerunt et eundem locum tam nobilitate sua quam et vitae merito decoraverunt. Unde factum est, ut ipse locus familiarior dominis rerum fieret, adeo ut sub tutela reges atque regine eum susceperunt.'

King Charles, who, according to the custom of his predecessors, as it were by hereditary right, from the very beginning of his reign took this monastery under his protection and safeguard (*familiaritas et defensio*)'.[63] Yet there can be no doubt about how the imperial grant of 825 was interpreted by Radbert and the synod: from the very beginning, Corbie had been given the privilege of electing its own abbot, and the freedom to dispose of its own estates. No doubt one of the documents they had in mind was the exemption granted in 664 by Bishop Berthefrid of Amiens: this had included the free election of the abbot without any episcopal intervention.[64]

Yet, for the synod of Paris in 846/7, Berthefrid's ancient privilege was not the main source of authority to be mentioned explicitly. Although Radbert and the bishops implied that the freedom of election had been an integral part of a continuous history of royal protection stretching from the Merovingian founders to Charles the Bald, they focused on the recent Carolingian royal privileges. Badly damaged, the charter issued by Louis and Lothar in 825 still survives, in a rare original that was unknown to Levillain, who suspected that it had been interpolated. The original became better known only when it was put up for private auction in 1991, and then again in 2004 and 2018.[65]

Whereas, in this royal grant, the free abbatial election comes as an afterthought, secondary to the immunity, in the synodal privilege of 846, the election had become of paramount importance, on a par with the protection of monastic property. The main aim was to ensure that the ruler would not hand out abbacies as a favour to their aristocratic followers, or even to the highest bidder, but this did not mean an end to royal influence: the king controlled the appointment of abbots and could send them packing if he chose.[66] What if the abbot's predecessor had been deposed for negligence because he happened to be 'less dutiful' (*minus officiosus*) towards the king? Even in such a case, the privilege of a free abbatial election should be upheld, the bishops argued, for it would not be right if 'the offence of one person overwhelms everyone', in the sense that

---

[63] *Privilege* (846/7), p. 144.

[64] Ewig, 'Das Privileg des Bischof Berthefrid'; Levillain, *Examen des chartes*, no. 4 (664), pp. 220–6.

[65] See the introduction to *MGH DD LdF* no. 243 (825), pp. 606–8; Morelle, 'Le diplôme original'. David Ganz informed me per email of 13 August 2018 that, after having been sold again in June 2018, the charter has now ended up in a suitable location, the Archives départementales de la Somme. A thirteenth-century dorsal notice on the original does mention Berthefrid's exemption, which by then had become mainstream once more. See Morelle, 'Le diplôme original', pp. 418–9.

[66] As pointed out by Gross, 'Abbés', pp. 576–7.

the sins would cause wrath to arise against everyone, and that because of one person, the church of Christ would lose its privileges.[67]

In other words, the sins of individual abbots should not be visited on their community. This could be read as a barely veiled allusion to Abbot Wala's sins during the rebellions of 830 and 833 against Louis. Had Corbie's right to elect its own abbot been ignored, or even suspended in the aftermath? It is possible. A pointed diatribe follows, against 'a wolf among the herd of sheep of the Lord' who would try to acquire the monastery for money, or because he found 'some favour with the lords'. This evokes the danger that Charles the Bald or his successors might give Corbie's abbacy to one of their great men, disregarding the monastery's hard-fought and still recent privilege.

As Radbert commented with hindsight, 'nowadays' – that is, in the 850s when he wrote the *Epitaphium*'s second book – laymen in charge of abbacies had become more common than they had been in Wala's day and age, even though 'the king had made a good start on these matters'.[68] This is a reference to Charles the Bald, rather than to his father Louis, for it was Charles who began his reign by supporting monastic immunity and property, but who, by the mid-840s, refused to accede to his bishops' demands. At the assembly of Epernay in June 845, the king put his foot down. The bishops were not amused. 'At this assembly, the most necessary admonition of the bishops of the realm about the affairs of the church was treated as if it did not matter a straw: practically never, since Christian times began, can reverence for bishops be found to have been so totally disregarded'.[69] Radbert could not have agreed more.

Wala's pronouncements on ecclesiastical property and its control bear the imprint of Radbert's own experiences as a participant in the synods of the 840s. These are a more likely context for the *Epitaphium*'s debates between churchmen and lay magnates than the late 820s, in which he situated Wala's interventions at the court. True, some of the critique of indiscriminate use of monastic property was already voiced at this early stage, yet Louis's right to have recourse to ecclesiastical lands for the good of the *respublica* remained unchallenged, and the same principle is still upheld in the synod's *privilegium*

---

[67] *Privilege* (846/7), p. 145, l. 27: 'Non enim iustum, ut unius culpa super omnes redundet, neque ullo pacto rectum posse est ut, uno peccante, super omnes vindicta consurgat aut causa unius ecclesia Christi sua privilegia perdat ... '.

[68] *EA* II, c. 4, p. 65.

[69] *Annales Bertiniani* s.a. 846, p. 68; Nelson, transl., *Annals of St-Bertin*, pp. 62–3, n. 1, with the suggestion that this is a later interpolation by Hincmar. See also the comment s.a. 866 (Nelson, transl., *Annals of St-Bertin*, p. 136) on Charles dividing monastic property 'among some of his men, with more detriment to his own soul than any benefit to them'.

of 846 for Corbie.[70] The question was not whether this was legitimate, but to what extent, and on what conditions. Mediating between churchmen who appealed to the 'honour of the churches' (that is, religious communities in the broadest sense of the word) on the one hand, and lay magnates on the other, who argued that the *respublica* could not survive without these resources, the 'Wala' of the *Epitaphium*'s second book took a moderate stance. If troops for the defence of the realm could really not do without the monastic property, bishops should be in charge of overseeing this, and ensuring that the transfer would be an orderly operation, for, 'according to the word of truth, whatever these holy bishops will bind on earth, shall also be bound in Heaven'.[71] Whereas the biblical text uses the singular, with reference to St Peter only, Radbert turns this into a plural which includes all bishops (*pontifices*). Exactly the same happened in the *Relatio episcoporum* of 833 which justified Louis's public penance and *de facto* deposition.[72]

This articulate discourse on the episcopal power of the keys, rendering all bishops joint successors of the apostles and vicars of Christ, surfaces only in 833, and then only as a minority point of view of the bishops allied to Lothar.[73] In the *Epitaphium*, however, it figures as an argument in favour of episcopal supervision of the use of monastic resources for the *respublica*. This fits the tenor of the synodal privilege of 846/7, but not what we know of Wala's own lifetime. The same holds true of the sharp rejection of lay abbots ascribed to Wala, and Radbert's frontal attack on royal exploitation of monastic wealth. In the second book, the gloves are off: 'I do not know which of our rulers might be saved, for whom nothing is quite as delightful as the robbing of churches, and nothing quite so gratifying, as it has been written: "Stolen waters are sweeter, and hidden bread is more pleasant".'[74] Had any of this been an important issue in the

---

[70] De Jong, 'Familiarity Lost'. My more extensive arguments in 'Familiarity Lost' (completed in 2011, forthcoming) are summarised in De Jong, 'Paschasius Radbertus and Pseudo-Isidore'. In a similar vein, see Breternitz, 'Ludwig der Fromme'. The case for an earlier start to the controversy about royal use of church property is made by Esders & Patzold, 'From Justinian to Louis the Pious'.

[71] *EA* II, c. 4, p. 64: 'Quod si secundum sententiam veritatis, quaecumque ligaverint isti sancti pontifices super terram, ligata erunt et in cęlis ... '. Cf. Matt. 16:19: 'et tibi dabo claves regni caelorum et quodcumque ligaveris super terram erit ligatum in caelis et quodcumque solveris super terram erit solutum in caelis.'

[72] *MGH Capit.* II, no. 197, pp. 51–2, ll. 39–1; transl. De Jong, *Penitential State*, pp. 271–7; on the textual transmission of this document, with a new edition, see Booker, 'A New Prologue'.

[73] De Jong, *Penitential State*, pp. 234–45; Patzold, *Episcopus*, pp. 188–92.

[74] *EA* II, c. 2, p. 63 (Teofrastus): ' ... nescio principum nostrorum quis salvus esse possit, quibus nihil tam dulcia sunt, quam predia ecclesiarum, nihilque tam suavia, sicut scriptum est: *Panis absconditus suavior est, et aquae furtivae dulciores*' (Prov. 9:17).

years preceding the rebellions against Louis, it surely would have been included in the list of accusations brought against the emperor in 833, as a legitimation of his subsequent penance, but this is not the case. With the second book of the *Epitaphium*, we enter a different era. It is more radical in tone and approach than the synodal privilege of 846/7, which steers a careful course between the affirmation of royal authority on the one hand, and pointed admonition of 'our sons and lords' on the other. Yet, with regard to the important role accorded to bishops as guarantors of the integrity of monastic property, the two texts are in total agreement. In different ways, both shed light on Radbert's abbacy and his tenacious fight for the integrity of Corbie's property.

To this end, in 846, Radbert enlisted the aid of the bishops gathered in Paris. In their confirmation of Corbie's rights, they explicitly referred to and cited a recent precedent, a privilege for the monastery of Moutiers-Saint-Lomer, issued only a few years before, in the autumn of 843, at the synod of Germigny. The two documents have similar turns of phrase in their opening sentences.[75] The synod of Germigny met in tandem with an assembly convened by Charles the Bald. With the consent of the king, the bishops present endorsed not only a now lost privilege issued by Louis the Pious for this community, but also a confirmation thereof by Charles himself, issued during this very assembly. They guaranteed the integrity of the monastery's possessions, as well as the right to choose an abbot from their midst, according to the precept of the Rule of Benedict.[76] The wording of the bishops' confirmation in Germigny largely followed that of the king's privilege.[77] As in the *privilegium* for Corbie granted three years later, Charles' consent is emphatically affirmed, which should preclude hasty conclusions in terms of an episcopal revolt against 'secular' power. In Paris in 846/7, the bishops admonished 'our sons and lords' to guarantee the integrity of ecclesiastical property, promising them the 'crown of eternal life and the glory of this Davidic, most felicitous and everlasting kingdom' as a reward.[78] This was not an attempt to undermine royal authority, but to harness it once more to the protection of religious communities.

The ensuing episcopal privilege is transmitted as part of Corbie's so-called oldest cartulary (Berlin, Staatsbibliothek 79, Phillipps 1776), which is a selective list of eight privileges for Corbie, four of them ecclesiastical, and four royal.[79] The four ecclesiastical documents are the exemption issued by Bishop Berthefrid of Amiens in 664, which included

---

[75] Hartmann, *Synoden*, pp. 201–2; *MGH Conc.* III, no. 1, pp. 1–6.
[76] *Regula Benedicti*, c. 64.4, p. 206.    [77] *MGH DD LdF*, Dep. no. 126, pp. 1117–18.
[78] *Privilege* (846/7), p. 146, ll. 31–5.
[79] Berlin, Staatsbibliothek 79 (Phillipps 1776), fols. 93–128. See the description in Rose, *Verzeichniss*, pp. 149–56; Ganz, *Corbie*, p. 146.

the free election of the abbot,[80] the synodal *privilegium* of 846/7, and then the two papal privileges obtained by Radbert's successor Odo, from Benedict III in 855 and Nicholas I in 863.[81] These are immediately followed by four Merovingian royal privileges, headed by Corbie's 'foundation charter', that is, a donation of property and the grant of immunity by Chlothar III (657–73) for his mother's foundation of Corbie.[82] None of the Carolingian royal privileges was included, which makes this a strange kind of cartulary. It would be better characterised as a selective list of ecclesiastical and royal privileges, compiled around 880. The episcopal *privilegium* of 846/7 is copied in a later version which includes the subscriptions of churchmen not yet in office when it was first issued, and still active in the late 870s.[83]

The privilege of 846/7 thus remained a living document to which later bishops committed themselves. Moreover, it became a crucial element in the subsequent self-perception of the monastery of Corbie and its rights, in which episcopal and papal privileges joined forces with Merovingian ones, while the Carolingian royal charters were left out of the collective memory of this institution.[84] When Radbert requested a confirmation of Corbie's rights from the bishops in Paris, he created one of the building blocks for this development, yet, when he did so, Carolingian royal grants of immunity remained of paramount importance. These were the documents worth mentioning explicitly. The episcopate in the kingdom of Charles the Bald manifested a new esprit de corps, and Corbie's abbot sought to harness this to the defence of his community's integrity. At the same time, royal support remained the key to survival. It was not a matter of having to choose between the ruler and the episcopate, but of having both: royal *tuitio*, guaranteed by bishops.

## 5     Radbert's Deposition (849–853)

In his commentary on Matthew, Radbert refers to losing Corbie's abbacy as a 'shipwreck' (*naufragium*), which suggests that there was more to it

---

[80] See above, n. 63.
[81] Levillain, *Examen des chartes*, no. 29, pp. 266–77; no. 32, pp. 282–8. See Boshof, 'Traditio Romana', pp. 8–11.
[82] *MGH DD Merov.* no. 86, pp. 220–4, with extensive arguments for the verdict 'unecht' by the editor, T. Kölzer; see also Kölzer, *Merowingerstudien*, p. 107, arguing for a *terminus post quem* of 769, and Brühl, *Studien*, p. 247, who opts for the middle of the ninth century. See now Barbier & Morelle, 'Le diplôme de fondation', who summarise the long discussion on this charter and add new insights on the new pressures on Corbie under Charles Martel and Pippin III.
[83] See above, pp. 58–9.
[84] On the implications of this manuscript transmission, see De Jong, 'Our Sons and Lords'.

than merely an old man bowing out with good grace.[85] The beginning of the *Epitaphium*'s second book is circumspect and non-specific, but also mentions 'unrelenting pressures' that had plagued Radbert.[86] Both the 'shipwreck' and the oblique reference to 'unrelenting pressures' hint at a serious conflict. The present consensus is that Radbert was deposed by Charles the Bald on account of a runaway monk named Ivo, who happened to be the king's relative (*propinquus*).[87] The evidence comes from two letters to Radbert from Lupus, abbot of Ferrières, dated by Levillain to 846.[88] Both have been interpreted as pertaining to Ivo's case, but to my mind, the first of these (no. 51) is neither about Ivo nor about Charles the Bald. Its contents are revealing, though, of other controversies that may have plagued Radbert during his abbacy.

These letters are worth a closer look, for they reveal much about the precarious position in which Radbert found himself at the time, be it in 846 or, more probably, a few years later. He had no direct access to the king, and had to use Lupus as a go-between, but even for the latter, approaching Charles the Bald was no straightforward matter. In a short note, he admitted to Radbert that he had not yet found a good opportunity to relay his friend's petition to the king, but promised to do so at the earliest opportunity and in the best way possible.[89]

This note seems to have been about the Ivo affair, for in a subsequent, longer letter to Radbert, Lupus' relief at the success of his carefully conducted intervention in this altercation is palpable. As he explains, he had now conveyed Radbert's petition to the king, requesting that Charles would no longer extend his protection to 'the monk Ivo', who had not returned to the monastery and showed no sign of heeding any form of discipline. If Ivo were to return to Corbie with Charles's backing, he would endanger himself as well as others there. It would be unworthy of Charles's royal dignity if he were to open the monastery to such wicked men, unless they had come to their senses. As Lupus proudly reports to Radbert, these arguments had proved effective. It would be best, the king had said, if Ivo were to be disciplined by the usual monastic custody before being readmitted to the community.[90] In other words, Ivo no

---

[85] *In Matthaeum* V, prologue, p. 463: ' ... praetermisso quietis bono, memet ipsum pene plurimis aurarum allisus impulsionibus in naufragium dedi'.

[86] *EA* II, prologue, p. 60.

[87] Mabillon, *Prolegomena*, c. 18, col. 14; Peltier, *Pascase*, pp. 71–3; tentatively, Ganz, *Corbie*, p. 32.

[88] Lupus, *Epistolae*, nos. 50–2, pp. 208–10; Levillain, 'De quelques lettres', p. 211. The argumentation is minimal; a redating of these letters in order.

[89] Lupus, *Epistolae* I, no. 50, p. 208.

[90] Lupus, *Epistolae* I, no. 52, p. 212: 'Ille, quo solet vultu cum gratiosis apparet, post quaedam alia, jure se ipse monacho deinceps negaturum auctoritas aditum respondit,

longer had access to royal protection but was obliged to return to Corbie, after a suitable time of penitential custody. Lupus reminded Radbert that this was even more than they could have hoped for. He had even told the king in no uncertain terms that Radbert would never divert from the precepts of the Rule of Benedict.[91] Everyone was now clear as to what had been agreed, and Lupus, pleased with his success, ended his letter with a reference to some top-quality fish that Radbert had sent him as a gift, presumably as a token of gratitude for his intercession.

Given that Charles had granted Radbert's petition, and that both king and abbot wanted Ivo disciplined and back in Corbie, it is difficult to see why the Ivo affair would have cost Radbert his abbacy. The other letter from Lupus to Radbert, which has been thought to show that Ivo was the king's kinsman (*propinquus*), in fact provides a more likely context for real royal displeasure. Again, one finds Lupus lobbying on Radbert's behalf, but with whom? With regard to Charles the Bald, directly or indirectly, Lupus assumed a deeply deferential tone, but this is totally absent here. Instead, he starts bluntly with a compromise he had managed to engineer with 'the man' on Radbert's behalf. After much argument, Lupus claims, he had

... brought the man to these terms: that there would be no harm done, but even the greatest good, if you [Radbert] would show kindness towards his kinsman (*propinquus*) who went away at a time of strife, but who might return now that the peace has been restored ...[92]

It has been assumed that 'the man' is Charles the Bald, and that the relative who had left at a time of strife (*tumultus*) must be the monk Ivo, who therefore was of royal descent; no wonder that this conflict had contributed to Radbert's involuntary retirement.[93] Yet it seems highly unlikely that Lupus would refer to Charles as this 'man' whom he got to agree to the following:

I confidently promised him that you [Radbert] would do this [receive his relative kindly] and that you would carry out anything else he saw fit to command,

quo hactenus uti contempserit, atque hoc sibi satius videri, ne pereat, ut constringatur convenienti custodia, priusquam societatis communionem recuperet.'
[91] Lupus, *Epistolae* I, no. 52, p. 212.
[92] Lupus, *Epistolae* I, no. 51, pp. 208–10: '... evolutisque ratiocinationibus multis ad hanc virum compuli condicionem, ut non modo noceat nihil, verum etiam prosit plurimum, si erga eius propinquum, que tempore tumultus discessit et instaurata pace reverteretur, benigne extiteris.'
[93] See Mabillon, *Prolegomena*, c. 18, col. 14, who also suggested the debate on Predestination as one of the causes for Radbert's disgrace, and discussed (cc. 16–17, col. 13) the possible complications surrounding Charles, son of Pippin II, who in 849 had been locked up in Corbie by Charles the Bald, but who had been enabled to flee in 854. Cf. Nelson, *Charles the Bald*, p. 179.

provided that you would enjoy his favour. I also insisted that he definitely promise not to oppose you in anything until he had first discussed the matter with me. I finally concluded my requests by asking him not to yield publicly to the rebels if they should sometimes request his support in their grievances, but to reserve matters of real importance for your moral judgement.[94]

Clearly 'the man' was a powerful figure, whose favour it was important to retain. His public support for the rebels was feared by Radbert, but he could also be persuaded by the suave and clever abbot of Ferrières to make promises and keep them, mainly about not undermining Radbert's authority by giving public support to 'the rebels' (*rebelles*). Apparently, Lupus was dealing with a mighty court-connected man who was nonetheless sufficiently equal to be negotiated with rather than deferentially petitioned, as one would in the case of one's own king and lord. Was it an important power broker at Charles's court, of the calibre of the king's cousin and archchancellor Louis, who held the abbacies of St-Denis, St-Riquier and St-Wandrille? Or perhaps the formidable representative of another Carolingian ruler?

This is a question I cannot answer, yet it seems that behind Radbert's loss of this glittering prize, the abbacy of Corbie, there was a more important controversy than one runaway monk. The more likely background to strife in Corbie, and closer to the years of Radbert's deposition (between the spring of 849 and April 853)[95] was the struggle for control between Charles the Bald and Louis the German over the kingdom of Aquitaine.[96] Although the rebellious Pippin II of Aquitaine was held at St-Médard, Radbert could well have become involved: in 849, Pippin's brother Charles was dispatched to Corbie by Charles the Bald as a monastic prisoner. When this Charles of Aquitaine escaped in 854, Radbert was no longer abbot, but the presence in his monastery of a young rebellious Carolingian surely contributed to the 'tremendous preoccupation with issues in the outside world' and the 'relentless oppression on all fronts' he had to contend with before relinquishing the abbacy.[97]

---

[94] Lupus, *Epistolae* I, no. 51, p. 210: 'Id vos et libenter facturos et in omnibus quae jubere dignaretur obsecuturos, dum eius gratia frueremini, fiducialiter spopondi; atque eo usque institi donec firmissime promitteret nihil se vobis offecturum, nisi prius mecum causam conferret. Itaque modum petitionis meae hoc fine terminavi, ut si quando rebelles eius favore suas querelas fulciri deposcerent, non vulgo acquiesceret, verum res duntaxat dignas vestrae conscientiae reservaret.' Note that, further on in the same letter, Charles is referred to as *rex*.

[95] See above, pp. 42–3.

[96] I am grateful to Jinty Nelson for alerting me to the possible Aquitanian complications and their impact on Corbie.

[97] *EA* II, prologue, p. 60.

There are other arguments for taking the letter about the *propinquus* as the one providing a background to Radbert's abdication. Whereas Lupus' letter about Ivo (no. 52) is the straightforward report of a successful petition, the other one (no. 51) is enigmatic and full of tension and secrecy. After relating that he has managed to persuade 'the man', Lupus tells Radbert that he has some information so confidential that he cannot communicate this by letter; he therefore proposes to meet with Radbert soon, on the pretext of other business.[98] All this looks like a much more explosive cocktail than the affair of the runaway monk Ivo, however well-connected he may have been. In any case, Radbert's position as an abbot was probably shaky from the very beginning. It is unlikely that the veritable chorus of criticism of Wala's abbacy in the first book of the *Epitaphium* suddenly ceased when Wala's man finally succeeded.

---

[98] Lupus, *Epistolae* I, no. 51, p. 210. At the time of writing, Lupus was part of Charles's retinue.

*Part II*

# Rhetoric

# 4  Lament and Dialogue

## 1  Radbert and Rhetoric

Radbert was admired for his eloquence,[1] an accomplishment on which he himself lavished fulsome praise in his epitaphs for Adalhard and Wala. His *Life of Adalhard* elaborates on the great abbot as the ideal orator. With a voice sweeter than that of a swan, Adalhard caressed the listener, yet his exposition was clear, brief and lucid, of the kind most highly praised by orators. His discourse was perfectly structured, so it could be remembered easily, and was utterly suited to persuasion or dissuasion. Captivating his audience instantly, he dispelled any boredom, and filled those present with a desire hotter than fire.[2] Wala's virtues as a public speaker are obvious as well, not just from extensive passages in which, in direct speech, he admonishes the emperor and his magnates, but also from the start of the *Epitaphium*'s first book, where he is immediately characterised as a superb speaker 'in both languages', that is, Old High German and Latin:

He possessed a very becoming eloquence in both languages (which often aids wisdom) and the fluency of speech to argue in favour of whatever course of action he wished. Being conspicuous for virtues such as these, therefore, he was universally loved.[3]

The implication is that eloquence mattered at the Carolingian court, which is confirmed by other evidence as well.[4] No wonder, despite

---

[1] Engelmodus, *Carmina* no. 3, *Ad Radbertum abbatem*, p. 62, ll. 1–8; p. 66, ll. 148–51.

[2] *VA*, c. 63, col. 1540A–C. Throughout, there is praise of Adalhard's *eloquentia*: *VA*, c. 14, col. 1516B; c. 23, col. 1520B; c. 56, col. 1537A; c. 57, col. 1537D; c. 77, col. 1546C.

[3] *EA* I, c. 1, p. 22: 'Eloquentiam quoque utrarumque linguarum, qua sapientia plerumque iuvatur, et copiam dicendi ad persuadendum quę vellet, modestam nimis habebat. Unde dum huiuscemodi reniteret bonis, ab omnibus amabatur.' Cf. *VA*, c. 77, col. 1546C: 'quis sine mentis scrupulo poterit epistolarum eius nitorem eloquentiae recitare? quem si vulgo audisses, dulcifluus emanabat: si vero idem barbara, quam Teutiscam dicunt, lingua loqueretur praeeminebat claritatis eloquio; quod si Latine, iam ulterius prae aviditate dulcoris non erat spiritus.'

[4] De Jong & Van Renswoude, 'Introduction', pp. 8–9; Vocino, 'Bishops in the Mirror'.

protestations that he could never attain Adalhard's level of proficiency, that Radbert presented himself as a man who could hold his own in a battle of verbal wits in high quarters. Early on in the first book, the total confusion of the entire political leadership is deplored, and the narrator Pascasius illustrates this as follows:

It is for this reason that almost two years ago, when I was deploying similar arguments against one of these people (a leading member of senate) so that he might correct his ways, defeated by my reasoning and scriptural citations, he said to me 'Are you listening? It is true that what you are saying was relevant to the conduct of life and had persuasive power in the age and at the time when we were born, but though these are the words of Scripture, in the age in which we live now there is no utility or reason to them. And so with these words we took our leave of one another, he striving to get what he was after, and I abandoning my efforts.[5]

This same Radbert, not just regretting a bygone age but also self-conscious about his public persona at the court, and proud of his occasional effectiveness, resurfaces in his account of his role as an emissary to Louis's court, shortly after Adalhard's death in January 826, when Wala's succession needed to be secured. He was challenged in jest by some of the great men at the court about Wala's suitability for this office: he would be far too austere and strict for the monks of Corbie. Radbert gave as good as he got, and better, for he silenced his opponents by citing an ambiguous biblical passage: 'And the Lord shall make thee the head and not the tail, and thou shalt be always above, and not beneath' (Deut. 28:13). As he proudly reports, the leader of this formidable pack of magnates 'smiled briefly at this, and reported it back – I believe – to the emperor. Following these discussions, I obtained absolutely everything that I wanted, just as I wanted it'.[6]

This suggests that Radbert was part of an elite for whom eloquence was an integral part of the ideal court, and necessary for any skilled leader, rather than merely a theoretical concept encountered in classical sources. Judging by these two proud stories about his encounter with secular magnates, it was entirely plausible that he would outwit them by a biblical citation without this falling on deaf or illiterate ears. Carolingian court culture had multiple roots in an authoritative textual past, but it was above all shaped by a shared knowledge of Latin Scripture embedded in

[5] *EA* I, c. 3, p. 25 (Pascasius): 'Hinc sane eorum aliquis ex senatoribus prior, cum contra eum ut se corrigeret ferme ante biennium depromerem, ratione superatus et sententiis divinis: Audisne? inquit. Profecto ista quae narras, licet divina, in eo saeculo, quo nati et quando nati sumus, locum agendae vitae habuere et vim dictorum: nunc autem in isto quo nunc sumus, scias nihil utilitatis et rationis inesse. His itaque dictis discessimus; ille post suum velle desudans, ego a meo posse quiescens.'
[6] *EA* I, c. 11, p. 39. See above, pp. 55–6.

patristic commentary.[7] In any competitive exchange of scriptural citations, a learned monk like Radbert would probably get the better of the average magnate, yet his hope that his adversaries would repeat his repartee to the emperor shows that he expected such verbal prowess to be appreciated in high quarters. Still, his portrait of Adalhard as an orator owes much to Radbert's enthusiastic reading of classical and late antique rhetoric in general, and Cicero in particular. In the *Vita Adalhardi*, he is hailed as the 'the king of Latin eloquence'.[8] For most of his life, Radbert had Corbie's exceptionally rich library at his disposal. Its holdings were already formidable in the late 820s, when he wrote his *Life of Adalhard*, but they expanded greatly in the following decades, especially after Radbert's involuntary retirement in the early 850s. With continued access to his monastery's growing collection of codices, the former abbot could now devote himself to an even more comprehensive reading of classical and patristic texts, and to completing a number of unfinished works. To this belonged not just the *Epitaphium*'s second book, but also the last eight books of his commentary on Matthew. A comparison of the earlier and later parts of this *magnum opus* shows how Radbert's textual horizon had broadened at this later stage. Whereas the first four books, written before 830, refer only to Cicero's *De inventione*, the later eight also cite *Cato Maior de senectute*, the *Laelius de amicitia*, and *De officiis*.[9]

As Radbert grew older, his knowledge of Cicero and other classical authors expanded, along with Corbie's formidable collection of codices. As a faithful student of Augustine's *De doctrina christiana*, it came naturally to him, as it did to contemporaries, to apply the principles of *De inventione* or *Ad Herennium* to the cause of biblical exegesis. A telling example is Radbert's prologue to the fifth and last book of his commentary on Lamentations, where he explains that it is the concluding summary of the preceding four books 'according to the principle of the rhetoricians' (*lege rhetorum*) who, in the conclusion of their plea, try to rouse the indignation or mercy of an equitable judge. In other words, Radbert interpreted this part of Lamentations as a perfect example of

---

[7] A massive literature is effectively summarised by Contreni, 'The Patristic Legacy'. On the literacy of the Carolingian court, see above all McKitterick, *Carolingians and the Written Word* and, by the same author, *History and Memory*; more recently, Screen & West (eds.), *Writing the Early Medieval West*, with a section on 'Texts and Early Medieval Rulers' (pp. 183–260).

[8] *VA*, c. 20, col. 1518C: 'Scribit namque Tullius, rex eloquentiae Latinae, in libro secundo de inventione rhetoricae artis . . . '; *In Matthaeum* I, prologue, p. 6, l. 158.

[9] Ganz, *Corbie*, pp. 82–3, who also notes new patristic reading; Bischoff, 'Hadoard and the Manuscripts of Classical Authors', especially pp. 49–51. Beda Paulus' list of works cited in the twelve books of the *In Matthaeum* is a good guide to the gradual expansion of Radbert's reading.

forensic rhetoric: its author, Jeremiah, bewails the dire fate of his people 'in the presence of the most clement judge', and thus 'brings to mind himself and his people, thrown in the deepest misery, in the manner of the orators'.[10] For Radbert and his Carolingian fellow exegetes there was nothing contradictory about perceiving biblical books as part of divine revelation, and at the same time as works produced by authors, that required textual analysis. As Augustine had shown, biblical exegesis also meant keeping abreast of divine rhetorical strategy.[11] This should be kept in mind in any discussion of Radbert's two epitaphs for Adalhard and Wala: he was a biblical commentator, first and foremost, who brought his knowledge of the rules of eloquence to his exegesis, but who also observed all human actions and endeavours through the prism of Scripture.

In this chapter and the next, I shall take this possible development into account, without in any way attempting to provide a more comprehensive picture of Radbert's expanding reading. Some of this can be quickly charted thanks to the exegetical works on which Radbert continued to work in his retirement, such as the commentary on Matthew just mentioned, or his exposition on Lamentations. As for his use of Corbie's library in his tributes to Adalhard and Wala, David Ganz's indispensable study of this monastery and its Carolingian manuscripts remains the first port of call.[12] Ganz has shown the extent to which Corbie's library was a precondition for intellectual innovation. My questions here are related, but more specific. Why did Radbert choose the genre of the *epitaphium*, or funeral oration, for his homage to his two monastic fathers, and what were the implications of this choice? How did dialogue work as a means of structuring his arguments, and what were his main sources of inspiration? These will be the main issues discussed in the present chapter, in which the *Vita Adalhardi* will also get due attention. With regard to this work and the *Epitaphium Arsenii* as funeral orations, I rely gratefully on Peter von Moos' seminal study of the late antique and medieval literature of consolation. This reveals Radbert's indebtedness, in both cases, to Ambrose's and Jerome's *epitaphia,* and should still be the starting point for anyone interested in these texts from this important perspective.[13] But as I shall explain, and as Von Moos himself saw very well, there are also limits to classifying Radbert's two biographical works in terms of lament and consolation, for, within this overall framework, there is a spirited defence of both Adalhard and Wala against the constant chorus of their enemies.[14]

---

[10] Paschasius Radbertus, *Expositio in Lamentationes* V, prologue, pp. 310–11.
[11] Cameron, 'Augustine and Scripture', pp. 203–5.
[12] Ganz, *Corbie,* pp. 103–120 and *passim.*
[13] Von Moos, *Consolatio* II, pp. 100–1 provides a provisional yet helpful overview of textual parallels between the *Epitaphium* and Ambrose's *De excessu.*
[14] Von Moos, *Consolatio* II, p. 141.

Recently, Matthew Kempshall has called attention to Radbert's use of judicial language in the *Epitaphium*, and has shown that, for his refutation of Wala's critics, Radbert deployed forensic rather than demonstrative rhetoric.[15] I shall build on this valuable insight in the next chapter, not least because the same turns out to hold true of Adalhard's *Life*. Yet, as we shall see in chapter five, there is more to Radbert's strategies of persuasion, even though forensic or judicial rhetoric did play a significant part in his pursuit of 'the truth about Arsenius'. In his analysis of Alcuin's dialogue between himself and Charlemagne, the *Disputatio de rhetorica et virtutibus*, Kempshall has shown that Alcuin's explanation of the principles of elocution, followed by a brief discussion of the four cardinal virtues, was less disjointed than has been assumed hitherto. On the contrary, if moral goodness (*honestas*) is required in all aspects of life, this is particularly true of words, 'because man's speech bears testimony to his character'.[16] The same could be said, with a vengeance, of Radbert's portrait of Arsenius in the *Epitaphium*, with its many instances of direct speech delivered by the great man. It also goes a long way towards explaining the choice of the dialogue as a medium to celebrate Arsenius' many virtues, for the very eloquence of the three confabulating monks was an indication of the truthfulness and wisdom of their utterances.

This claim is made from the start. In the opening sentences of the *Epitahium*'s prologue, the narrator Pascasius compares himself to the painter Zeuxis, who had used the five most beautiful maidens of Kroton as a single model, because all the components of perfect beauty could never be combined in one person.[17] Radbert was fond of this anecdote from Cicero's *De inventione*.[18] He had already cited the story at greater length in his *Vita Adalhardi*,[19] and, for the very first time, in his prologue to the first book of his commentary on Matthew.[20] Zeuxis' plight expressed the author/narrator's difficulty in doing justice to his illustrious subject, but also his total commitment to veracity, despite the fact that true virtue was a complex matter. Accordingly, a portrait of Arsenius could not be based on only one model, 'since in his actions he exhibited the moral excellence of many famous people': not just the Arsenius of yore, after whom he was named, but also St Benedict and the prophet Jeremiah.[21] Yet, there was another reason why the story of Zeuxis may have appealed to Radbert: he was nothing if not eclectic. Cicero invoked

---

[15] Kempshall, *Rhetoric*, pp. 202–8.
[16] Kempshall, 'Virtues of Rhetoric', p. 22. For a discussion of the virtues in the *Epitaphium*'s first book, see Verri, 'Il libro primo'.
[17] *EA* I, prologue, pp. 18–19.     [18] Cicero, *De inventione* II.1, p. 166.
[19] *VA*, c. 20, cols. 1518–19.     [20] *In Matthaeum* I, prologue, p. 6.
[21] *EA* I, prologue, p. 20.

the beauty of the maidens of Kroton to point out that the discipline of eloquence had a rich and varied tradition which he intended to make the most of, without committing himself to any particular school. This was also how Radbert approached his weighty task of depicting his two fathers, using the genre of the funeral oration as a flexible framework that enabled its author not just to grieve and console, but also to commemorate and to praise, and above all, to pursue his central aim: establishing the truth about two controversial men and persuading a potentially hostile audience to change its position.

## 2     Epitaphium

Although Radbert's tribute to Adalhard is entitled the *Vita Adalhardi* in the ninth-century manuscript from Corbie that is the earliest surviving version of this text, Radbert called it an epitaph.[22] Declaring that he would follow the example of Ambrose, Jerome and other saintly men who had written eloquent funeral orations (*epitaphia*), he makes this clear by citing Ambrose's *De obitu Valentiani*.[23] The theme in question, the consolation of memory, dominates Radbert's own conception of this genre. Writing about the loss of a beloved one may increase one's grief, yet the act of recalling the one for whom we grieve gives comfort, and evokes his presence.[24] By the time he embarked on his *Epitaphium Arsenii*, this needed no further explanation or legitimation. The term *epitaphium* occurs in the title, and twice in the main text. In the first book, it is the metaphorical funeral monument (*epitafium*) which the monks of Corbie sprinkled with their tears, for Arsenius died far away, in Italy;[25] in the second, the prologue refers to the completion of 'the form of our father's epitaph, which we earlier began to commit to writing'.[26] Whether textual or tangible, as in a grave monument with an inscription, an

---

[22] See above, p. 10.

[23] *VA*, c. 2, col. 1509A: 'Quapropter officiosissimum est, sicut dixi, sanctos imitari viros, videlicet praefatum Ambrosium, et beatum Hieronymum, reliquosque sacros imitabiles viros, qui suis epitaphia charis facundissime condiderunt.' Jerome even called his *De viris illustribus* 'epitaphia', for which he was corrected by Augustine; cf. Von Moos, *Consolatio* I, pp. 43–4.

[24] *VA*, c. 1, col. 1507D: 'Quoniam, sicut beatus Ambrosius in opere super Valentinianum dixit: "Etsi incrementum doloris sit id quod doleas scribere, tamen plerumque in ejus, quem amissum dolemus, commemoratione requiescimus; et dum scribendo mentem in eum dirigimus, intentionemque defigimus, videtur nobis in sermone reviviscere, et totus medullam mentis nostrae influere."'
     Cf. Ambrose, *De obitu Valentiniani*, c. 1, p. 329; Liebeschuetz, transl., *Ambrose of Milan*, p. 364.

[25] *EA* I, prologue, p.19 ('... epitafium scilicet more priorum lacrimis inorare ...'). This is metaphorical, for Wala was buried in Bobbio.

[26] *EA* II, prologue, p. 60.

epitaph was a literary expression of grief, according to authoritative examples provided by classical and patristic authors: the funeral oration. Ambrose, Jerome and also Sulpicius Severus were the late antique Christian masters of the genre.[27]

The *epitaphium* is one of three types of funeral oration: it is different from lament (*monodia*) and consolation because it puts more emphasis on praise, at the expense of the former two elements, but these are present nonetheless.[28] The most exemplary exponent of the *epitaphium* as a genre is the rhetorician Menander of Laodicaea, who worked in the late third or early fourth century AD, in the tradition of ancient demonstrative or epideictic oratory. The funeral speech praised the deceased's family, birth, nature, upbringing and conduct, and usually included consolatory words for the bereaved as well as lamentations meant to provoke pity.[29] Yet this Menandrian template was in no way rigid, since it already served as a flexible point of reference for Menander's contemporaries. It is no surprise to find it also used freely by Radbert's patristic authorities, Ambrose and Jerome. As Andrew Cain explains, bending the rules of the traditional funeral oration was a way in which skilled writers such as Jerome displayed their literary prowess.[30] The church father's tribute to his Roman friend and follower Paula, the *Epitaphium Paulae*, has a strong biographical component, which, however, allows for the introduction of elements from other literary genres, resulting in a hybrid composition. Jerome's epitaph is presented as a consolation for Paula's bereaved daughter Eustochium, but in fact laid a rich textual foundation for the cult of Paula in Bethlehem.[31] Cain calls it 'a veritable potpourri', in which Jerome displays both his literary and exegetical skills. Radbert probably knew this work, and he was certainly familiar with Jerome's equally idiosyncratic *In Consolation of Heliodorus* (Ep. 60).[32] Jerome made it crystal clear that he knew the rules of the funeral oration but did not feel bound by them: 'For my part, in praising Nepotianus' soul I shall not concern myself with physical advantages, which he himself always despised, nor shall I boast about his family ... '.[33] This was not a patristic innovation, but a masterful attitude he shared with his contemporaries, be they Christian or not.[34]

---

[27] Von Moos, *Consolatio* I, pp. 43–4.    [28] Cain, *Jerome's Epitaph on Paula*, pp. 9–10.

[29] Cain, *Jerome's Epitaph on Paula*, pp. 6–7; Menander Rhetor, II.11, pp. 171–9. See also Heath, *Menander*.

[30] Cain, *Jerome's Epitaph on Paula*, pp. 7–12. On Ambrose's free use of the genre: Biermann, *Leichenreden*, pp. 99–128.

[31] Cain, 'Jerome's "Epitaphium Paulae"'.

[32] Cited in *VA*, c. 4, cols. 1509D–1510A; Berschin, 'Epitaphium', pp. 50–1.

[33] Scourfield, *Consoling Heliodorus*, p. 30; Jerome, *Ep.* 60, c. 8.1, ed. Scourfield, p. 52.

[34] I am grateful to Robin Whelan for pointing this out to me.

When Radbert decided on writing his tribute to Adalhard as an *epitaphium*, therefore, he had authoritative patristic models that allowed him considerable leeway, for the *patres* had taken this themselves. There was no problem with a funeral oration that was also a biography, for Jerome had already led the way. Given that Adalhard's byname was Antony, the *Vita Adalhardi* might as well have been called the *Epitaphium Antonii*.[35] Was this a deliberate decision on Radbert's part to steer clear of traditional hagiography and its 'dramatic miracles'? When he did (re)write hagiography, as he did in the *Passio* of the late antique martyrs Rufinus and Valerius, he expressed his misgivings about the ostentatious – that is, material – aspects of the cult of relics and its concomitant miracle stories.[36] To these tales about Roman martyrs, he preferred the historians of late antique Christianity as a more reliable source of information. This is not to say that Radbert did not have the deepest veneration for miracles. Their sudden intensification during the crisis of Louis's reign signalled no less than a divine warning, and these were 'miracles of such quality and quantity as are never heard to have been performed at the relics of the saints at one time since the beginning of the world. For all the saints who have been carried hither and thither to this kingdom roused one another, as if at cockcrow, to sing together in harmony'.[37] Crisis precipitated a general alert of the saints, expressed by an upsurge of miracles. All the same, his new version of this *Passion* was seven times as long, so was meant for reading rather than for the liturgy, and highlighted above all the Roman history of Rufinus and Valerius.[38] He adds an interesting disclaimer, namely that these saints did not need the cheap paint and ornaments of rhetoric,[39] a protestation we also find in the explicitly rhetorical *Vita Adalhardi*.[40] What Radbert meant to say is that he was a Christian orator who practised a pure form of this art of eloquence, and that all his illustrious subjects deserved such a treatment.

As Gerda Heydemann has suggested, a strong sense of the overlap between an authentic Christian past and the Carolingian present underlies both the *Epitaphium Arsenii* and this particular hagiographical work. Radbert stressed in his prologue to his *Passio* that it was his task to write a *historia sanctorum*, rather than to stimulate the vain veneration of jewel-encrusted

---

[35] Berschin, *Biographie*, III, p. 308.

[36] Paschasius Radbertus, *Passio Rufini et Valerii*; Cf. Berschin, *Biographie* III, pp. 304–8, who thinks the text dates to Radbert's abbacy of Corbie.

[37] *EA* c. 2, p. 62: 'Nequaquam igitur dixerim sine causa miracula sanctorum longe diu in Christo quiescentium nuper coruscasse, quanta et qualia nunquam sunt audita a saeculo facta uno in tempore ad reliquias sanctorum, quia omnino, quasi in gallicinio, sancti hoc in regno huc illucque delati, se invicem excitarunt quasi ad concentum cantus.'

[38] Berschin, *Biographie* III, pp. 306–8.

[39] Paschasius Radbertus, *Passio Rufini et Valerii*, col. 1490C.    [40] *VA*, c. 85, col. 1551B.

*simulacra* (relics) that would not help the cause of the realm in any way.[41] In other words, Radbert's two epitaphs were quite different from the prevailing tradition of cult-oriented miracle stories, but much less so if one takes his own conception of saintly history into account.[42] Both the *Vita Adalhardi* and the *Epitaphium Arsenii* contain hagiographical traits, such as the contentious break with the world, and the innate virtues that were present from youth,[43] but then again, the theme of early perfection maintained throughout life is not just a topos in saints' lives. It also surfaces in Ambrose's funeral oration for Valentinian.[44]

This epitaph for an emperor was the model that most inspired the *Vita Adalhardi*. Radbert's frequent citations of the Song of Songs in his tribute to his deceased abbot, for example, are also a salient feature of Ambrose's *De obitu Valentiniani*. Another text often cited by Ambrose is Lamentations, as, for example, in a short dialogue between a weeping *ecclesia* and a consoling Valentinian. This may have sharpened Radbert's interest in a biblical book on which he would in due course write an extensive commentary.[45] In order to facilitate my further discussion of some aspects of the *Vita Adalhardi*, I provide a simplified overview of its structure:[46]

**cc. 1–6** On Christian lament and praise; joy and sorrow.

**cc. 7–29** Adalhard's life, career and virtues up to 814.

**cc. 30–54** Exile and return.

**cc. 55–64** *Figura nobilitatis/characterismos.*

**cc. 65–67** Founding Corvey.

**cc. 68–72** Adalhard as abbot.

**cc. 73–88** Illness, death, burial.

**c. 89** *Ecloga duae sanctimonialium.*

---

[41] Heydemann, 'Relics and Texts', pp. 196–7. On late antique critique of relics taken on board by Carolingian authors, see first and foremost Raaijmakers, 'I Claudius' and 'Studying Jerome'.

[42] See Ganz, *Corbie*, p. 102, who emphasises the non-hagiographical novelty of Radbert's epitaphs, and Verri, 'L'arte di ritratto', who highlights the hagiographical aspects of the *Vita Adalhardi*.

[43] See above, pp. 21–3.   [44] Duval, 'Oraisons funèbres', p. 264.

[45] Ambrose, *De obitu Valentiniani*, cc. 8–9, transl. Liebeschuetz, pp. 368–9; Duval, 'Oraisons funèbres', pp. 262–3; Matter, 'Lamentations Commentaries'.

[46] For a fuller discussion, see Berschin, *Biographie* III, pp. 309–18; Von Moos, *Consolatio* I, pp. 137–46; Ganz, *Corbie*, pp. 103–12. Von der Nahmer, 'Die Bibel im Adalhardsleben'; Verri, 'L'arte di ritratto'.

Radbert's epitaph for Adalhard had much in common with the one he wrote for Wala: he portrayed both his much-lamented abbots as men who spoke unmitigated truth to power, and whose unflinching loyalty met with royal ingratitude and disfavour. Both texts are dominated by the two protagonists' undeserved exile from the court, and by their perseverance in the face of the animosity and persecution of those who ousted them from Louis's court. Above all, both brothers tried to save the realm but were thwarted by their enemies. Adalhard 'bore his exile for the benefit of the *respublica*'.[47]

Adalhard's epitaph is not structured as a dialogue, yet Radbert added to his *Vita Adalhardi* the *Ecloga duae sanctimonialium*, an elegiac poem in the form of a dialogue between two nuns, who poetically and alternately express their sorrow for and praise of their abbot. Galathea and Phillis, two names from Virgil's *Eclogues*, stand for *vetera et nova Corbeia*, Corbie and Corvey, the mother and the more recently founded daughter. The first had been wed to Adalhard in the manner that Christ had married his church, while the second had been generated by him according to monastic discipline. Both lament their beloved abbot's death and comfort each other, with Corvey most often in the role of the one who needs to be consoled by Corbie.[48] Together, the prose *Life* and the poem form a so-called *opus geminatum*, and as such the work reflects Radbert's far-reaching literary ambitions.[49] Still, it should also be read against the background of Wala's contested succession to Adalhard after the latter's death on 2 January 826; keeping the mother and daughter together and delivering them into Wala's capable hands had not exactly been easy. The separation dreaded so much by Radbert would become effective in 833, when Warin became abbot of Corvey.[50]

From the *Vita Adalhardi*, one gets a sense of a brilliant author coming into his own, bringing all his formidable knowledge of the classics and late antique authors to his first major attempt at a biography of Adalhard. Meanwhile, there is no reason to think that Radbert's 'rhetorical bravura', as Chiara Verri expresses it, detracted in any way from his staunch adherence to a biblical and patristic world view.[51] 'Bravura' is the right word, for in the *Vita Adalhardi* one encounters a younger author who is still experimenting, in awe of Cicero as the King of Eloquence. The text opens with a legitimation of the entire enterprise: first there is an announcement that the author intends to follow the rules of the Christian epitaph, by imitating

---

[47] *VA*, c. 32, col. 1526A: ' ... ob beneficium reipublicae exsilium tulit ... '.
[48] Von Moos, *Consolatio* I, pp. 138–9; for a translation and commentary, see Harrison & Leon, 'The Pastoral Elegy'.
[49] Klopsch, 'Prosa und Vers'.    [50] See above, pp. 50–2.
[51] Verri, 'L'arte di ritratto', p. 651.

those highly learned men who had not only wept for the dead but also pursued them with praise; then there is the extensive citation of Ambrose's funeral oration for Valentinian.[52] Halfway through the *Vita*, there is an extensive section on Adalhard's *characterismos* or *figura nobilitatis*,[53] another sign that Radbert was emphatically playing by the rules of the *epitaphium*. He took some time explaining what he was up to, and informed his readers that, according to the rhetoricians, a perfect man's qualities should be discussed in a set order, starting with his name, country, family, status, fortune, outward appearance, education, conduct and diet, and ending with his entire *habitus*, both inward and outward.[54]

This catalogue of characteristics stems mainly from Fortunatianus' sixth-century *Ars rhetorica*, while Cicero's *De inventione* (1.34–36) also had some impact; the notion of a *characterismos* or *figura nobilitatis* was also transmitted by Isidore of Seville and Cassiodorus.[55] The word *charakterismos* was usually written in Greek letters, and Radbert followed suit. It was his faithful adherence to these rhetorical precepts that made him insert this set piece. One might argue that it forms a bridge between the section on Adalhard's exile and the follow-up on the foundation of Corvey. In my view, this also marks a younger author who experimented with his rhetorical knowledge, and wanted to be seen as adhering to his authoritative models. This is much less the case in the *Epitaphium Arsenii*, where the genre of the funeral oration is both adopted and adapted, without further justification.

Here, the influence of Ambrose's tribute to the deceased Emperor Valentinian also makes itself felt, as does his treatise *De bono mortis*, yet by far the greatest impact on the *Epitaphium Arsenii* comes from Ambrose's *De excessu fratris*. This two-book funeral oration was written on the occasion of the death of Satyrus, the bishop of Milan's elder brother.[56] Its first book is the written version of an oration delivered in 379 at the funeral of Satyrus, who had succumbed to an illness[57]. It is

---

[52] *VA*, c. 1, col. 1507 C–D: 'Pretium operis est viros quosque doctissimos imitari, qui pio mentis affectu, charorum in Christo funera pietatis opere deflevere, flendo quoque miris eos prosecuti sunt laudibus.' For the citation from *De obitu Valentiniani*, c. 1, see above, n. 24.

[53] *VA*, c. 55, col. 1536C: 'Caeterum, si figuram nobilitatis ejus a puero describere voluero, quae Graece χαρακτηρισμὸς dicitur, ero inefficax.'

[54] *VA*, c. 55: 'Consideratur enim perfecti viri qualitas, juxta oratores, nomine, patria, genere, dignitate, fortuna, corpore, institutione, moribus, victu; si rem bene administret; qua consuetudine domestica teneatur; affectione mentis, arte, conditione, habitu, vultu, incessuque, oratione, affectu.'

[55] Berschin, *Biographie* III, pp. 313–14; Von der Nahmer, 'Die Bibel im Adalhardsleben', pp. 45–54; Cizek, 'Der Charakterismos'.

[56] Ambrose, *De excessu fratris*, transl. de Romestin et al. (*On the Death of Satyrus*); Duval, 'Oraisons funèbres'; Biermann, *Leichenreden*, pp. 57–62; Ganz, *Corbie*, pp. 115–7.

[57] McLynn, *Ambrose*, pp. 69–78.

a meditation on the limits of justified grief, and tries to distinguish between necessary tears, which are a source of consolation, and excessive versions thereof. The latter are unchristian, and not mindful of the constant presence of the beloved dead through commemoration and enduring affection. Moreover, how can one grieve for one's loss, given that death is nothing but a kind of sleep, awaiting resurrection? In Ambrose's first book, these arguments for allowing oneself to be consoled are regularly overwhelmed by sorrow, while in the second, a more reasoned approach to consolation prevails: death liberates the immortal soul from the constraints of the body.[58] The expectation and nature of eternal life form Ambrose's central theme, in a speech that was allegedly delivered a week after his brother's death. Since eternal salvation is to be preferred vastly over life on earth, there are no reasons to deplore the loss of one's beloved brother. How can one feel sorrow if someone has passed on to a better existence? The general tenor of the entire work is one of self-consolation, with Ambrose reminding himself that he should rejoice about having had such a brother, rather than grieve about losing him.

Ambrose's oration revolved around St Paul's discussion of the limited power of death and loss in the face of salvation: Christ had conquered death, the last enemy (1 Cor. 15:26). This offered Radbert an inspiring example of how to achieve, as David Ganz aptly expressed it, 'a heroic restraint which does not diminish the strength of his feelings of grief'.[59] This reflection on the tension between loss and hope was entirely pertinent for Radbert and his fellow monks who had lost their abbot, while the funeral oration also provided an established and exacting standard of eloquence. By citing De excessu extensively, and borrowing its two-book structure, Radbert could pay tribute to this great bishop and orator, and associate himself closely with an epitome of orthodoxy. Towards the end of the Epitaphium's second book, in a summary of the essence of Ambrose's and his own views on death, Radbert signals his indebtedness to another work by the church father: 'And therefore the blessed Ambrose has also published a most needed book on the goodness of death. If, therefore, on the occasion of the death of such a great father [Wala/Arsenius] we lament various saddening things and his many sufferings, let us rejoice with him that for him living was Christ, and to die is gain'.[60]

Although Ambrose's De excessu was based on two distinct orations, these were published as one work. Presumably, this was also what

---

[58] Duval, 'Oraisons funèbres', pp. 237, 254–5.     [59] Ganz, Corbie, p. 116.

[60] EA II, c. 23, p. 96: 'Et ideo etiam beatus Ambrosius de bono mortis edidit librum satis pernecessarium. Quapropter si planximus in obitu tanti patris, varios rerum merores et ejus labores plurimos, gaudeamus cum eo, quia ei vivere Christus fuit et mori lucrum.' See Phil. 1:21.

Radbert had in mind, right from the beginning, when he decided to use this work as the basic structure for his reflections on Wala's life and death. Significantly, almost all citations in the *Epitaphium*'s first and second books, respectively, were taken from the corresponding two books of *De excessu*.[61] This should dispel any doubt as to whether the *Epitaphium* was intended as one work, but there is more to this matching of citations and books than a brilliant instance of 'background style' or early medieval intertextuality.[62] Most of the citations from or references to *De excessu* occur in the first book, and predominantly in the first half of it. As for the *Epitaphium*'s second book, all borrowing from Ambrose is concentrated in the final part that follows the narrative about Wala's death in Italy. This section of the second book reads like a brief funeral oration in its own right. The reason for this uneven distribution is obvious: whenever Radbert relies on Ambrose's model, he does so in the context of the theme of grief and lament. In the first book, this is a theme he still regularly returns to, but in the second, lament about the loss of Wala mostly recedes into the background, until the very end of the work, which revolves around Wala's death in distant Italy, and the inability of his northern disciples to attend to his death bed and grieve properly. Here, Radbert returns to his original theme, reminding his reader that his work had once started off as a funeral oration, and has now come full circle.

In between, however, other concerns prevail. The *Epitaphium*'s dependence on Ambrose's commemoration of his elder brother is undeniable, but it has perhaps been emphasised too much, obscuring other important features of this text in the process. First of all, Radbert rarely cites Ambrose verbatim, and if he does, it is mostly a matter of shorter sections that are woven into the tapestry of Radbert's own narrative. Even the extensive cluster of citations at the end of the second book is by no means precise, to such an extent that it has been doubted whether it was based on the full text or a florilegium, or even whether Radbert himself had been the author of this Ambrosian addition.[63] The estimated date of the *Epitaphium*'s one manuscript, close to the tentative year of Radbert's death (860), suggests that it was the author himself who brought his funeral oration full circle by returning emphatically to Ambrose when he treated Wala's death and funeral. At this later stage of his narrative, the imitation of *De excessu* became relevant once more.

---

[61] See Von Moos, *Consolatio* II, pp. 100–1. Six instances in cc. 1, 2 and above all c. 5; also in cc. 8, 10, 12, 15, 17, 28 and 31; *EA* II cc. 22 and 23 have *De excessu* and one instance of *De obitu Valentiniani*, and Radbert refers explicitly to Ambrose's *De bono mortis* in *EA* II, c. 23, p. 96.

[62] Berschin, 'Epitaphium', p. 52.

[63] *EA* II, c. 23, pp. 95–6; Von Moos, *Consolatio* I, p. 140.

Jerome had departed from the classical structure of the funeral oration as a combination of consolation and praise, and the same is true of Radbert's even more important model Ambrose. *De excessu fratris* is no exception. The deviations in its first book were precisely the choices that made this text an attractive model to Radbert when he embarked on his epitaph for Wala in the late 830s. Rather than delivering a traditional eulogy of his brother, Ambrose eulogises his own close relation with Satyrus, and the happy times they spent together. Praise of the deceased is an integral part of the traditional epitaph, of course, but rather than offering the usual rhetorical topoi, Ambrose commemorates a togetherness now lost. This has become bearable through the awareness, inspired by St Paul, that death and grief pale into insignificance in view of the consolation of eternal salvation.[64] This emphasis on a lost communal life, as well as the shared grief for Satyrus, made *De excessu* the best possible model for an author like Radbert, who wished to express a collective sorrow about the loss of Arsenius.[65]

This having been said, there were limits to lament. It would go too far to say that lamentation serves merely as a cover for more daring and potentially offensive pronouncements, but this genre certainly permitted Radbert to defend Wala and attack the great man's enemies within an apparently inoffensive framework. Throughout the first book, there are reminders that lamenting Arsenius is the business at hand. The monks' first duty was bewailing Arsenius' death and praising his exemplary life: 'He alone is to be commended to our tears'.[66] Yet Pascasius, the narrator, begs forgiveness for giving way to the secret shedding of tears in their secluded confabulation, for even this might give offence to those who hated Arsenius.[67] Especially in the first book, collective lament at times seems to function like a default option. Whenever the discussion gets too heated and outspoken, one of the participants can recall the others to the original purpose of their confabulation. Usually, it is the narrator Pascasius who intervenes, reining in his two fellow monks, who tend to cross the line.[68] Speaking more carefully means grieving more deeply.[69] Meanwhile, there is an almost imperceptible shift from commemorating Arsenius and grieving for his absence, to lamenting the evils of Radbert's own day and age. In the middle of Pascasius' meditation on the comfort of remembering the loved one, a very different note is struck: 'For everywhere there is grief,[70] everywhere sorrow and mourning,[71] because not

---

[64] Biermann, *Leichenreden*, pp. 57–81; the key biblical text is 1 Thess. 4:13–18.
[65] On this aspect of *De excessu fratris*, see Duval, 'Oraisons funèbres', pp. 244–6.
[66] *EA* I, c. 20, p. 49: '... solus fletibus commendandus est ... '.
[67] *EA* II, c. 5, p. 27: 'quo velim ignoscant, si prolabimur ad lacrimas secretius in secessu ... '.
[68] *EA* I, c. 17, p. 47; I, c. 20, p. 49; I, cc. 21–2, p. 52.    [69] *EA* II, c. 11, p. 39 (Pascasius).
[70] Virgil, *Aeneid* 2.368–9: '... ubique luctus, ubique pavor ... '.    [71] Isa. 35:10; 51:11.

daily, I tell you, but by the hour one hears of evils everywhere, and nothing but confusion is reported.'[72] In the second book, bewailing the terrible events of the 830s would become the predominant theme. This is anticipated in the last two sentences of the first book, which first echo Ambrose on the consolation and joy of remembrance, and then confront Arsenius' (and Radbert's) political enemies: he and his fellow monks refuse to be intimidated by slander, although nowadays even men of high standing (*honestiores*) speak up against what is good.[73]

Towards the end of the *Epitaphium*, the return to the original theme of sorrow and consolation is initiated by the monk Adeodatus, who functions as the game-changer throughout the entire work.

Yet now that we have grieved about the deeds of the past and mourned what happened, Pascasius, and bewailed so many catastrophes[74] and their diverse consequences,[75] recounted the tribulations, and, lamenting, enumerated the various aspects of the case, now it remains to concentrate upon the end and on his death ...'[76]

Admittedly, 'the various aspects of the case' is a deliberately vague translation of *varia causarum negotia*, an expression with technical connotations. *Causa* may be synonymous with *negotium*, and pertain to the detailed subject matter underlying a rhetorical representation,[77] but it can also have judicial inflections, and refer to a lawsuit.[78] After having operated at this level for most of the second book, it is now time for the speakers to return to lament and citing Ambrose, but in the middle of this, the narrator Pascasius interjects his confirmation of Adeodatus' assessment of what the confabulators have been up to in the second book: they have 'lamented justly, while we bewailed the various attacks on him, enumerated manifold tribulations and also explained the misfortunes'.[79] As a summing up of

---

[72] *EA* I, c. 17, p. 47 (Pascasius), in a passage that freely cites Ambrose, *De excessu* I, c. 6, p. 212 and c. 21, p. 221.

[73] *EA* II, c. 28, pp. 59–60: 'Hinc consolemur interdum nos gaudio conscientiae, quod talem eum tantumque cognovimus et habuimus, de quo gaudere in Domino non veremur. Et ne ullis frangamur infamiis praevidendum: quia nunc in tempore plurimi etiam honestiores obloquuntur bonos, ita ut nullus exire intactus possit.'

[74] Virgil, *Aeneid* 2. 204–5: 'Per varios casus, per tot discrimina rerum/tendimus in Latium.'

[75] Cicero, *De inventione* I, 28.42, p. 82 on *eventus* as consequences of actions.

[76] *EA* II, c. 22, p. 92 (Adeodatus): 'Sed quoniam retro quae gesta sunt, quae contigerunt, Pascasi, doluimus, rerum discrimina et varios eventus deflevimus, tentationes quoque recensuimus, et varia causarum negotia plangentes enumeravimus: nunc restat ad finem intendere, eiusque obitum ... '.

[77] On definitions of *causa* and *negotium*, together with their relation to a rhetorical *quaestio*, see Quintilian, *Institutionis oratoriae* III.5.17–18, p. 142; also, Cicero, *Topica* 21.80, p. 444. On the pertinence of these concepts to Alcuin, see Kempshall, 'Virtues of Rhetoric', p. 8, with n. 6.

[78] Cicero, *De inventione* I.3.4, p. 8.

[79] *EA* II, c. 23, p. 95 (Pascasius): 'Et si planximus iure, dum varias eius deflevimus impulsiones, et tentationes multiplices dinumeravimus, casus quoque exposuimus ... '.

the second book, this cannot be faulted, but it was not how Radbert started off initially, when he undertook his epitaph for Arsenius. As I shall explain in the next chapter, the funeral oration had become a vehicle for Wala's defence, including a pointed attack on his enemies.

## 3     Dialogue and Monastic Confabulation

Radbert's choice to structure this work as a dialogue gave him the freedom and flexibility to combine lament, praise, defence and invective, and to switch between these registers in order to support his central argument: that Wala, the perfect abbot and magnate of the first book, could have saved the Christian polity in the early 830s, according to the second book, and yet had been unjustly accused of infidelity. The medium of the dialogue allowed the author to present different and even conflicting viewpoints, including those of Arsenius' critics. One of the discussants, more often than not the monk known as Adeodatus, will report or raise an objection against Arsenius' conduct, which is then refuted at some length.

Such contrary remarks often serve to trigger another bout of praise, but they also address controversial aspects of Wala's reputation. When the narrator, Pascasius, waxes eloquent on the general approval the younger Wala has enjoyed as one of Charlemagne's courtiers, Adeodatus asks him 'to explain to me why he often lamented that he had been born a man of strife and a man of contention, especially since, as you say, he was loved by everyone' (Jer. 15:20). Pascasius explains that at that particular time, the realm had grown and prospered. In other words, Arsenius had every reason to rejoice, rather than to lament like Jeremiah.[80] For his own community as well as others, the highly contentious abbot of later years tended to obscure the earlier and happier parts of his career. Radbert sought to highlight the heyday of Wala as second only to the emperor. By having Adeodatus raise an objection, he created room for himself in his guise as Pascasius, the narrator, to elaborate. This is one of many of such interventions on Adeodatus' part, and they continue into the second book: if Arsenius was so humble and dead to the world, why did he then speak boldly to the emperor and all of the leading (church)men of the realm?[81]

Throughout the *Epitaphium*, three monks of Corbie sustain the dialogue. In both books, the narrator Pascasius and the monk Adeodatus are

---

[80] *EA* I, c. 1, p. 22.

[81] *EA* II, c. 5, p. 65: 'Nam cum esset tam humilis, quo nullus humilior, nullusque magis mortuus mundo videretur, quid est quod tam inter summos ecclesiarum, praesulum videlicet et senatorum, consules, in senatu coram augusto consulte constanterque loquebatur?'

a constant presence. Pascasius represents the author Radbert, while Adeodatus, at least in the first book, is a younger monk whose character may have been inspired by one of Radbert's pupils. This was the name of Augustine's son, who was his discussion partner in the dialogue called *De magistro*, and also of an abbot mentioned in passing in the *Life of Benedict* by Gregory the Great;[82] the name has the more generic meaning of 'given by God', and there are associations with David as well.[83] Adeodatus is the interlocutor who prompts Pascasius to start his narrative, and who then keeps it going by one question after another, interspersed with some challenging comments of the kind just mentioned. What is so special about a monk that you must praise Arsenius for being one?[84] If he were such a man of charity and holiness, why do they sometimes insist that he was austere and harsh?[85] The general impression conveyed is that Adeodatus is younger and therefore knows little of Wala's earlier life before he entered Corbie in 814. He is also pictured as someone who has never been an intimate of the great man, and who therefore wants to know more, especially when it comes to the criticism he has picked up. I suspect that in the first book Adeodatus stands for the younger monks of Corbie and Corvey who had heard of Wala's exploits in the 820s and 830s, but had never known him personally.[86] The two older and experienced monks who respond to his insistent queries are Pascasius, who was Arsenius' constant companion during these years, but also Severus, who, unlike his friend Pascasius, had remained staunchly inside Corbie's cloister, and therefore counted as an expert on Arsenius' qualities as an abbot.

Apart from Pascasius, who represents Radbert himself, Severus is the only other interlocutor who can be identified. Radbert dedicated his commentary on Lamentations to 'Odilman Severus', with a preface in which he spoke of himself as an elderly man.[87] This means that the Lamentations commentary was completed during a later phase of Radbert's life, but before he embarked on the second book of his *Epitaphium*, for by then, 'the happy Severus' had 'entered the way of all

---

[82] Augustine, *Confessiones* IX, c. 6, p. 141; Augustine, *De magistro*; Gregory, *Dialogi* II, c. 2, 4, p. 132.

[83] De Jong, *In Samuel's Image*. An Adeodatus is one of David's heroes in the battles against the Philistines: 2 Kgs (= 2 Sam.) 21:9; 1 Par. (= 1 Chr.) 20:5; Hrabanus, *Commentaria in libros II Paralipomenon* II, c. 20, col. 374, interprets Adeodatus as the *typus* of David. The name was not uncommon: there was a Pope Adeodatus (570–618), also known as Deodatus or Deusdedit. On the *Epitaphium*'s discussants, see also Ganz, *Corbie*, pp. 112–13 and De Jong, 'Becoming Jeremiah', pp. 191–2.

[84] *EA* I, c. 10, p. 36.   [85] *EA* I, c. 22, p. 53.   [86] Cf. *EA* I, c. 12, p. 41.

[87] Paschasius Radbertus, *Expositio in Lamentationes* I, p. 4: 'Pascasii Radberti monachorum peripsema votorum liber primus fletibus explicandus seni Odilmanno Severo opera pretio consecratus.' All five books were offered to Odilman/Severus.

flesh'.[88] Probably Odilman was older than Radbert, but not by much. In the *Epitaphium,* as Severus and Pascasius, both play a central role as witnesses to Arsenius' life, albeit from different perspectives. Whereas Pascasius, the constant companion, is the one to report on the great man's exploits outside Corbie, such as the foundation of Corvey in Saxony in 822, Severus is the expert witness concerning Arsenius as the abbot and disciplinarian of his community in Corbie. Furthermore, Severus is the gruff and outspoken older monk who tells it straight, doing justice to his name: 'Severus' is characterised by the severity of his judgement, and by his frank delivery of harsh and uncompromising truths.[89] As a typically cloistered figure, Severus is the opposite of Cremes, a well-travelled monk named after a central character from Terence's comedies.[90] He had been in Italy with Wala in 823–5, and makes some substantial appearances in the first book in order to share his knowledge of Arsenius' dispensing justice there as Lothar's right-hand man. Finally, to complete this brief overview of the interlocutors of the first book, there is the unique and intriguing intervention of Allabigus, an illiterate monk whose passionate praise of Arsenius makes him, suddenly and spontaneously, burst out in fulsome Terentian prose.[91] He embodies the saintly simplicity that features frequently in early medieval hagiography and visionary literature.

That much time had passed by the time Radbert added his second book is made emphatically clear from the outset. Once more, Adeodatus is the one to get the conversation going again, hinting at all the troubles that now lie behind them, but with an explicit reference to Pascasius' retirement from the abbacy of Corbie:

After the countless anxieties of duty within the monastery, and the weighty issues to attend to outside it; after the ups and downs of circumstances and affairs, and the hardships of life; after the long weariness of sundry travel hither and thither and running about everywhere; after unrelenting pressures on all fronts: at long last, Pascasius, now that all of this has been left behind and tranquillity and freedom of mind have been restored to you by the disposition of divine judgement, it is time to recall what we formerly omitted, so that going forward, we may complete the form of our father's epitaph, which we earlier began to commit to writing. For it would have been more respectable not to have started than to leave unfinished what we began.[92]

[88] *EA* II, prologue, p. 60.
[89] *EA* I, prologue, pp. 20, 21; c. 2, p. 24 ('Acriter invehis, frater Severe … '); c. 17, p. 47 (' … tu more agis, qui severe alios antequam corripias … '); Ganz, *Corbie,* p. 113.
[90] De Jong, 'Heed That Saying', pp. 284–7. A role for a Chremes is part of Terence's *Phormio, Andria* ('The Women of Andros') and *Heauton Timorumenos* ('The Self-Tormentor').
[91] See below, pp. 114–6.
[92] *EA* II, prologue, p. 60 (Adeodatus): 'Post innumeras intus officii curas, post immensas exterius occupationum causas, post varios rerum negotiorumque eventus et vitae dispendia, post longa huc illucque diversi itineris fatigia et concursus ubique, post indefessas

It is made clear not only that Severus has died, but also that 'Cremes has now disappeared in the midst of our crisis'.[93] Pascasius and Adeodatus represent the continuity of the narrative and guarantee the unity of the work as a whole, yet the young and inquisitive Adeodatus of the first book has now become an older and experienced member of his community, who shares his memories of the more recent past with Pascasius and helps to verify the latter's narrative of Wala's role in the rebellions by his own well-informed testimony. Now that Severus has gone the way of all flesh, a new discussion partner has had to be found. In the words of Pascasius:

> ... we need to choose (in the manner of the sacred fathers) one of those who lived with him as we did, so that through him the truth may be more strongly sanctioned (by the testimony of three witnesses, as it were), and our lament will not be found different even in the number of participants.[94]

Adeodatus is then charged with making this choice, and comes up with Teofrastus, another monk from Corbie, named after Aristotle's successor as the leader of the Peripatetic school, who figures in Cicero's *Tusculan Disputations*, and in a great many of Cicero's rhetorical works.[95] There is also a Theophrastus in Jerome's *Ad Iovinianum*, who had allegedly written an elegy about marriage which Jerome included in his treatise on this topic; possibly this fictional figure was also named after the famous Greek philosopher, which would have made this an even more meaningful byname.[96] Radbert's deliberately 'Greek' spelling of this name shows that he was well aware of this philosopher's identity. From the outset, Teofrastus positions himself as a worthy successor to the outspoken Severus, although, as we shall see, he pushes the limits of frankness to new extremes. As Adeodatus comments, after the new interlocutor's first outburst, if this intemperate man had joined the discussion at an earlier stage, he would have exposed and betrayed the discussants, for he cannot

---

omnium pressuras, tandem divino dispensante iudicio, relictis omnibus, quia tibi, Pascasi, reddita est quies et libertas animi, recordari oportet quod omisimus olim, quatenus deinceps aliquando epitaphii patris formam expleamus, quam commendare litteris coepimus pridem. Alioquin esset honestius non inchoasse, quam inchoata non explere.'

[93] *EA* II, prologue, p. 60.

[94] *EA* II, prologue, p. 60 (Pascasius): 'Sed quia interdum Severus ingressus est felix viam universae terrę, et Cremes inter discrimina nostra iam discessit, necesse est unum eligamus de his more sanctorum patrum, qui nobiscum cum eo versati sunt, quatinus per eum et veritas, quasi sub tribus testibus, melius commendetur, et noster planctus non diversus vel numero inveniatur.'

[95] Aristotle's successor as leader of the Peripatetic school, who came to Athens as a young man. It is no coincidence that he figures in Cicero's *Tusculan Disputations*. Some scholars attribute the origins of the *genera dicendi* to Theophrastus: Quadlbauer, 'Genera dicendi', p. 64, n. 86.

[96] Jerome, *Adversus Iovinianum* I, c. 47, cols. 288–91.

hold his tongue.[97] This helps to mark the difference between the two books: at first, the monks engaged in dialogue had been compelled to watch their words, but now they can afford to have someone like Teofrastus on board.

Or was the contrast between the two books a matter of clever construction and editing when the entire work was completed? There is much that argues against this. To begin with, there is a new chronological perspective throughout the second book, with its marked contrast between 'now' (*hodie*) and then (Wala's lifetime), and the transition from relative reticence to emphatic outspokenness just noted. But apart from this, the rhythm and spirit of Radbert's dialogue seems to have changed altogether. Whereas the first book's discussion among the three monks is at times lively and even bantering, with challenging interventions and short repartees, the second features ever longer monologues by Pascasius, while his two interlocutors serve as a chorus of sharp disapproval of the shocking events related by their narrator, and as the ones who draw the inevitable conclusion from his terrible tale. In his reactions, Adeodatus is no less bold than his frank fellow discussant Teofrastus: 'Insofar as it is in our power to understand, the likes of them at the time were neither counsellors nor overseers of their fatherland, but robbers whose narrow minds the darkness of present concerns had blinded . . .'.[98]

This comment not only underlines the distance in time, but also sharply condemns the depravity of those who opposed Wala's defence of ecclesiastical property. Another striking change has to do with Radbert's use of classical sources. In the first book, Virgil, Seneca, Statius and above all Terence are emphatically cited, in a way that is sometimes reminiscent of the exuberant one-upmanship of the schoolroom. With a sovereign disregard for the original meaning of Terence's comedies, Radbert intersperses Pascasius' and especially Severus' discourse with snippets and sentences from 'the comic', in the way he had encountered them in the works of Jerome and Augustine. The second book no longer displays this knowledge of the classics. The emphasis is now almost entirely on biblical citations, with a marked preference for Isaiah, Matthew and Paul. When Radbert broaches the painful topic of Louis the Pious's public penance of 833, he intersperses Pascasius' narrative with words and expressions taken from the Book of Job, borrowing from this authoritative prose as he had earlier used Terence.

---

[97] *EA* II, c. 1, p. 62.

[98] *EA* II, c. 6, p. 66 (Adeodatus): 'Quantum datur intelligi, tales qui tunc fuere, non consules, non provisores patriae fuerunt, sed latrones, quorum mentes angustas praesentiarum caligo caecavit . . .'.

At times, the lively dialogue of the first book is reminiscent of an actual conversation between monks. It is tempting to hear the echoes of a schoolroom once shared by the two friends Radbert and Odilman, or by the *magister* Radbert and his more advanced pupils, who knew their Virgil and Terence, and were proud of it. Yet even though the identities of Pascasius and Severus are known, it would be a mistake to take their exchanges in the *Epitaphium* as a direct reflection of actual conversation. This would mean a return to an older dichotomy that has been effectively challenged over the past years, between dialogues that represent 'real' and open-ended debates and those that are literary artifices with a primarily didactic purpose. It has been mostly the classical dialogues according to the Socratic model that have been understood as a more or less faithful reflection of actual public debates, while their Christian successors tend to be qualified as educational constructions geared towards the mainte-nance of orthodoxy and the suppression of heretical dissent. This view has recently come in for criticism, and rightly so, if only because all the dialogues known to us are transmitted in a literary form: the classical Greek and Roman dialogues that have served as a yardstick may have been just as fictitious as their Christian successors. In fact, the genre of the literary dialogue flourished in the fourth and fifth centuries, including imaginary debates which allowed the author and his audiences to engage with patristic tradition in a creative way, and to address contemporary religious controversies. Even if the scales were *a priori* weighted on the side of orthodoxy, such dialogues still sustained the persistent cultural notion that truth could be found by articulating controversy and persua-sively discussing opposite points of view.[99]

In keeping with the more general idea that the rise of Christianity spelled the end of dialogue, Richard Lim has argued that this genre belonged to the elitist literary culture of *paideia*. It was highly influ-ential, yet also a 'boutique literary genre', and therefore very different from the inclusive Christian *sermo humilis* that aimed to reach as many people as possible, including those from lower social strata. The inherent elitism of the dialogue, as Lim called it, was ill suited to a religious communication that aimed at the masses, so the demand for this particular literary form gradually disappeared.[100] Recently, the view that Christianity and dialogue were incompatible has come in for criticism from both late antique historians and early medieval-ists, partly thanks to productively provocative titles such as *The End*

---

[99] On this theme, see now Whelan, 'Imaginary Dialogue', with extensive references to older literature.

[100] Lim, 'Christians, Dialogues and Patterns of Sociability', with p. 171 on the 'boutique genre'.

*of Dialogue in Late Antiquity.*[101] For those familiar with Alcuin's disputations, Radbert's *Epitaphium* or the work of Agius of Corvey,[102] it must come as something of a surprise that dialogue is supposed to have vanished, as does the notion that Christian dialogue is invariably catechism-like and educational, and therefore meant to produce only fixed answers.[103] And of course this is not the case: the very suggestion of an end to dialogue in late antiquity yielded a collection of articles in which some authors did something of a demolition job on this point of view, even with regard to the early Middle Ages. As Kate Cooper and Matthew Del Santo put it, without much ado, 'Christians did dialogue in the later sixth and seventh centuries as they had in earlier centuries; and the literary dialogues this created actually reflect a real socio-historical context of debate, dissent and disputation'.[104] On the other hand, in the same volume, Gillian Clark explains why Augustine produced so little dialogue to speak of: as a busy pastor, he had to address all his flock through sermons, rather than sharing the delights of a literary dialogue with the happy few.[105]

Something similar may have pertained to busy Carolingian bishops and abbots, yet only up to a point. They were certainly not excluded from the biblically oriented Carolingian culture in which the 'boutique genre' of Latin literary dialogues flourished. This was elitist, in the sense that it was shared by religious communities, the court and the highest echelon of the secular clergy and laymen and women. To a considerable extent, a high-level Latin literacy defined and demarcated this court-connected ninth-century elite; it was built during Charlemagne's reign, and continued to expand during those of his son and grandsons. As a polemical treatise that addressed the fall and exclusion of one of this group's most prominent members, the *Epitaphium Arsenii* is a precious witness to this milieu, in which one might have the reasonable expectation that one's biblical witticisms would be reported to the emperor, and duly appreciated.

For his *Epitaphium*, Radbert could rely on this rich legacy of late antique Christian dialogue, which partly overlapped with a varied

---

[101] Cameron, *Dialoguing*, especially pp. 10 and 37; Van Nuffelen, 'The End of Open Competition?'; De Jong & Van Renswoude, 'Introduction', and the articles published in the themed issue of *Early Medieval Europe* 25 (2017) on Carolingian cultures of dialogue, debate and disputation, in which Whelan, 'Imaginary Dialogue' introduces the role of these texts in patristic culture.

[102] On Agius' *Dialogue* for Hathumoda of Gandersheim, see Von Moos, *Consolatio* I, pp. 149–84.

[103] Goldhill, 'Why Don't Christians Do Dialogue?', p. 5. On court-connected debates around 800, see Van Renswoude, 'The Art of Disputation'.

[104] Cooper & Dal Santo, 'Boethius, Gregory the Great', p. 182.

[105] Clark, 'Can We Talk?', pp. 133–4.

tradition of monastic dialogic education. This holds true for older and influential examples of monastic dialogues such as John Cassian's *Conferences*, the *Apophthegmata patrum* or the *Rule of the Master*, as well as for Alcuin's remarkable dialogues, in which Charlemagne and his son Pippin figure as pupils.[106] These dialogues certainly belonged to a 'boutique genre' aimed at a discerning readership, and the same could be said of early medieval dialogues stemming from various monastic milieus, ranging from the apparently vulgarising but in fact highly polished *Dialogues* of Gregory the Great to the riddle-like Old English colloquies with which Alcuin was familiar.[107]

Apart from these elitist literary genres, to be shared and enjoyed, first and foremost, by the best and brightest members of courtly and religious communities, there was also the monastic practice of *confabulatio* that should be taken into account: a religious conversation within an intimate and restricted circle of learned and learning participants. Very occasionally, something of the practice of such conversations can be glimpsed, when an abbot is said to have called his *scholastici* to his private chambers to discuss the metrical version of a saint's life that would be far too demanding for ordinary members of his community,[108] or when three elite members of the community of St Gall are depicted as excluding an illiterate eavesdropper from their conversation by switching to Latin as soon as they suspect his presence.[109] Monastic intellectual training was a possible venue for competitive disputation, but not necessarily in the formal setting of the 'schoolroom' so often imagined by modern historians of religious culture.[110] The informal interaction between a *magister* and the most talented of his pupils was a more likely setting for the kind of dialogue Radbert evoked in his first book, and given that he was a teacher himself, it stands to reason that this experience had an impact on the way he fashioned a highly experimental literary dialogue.[111]

The type of monasticism established in the Carolingian realm emphatically privileged early recruitment, be it through child oblation or less formal types of entry into the community that might eventually result in

---

[106] Alcuin, *Disputatio de rhetorica et virtutibus*; see Kempshall, 'Virtues of Rhetoric'; Bayless, 'Alcuin's *Disputatio Pippini*' offers a commentary and edition. On the terminology re. dialogue, debate and dispute, see De Jong & Van Renswoude, 'Introduction', pp. 14–16.

[107] On the fourth book of Gregory's *Dialogi* as a sophisticated attempt to rebut contemporary scepticism of the cult of the saints, see Dal Santo, *Debating the Saints' Cults*, pp. 88–107.

[108] De Jong, 'From *scholastici* to *scioli*'.

[109] Ekkehard, *Casus S. Galli*, cc. 35–6, pp. 80–4; De Jong, 'Internal Cloisters', p. 218.

[110] For a pertinent critique, see Illmer, *Erziehung*, pp. 35–66, 179–88.

[111] On Radbert as a teacher, see above all the praise poem by his pupil Engelmodus.

a profession.[112] Apart from the spiritual and social benefits of giving one's child 'to God in the monastery', this practice owed much to the ideal of ascetic purity from childhood onwards. Furthermore, there was the practical experience that in order to become well and truly versed in Latin-Christian written tradition, monks and nuns needed to be trained *ab incunabulis*: that is, almost from the moment they could walk and talk. Unsurprisingly, as the product of such an education, Radbert fully subscribed to these tenets of monastic recruitment and formation. His portrait of Wala as an innocent and prematurely wise young member of Charlemagne's entourage shows how the ideal of the untainted *puer senex* could spill over from the monastery to the court.[113]

The members of the big Carolingian monastic communities tended to be classified according to three interconnected criteria: their seniority (in terms of their entry into monastic life), their level of literacy, and their relation to the *claustrum*, the inner and secluded part of the monastery that maintained the community's stability.[114] The *Epitaphium*'s first book is a case in point. Whereas Severus is a diehard of the cloister, a highly learned man who has interiorised monastic rules so well that he can afford to make up his own mind, Adeodatus is still feeling his way towards such certainty; Pascasius has seen much more of the world outside the monastery, and especially of the court, but not quite as much as the widely travelled Cremes, who witnessed Wala in his capacity as Lothar's deputy in Italy. As for the illiterate Allabigus, he is the exception who proves the rule of Carolingian monasticism, namely that literate monks formed an undisputed elite. As an *idiota* who suddenly cites Terence, he represents the saintly simplicity that also remained an integral part of religious ideals. Pascasius, on the other hand, shows that for monastic leadership, different qualities were required, such as being able to hold one's own at the imperial court and deal with formidable magnates.

The monks in the *Epitaphium* have their own distinctive voices in this dialogue, but it is no longer possible to detect actual personalities; what prevails are monastic 'types' or characters. These were not dissociated from actual practice or experience: Carolingian monasticism allowed for a limited number of social roles, which needed to be recognised by Radbert's audience, and by the readership of other monastic authors as well. It is no coincidence that Ekkehard's *Casus sancti Galli*, written in the mid-eleventh century but still in a world dominated by Benedictine religious life, also has three monastic heroes of whom one, Radpert, is the typical 'old boy' who prides himself on never having left the cloister,

---

[112] De Jong, *In Samuel's Image*, pp. 126–55; 'Growing Up'.    [113] See above, pp. 25–7.
[114] De Jong, 'Internal Cloisters'.

while another, Tuotilo, has travelled far and wide, just like the opposites Severus and Cremes in the first book of the *Epitaphium*.[115] Here, Severus is the older monk who refuses to mince his words ('Yours is a fierce invective, brother Severus!'). Odilman may have earned the byname Severus because of relentless asceticism and his prickly nature, but perhaps also with reference to Sulpicius Severus, the well-known and much-admired author of the *Life of St Martin*. Sulpicius Severus also wrote a dialogue on the virtues of Martin, the so-called *Gallus*, that may have served as one of the models for the *Epitaphium*.

## 4    Models for Dialogue: Terence, Jerome, Sulpicius Severus

Radbert's idiosyncratic dialogue cannot be pinned down to one particular model, so what I discuss here are some possible influences and reso-nances, for others to build on in future research. Clearly, he was familiar with a host of classical and patristic literary dialogues: he knew Cicero's *Cato Maior de senectute*, which also had three interlocutors, and also the *Tusculan disputations*, as well as Boethius' *Consolation of Philosophy*, and a number of dialogues by Augustine and Jerome. Yet the at times lively exchanges between Pascasius and his fellow monks in the *Epitaphium*'s first book do not resemble Cicero's dialogues, with their ponderous monologues and the elaborate discourse of 'M' – that is, Marcus Cicero himself. Participants in Cicero's dialogues did little more than prompt the conversation and move it forward, without contributing all that much to the central points and issues argued by the author. Given Terence's marked presence in the first book, it seems likely, as Courtney Booker has argued, that these ancient comedies have helped to shape Radbert's dialogue.[116]

I fully agree that Radbert had an intimate knowledge of Terence's comedies, and had sufficiently internalised them that he was able to use these texts for his own purposes, freely and playfully. It is also to be expected that the lively dialogue of the first book owed something to 'the comic', even though much of it still fairly monologic compared to Terence's firework-like exchanges. After all, the narrator Pascasius needs considerable room to tell his story, also in the first book. Recently, Booker has shown how ninth-century knowledge of ancient drama was harnessed to the exegesis of biblical texts on hypocrisy, notably Matthew's Gospel

---

[115] Ekkehard, *Casus S. Galli*, cc. 33–4, pp. 76–8; De Jong, 'Internal Cloisters', pp. 217–18.
[116] Booker, *Past Convictions*, pp. 42–50, to which I responded in De Jong, 'Heed That Saying'; see now Booker, 'Hypocrisy', pp. 187–94. For a semantic history of hypocrisy, see Amory, 'Whited Sepulchres'.

on the Pharisees (Matt. 23). This is a pertinent observation, but I am not convinced that Radbert's *Epitaphium* can hence be categorised as a 'typological drama' about recent history in which all the theatrical resources of Terence's comedies are mustered.[117] And did this fit 'a court culture replete with political protocol, liturgical ritual, public processions and the like'?[118] Booker and I are both intrigued by the awareness of Radbert and some of his contemporaries of a potentially dangerous disparity between inner feelings and outside comportment; the public promises made in 830 by Louis the Pious without any inner conviction are a salient point in case. Yet I doubt whether the notion of a generally 'performative' Carolingian culture is helpful in understanding Radbert's sensitivity to this discrepancy. He was, after all, a monk who lived under the Rule of Benedict, with its twelve degrees of humility culminating in the perfect harmony of the heart and the body: both had learned humbleness through a process of daily discipline.[119] The mid-ninth-century commentary of Hildemar of Corbie/Civate elaborates on Benedict's Rule in a way that fully accords with Radbert's view of the matter:

If this bowing of the head does not proceed from the mortification of the interior man, it is worthless; there are many who go about with *bowed head* but that profits them nothing, since it does not proceed from the mortification of the interior man. To bow the head truly is to judge oneself frail and to believe oneself to be dust and ash.[120]

The education of Hildemar's child oblates aimed at their gradual interiorisation of what started as the merely outside gesture of bowing one's head: this was what the principles of *custodia* and *disciplina* were all about.[121] Much as I am convinced of the significance of Terence for Radbert, possibly also with regard to a heightened sensitivity to role-playing and hypocrisy, I doubt whether it was the dramatic qualities of the plays themselves that deserve most of our attention. To focus entirely on the *Epitaphium*'s lively dialogue and typecasting means ignoring the fact that its manuscript does not have a layout that emphasises its supposedly dramatic nature. Furthermore, there is the question of why Radbert

---

[117] Booker, 'Hypocrisy', pp. 189–90.    [118] Booker, 'Hypocrisy', p. 193, 197.

[119] *Regula Benedicti*, c. 7, pp. 62–70.

[120] Hildemar, *Expositio*, c. 7, p. 265: 'Ista *inclinatio capitis* si ex mortificatione interioris hominis non processerit, nil valet; nam multi sunt, qui *inclinato capite* incedunt, sed nil illis proficit illa *inclinatio capitis*, quia non procedit ex mortificatione hominis interioris; *inclinare* enim veraciter *caput* est, fragilem se esse aestimare, pulverem et cinerem se esse credere.' (Cf. Gen. 3:19). I follow the translation offered by the Hildemar project (www.hildemar.org).

[121] De Jong, 'Growing Up', 'Internal Cloisters'.

deploys 'the comic' extensively in the first book, and not at all in the second. Finally, and most importantly, his 'citations' from Terence are in fact borrowings of words, expressions and half-sentences which are then integrated flexibly into the dialogue. This prompts the question of whether, in this brilliant display of knowledge of Terence, usually detached from the original contents of the plays, Radbert was following older models. My attempt to find some answers led to the discovery that Terence entered the Carolingian cultural bloodstream via late antique grammatical texts as well as patristic writing.[122] Thus, the comedies gained the kind of authority that kindled a direct interest in his plays in Corbie and other West Frankish monasteries, and also at the court of Louis the Pious, which meant that the entire plays were now read and discussed. Surely Radbert was in the forefront of this, yet it is the typically patristic uses of Terence that we encounter in the *Epitaphium*. Radbert was confronted with a vast legacy of harnessing Terentian vocabulary and idiom to Christian strategies of persuasion, of which he makes the most in the first book.

In late antique Latin literature, Terence is cited more often than any other classical Latin poet, with the exception of Virgil, who was also a school author. Terentian maxims such as *Ne quid nimis* were cited so often that they had lost all connection with their original context.[123] Christian authors of the fourth century cited them frequently, for moralistic purposes but also in biblical commentary. When Augustine discusses the problematic words 'Jesus Christ who died' and distinguishes the *percontatio* from the *interrogatio*, he relies on grammatical commentaries on Terence's *Andria* by Donatus and Quintilian.[124] Augustine cites Terence throughout his correspondence and theological work, including the *City of God*. He also resorts to Terentian language in order to evoke contemporary realities.[125] And yet, no author, whether pagan or Christian, refers to Terence's comedies more often than Jerome, who ranked the poet alongside Homer, Virgil and Menander. As Andrew Cain explains, Jerome used Terentian expressions to gloss biblical texts, but also to perform a specific rhetorical function within a narrative. Cain then gives an example from a preface to Jerome's commentary on Micah, in which he hits back at unnamed enemies who have accused him of

---

[122] De Jong, 'Heed That Saying'; I wrote this article in 2011. At the time I would have profited greatly from Andrew Cain's excellent overview, 'Terence in Late Antiquity', which appeared two years later. See now also Villa, 'Terence's Audience'. My mainstay was (and remains) Hagendahl, *Latin Fathers and the Classics*.

[123] Cain, 'Terence in Late Antiquity', p. 387.

[124] Augustine, *DDC* III.12, p. 136; Hagendahl, *Augustine and the Latin Classics*, pp. 380–1.

[125] Cain, 'Terence in Late Antiquity', pp. 390–1.

plagiarism. This 'densely packed pastiche of Terentianisms', as Cain aptly calls it, strongly resembles the uses of Terence in the *Epitaphium*'s first book, where the comic's language is integrated flexibly and eclectically into a polemical discourse.[126]

Given Radbert's deep and enduring admiration for Jerome, to which Augustine only came second, it seems likely that Jerome's deft use of Terence was his most influential example. In his exegetical work, Radbert also took a leaf out of Jerome's book, by adapting his biblical sources, phrasing them in a more precise manner, elaborating, abbreviating and correcting them, welding them together, and, last but not least, borrowing their language to express his own thoughts.[127] This borrowing of language was also what both Jerome and Radbert did with Terence's comedies. But to what end? As Cain points out, Jerome was doing more than combatting his literary enemies by harnessing Terence's words to his cause. He was also legitimating his counter-attack by adopting Terence's polemical *persona* and, like Terence, he does not deign to name his enemies, so they will receive no recognition whatsoever.[128] Something very similar underlies Radbert's use of Terentian language: it infuses his dialogue with a special authority, especially when the discussion moves into contentious areas.

The ways in which Radbert resorts to Terence when he needs to refer obliquely to painful truths will be further discussed in the next chapter, as will the reasons why Terence features in the first book and not in the second. Here, I simply reaffirm my view that Radbert's 'citations' of the comic are best understood in the context of a long and authoritative tradition legitimated by the *patres*. Their deep respect for Terence, and their vivid examples of deploying Terentian references as a strategy of persuasion, were the models Radbert followed in the *Epitaphium's* first book. This had little to do with lively dialogue, and everything to do with assuming an authorial voice that would carry weight and authority, albeit derived from comedy, not from tragedy. As we shall see, this distinction matters.

To sum up: Jerome was one of Radbert's main models for his dialogue. Jerome's fierce altercation between Atticus and Critobolus, usually known as the *Dialogue against the Pelagians*, deserves some special attention, for Corbie had an early ninth-century manuscript.[129] It is entirely

---

[126] Cain, 'Terence in Late Antiquity', pp. 392–3.

[127] In his edition of Radbert's commentary on Matthew, Beda Paulus gathered a number of illustrative examples; cf. Paschasius Radbertus, *Expositio in Mathaeo*, pp. xx-xxv; Ganz, *Corbie*, p. 82.

[128] Cain, 'Terence in Late Antiquity', pp. 393–4.

[129] Paris, BnF lat. 13352, s. ix in.; Ganz, *Corbie*, pp. 76, 138–9; Bischoff & Ebersperger, *Katalog* III, p. 205; on this text and its misleading modern title, see Whelan, 'Imaginary Dialogue', pp. 28–9, with reference to Jeanjean, 'Le *Dialogus Attici et Critobuli*'.

possible that Jerome's dialogic attacks on heresy were on Radbert's mind when he turned to dialogue himself, and surely Jerome had more to offer by way of sharp and quick-witted exchange than Cicero. On the other hand, the *Epitaphium* is not in any way a *Kontroversdialog,* as German scholars have labelled the agonistic dialogues of Christian late antiquity,[130] for the three discussants are united in their effort to lament, praise and defend Arsenius. A more likely and generally accepted model is Sulpicius Severus' *Gallus,* a dialogue about the virtues of St Martin written between 397 and 401.[131] Like the *Epitaphium,* the *Gallus* presents a discussion with three main participants. Apart from Sulpicius Severus himself, the host and the leader of the conversation, there is Postumianus, a cultivated aristocrat who has just returned from a long voyage to monasteries in the eastern empire, and Gallus, a monk from Gaul who extols Martin's miracles in this region. The general contention is that, as a miracle worker, Martin was much more effective than anyone in Postumianus' report from the East, a claim supported by the occasional interventions of a priest called Refrigerius, who is called in as a witness from the outside world and is prepared to swear to the truth of Martin's great reputation.[132]

At the beginning of his second book, Radbert makes it clear that in order to continue the conversation, 'we need to choose (in the manner of the sacred fathers) one of those who lived with him as we did, so that through him the truth may be more strongly sanctioned (by the testimony of three witnesses, as it were), and our lament will not be found different even in the number of participants'. As we have seen, these arguments introduce the deceased Severus' replacement by Teofrastus. The need for 'two or three witnesses' is a recurrent theme in the New Testament, with some juridical inflections of which Radbert was well aware, for he elaborated on this theme in his exegesis of Matthew.[133] Furthermore, as the author of the *Vita S. Martini,* Sulpicius Severus would surely qualify as a 'sacred father', and his aim with his *Gallus* was similar to that of Radbert in his *Epitaphium*: namely, to extol the virtues of their illustrious subject. On the other hand, there are some real differences between these two texts. To begin with, whereas *Gallus* is a truly hagiographical dialogue,

---

[130] Schmidt, 'Zur Typologie,' p. 150.

[131] Verri, 'Il libro primo', pp. 34–5, n. 4; Von Moos, *Consolatio* I, p. 141.

[132] Sulpicius Severus, *Gallus* II, c. 14.5, p. 284, and III, c. 1.3, p. 288: '... quasi sub testibus consignatam abs te accepturus est vertitatem ... '; Schmidt, 'Zur Typologie', p. 152.

[133] 'And if he will not hear thee, take with thee one or two more: that in the mouth of two or three witnesses every word may stand' (Matt. 18:16); 'For where two or three are gathered together in my name, there am I in the midst of them' (Matt. 18:20); 'In the mouth of two or three witnesses shall every word stand' (2 Cor. 13:1). Paschasius Radbertus, *In Matthaeum* VIII, pp. 892–3, ll. 3073–95.

featuring the saint as miracle worker, in the *Epitaphium* there is not a miracle in sight. Radbert's Arsenius has many virtues, some of them saintly, but first and foremost he is an ideal abbot and a formidable royal counsellor. Secondly, Sulpicius addresses his friends in the first person, and also uses the persona of Gallus to address his audience, in order to refute Postumianus' glowing report of monastic greatness in the East. By contrast, Radbert keeps some distance between himself and Pascasius by writing of the narrator and his alter ego in the third person, and in spite of some occasional banter, his fellow discussants are never presented as an opposition that needs to be taken to task.

Sulpicius Severus adheres to a Ciceronian tradition by suggesting that the dialogue proceeded in three stages close to each other in time, with Sulpicius taking the initiative and inviting his interlocutors to continue, as guests in his villa. In the *Epitaphium*, there is no indication of any location where the monks conduct their confabulation, and once this is resumed in the second book, it is made eminently clear that much time has passed. The *Gallus* was also Ciceronian in its uninterrupted narratives, both on Postumianus' and on Gallus' part. These are more extensive than any of Pascasius' indignant monologues on Arsenius' enemies in the *Epitaphium*'s second book. Compared to the *Gallus*, this still remains an exchange of views between three interlocutors, although the narrator gets a bigger part than before.

I have not been able to identify any direct reference to the *Gallus* in the *Epitaphium*, nor have I found a manuscript of this work that is connected with Corbie. Others may be more successful in this respect, and it would not surprise me, for there are also some striking parallels. By rounding off his *Gallus* with a brief elegy, Sulpicius Severus frames his dialogue as an expression of grief: the discussants go their way, 'having moved everyone to tears by our laments'.[134] Both Sulpicius Severus and Radbert, more-over, introduce extra interlocutors – namely, the priest Refrigerius and the monk Cremes – as faithful witnesses to their hero's activities in areas beyond the core discussants' experience. It has been suggested that, by his eloquent testimony to Martin's exploits outside the community, Refrigerius creates a bridge between monastic and lay audiences.[135] Perhaps this also holds true of Cremes, but he certainly addresses a controversial phase of Wala's career, of which none of the other con-fabulators had any direct experience: namely, his years in Italy (822–5) as Lothar's deputy. While in perfidious Ausonia, had their abbot also been

---

[134] Sulpicius Severus, *Gallus* III, c. 18, p. 364.
[135] Schmidt, 'Zur Typologie', pp. 152–3.

corrupted, as his enemies had it, or had he been the embodiment of Christian and Frankish justice?

The most important similarity, however, is that both the *Gallus* and the *Epitaphium* are characterised by 'the tone of a defensive plea', as Von Moos has expressed it.[136] It is no coincidence that, towards the end of the fifth century, Gennadius, in his continuation of Jerome's *De viris illustribus*, characterised the *Gallus* as 'a conference between Postumianus and Gallus, in which he [Sulpicius] himself acted as mediator and judge of the debate. The subject matter was the manner of life of the oriental monks and of St Martin, conducted in the manner of a dialogue'.[137] Gennadius' near-contemporary reading of the *Gallus* should be taken seriously, and not just because it was among the Merovingian manuscripts written in Corbie, and available to Radbert.[138] The *Gallus* is not a hagiographical dialogue devoted to extolling the saint's virtues: the text is structured as a defence of the saint against his enemies. Among the latter, the bishops of Gaul figure prominently, opposing the saint whenever they can, and spreading evil gossip about him at the court. The emperor sees sense, however, and Martin studiously avoids attending synods.[139] Both Martin and Arsenius are depicted as the emperor's most faithful counsellors and defenders, who found no public recognition for their efforts. Dialogue was the ideal medium to accomplish this, with interlocutors who act as witnesses for the defence, first and foremost. Their veracity is carefully established, and their claim to truth constantly underlined.

---

[136] Von Moos, *Consolatio* I, p. 141.    [137] Schmidt, 'Zur Typologie', p. 172.

[138] BnF lat. 12161; Ganz, *Corbie*, p. 162 and Plate 2.

[139] Sulpicius Severus, *Gallus* III, c. 11, pp. 328–36; c. 13, pp. 340–2. See also I, c. 24, p. 200, on Martin 'in medio coetu et conversatione populorum, inter clericos dissidentes, inter episcopos saevientes . . . '.

# 5    Strategies of Persuasion

## 1    *Assertor veritatis*

Throughout the *Epitaphium,* there is a background chorus of Wala's enemies, who accuse Arsenius of worldliness, corruption and infidelity. Radbert presents himself as the advocate of his much maligned mentor, who has to convince a disbelieving audience of Arsenius' staunch virtue and unwavering fight for his emperor and the common weal.[1] In the best tradition of Roman forensic rhetoric, the *Epitaphium* offers a point-by-point refutation, combining formal lament with a judicial pursuit of the truth.[2] However, the format of the funeral oration is more than merely a formal framework; along with consolation and praise, lament remains a recurrent theme in the first book, and one that Radbert returns to at length towards the end of his work. Furthermore, forensic or judicial rhetoric, however important, should not be treated as the only key to this text. Radbert's outlook was dominated by biblical precepts and narratives, which went very well with his admiration for Cicero. Apparently effortlessly, he used his rhetorical tools for the purposes of biblical exegesis, while harnessing the resources of Scripture to his strategies of persuasion. It is the joint forces of classical eloquence and biblical narrative that make the *Epitaphium* such a powerful text.

Radbert's judicial language is as good a reason as any to assume that the *Epitaphium* was more than a text for an internal and purely monastic audience. For Cassiodorus and Alcuin, the art of rhetoric dealt with civil issues (*quaestiones civiles*), that is, matters that were 'political' in that they pertained to the pursuit of goodness and equity in human society.[3] The *Epitaphium*'s varied strategies of persuasion, including the use of forensic rhetoric, all suggest that Radbert operated within the same broad parameters of social order, and that his dialogue addressed a wider debate on public virtues

---

[1] Kempshall, *Rhetoric*, pp. 198–208, especially pp. 200–1.
[2] Kempshall, *Rhetoric*, pp. 206–7; on the strong connection between rhetoric and forensic practice in Late Antiquity, see Humfress, *Orthodoxy and the Courts*.
[3] Kempshall, 'Virtues of Rhetoric', pp. 9–11.

within the highest echelon of the Carolingian leadership.[4] At stake was the moral worth (*honestas*) of the orator Radbert and his beloved abbot, and, above all, their truthfulness. There was nothing particularly monastic about those who criticised Wala, or their means of attack. However briefly and elusively, the accusations which the *Epitaphium* sought to counter also surface in other sources concerning the crisis of the reign of Louis the Pious, especially corruption and disloyalty to the emperor.[5] Telling the truth about Arsenius was not just a matter of exculpating him from allegations of disloyalty and self-interest, but above all a matter of showing that the choices the great man had made were divinely approved, as well as in accordance with the values that prevailed in the Carolingian leadership, regardless of the political positions they had taken in the rebellion era: justice, loyalty and truthfulness. Radbert's pursuit of truth is certainly couched in judicial language, and served by his knowledge of forensic oratory, but it goes well beyond exculpating Wala, or a systematic rebuttal of hostile allegations. Instead, he presents his subject as the very embodiment of the 'defender of truth' (*assertor veritatis*). The *Vita Adalhardi*, composed at least a decade before the *Epitaphium*, may at first glance look more like a conventional epitaph,[6] but in fact it is as full of judicial language as its successor. Both Adalhard and Wala are depicted as intrepid truth-tellers. In both works, this is their most outstanding virtue, and one with which their biographer emphatically associates himself.

In the prologue of the *Vita Adalhardi*, Radbert declares that he will never abdicate the 'rights of truth' (*iura veritatis*); he then proceeds to paint a portrait of Adalhard as a 'friend of justice and truth', who staunchly refused to consent to Charlemagne's repudiation of Desiderius' daughter.[7] He always kept his promises and had 'recently' sent a letter admonishing the Emperor Lothar on the importance of loyalty (*fides*) among men and the inviolability of a Christian oath sworn truthfully; a violation would imply contempt, not of man, but of God 'as a witness and my truth'.[8] When Louis

---

[4] De Jong, 'For God, King and Country'; see below, pp. 185–92.

[5] On Wala's alleged corruption: Amalarius, *Opera omnia* I, p. 361; Weinrich, *Wala*, p. 52, n. 58; the Astronomer underlines Wala's disloyalty to Louis: *Vita Hludowici*, c. 21, pp. 346–8 (on 814); c. 45, p. 461 (on the revolt of 830); c. 55, p. 506 (as Lothar's emissary to Louis in 834); c. 56, p. 512 (death from epidemic illness of those who followed Lothar to Italy in 836).

[6] Kempshall, *Rhetoric*, p. 198. For differing opinions about the degree of conventionality or originality of both works, see the references and rightly dismissive comments of Von Moos, *Consolatio* II, p. 97–8.

[7] *VA*, c. 7, col. 1511B: ' ... elegit magis iustitiae fore et veritatis amicus quam in illicita consentire ...'.

[8] *VA*, c. 18, col. 1518A: ' ... quantum valere debeat foedus Christiani in veritate promissum? non te decipiat aliquis, obsecro, inquit, imperator, quia fides cum contra aliquem violatur, non homo, sed Deus testis et veritas mea contemnitur.'

succeeded his father in 814, *veritas* was shaken, because of the envy of
Adalhard that was stirred up by the devil; this was nothing new, for the
wicked treat the truth as an enemy, and justice is destroyed by the foolish.
They plotted to remove Daniel from the king's side (Dan. 6:4) and succeeded: Adalhard was punished without an accuser, an assembly, a hearing
or a verdict. 'Stripped of his possessions, robbed of his dignity, defiled by
popular opinion, he bore exile for the benefit of the republic ... '.[9] As in
Wala's case, this infamous exile sums up all the other injustices committed
against Adalhard; the author's diatribes against the great man's perfidious
adversaries are fine specimens of passionate forensic oratory.

Already in his *Vita Adalhardi*, Radbert combined the overall structure
of the epitaph with praise and lament, as well as with interludes of forensic
fury against those who had maligned and exiled the great man. In fact,
lamentation was integrated deftly into passages full of judicial language.
Amidst all the conflicting accusations, Adalhard was the only competent
advocate present. Who could keep a stony heart and refrain from weeping? All cried out in lamentation about the blindness that sent Adalhard
into exile; no other Frank would come after him who would be such
a great champion of charity and truth.[10]

Radbert built his portrait of Adalhard around the abbot as an *assertor
veritatis*, who saw and spoke truth where others were blinded, and who
intrepidly announced the dismal truth he detected to the world around
him.[11] Radbert, the pupil who wrote Adalhard's epitaph, acted as the
fearless advocate of his illustrious subject and, by association, as an orator
appealing to an audience whose eyes needed to be opened to the unveiled
truth. He was not the only one who deeply admired the grand old man's
powerful speeches during assemblies. Agobard of Lyon gives a vivid
depiction of Adalhard addressing the gathering at Attigny in
August 822.[12] During this very assembly, Louis the Pious performed
a public penance, to atone for his harsh treatment of his half-brothers
and his nephew Bernard of Italy, but also to cement his reconciliation
with Adalhard and Wala one year before.[13] He was hailed by some as
a new Theodosius,[14] but Radbert was not impressed:

---

[9] *VA*, c. 30, col. 1524B: 'Quo factum est, ut sine accusatore, sine congressu, necnon sine
audientia atque sine judicio, justitia plecteretur in eo. Qui pulsus praesentibus bonis,
dignitate exutus, vulgi existimatione foedatus, ob beneficium reipublicae exsilium tulit.'

[10] *VA*, c. 38, col. 1529 B–C: ' ... neque Francorum quisquam ei similis tantusque charitatis
ac veritatis invenietur assertor.'

[11] *VA*, c. 51, col. 1535A ('assertor veritatis'); c. 47, col. 1533B ('veritatis amator').

[12] Agobard, *De dispensatione*, c. 2, p. 121.

[13] De Jong, *Penitential State*, pp. 125–8; Depreux, 'Penance of Attigny'.

[14] Astronomer, c. 35, p. 406.

What else? The glorious emperor himself undertook a public penance because of his many sins. He who as it were by royal haughtiness had been his own worst tempter was made the humblest of all, so those whose eyes he had offended by sin would be healed by a royal satisfaction. Doubtless all were particularly intent on his willingness and clearly observed his unwillingness. Had the speaker of truth not returned, it would not have become evident at all how oppressed by lethargy they were. Hence ripe old age cured the wound of their blindness, by persuading them to be treated medically with the salubrious antidote of Christ, by means of persuasion.[15]

This is the most explicit statement about Adalhard as an *assertor veritatis*, and one of the more outspoken attacks on Louis as a ruler who attempted to capture the moral high ground, but who was no match for men of the calibre of Adalhard and Wala. As we shall see, royal religious authority was a real threat to Radbert, who felt strongly about the *cultus divinus* being the prerogative of religious experts embedded in a clerical hierarchy: rulers should not occupy themselves with the liturgy, or lord it over their palace chaplains, who were accountable only to the king.[16] That Radbert could pen his critique of Louis's penance in Attigny shortly after Adalhard's death in December 826 says a lot about Wala's powerful position at Louis's court during these years. Radbert could attack Adalhard's exilers with impunity, for despite formidable opposition, Wala had succeeded his half-brother as abbot of Corbie shortly after the latter's death.

By the time he embarked on the first book of his epitaph for Arsenius, Radbert's position had become very different. Wala was dead, and Radbert had not yet become his successor. Time and again, the confabulating monks draw back from saying too much. In loud stage whispers, and constantly urging restraint, they intimate that great injustice has been committed against Wala. In due course, a time will come when all can be told, but it has not yet arrived. The first book is full of such 'raging silences'(*silentia furibunda*), as Radbert, citing Statius, expresses it through his learned fellow monk, Severus.[17] This self-imposed silence was more than a rhetorical device – certainly if he wrote the first book

---

[15] *VA*, c. 51, cols. 1534D–1535A: 'Quid plura? ipse gloriosus imperator publicam ex nonnullis suis reatibus poenitentiam suscipiens, factus est omnium humillimus, qui quasi regali elatione sibi pessimus persuasor fuerat: ut quorum oculi offenderant in delicto, satisfactione regia sanarentur; praesertim quod ejus velle cunctos considerare, ejusque nolle conspicere manifestum non ambigitur. Sed nisi reversus esset veritatis assertor, interea minime paruisset, quo lethargico spiritu premerentur. Unde etiam matura senectus caecitatis eorum vulnus salubri Christi antidoto mederi persuadendo curabat.'

[16] *EA* II, c. 2, p. 62; c. 5, p. 66.

[17] *EA* I, c. 3, p. 25 (Severus): ' ... sed in omni negotio et verbo, in omni re et consensu, amicam sibi scrutabatur inesse veritatem, et quasi ab ungue singulas rerum disquirebat negotiorumque causas, ne forte rimam in aliquo falsitas praecidisset.'

before Louis's death, as seems highly likely. But even if this was not the case, and the old emperor's demise opened a window of opportunity, so to speak, there was every reason for Radbert to hedge his bets, for the outcome of the sons' fight for succession was by no means certain.

Meanwhile, like the painter Zeuxis, he patiently built a complex portrait of his deceased abbot as the embodiment of truthfulness. This is how Arsenius is introduced at the very beginning of Pascasius' narrative:

> It is true that from boyhood onwards he expanded upon the glory of the earlier Arsenius through military service and high office. For he was a cousin of the greatest of emperors and was favoured by him above all others; he was truthful in speech (as is said of the one whose ashes, recently brought here, were resplendent with such great miracles[18]), just in judgement, having foresight in counsel, and absolutely faithful with what had been entrusted to him.[19]

With his stellar career at Charlemagne's court, allegedly as a general and the head of the royal household, Wala had surpassed his late antique namesake, who had merely been the tutor of Theodosius' son Honorius. The four virtues ascribed to Arsenius, truthfulness, justice, foresight and loyalty, are a variation on the cardinal ones of prudence, courage, temperance and justice. Together, these virtues credited to Arsenius constituted the hallmark of an ideal royal counsellor. These qualities resonated with late antique as well as with contemporary veneration of the martyrs, for they were derived from the *Acts of Saint Sebastian*. In 826, Sebastian's remains had been transferred from Rome to St-Médard of Soissons, at the behest of Louis's archchancellor, Hilduin; in the formidable presence of Sebastian, in October 833, Louis the Pious had submitted to the public penance that was meant to exclude him from wielding imperial power.[20] It is no coincidence that the first virtue listed is being truthful in speech (*sermone verax*). Like Adalhard, and unlike his enemies, Arsenius had the truth as his constant companion, and even his friend: ' ... in every deed and word, in every affair and every agreement, he was accustomed to seek out the presence of truth as his friend and diligently investigate every point at issue in any matter or dealing, down to the last detail, as it were, lest by chance falsehood should open a crack in anything'.[21]

When it came to fearlessly defending *veritas*, Wala shares some biblical models with Adalhard, such as Elijah or John the Baptist, but not Jeremiah.

---

[18] *Acta S. Sebastiani*, c. 1, *AASS* Ian. II, col. 265; Smith, 'Old Saints', pp. 322–4; Lanéry, 'La tradition manuscrite'.

[19] *EA* I, c. 1, p. 22: 'Verum quod prioris Arsenii a puero ex militia et dignitate gloriam ampliavit. Fuit enim consobrinus maximi augustorum eique pre cunctis acceptior, in sermone verax (ut de illo dicitur, cuius apud nos nuper delati cineres, tantis coruscarunt miraculis), in iudicio iustus, providus in consilio, et in commisso fidelissimus.'

[20] De Jong, *Penitential State*, p. 274; *Relatio episcoporum* (833), p. 53.     [21] *EA* I, c. 3, p. 25.

Only Wala is closely associated with this prophet; both suffered enmity because of their fierce invectives, which, however, did not spring from hatred but from love.[22] The monk Severus adds, addressing Arsenius' enemies: 'Although they may not believe it, we who knew him should be in no doubt that the promises of Christ are not withheld from one who endured such difficult struggles for the sake of the truth'.[23] No explanation is needed: like the prophet, Wala had warned his people of the dire consequences of their disobedience to God, and like Jeremiah, he had been rewarded for his efforts by imprisonment and exile. That Wala was like Jeremiah is signalled from the very beginning of the first book, when the narrator, Pascasius, reminds his fellow monks that he might give offence by giving in to their request that he tell them about Arsenius: 'Or are you unaware, Severus, that the age of our wretched life brought forth another Jeremiah from him?'[24] Once, their beloved master had not yet been aware of the damage that the state had suffered recently. On the contrary, as a younger man, Arsenius had rejoiced in the growth of the *respublica*, and had cultivated friendships with the noblest and holiest men, 'rather than to bewail, like Jeremiah, our sins and the injuries to the state, which had not yet grown so bad'.[25] From a powerful centre of court-connected networks, Wala had changed into an outsider and a prophet of doom.

Arsenius in his guise as the fearless and uncompromising Jeremiah comes into his own only in the second book, where Radbert, his subject and the prophet increasingly speak with one accusing voice. The Jeremiah of the first book is above all the prophet who lamented the fall of his city and then took up praise, although forbidden to do so,[26] and the innocent victim of his relentless enemies.[27] That Jeremiah/Arsenius was also an intrepid speaker of truth is hinted at by Severus, who declares that 'the harsh invectives that both of them delivered against the people arose not from hatred, but from love'.[28] Here, though, the emphasis is on Arsenius'

---

[22] *EA* I, c. 2, p. 24 (Severus): 'Fateor quod non tantum pro nobis, verum etiam et pro his, uti et ille, quos inimicos pertulit, intercessor erit, quia utrorumque invectio illorum tam severa contra populum, non de odio, sed de amore fuit.'

[23] *EA* I, c. 2, p. 24 (Severus): 'Ista licet minus credant, tamen nos qui eum agnovimus, dubitare nequimus, quod his qui pro veritate tantos pertulit agones, Christi promissis minime privatur.'

[24] *EA* I, prologue, p. 19 (Pascasius): 'An ignoras, Severe, quod nostrae hunc infelicissimae vitae saecula Jeremiam alterum tulerunt ab illo?'

[25] *EA* I, c. 1, p. 22: 'Necdum enim praesentiarum reipublicae detrimenta noverat, quam augmentari gaudebat. Et ideo plus firmissimas nobilium societates, sanctissimasque plebium amicitias studebat, quam, secundum Jeremiam, peccata et detrimenta rerum, quae necdum adeo excreverant, deplorare.'

[26] *EA* I, c. 2, pp. 23–4 (Severus).

[27] *EA* I c. 21, p. 50:' ... qui de corde sibi falsa locuntur ... '.

[28] *EA* c. 2 p. 24: ' ... quia utrorumque invectio illorum tam severa contra populum, non de odio, sed de amore fuit.'

refusal to conform his behaviour to anyone else's but that of Christ, whose suffering was not unlike that of Job.[29] This also entailed a rigorous truthfulness to himself, which, as in Jeremiah's case, distinguished him from his enemies, who spoke 'falsehoods to themselves from their hearts'.[30] Arsenius's self-knowledge and his opponents' lack thereof is a theme that runs through the entire work.[31] It surfaces early on, when Pascasius declares to his fellow monks, in a dig against Arsenius' as yet nameless enemies: 'Let those of our number consider this, therefore, who seek to slander him and charge him with crimes of which he is innocent, when he exercised such severe scrutiny over himself'. In a similar vein, Severus explains that it is much more difficult to observe oneself than others.[32] Monks were trained to watch themselves and others constantly. This basic attitude was not restricted to the cloister, but also prevailed in Louis's court, the moral hub of the realm, which required its own version of self-discipline and self-examination.[33] If Dhuoda's instructions for her son William are anything to go by, these qualities were a yardstick by which high-level aristocrats measured themselves and others, however much they may have fallen short of these norms.[34] An uncompromising and self-referential love of truth is highlighted not just in Arsenius' exemplary conduct as an abbot (never harsher to others than he was to himself!), but also in the chapters on how he governed Italy. Praising 'how diligent he was in seeking out the truth, how energetic in pronouncing judgement, how forceful against the highest judges of iniquity, how effective against those who were corrupted by gifts', the monk Cremes, expert on Italian corruption, embarks on a lengthy narrative about Wala's staunch defence of a widow robbed of the property she had entrusted to her legal guardian (defensor).[35] When the widow appealed to the emperor, her persecutors, who even included some bishops, conspired in a cover-up and murdered the woman. But then the conspirators fell out, and the defensor had the other two killed. Although Arsenius used all manner of proof to get at the truth, all of Ausonia, corrupted by bribes, tried to prevent this. Wala was challenged to submit to an ordeal, and accepted; his prayers and trust in God made the guilty guardian confess, and point the finger at all others involved. As Cremes explains, blinded and

---

[29] EA I, c. 25, 54–5.     [30] EA I, c. 21, p. 50.

[31] As observed by Booker, Past Convictions, pp. 37, 48; more generally, in relation to the self-scrutiny of penance, Booker, 'Hypocrisy', pp. 184, 199–201. On monastic self-scrutiny, see Diem, Das monastische Experiment.

[32] EA I, c. 4, p. 27.

[33] Innes, 'A Place of Discipline'; Nelson, 'Aachen as a Place of Power'; De Jong, Penitential State, pp. 185–205; Stone, Morality and Masculinity, pp. 27–68.

[34] See below, pp. 213–5.     [35] EA I, c. 26, pp. 56–7.

confused, the members of the tribunal handed the culprit over to do penance.[36]

Severus is not surprised or impressed by this report, for, as the oldest monk present, he has experienced Arsenius as the perfect leader of his community, who could fathom the recesses of the heart so well that nothing remained hidden from him. Cremes agrees, but points out that, whereas in the monastery Arsenius had others who helped him get at the truth, in Italy he was all by himself, up against an overwhelming majority ready to condone the crimes and help the criminals to get away with it. For good measure, Cremes then adds another of Arsenius' judicial feats: a man made off with someone else's will *(testamentum hereditatis)*, hid it in a scabbard, and then swore, with oath-helpers, that he had returned the document which proved the other's rights of property. When the oath was inconclusive, 'our Arsenius smiled and ordered the guilty man to come forward, as if he were already aware of the nature of the crime. "Unhappy man," he said, "how did you think up such a clever trick?" And that man, seeing that he was as good as caught, fell at his feet and revealed what he was hiding'.[37] In this case and that of the guilty *defensor*, Wala is portrayed as deploying a time-honoured monastic practice: identifying sinners by harnessing the entire community to their detection, and inducing sufficient guilt through group pressure that culprits would confess. The implication of Cremes' interventions is that, as an uncompromising friend of truth and The Truth, the abbot had access to the resources of divine justice, while his enemies got stuck in their oaths and ordeals because of their obvious falsehood. Wala/Arsenius was able to see into people and find truth, appealing to their conscience in a way that nobody could really stand up to. The teller of truth was also a finder of truth, within himself and others.

## 2    Telling the Truth about Arsenius: The Prologue of the First Book

When it comes to lively dialogue, the opening of the first book is one of the highlights of the entire *Epitaphium*. The three main interlocutors are introduced by a barrage of banter, and immediately they establish their claim to the truth. What they are up to in this dialogue is not telling fables, but telling the history of what happened *(rei gestae historiam)*.[38] The three

---

[36] On penance as a punishment in the early Middle Ages, see Kottje, 'Busse oder Strafe?'. I further explored this topic in 'Monastic Prisoners'; with regard to Late Antiquity, see Uhalde, *Expectations of Justice*, and now the fundamental study of Hillner, *Prison, Punishment and Penance.*
[37] *EA* I, c. 27, p. 58.    [38] *EA* I, prologue, p. 22.

monks are expert witnesses who each have their own role in Arsenius'
defence. As we have just seen, Cremes knows the details about Wala's
exploits in Italy. Together with Pascasius, Severus has experienced their
mentor's rigorous discipline, but as a steady resident of the cloister, the
older monk has seen more of it, and so is called upon to testify to Arsenius'
impeccable monastic leadership.[39] For the period from 821 onwards,
when Adalhard had returned from exile and the two brothers had proceeded to found Corvey a year later, Pascasius himself, the 'third man'
who was often at their side, becomes the key witness.[40] He makes it
evident, discreetly but emphatically, that he was once Wala's special
emissary to Louis's court, as well as someone who was sent on business
trips by the emperor himself.[41] He has much to tell, therefore; by contrast,
in the first book, Adeodatus mostly functions as the one who moves the
testimony forward, either by his questions or by provocative comments
that repeat what is being said by Arsenius' detractors. Together, the
threesome defend the claim to truth that they elaborately established at
the outset. This is where Zeuxis comes in, and Radbert's protest that he
himself was a contemptible painter, unable to live up to his ancient
predecessor and incapable of doing justice to his illustrious subject.

Although the manuscript of the *Epitaphium* has no chapter divisions,
the narrative about Arsenius' life is preceded by an extensive discussion of
what this confabulation is all about, and what it seeks to achieve.[42] This
functions as a prologue or *exordium*, and is worth examining more closely.
Pascasius, citing Terence right from the start, declares that he will 'relate
partly what I saw with my own eyes, and partly what I heard with my
ears,[43] and understood more completely in my mind'; in response,
Severus establishes Pascasius' position as Arsenius' imitator, and his
own as the great man's disciple. Adeodatus confirms the obligation to
commemorate their deceased abbot, but Pascasius warns him that by
trying to please his friends with information, he is likely to offend many
others. Arsenius had tried to put out the flames, but the blaze was stoked
again, as Pascasius had once seen in a dream, a portent of the ensuing
disasters. Severus is scathing about something as dubious as dreams. He
contends that Pascasius would never have testified to the truth if he had
not been asleep, and warns his fellow monks that this should be a serious
discussion. Had not Adeodatus asked for a lament? Severus then returns

---

[39] *EA* I, c. 4, p. 26.     [40] *EA* I, c. 14, p. 43.
[41] *EA* I, c. 8, p. 33 (dispatched by the emperor on an errand); *EA* I, c. 11, p. 39 (sent to the
court to negotiate Wala's succession to the abbacy).
[42] *EA* I, prologue, pp. 18–22. For the entire text in translation, see De Jong & Lake,
*Confronting Crisis*, forthcoming.
[43] Terence, *Hecyra* 3.3, ed. Barsby, p. 184, ll. 361–3.

to the theme of Zeuxis and catching Arsenius' likeness: his portrait has the features of his older namesake, but also of St Benedict, and on occasion 'he took on the role of Jeremiah, with his steely visage and fierce determination, though in truth he was gentle in spirit and the mildest of men'. Pascasius retorts that if he were to continue in this vein, hardly anyone would believe it.

At this point, Adeodatus asks a provocative question: who has ever required a historian to produce witnesses? Here, Radbert cites Seneca's *Apocolocyntosis*, a satire on the deification of the Emperor Claudius. From then on, the three monks concentrate on establishing that their conversation has nothing to do with 'stories' (*fabulae*) and everything to do with re-establishing a truth that has been 'trampled underfoot and driven out of these kingdoms'. Pascasius is ready to testify to Arsenius' resemblance to St Benedict, but once more doubts that anyone will listen. He admits that the monks must grieve for Arsenius, yet the envious will be prepared to swear against it, especially if they realise who the subject of this story (*fabula*) is. Then Severus gets up in arms: are you now telling me that you will not provide us with a history of actual events, but merely with a *story*?[44] Adeodatus chides Severus for his intemperate outburst and explains that Pascasius was referring to these others, who think of the history of Adeodatus as if it were a story, and not something which can be read in one's conscience, as Pascasius does. The latter agrees: what will outsiders do, if we are accused by one of our own?[45]

Radbert continues to push his point by a much longer reference to the *Apocolocyntosis*. When the man who swore in the Senate that he had seen Drusilla ascending to heaven met with general disbelief, he took an oath never again to tell anyone what he had witnessed, even if he saw a murder committed in the Forum. Seneca's comedic satire mocked untrustworthy eyewitnesses who would tell you things in private which they would never vouch for in public,[46] but for Radbert, this anecdote is about something entirely different: namely, his own veracity in the face of overwhelming

---

[44] *EA* I, prologue, p. 22. (Severus): 'Nonne dixisti morum imaginem te picturum, et quasi rei gestam [*l.* gestae] historiam texere; nunc autem nobis fabulam adportas.' For the distinction between *historia* and *fabula*, see Cicero, *De inventione*, I.19.27, p. 55: *Fabula* is a narrative in which the the events are not true and have no verisimilitude; *historia* is an account of actual occurrences remote from the recollection of our own age; and then there is *argumentum*, fictitious narrative which nevertheless could have occurred; see also the recapitulation in Isidore, *Etymologiae* I.40–1. Radbert here stakes his claim that the monks are engaging in *historia*.

[45] *EA* I, prologue, p. 21 (Adeodatus): 'Mirum, Severe, quod tam assuetis uteris semper verborum acrimoniis. Nam mihi videtur fabulam dixisse, non tibi, sed illis quibus totum fabula est et ludus, quod veritate fulcitur. Historiam autem huius tua in conscientia legis, unde non fabula tibi, sed veritas declaratur.'

[46] Weisweiler, 'Unreliable Witness'.

disbelief, and his hesitation to relate a true history that is likely to cause offence. In other words, in Radbert's rendering, the man who saw Drusilla go to heaven is the exact opposite of what he was in Seneca's satire: an author prepared to tell the truth but full of trepidation about doing so in public. It takes Adeodatus to elicit from Pascasius an impassioned invocation of all those who had not believed Christ, and the many apostles, martyrs, confessors and virgins whose testimony and miracles were witnesses of the truth.

This introductory exchange alerts the reader to three central and interconnected themes of the *Epitaphium*. To begin with, all discussants are expert witnesses, committed to telling the truth about Arsenius; second, this can be a dangerous pursuit, and should be done judiciously; third, Arsenius himself was an indomitable champion of truth, whose example Pascasius and his fellow interlocutors are attempting to imitate, but can never emulate. To his own rhetorical question as to whether a historian needs witnesses, Adeodatus replies that these should be 'men of unimpeachable character who will present their right hands to swear by what you have said'. Urging Pascasius onwards, he adds: 'It is unseemly, therefore, to seek to evade a friend of the truth, and to maintain a cowardly silence in the face of those who are seeking the truth from you.' Pascasius himself protests loudly and at regular intervals: 'hardly anyone will listen to what I say, though it is the unblemished truth.' But young Adeodatus concludes that the narrator has more reservations than were warranted. He cannot please everyone, and what is more true than the message that Christ returned from the dead? The apostles, martyrs, confessors and virgins have all been witnesses to this glorious truth, in the face of disbelief and rejection, so Pascasius has no reason to complain.

## 3    Silence and Speech

The prologue firmly establishes Radbert's claim to be a speaker of truth according to the example set by Jeremiah and Arsenius, yet it also introduces a tension between silence and speech that is maintained throughout the entire first book. The three monks have to hold their tongues because the political wind is against them, but this reticence is challenged regularly, especially by Severus, who lives up to his name. Early on in the conversation, he reveals that Arsenius was like Jeremiah, uttering fierce invective out of love, and he urges the great man's detractors to keep silent and cease their slanders, lest their own evil deeds should become manifest.[47] When Pascasius warns that Arsenius 'is attacked on all sides

---

[47] *EA* I, c. 2, p. 22.

by hatred and envy', and can be praised only sparingly in a world where truth is stifled, Severus answers: 'I suppose that if you had lived during the age of the persecutions, you would either have claimed to know nothing about Christ, or at any rate you would have stayed silent.'[48] Having been urged by his Severus to be unafraid and true to his love for Arsenius, Pascasius decides to steer a middle course: he will narrate a 'fable', as outsiders call it, that is already known to the entire world; even though more ought to be said, there can be no offence in relating what is already in the public domain. This then leads into a discourse on Arsenius' virtues as a youth at the court.[49] Whereas Severus refuses to mince his words, Adeodatus is often the one who reminds the others of the need to be careful, and who thus keeps the issue of silence versus speech on the agenda. Typically, he is 'afraid that those who rail against a man such as this may feel that we are discussing too openly one of whom you proposed to speak obliquely (*enigmatice*)'. Pascasius then expresses his hope that there will come a time when he can divulge the entire truth about Arsenius:

Because I have not yet applied my lips to these affairs and keep silent about what is secret, there will come a day, I am certain, when I will be allowed to assert openly the facts about him, and to explain more clearly what is most important about him. In the meantime, though, as you advise, we would do well to speak more carefully, lest we step over the line, and to grieve more deeply that we live without him, when it would have been better to die with him ...[50]

This is another example of the return to lament as a possible retreat from saying too much: the epitaph as the 'default option' that I discussed in the previous chapter. The 'affairs' mentioned concern Wala's exile from the court, following the rebellion of 830 in which he took a leading part, as a punishment for his alleged breaking of his oath of fidelity to Louis. This undeserved ignominy and the need to restore Wala's reputation underpin the entire first book, but they are only hinted at. Yet there is one intriguing exception, when Pascasius recalls his horror and shock at suddenly learning of his abbot's disgrace. Having been sent on a mission by the emperor, he found himself in the refectory of a monastery in Cologne when the news broke, in less than sympathetic company: 'Broken in grief, I fainted,

---

[48] *EA* I, c. 9, p. 34 (Severus): 'Forsitan persecutorum si esses, de Christo aut nescire te quicquam te asseres, utique aut mutus esses.'

[49] *EA* I, c. 9, pp. 34–5.

[50] *EA* I, c. 11, p. 39 (Pascasius): 'Sed talibus quia necdum apposui labra, et condita sub silentio servo, erit, ut credo, illa dies, mihi cum liceat eius aperte dicere facta, et quę potiora sunt de illo, manifestius explicare. Interdum vero, sicut mones, ne quid nimis fiat, cautius loqui iuvat, et uberius deplorare, qui sine illo vivimus, cum quo melius mori duxerim ... '.

to the astonishment of all. Some were speaking of what had happened; others imagined that I was an accessory to his guilt.'[51] This elicits a wry comment from Severus about those who once paid court to Arsenius and then revealed themselves as his enemies, foreshadowing 'the unspeakable deeds of future men'. At this point, Adeodatus steers the others away from this dangerous territory and back to lament, with the complaint that the conversation goes in all directions, and that the 'order of speaking is not preserved'.[52] This then signals another retreat to the safer territory of lament and praise, of the kind that punctuates the text at regular intervals.

However, Radbert had other tactics at his disposal to make sure that his criticism would remain subtle, and this is where Terence comes in. It is not just the youngest discussant, but also Pascasius/Radbert who occasionally puts the brakes on, warning his old friend Severus that his 'invective is too fierce'.[53] He reminds him of a well-known maxim of Terence, 'nothing in excess',[54] and of the suspicious nature of those with a guilty conscience: 'They take everything as an insult, and always think that they are being blamed for their actions.'[55] Beyond the ubiquitous *ne quid nimis*, cited by just about every authoritative late antique author, up to the Rule of Benedict, Pascasius' short rebuttal also contains partial sentences and expressions from Terence's comedy *Adelphoe* (*The Brothers*). As in other instances, Radbert's use of Terence can hardly be described as quoting; rather, it seems as if he chose bits of Terentian language randomly, from a wide range of comedies, and integrated these into his dialogue. Yet there is some method to this, for Terence usually crops up when outspokenness is being pushed to its limits and needs to be tempered, either by a joke or by deliberately oblique speech made up of a patchwork of citations.

One of the most striking instances of this is the appearance of Allabigus, brought into the discussion, together with Cremes, to testify to the life Arsenius had led before he entered Corbie, and when he was outside the monastery. Like Cremes, Allabigus does not belong to the inner circle of the discussants. Whereas Cremes is a sophisticated traveller who sees through all the tricks of the Italians, Allabigus is a very different figure: bald, illiterate and entirely lacking in eloquence, he seems to be the 'type' of the uncultivated monk who converted only late in life, and therefore could never become a member of the literate inner circle of the cloister. Or was he conceived of as a layman? It is difficult to say. Allabigus, an unusual name that I have been unable to identify, and which is apparently

---

[51] *EA* I, c. 8, p. 33.    [52] *EA* I, c. 9, p. 34.    [53] *EA* I, c. 2, p. 24.
[54] Terence's most frequently cited maxim: De Jong, 'Heed That Saying', pp. 284–6; this includes the *Regula Benedicti*, c. 64.12, p. 208.
[55] Terence, *Adelphoe* 4.3, ed. Barsby, p. 320, ll. 605–7.

attested only in this text, may be an alias for someone who followed Wala from the secular world into Corbie: an old retainer who stuck with his master. His bald pate suggests that he was an elderly man, but not necessarily a monk. Whatever the case, in the *Epitaphium*, the illiterate Allabigus responds to a highly literate challenge by Severus, who nettles the others for their lack of decisiveness: 'Perhaps, like certain philosophers, we hold everything to be doubtful and theorise that nothing can be known for certain'.[56] It is time for some straight talk, but first Cremes bores everyone with a dutiful report on Arsenius' exemplary use of tithes, and to add insult to injury, he mocks the impatient bald man who fidgets and scratches his head. Then the latter barges in, with a passionate outburst that is interspersed with expressions from Terence's *Eunuch*:

Why, then, do you bandy such nonsense as if it were in jest? And if I appear bald to you, why do you mock Elisha? Or are you unaware, Cremes, that many winds have blown upon me? Perhaps I have brought this down on myself by swearing upon this head. Now, however, since they don't believe [me], I have found this new thing, as Terence puts it, namely, to latch onto those who want to be foremost in everything but are not. When they laugh, I laugh along with them and admire their cleverness. I praise whatever they say, and if they contradict themselves I praise it again. Whatever anyone denies, I deny. What they affirm, I affirm. I have steeled myself to go along with everything, since this way of making a living is now so lucrative.[57]

Allabigus then sings his master's praises, sounding the horn of truth and declaring his undying loyalty. Despite his lack of eloquence and inability to speak at great length, he declares himself unashamed to mourn the great man, even in public.[58] When Allabigus has fallen silent, Pascasius remarks that this bald man, who seemed to be illiterate, has suddenly been transformed into a philosopher of lamentation. Without any doubt he had been touched by the spirit of 'him, for whom we grieve', and been turned into a deliverer and herald of the truth (*invector ... precoque veritatis*).[59] This reaction underlines some important aspects of Allabigus' role in the dialogue. First of all, his *sancta simplicitas* gives

---

[56] *EA* I, c. 8, p. 32: 'Fortassis ergo ut quidam filosophorum omnia dubia tenemus, nihilque certum posse conprehendi philosophamur'.

[57] *EA* I, c. 8, p. 32–3: 'Quid igitur ludicra iocose seritis? et si calvus vobis videor, Heliseum quid contemnitis? An nescis, Cremes, quia multi me venti flaverunt? fortassis ergo iurando per hoc caput ista contraxi. Nunc autem quia non credunt, *hoc novum* repperi iuxta Terrentium, ut consector eos, *qui se primos omnium esse volunt, nec sunt*: et cum riserint, *adrideo, eorum*que *ingenia admiror,* vel *quicquid dicunt, laudo*; et *si negant, laudo*; quid *quisque* negaverit, *nego*; aiunt, *aio*. Deinde *imperavi mihi omnia adsentari, quia is questus nunc est* valde *uberrimus.* Tamen saltim parvam adhibeam fidem, qui mihi de illo quam bene sum conscius, nihilque falsi fingam, quoniam meo cordi nullum cariorem invenio.'

[58] *EA* I, c. 8, p. 32.      [59] *EA* I, c. 8, p. 33.

him a direct access to divine truth that is denied to the learned. His passionate declaration of loyalty is meant to counterbalance doubt about Arsenius, and especially philosophical doubt – always a dangerous temptation in Carolingian monastic life. It was precisely his lack of eloquence that made Allabigus a 'herald of truth'. As for his suddenly spouting Terence, this is reminiscent of the many illiterate visionaries of the period, celebrated for their simple acceptance of what God deigned to reveal to them, even though their experiences had to be written up by clerical experts.[60]

In the first book of the *Epitaphium*, Terence is invoked not only when potentially offensive pronouncements have to be toned down, but also when, more generally, the tension between silence and speech needs to be addressed. Allabigus claims he has 'found this new thing, as Terence calls it', and then, in sentences taken from the *Eunuch*, he savagely mocks those who will say whatever is dictated by those in power, however stupid. It is no coincidence that this intervention is situated right before Pascasius' recollection of the traumatic memory of his discovery, in Cologne, of Wala's exile: Allabigus' impassioned speech creates the space required for the narrator's subsequent memory of his one-time despair. It should be kept in mind that whenever Radbert borrows language from Terence's plays, the original meaning seems largely irrelevant, or even gets lost completely. Terence's trickster Gnatho has his audience in stitches because of his misguided self-confidence, yet in the mouths of Allabigus and Severus these passages from the *Eunuch* signal the tragic impossibility of speaking in public about good men, in a world which has become infested with faithless flatterers. An even more striking example of such an inversion, also involving the *Eunuch*, can be found in the letter by which Radbert dedicated the first version of *De corpore et sanguine* to his former pupil Warin, the future abbot of Corvey. As Radbert puts it, Wala 'suffers exile because of *fides,* in the manner of that writer of comedy, because he was full of leaks (*plenus rimarum*), and knowing the truth he did not want to remain silent'. In Terence's play, the slave Parmeno says he leaks like a cracked pot and will be silent only about true secrets.[61] This is exactly the opposite of what Radbert states about Wala (and, implicitly, himself): knowing the truth, he could not be silent. In other words, Arsenius' 'leaks' were those of a compulsive truth-teller on a divine mission.

---

[60] A classic example is Einhard's *Translatio SS Petri et Marcellini*, especially the third and fourth books; Dutton, *Charlemagne's Courtier*, pp. 92–130; Dutton, *The Politics of Dreaming*, pp. 91–8.

[61] Paschasius Radbertus, *De corpore*, pp. 3–4; Terence, *Eunuchus* I.2, ed. Barsby, p. 324, l. 105: '... plenus rimarum sum, hac atque illac perfluo. proin tu, taceri si vis, vera dicito.'

## 4     Why Terence?

It is time to return to the question of why Terence is so prominently present in the first book, and totally absent from the second. The latter book has some echoes of classical texts, but none of the explicit references that abound in the earlier part of the *Epitaphium*. Did Radbert have a change of heart, turning away from his youthful enthusiasm for the 'king of rhetoric' and other classical authors? Apart from the fact that Radbert was hardly a youngster when he wrote the first book, there is no indication in his later exegetical work that he turned his back on Cicero or other classics. On the contrary, it looks as if, during the years of his own abbacy and the decade thereafter, Corbie steadily extended its classical holdings, under the aegis of Radbert himself. Monks in Corbie may not have started learning 'the comic' at age ten to twelve, as Roman upper-class children did, but they certainly came across the poet in grammatical treatises and patristic writing early enough to interiorise sentences, sayings and expressions. As we have seen in the previous chapter, Christian authors such as Augustine had invoked Terence as an expert on human life in general and moral dilemmas in particular, and this was how ninth-century youngsters first met Terence, beyond the use of his language as a model for Latin grammar.[62] Like some biblical texts learned early, Terence tended to stick in the memory. The suggestion that Radbert did not use Terence in his second book because, after his deposition, in temporary exile in St-Riquier, he did not have access to the Corbie copy, can therefore be safely discarded.[63] Radbert had enough Terence in his head to last him a lifetime, so why did he not use the poet in his second book?

At one time, I thought the answer should be looked for in the first book's more monastic focus. Whenever Pascasius and Severus are presented as playfully throwing Terence back and forth, there is indeed a whiff of the one-upmanship between learned monks who had known each other since they shared the Corbie schoolroom. There may still be some truth in this, but not because Terentian pastiches could be appreciated only by learned monks. One of the more famous copies of Terence's comedies was produced at the court of Louis the Pious, so at least some non-monastic interest in the playwright must be taken into account.[64] Distinguishing between

---

[62] On early medieval teaching of grammar and some of the key manuscripts, such as the famous codex Berlin, Deutsche Staatsbibliothek, MS Diez B. Sant 66, see Villa, 'Cultura classica', 'Die Horazüberlieferung'; McKitterick, *Charlemagne*, pp. 365–8.

[63] Booker, *Past Convictions*, p. 298, n. 178. This contradicts Booker's more plausible suggestion (*ibid.*, p. 45) that Radbert cited Terence mostly from memory.

[64] For the bibliography on this, see De Jong, 'Heed That Saying' and Booker, 'Hypocrisy'.

Carolingian monastic and court cultures is far from easy, and in Radbert's case, with his wide experience of both worlds, this is particularly difficult. It is not a good idea to ascribe dissimilar levels of learning to the two books of the *Epitaphium*, therefore, and to connect these with different audiences. After all, the text as it was copied into one codex and carefully corrected contained *both* books, which were meant to make sense together. In fact, the meaning of the work as Radbert completed it in the 850s depends on the contrast between the reticent first book and its outspoken sequel. As I have argued above, this is not merely a matter of literary artifice. There is enough internal evidence to suggest that the two parts were written some decades apart, and in different circumstances. Above all, it was Radbert's changed position that set the constraints within which he could write, but these also helped to determine his widely varying literary approach to his main aim: namely, telling the truth about Wala.

The episode with Allabigus discussed above offers some clues as to why Terence was so important in the first book. Assuming Terence's voice, full of banter and allusion, Radbert could push against the limits of what might be said, and maintain the deliberately low-key tone he had assumed from the beginning, despite the seriousness of his subject. By contrast, in the second book, he adopts the thunderous voice of the prophet Jeremiah. Here, the Book of Job is used in the way Terence was deployed in the first book: namely, to address deeply contentious issues in an oblique yet authoritative manner.[65] Radbert's account of Louis's public penance in 833 is phrased partly in language derived from Job 12:14–25, the passage in which Job, responding to Sophar's challenge, praises God's wisdom and strength, and the utter dependency of the leadership, kings as well as priests, on divine succour. In this case, Radbert weaves Job's idiom into a long monologue by his alter ego, Pascasius, on the failure of the rebellion of 833, announcing Arsenius' departure for Italy. He adopts biblical language in order to refer to events too painful to speak about openly and directly.

These choices may have been influenced by Radbert's knowledge of the three rhetorical styles (*genera dicendi*). I shall explore this possibility in the rest of this chapter, along with some related strategies of persuasion.

---

[65] De Jong, 'Political Discourse and the Biblical Past', with on pp. 74–6 a translation of the relevant text: *EA* II, c. 20, pp. 91–2 (Pascasius).

## 5 Stilus modestus

In an intriguing passage in the *Epitaphium*'s prologue, Adeodatus implores Severus to temper his eloquence and wit, and to adapt himself to the joint purpose of the dialogue:

You frequently employ the subtleness of Chrysippus, Severus, and parry even well-chosen jests with the sword of your eloquence. I ask you not to treat us with the severity that your name portends, but rather to work together with us to fashion an image of our father with a modest pen in a restrained style.[66]

What did Radbert mean by the *stilus modestus* that the monks had to use – even the sharp-witted Severus, who was as eloquent as the proverbially clever Stoic philosopher Chrysippus?[67] Is this indeed an indication that Radbert wrote in a mixed rather than a simple style, in accordance with his writing enigmatically and allusively, as Kempshall has suggested?[68] Possibly, but I doubt that *modestus* is a technical term in this particular context. Furthermore, in the *Epitaphium*, the word *stilus* seems to refer to the pen as a metaphor for the act of composition,[69] while the expression *modestus* does not belong to the vocabulary of the three styles. I am inclined to interpret this passage, therefore, as a non-technical declaration that our author intended to keep his dialogue low-key, with the pen paying a modest homage to the great Arsenius. Yet, even if in this particular passage the styles did not play a part, they can still help to explain some of the striking differences between the *Epitaphium*'s two books.

The basic principles of the three styles of speech can be found in the *Rhetorica ad Herrennium*, traditionally ascribed to Cicero, and in Cicero's *Orator*, two texts Radbert had at his disposal in Corbie's library.[70] The terminology varied: Cicero's referred to the three *genera dicendi* as *subtile*, *modicum* and *vehemens* (or *grave*), while the author of the *Ad Herrennium* called these *genera* 'figures' and referred to them as *extenuata*,

---

[66] *EA* I, prologue p. 20 (Adeodatus): 'Uteris frequenter, Severe, Crisippi acumine et iocose etiam eximios eloquii tui refellis mucrone. Quaeso ne iuxta tui praesagium nominis severius agas, quin immo nobiscum age, ut imaginem patris stilo formemus modesto'.

[67] Chrysippus of Soli (c. 280–c. 204 BC), the third head of the Stoic school at Athens, was renowned for his sagacity and quickness of intellect; see Jerome, *Epistolae* 57.12 and 61.3.

[68] Kempshall, *Rhetoric*, p. 199.

[69] *EA* I, c. 9, pp. 33–4: 'Dum varia rerum incidunt negotia, in colloquio confunditur stilus, nec ordo dicendi servatur, nec flendi copia pectoris de fonte uberior hauritur'; *EA* I, c. 27, p. 59: 'Quibus ita dictis, quia tandem ad Gallias rursus stilum vertimus, finem libri ponamus'; *EA* II, c. 15, p. 82: 'Quae profecto mala omnibus tunc et deinceps in manifesto venerunt maiora et atrociora, quam quae noster stilus fluendo prosequi velit aut possit.'

[70] *Ad Herrennium*: Paris, BnF lat. 7714. Cicero, *Orator*: Avranches, Bibliothèque municipale 238.

*mediocris* and *gravis*.[71] Yet the division between the three styles remained the same, and I shall refer to them here by the conventional terms most often found in the secondary literature on rhetoric. The lowest, the *genus humile* or restrained style, is direct and conversational, and the opposite of the 'grand' style, the *genus grande* (or *vehemens*) used for passionate oratory; in between, there was the mixed or intermediate way of speaking, the *genus medium* or *modicum*.[72] Among the ancients there was much debate, as there still is nowadays among specialists, about which style the orator should choose for a given topic. The master of forensic oratory, Cicero, thought the restrained style appropriate for simple matters of proof, while audiences and judges should be entertained in the intermediate and convinced in the grand style.[73] Disagreement on details notwithstanding, in the Roman world it was agreed that there was an intimate connection between style and discourse, and that the grand style should be reserved for passionate and powerful oratory on important subjects. This had been a set principle since Aristotle, also with regard to demonstrative rhetoric, but in Roman treatises on rhetoric, it was forensic oratory that was the main context for the most brilliant feats of the grand style of speaking.[74] This could entail the use of ornate language, but the main characteristic of the *genus grande* was that it managed to sway opinion through an emotional appeal to the audience.

In his *Orator*, a work written towards the end of his life, Cicero helpfully elaborates on the close connection between the topic and the style of speaking. The restrained speaker should by no means represent the state, and his delivery should not be theatrical or tragic; he can use humour and wit, and sprinkle his speech with pleasantry, as long as he resorts to ridicule and jest with moderation.[75] By contrast, affairs of the state should not be addressed in restrained speech, but in the grand style; the middle style is particularly suited for discussing philosophical issues, and those who practise it would be wise to study Aristotle and Chrysippus. The ideal orator, Cicero claims, is he who can speak subtly about humble affairs,

---

[71] *Ad Herrennium* IV, 8, p. 252. On the Latin terminology, see Lausberg, *Handbuch*, 1079–82, pp. 519–25.

[72] Cicero, *Orator* 21.69: 'Erit igitur eloquens – hunc enim auctore Antonio quaerimus – is qui in foro causisque civilibus ita dicet, ut probet, ut delectet, ut flectat. Probare necessitatis est, delectare suavitatis, flectere victoriae: nam id unum ex omnibus ad obtinendas causas potest plurimum. Sed quot officia oratoris, tot sunt genera dicendi: subtile in probando, modicum in delectando, vehemens in flectendo; in quo uno vis omnis oratoris est.' This is the opening of a long digression on the three styles.

[73] On the development of Cicero's views on the three styles between *De oratore* and the *Orator*, see Quadlbauer, 'Genera dicendi', pp. 82–90.

[74] Shuger, 'Grand Style', pp. 3–10. Quadlbauer, 'Genera dicendi', pp. 60–1, 64–8. Forensic passion should be expressed in the *genus grande*.

[75] Cicero, *Orator* 25.85–6; 26.87–90, pp. 368–70.

grandly (*graviter*) about the highest things, and temperately about what was in between (*mediocre*).[76] Having acknowledged that this can only be an ideal, the old pro then proceeds to give pages of examples from his own speeches to show how ideal oratory actually works. One important piece of Cicero's advice should be kept in mind: within speeches, styles should be varied. The orator in the grand style is the greatest of all, but if he is only capable of this, he should be despised. By carefully moderating the *genus grave* by the other two more temperate styles, he should gradually transport his audience to a fiery passion, otherwise they will think he is drunk.[77]

Cicero's counsel makes sense, also for modern historians tempted to detect one particular style in the *Epitaphium Arsenii*, or in either of its books, for that matter. Still, the fact that Terence is emphatically present in the first book as 'the comic', along with the conversational directness in the dialogue, does suggest that here, as far as style is concerned, Radbert was aiming for a lower register. This may not necessarily or consistently have been the *genus medium*, which in any case is the most difficult of the three *genera dicendi* to identify. By the end of antiquity, *stilus* could indeed refer to a style of speech, but *modestus* was not a term to designate the mixed style. It is better to take a helicopter view of the entire issue of styles in the *Epitaphium*, and to recognise that it is not just 'the comic' himself whose presence is already announced in the prologue. There is also the extensive reference to Seneca's vicious satire on the death of Claudius. As we have seen, Radbert used the story of the man who saw Drusilla ascend to heaven for different purposes: to address the disbelief of his audience, who would not listen to anything he had to say, and to convey his certainty that Wala was now up there, among the blessed, and praying for his bereaved monks. None of this had anything to do with the original meaning of Seneca's satire,[78] yet Radbert's emphatic introduction of comic genres into the prologue may have owed something, at least, to a tradition that associated speaking grandly with tragedy, and comic genres with more restrained forms of speech.[79] Terence certainly counted as a master when it came to a lively portrayal of characters, in a way that was aimed at pleasing (*delectatio*): allegedly the province of demonstrative oratory, and of the mixed or intermediate style.[80]

---

[76] Cicero, *Orator* 29.100, p. 378.    [77] Cicero, *Orator* 28.97–9, pp. 374–8.

[78] Contra De Jong, 'Heed That Saying', p. 277.

[79] For an example, see the opening chapter of Cicero's *De optimo genere oratorum* (I.1–4), where different forms of poetry are loosely compared with the three *genera*. Quadlbauer, 'Genera dicendi', pp. 70–71.

[80] Cicero, *Orator* 37.128, pp. 400–2.

Whether Radbert had all this fascinating theory foremost in mind remains unclear, but he surely expressed an interest in Roman drama, and knew the difference between tragedy and comedy.[81] It is likely that his emphatic introduction of Terence's comedy and Seneca's satire sent out a clear signal, namely that the defence of Arsenius would be *modestus*, in a style that was most often colloquial and understated, and that an attempt would be made to delight and entertain the audience. This would not be incompatible with forensic oratory, for the orator might start off with an amusing story to get his audience in a good mood, prior to resorting to heavier ammunition.[82] The anecdote about Drusilla seems to serve this purpose, but there is also more to it. The monk Adeodatus is quick to point out its deeper and very different significance: 'If it comes to that, what is more glorious, more joyful, and (of greater importance) more true than the message that Christ returned victorious from hell and entered heaven in the flesh?'[83]

## 6     Radbert, Augustine and the Christian Orator

Radbert was a Christian orator, for whom Augustine, in the fourth book of his *De doctrina christiana*, had laid down the ground rules. There is no doubt that he read Cicero and other classical texts on eloquence through the prism of Augustine's great defence of rhetoric for Christian purposes. The church father had much to say on the *genera dicendi*, drawing his copious examples from Scripture or from Christian authorities such as Cyprian or Ambrose.[84] His insights into the three styles and their purposes are based on a practice of preaching and writing: for Augustine, it is clear that Old Testament prophets as well as St Paul knew the *genera* and used them to great effect. He agrees with Cicero that eloquence is all about instructing, delighting and moving the listener.[85] Styles of speaking should correspond, but not according to the importance of the topic, or the social status of those concerned, in the sense that the restrained or humble style is mainly suited for straightforward matters and simple folk.

In purely secular forensics, this is a defensible view, Augustine argues, but not for Christian topics, because these have to do with eternal salvation, however small and humble they might be. For Christians, to be

---

[81] Booker, 'Hypocrisy', pp. 197–8, provides the relevant references.
[82] Kempshall, *Rhetoric*, pp. 192–3.     [83] *EA* I, prologue, p. 21.
[84] Augustine, *DDC* IV.75–160, pp. 228–280. On Augustine's work in Corbie, cf. Ganz, *Corbie*, pp. 96–102.
[85] Augustine, *DDC* IV.74, p. 228. See Cameron, 'Augustine and Scripture', pp. 203–5, on divine rhetorical strategy; on *De doctrina christiana* and its aims, Vessey, 'Augustine', pp. 249–53.

trustworthy even in small matters is a big issue, which is all about the core values of justice, charity and piety. Augustine gives a telling example of St Paul (1 Cor. 6:1–9) speaking grandly about small matters, and adds that a preacher does not use restrained speech simply because he is dealing with minor sins.[86] But neither should the grand style be used in any situation where religious purposes are served. The *doctor*, the learned Christian preacher or writer, should use the restrained style when teaching, and the intermediate one when censuring or praising something. But when action needs to be taken and he is faced with an unwilling audience whose minds need to be changed, 'then we must speak of what is important in the grand style, the style suitable for moving minds to action'.[87]

Like Cicero's ideal forensic orator, his Christian counterpart should vary his styles, starting in a restrained manner and only then proceeding to speaking *granditer*, yet this should not be kept up unremittingly, without any breathing space for the listeners.[88] In order to sway his audience and win the case, he requires the grand style, of the kind used by Jeremiah against his sinful people, and fervently admired by Augustine: 'What eloquence – all the more terrifying for its purity, and all the more forceful for its vehemence!' (*O eloquentia tanto terribilior quanto purior, et quanto solidior tanto vehementior*).[89] What Radbert learned from Augustine, and brought to his own exegesis, was an understanding of biblical authors as fellow writers, who had followed the same rhetorical and stylistic rules. Doubtless, Augustine's reading of Scripture with the three styles in mind greatly enhanced Radbert's admiration for 'the king of rhetoric', and it must also have influenced his own biblical commentary.

The role of rhetoric in Radbert's biblical exegesis merits further research. Here, I am concerned with the question how the three styles helped to shape the *Epitaphium*, if at all. It is the mixed or intermediate style that is most difficult to pin down, also for Augustine, who after much deliberation comes up with the following distinction: whereas the restrained speaker persuades people of the truth, the intermediate style aims at being listened to with pleasure, while the grand style hammers home what is already known, but now gets people to obey and act accordingly. As soon as this has been established, Augustine challenges his own classification, maintaining that persuasion, pleasure and obedience should be the aim of any Christian speaker, whatever style he chooses.[90]

[86] Augustine, *DDC* IV. 98–9, p. 240.        [87] Augustine, *DDC* IV. 10, p. 244.
[88] Augustine, *DDC* IV. 134, p. 266.
[89] Augustine, *DDC* IV.81–2, p. 233; here I diverge from Green's translation.
[90] Augustine, *DDC* IV. 141–8, pp. 270–4.

When it comes to distinguishing between styles, Augustine's concrete examples are more instructive: St Paul in his restrained mode anticipates questions, of which one leads to the other, and then is refuted by the debater (Gal. 4:21–6), while at the intermediate or mixed level he is delivering a monologue, as a preacher. St Paul speaking grandly and ornately is also monologic (2 Cor. 6:2–11; Rom. 8:28–39), but the difference is that his speech is inflamed by heartfelt emotion.[91] This is what singles out speaking *granditer*, even when it is not done ornately, in elaborate speech: the emotional fervour (*motus animi*).[92] Augustine points out that St Paul at times combines the mixed style with speaking grandly, when he inserts passages of powerful emotion (Gal. 4:10–20), without any attempt at elaborately ornate language.[93] He then moves on to examples from Cyprian and Ambrose, and the differences between the three styles become even clearer. Whereas the restrained style is for teaching, and especially for demonstrating points with the aid of factual evidence, the mixed one is for instruction and admonition, as in exhorting virgins to lead an exemplary life, but if you denounce 'painted women' with a full blast of vituperation about their evil ways, this is the grand style.[94]

On the strength of this, it could be said that the lively yet reticent dialogue of the *Epitaphium*'s first book tends towards the restrained style, while the polemical second book, with its invective against Justina and Naso, goes overboard in the other direction, but it is not as if one clear style can be assigned to either book. They are a mixed and rather eclectic bag. Still, the allusive witticisms and display of intellectual brilliance of the first book give way in the second to the kind of speech that Augustine associated with the prophets, first and foremost. There was Amos, who might seem rustic to some, but who still followed the rules of eloquence when he ardently laid into the wicked, the proud and the indulgent. What more could anyone want, except for 'the invective, crashing with an explosive roar upon the sleepy senses to awaken them . . .'.[95]

The grand style is all about passionate delivery, including invective, and this is what distinguishes the second book from its predecessor. Initially, be it in a restrained or mixed style, or a combination thereof, Radbert carefully avoids any outright discussion of the shame of Wala's exile from the court, mentioning it only obliquely, as a personal memory of the narrator that was judiciously introduced by Allabigus' innocent and

---

[91] Augustine, *DDC* IV.107–21, pp. 244–54.
[92] This holds true also for the speech of tragedy: Quadlbauer, 'Genera dicendi', pp. 80–1.
[93] Augustine, *DDC* IV.112–13, pp. 254–6.
[94] Augustine, *DDC* IV.127–33, pp. 258–62.
[95] Augustine, *DDC* IV. 49–51, pp. 216–18.

illiterate frankness. By the time the ex-abbot resumed his unfinished work, this had changed. Radbert switches from an emphatically low-key register to a grand prophetic style. This does not prevail all the time, for the audience deserved some light relief, but by the mid-850s they got very little of this. It was now time for frank and compelling rhetoric, of the kind that drove the truth home relentlessly, and would attack the moral integrity of the enemy, leaving him speechless.

## 7    Becoming Jeremiah

The passing of time, but above all the different tone of the second book, is marked by the introduction of the new interlocutor, Teofrastus. This replacement of the deceased Severus is chosen by Adeodatus, with the caveat that 'we are not looking for a philosopher for our lament, but for one whose pious remembrance or emotion will move us to tears'.[96]

Three messages are packed into this sentence, which is part of the agenda-setting prologue to the second book: it calls to mind the philosopher to whom this new discussant owes his byname, it reminds the reader that this is still a funeral oration, and it announces that the aim of the continued confabulation is to move the audience to emotion (*affectus*).[97] The tone is then lightened by a joke about Teofrastus' beardlessness, but the newcomer is not amused, and this is the last of any such monastic banter in the entire second book. Pascasius defines the aim of the operation once more – namely, lamentation and truth (*threnos et veritatem*) – but then Adeodatus proposes postponing the lament (*lamentum*), for he first wants to hear about 'the beginning of this major crisis, because there is nobody in his right mind who believes that all this happened among the people without God being offended'. Pascasius hesitates, claiming that not all should be revealed to everyone, especially not to those who hate the truth and delight in wickedness. Thus, he positions himself versus the nameless enemies of *veritas*; before he embarks on his narrative of Wala's intervention during the winter meeting in the palace in Aachen in 828–9, however, which is to dominate the next pages, a brief debate ensues which clarifies that Teofrastus' presence implies a novel kind of frankness. When Adeodatus explains that the new interlocutor is so intemperate that he could not have taken part in the earlier conversation without having exposed the others as traitors, Teofrastus points out that Arsenius was unafraid to expose the sins of the people: an example that should be

---

[96] *EA* II, prologue, p. 60 (Adeodatus): 'Non enim philosophum ad lamentum rite quaerimus, sed eorum aliquem, cuius aut memoria pię recordationis, aut affectu ad lacrimas incitemur.'
[97] *EA* II, prologue, p. 60.

followed, so that it may serve 'as a warning for correction, if not for us, then for future generations'.[98]

The scene has been set, and opens the way for Radbert's depiction of Arsenius' fiery and uncompromising speeches during the gathering in Aachen. As I have argued above,[99] this vivid evocation of Wala at the court of Louis the Pious has as much, or perhaps even more to do with the way in which Radbert himself and his fellow reformers confronted Charles the Bald during debates about church property, but this is not the issue here. Radbert's depiction of Wala's address to this restricted assembly of the leading men of the country is forensic oratory at its finest, in a style that is both passionate and emotive.

This is the first of many occasions in the second book when the grand style takes over. A key to this is Arsenius' and Radbert's ever closer association with Jeremiah. That the troubles of his time had 'brought forth another Jeremiah' from Arsenius had already been announced in the first book, but in the second, it becomes clear what this Jeremiah was like: he was someone who, like the prophet he was likened to, spoke truth to power without hesitation or fear. The monk Adeodatus spells it out in the course of the opening narrative about Wala's interventions during the crisis meeting in Aachen in the winter of 828/9:

As I understand it, it was not without justification that you referred to him as another Jeremiah for the constancy of his faith and the hardness of his head,[100] since he so boldly inveighed against the idleness of luxury and the wicked habits of kings to the emperor (as we saw), since he had neglected his duties because he was preoccupied with things of no importance.[101]

This 'constancy of faith' (*constantia fidei*) is worth keeping in mind, for in subsequent passages that identify Wala with Jeremiah, this idiom crops up again: the great man spoke resolutely (*constanter*), like another Jeremiah.[102] This is Pascasius' answer to a revealing question on Adeodatus' part: if Arsenius was indeed so humble, why then did he

---

[98] *EA* II, c. 1, p. 62 (Teofrastus): 'Propterea igitur, ni fallor, isto denotanda et plangenda sunt loco, ut si non nobis, saltem posteris veniant correctionis ad exemplum.'

[99] See above, pp. 60–3.

[100] Ezek. 3:8: 'Ecce dedi faciem tuam valentiorem faciebus eorum, et frontem tuam duriorem frontibus eorum.'

[101] *EA* II, c. 2, p. 63 (Adeodatus): 'Ut sentio, non immerito tu altrum eum Hieremiam dicebas, ob constantiam fidei et frontis duritiam, qui tam audenter augusto invexit, tanta quae vidimus, ob luxus desidiam, necnon et pessimas regum consuetudines, officii sui negotia, cum esset preoccupatus vanis rebus, pretermisisse.' See also Pascasius at the beginning of c. 2, p. 62: ' ... acsi Hieremias alter ostenderet, in quibus Deum omnes offenderant: et monuit constanter caritatis officio, ut mala quae admiserant, destruerent, dissiparent et evellerent ... '.

[102] *EA* II, c. 5, p. 66 (Pascasius): 'Propterea igitur talia et quamplura, veluti alter Hieremias, constanter loquebatur.'

speak so forcefully and resolutely in front of all the leading men and the emperor himself?[103]

Again, the word *constanter* is used, which signals that Radbert inserted himself into the long tradition of *parrhesia*, or frank speech. Irene van Renswoude has recently written an illuminating study about the continuity and persistence of notions of free speech in late antiquity and the early Middle Ages, in which she shows that, regardless of major changes in social setting and terminology, the phenomenon of *parrhesia* did not disappear.[104] *Constantia* became one of the Latin terms used to designate occurrences of *parrhesia* in the Greek New Testament, and thus an important expression in the Christian discourse of free speech.[105] In the post-Roman West there continued to be those who dared to speak truth to power, emphatically positioning themselves as harmless outsiders. Excluded from the political order and devoid of institutional power, they dared to challenge the powerful by their fearless rebukes.

The classical parrhesiast had been a philosopher, but in late antiquity, intrepid bishops such as Ambrose had adopted this guise as part of their public persona: Ambrose's confrontation with Theodosius is the best-known case in point, and an enduring part of the the legacy of Christian free speech that would become highly influential in the Carolingian world and beyond. Even before Ambrose had become regarded in the ninth century as the epitome of the bishop admonishing his ruler in order to save the latter's soul, Old Testament prophets had become influential models for frank speech. In the standard biblical repertoire that underpinned the Christian discourse of admonition, Ezekiel 3:17–19, was no doubt the most important text: warning sinners was a duty of the 'watchmen of Israel', and if they neglected to do so, the sin and its consequences would be on their own head.[106] It was through this biblical text, first and foremost, that in 833 the rebellious bishops justified the public penance that they imposed on Louis the Pious.[107] As Van Renswoude has argued, the key element in the early medieval continuity of free speech was the voice of the prophet, replacing the philosopher who had filled this role in

[103] *EA* II, c. 5, p. 65 (Adeodatus): Nam cum esset tam humilis, quo nullus humilior, nullusque magis mortuus mundo videretur, quid est quod tam inter summos ecclesiarum, praesulum videlicet et senatorum, consules, in senatu coram Augusto consulte constanterque loquebatur?'.

[104] Van Renswoude, 'Licence to Speak'. On early medieval *parrhesia*, see also Garrison, 'An Aspect of Alcuin'.

[105] See above, pp. n. 102.

[106] The central biblical texts are Ezek. 3:17–19; Pss. 118:46; Isa. 58:1 and 2 Tim. 4:2, but above all Ezekiel; De Jong, *Penitential State*, pp. 114–118; Booker, *Past Convictions*, pp. 142–4; Van Renswoude, 'Licence to Speak', pp. 131–5; see also Van Renswoude, *Rhetoric of Free Speech* (forthcoming).

[107] *Relatio episcoporum* (833), p. 52 (Ezek. 3:18).

antiquity. The prevailing image of the Old Testament prophet was that of
the divinely inspired outsider who warned kings and peoples of God's
displeasure and impending wrath, raising his voice time and again at his
own personal risk.[108] Authors who assumed this voice often posed as
outsiders, even if they were well-established bishops. In his *Libri apologetici*, Agobard of Lyon calls out 'with the bellowing voice of the
prophet',[109] yet in other works Agobard adopts a different register of
the prophetic role, namely that of the flawed speaker who is 'only
a mumbler', like Jeremiah, who could speak without a stutter only when
God spoke through him, or another prophet, Ezekiel, whose power of
speech was equally dependent on divine favour.[110] In the Old Testament,
Jeremiah has different faces, all of which correspond conveniently with
Wala's history in the 830s. The prophet had fearlessly delivered divine
warnings to Jerusalem, and thus became the victim of persecution, to the
point where he was thrown into a cistern; when his prediction of the city's
destruction came true, he became an exile in Egypt, where, according to
tradition, he recorded the fall of his people after the event, like
a retrospective prophecy, and wrote his Lamentations. In Radbert's portrait of Wala as Jeremiah, a martyr-like persistence in the face of persecution is closely linked to speaking *constanter*, like another Jeremiah:
nothing, including threats, force or rewards, could keep him 'from the
charity of Christ and love for his fatherland and people, from love for the
churches and loyalty to the emperor'.[111] This connection between truth-
telling, persecution and exile is also at the heart of Radbert's literary
creation, in which he combines a funeral oration with a defence of
Wala. In the second book, when Jeremiah the victim is fully transformed
into Jeremiah the frank speaker, Adeodatus elucidates the change of focus
from lamenting Arsenius' death to writing an epitaph for his era: 'It is not
so much this man but these events that we must continuously bewail, so
that God's wrath may be turned away from us.'[112] The reader is also
reminded of the two faces of the prophet, lament and frank speech, and
their intrinsic connection in the *Epitaphium*:

And lest anyone say that such things should not be heaped up or repeated in
a lamentation, let him know that there is no place where this is more appropriate,
especially when such terrible evils are appearing, when the truth is persecuted by

[108] Van Renswoude, 'Licence to Speak', pp. 313–33.
[109] Van Renswoude, 'Licence to Speak', p. 329.
[110] Van Renswoude, 'Licence to Speak', pp. 313–4; Jer. 1:6; Ezek. 3:26. Agobard, *Epistolae*
no. 4, p. 164.
[111] *EA* II, c. 5, p. 65–6.
[112] *EA* II, c. 8, p. 70 (Adeodatus): 'Neque enim ille tam plangendus est, quam iugiter ista
deploranda, ut avertatur ira Dei a nobis.'

hatreds, and when justice is under assault. This is the reason why the prophet Jeremiah – after rebukes, persecutions, and attacks – turned to lamentation and mourned bitterly for everything that happened as a punishment for sin.[113]

## 8      Speaking Grandly about the State

Against this slander, a counter-attack was the best defence, both for Wala and for Radbert himself. His onslaught comprises most of the *Epitaphium*'s second book, and speech in the grand style was an integral part of this operation. There are many examples of passionate speech intended to change the readers' views, voiced by Wala/Arsenius as well as by narrator Pascasius and his two fellow discussants. An obvious and telling example is Wala's alleged address to the emperor and 'his loftiest magnates' during the winter assembly of 828/9, admonishing them, 'like another Jeremiah', about the ways in which they had offended God. Apart from the use of direct speech, which allows the prophetic voice to bellow even more loudly, there is the subject matter at hand: the well-being of the *respublica* in the face of impending divine wrath. As we have seen, both Cicero and Augustine posited a connection between content and style: in Cicero's view, the restrained speaker should not represent the state.[114] By contrast, the grand style is 'magnificent, opulent, stately and ornate' (*amplus, copiosus, gravis, ornatus*), and is the most powerful: who attains this kind of brilliance gains the admiration of many nations and states, and the despairing envy of those who will never manage to speak in this way.[115] Of course, Cicero then goes on to give some examples of his own brilliant oratory, and explains that he used every kind of rhetorical amplification when it came to upholding the dignity of public law.[116] Radbert seems to have taken a similar course. Whereas the first book never mentions *respublica*, or *imperium* for that matter, these notions dominate the second, for this book highlights Arsenius' valiant yet fruitless attempts to save the state.

These are precisely the passages in which the author, as Pascasius, speaks directly to his reader in the grand style. I have called these sections 'monologic', because the narrator tends to take over most of the dialogue, yet there is nothing dull about such monologues. On the contrary, they provide room for emotive oratory in this higher register, of which the

---

[113] *EA* II, c. 8, pp. 70–1 (Adeodatus): 'Et ne dicat aliquis, in threnis quod talia non sint coacervanda neque replicanda, sciat quod nullo in loco amplius, maxime quando talia crebrescunt mala, quando veritas insectatur odiis, quando iustitia debellatur. Sic itaque Hieremias propheta post increpationes, post persecutiones et impulsiones, ad lamenta se convertit, et omnia quae acciderunt pro delictis, amarissime deflevit.'
[114] Cicero, *Orator* 25.85, p. 368.      [115] Cicero, *Orator* 28.97, pp. 374–6.
[116] Cicero, *Orator* 29.102, p. 380.

*Epitaphium*'s second book contains many instances. A telling case in point is in the vicious invective directed at the undisputed villain of the piece, Bernard of Septimania, who replaced Wala in August 829 as the most powerful man at Louis's court. He was branded as having abandoned all honour in life and in his office, and plunged himself into every filthy sty. 'Like a wild boar, he turned the palace upside down, put an end to counsel, and destroyed all the laws of reason.'[117] Meanwhile, Teofrastus has fallen into a steady rhythm of hammering home why divine punishment had struck the leadership of the Frankish realm with total blindness, so that they were unable to recognise good warnings and advice when they encountered it.[118]

A distinctive part of the grand and emotive oratory of the second book is formed by a series of formulaic pronouncements about 'what Arsenius believed in'. Although not entirely identical, these declarations of loyalty contain the same key objects of allegiance, such as God, the churches, the state and stability of the realm, the emperor and his sons, the fatherland and its 'citizens' (*cives*). There are no fewer than twelve such mantra-like assertions, in which Wala's staunch adherence to the core values of the Frankish political elite are affirmed and reaffirmed.[119] These are connected not only with Radbert's passionate defence of Arsenius, but also with the latter's role as 'another Jeremiah', and with speaking *constanter*. They tend to crop up at crucial turns of the narrative: for example, in 830, when a reluctant Wala allowed himself to get involved in an attempt to oust Bernard and Judith from the palace. A delegation of the great and powerful travelled to Corbie, weeping and lamenting, and declared 'resolutely' (*constanter*) that only Arsenius could assist them in this dire predicament, namely a court that was given over to sinful and sinister practices:

Having accepted this counsel, therefore, at the urging of many people, together with the most distinguished and eminent men he sent himself into great danger on behalf of the faith of Christ, the preservation of the empire, the peace of the churches, the love of king and realm, and the well-being of his sons, fired with love for God lest the deceit of the devil prevail, and so that the dignity of the fatherland would be maintained and prosperity would be preserved for its inhabitants. And for the sake of justice and fidelity he devotedly offered up his own security in the interest of everyone's freedom.[120]

[117] *EA* II, c. 7, p. 67.    [118] *EA* II, c. 7, p. 67.
[119] *EA* II, c. 5, p. 66 (2x); c. 8, pp. 69 and 70; c. 9, pp. 71 and 72; c. 10, pp. 73, 75, 76, 77; c. 10, p. 78; c. 14, p. 81 (2x). All these are voiced by Pascasius, except c. 10, p. 77; see De Jong, 'For God, King and Country', pp. 109–11.
[120] *EA* II, c. 8, p. 70: 'Ita siquidem multis exortantibus accepto consilio, una cum electissimis et clarissimis viris misit se pro fide Christi, pro statu imperii, pro pace ecclesiarum,

Such emphatic and repetitive assertions partly derive from a vocabulary of public authority also found in contemporary royal documents such as capitularies and privileges of immunity for monasteries,[121] yet they are also characteristic of those parts of the narrative where emotive and grand oratory is the main strategy of persuasion. With one exception,[122] it is the narrator, Pascasius, who pronounces these statements. He does so first of all in his guise as Wala's passionate advocate, but also as the author/orator who reminds his audience that he speaks about the gravest matters there can be, which deserve the grand and weighty style: the well-being of a realm and a ruler accountable to God.

Thus, the main difference between the two books of the *Epitaphium* is not that the first cites the classics and Terence, while the second is more biblically oriented. On the contrary, the density of biblical citations, including those from Jeremiah and Lamentations, is greater in the first book. Citing Terence serves two main purposes: it guarantees that the style of speech remains light, and that a lot is in a loud stage whisper: 'We are keeping as quiet as we possibly can!'. By contrast, the second book addresses affairs of the state, which, according to Cicero, are especially suited to being dealt with in grand speech, and with the full brilliance of forensic oratory. Here, Radbert resorts to various strategies of speaking both frankly and grandly, but he does so judiciously, in a way that will be recognised as appropriate by his readers. In portraying Arsenius as a latter-day Jeremiah, he adopts the prophetic speech that, according to Augustine, is eminently well-suited to speaking authoritatively and *granditer* on matters of the greatest importance. This also creates more room for Pascasius, the narrator, who now comes into his own as the advocate of his beloved abbot, and as a Jeremiah in his own right.

---

pro amore regis et regni, pro salute filiorum eius, zelo Dei succensus, ne fraus prevaleret adversarii, ut dignitas servaretur patriae, salus maneret civibus, in magnum discrimen; et salutem suam pro iustitia et fide devotus ob omnium libertatem obtulit. '
[121] De Jong, 'For God, King and Country', pp. 110–11.
[122] *EA* II, c. 10, p. 77 (Adeodatus).

# 6    What's in a Name?

## 1    Nicknames, Bynames, Pseudonyms and Aliases

Nicknames or bynames are a central feature of the *Epitaphium Arsenii*. In both books, the discussants are identified by their monastic names, as is the illustrious subject of their confabulation. As we have seen, it is difficult to pinpoint when and where Wala gained his byname Arsenius, except that it was connected with his tonsure in 814, as well as with his mentorship of Lothar from 821 onwards. Possibly the latter reinforced the former.[1] As for Wala's brother Adalhard, it was no less than Alcuin of York who bestowed the nickname 'Antony' on him, after the founder of monasticism and celebrated desert saint. Alcuin wrote letters to Adalhard in which he referred to himself as Paul, Antony's fellow hermit, to whom Jerome devoted a well-known *Life*.[2] Once named, someone might identify with his nickname, as Hraban seems to have done when, as an adolescent at Charlemagne's court, he was called 'Maurus' by Alcuin. This name derived both from the blackness of 'Hraban' (a raven, in Old High German), and from Benedict's favourite pupil, mentioned in the *Dialogues* of Gregory the Great.[3] For the rest of his life, Hraban referred to himself as Maurus, both in his correspondence and his verse. In some of his biblical commentary, he distinguishes his own interpretation from that of the Fathers by identifying it with the letter 'M' in the margin.[4]

The choice of bynames varied. Alcuin's letters, for example, display dazzling wordplay on the names of his friends and pupils, and a penchant for naming them after animals, but names could also be inspired by well-known figures from written tradition, be it biblical, profane or patristic.[5] This naming practice presupposes a community with a shared knowledge of a corpus of texts and their interpretation. Bynames invited comparisons

---

[1] See above, pp. 31–2.    [2] Garrison, 'Social World', pp. 73–6; Jerome, *Vita Pauli*.
[3] Gregory, *Dialogi* II, c. 3.4, p. 150 and II, 5.2, p. 156.
[4] De Jong, 'Empire as *ecclesia*', pp. 202–3; 'Becoming Jeremiah'.
[5] Garrison, '*Praesagum nomen tibi*'. On Alcuin and his correspondence with his pupils, see also Steckel, *Kulturen des Lehrens*, pp. 148–95.

with people and events from an authoritative past, and connected 'the profane everyday time with a realm of transcendent meaning', as Mary Garrison puts it in her perceptive analysis of Alcuin's naming strategies.[6] Bynames originated in specific social groups and circumstances, such as monastic communities or royal courts; they reinforced in-group sentiments and consolidated pre-existing relations of friendship. The banter between Pascasius (Radbertus) and Severus (Odilman) in the *Epitaphium*'s first book suggests a close relationship based on a shared youth in Corbie, even though Severus is clearly the older of the two.[7] Yet such names also functioned as a typology, for they helped to define the moral status of the person in question by revealing an underlying reality more significant than what could be observed on the surface. Along the lines of Isidore of Seville's linguistic realism, there was a connection between the byname and a person's nature.[8] Accordingly, the young Adeodatus implores Severus not to act with the severity that his name portends.[9]

Arsenius, Antony, Pascasius, Severus and Adeodatus: these are all names derived from an authoritative late antique Christian tradition that infused Radbert's work as well as his life. The extent to which the patristic past was also the present for him emerges from his treatise *Cogitis me*, written for the nuns of Nôtre-Dame of Soissons who had educated him as a child. Radbert wrote this meditation on the Assumption of the Virgin as 'Jerome', calling it a 'letter from the Blessed Jerome to Paula and Eustochium', addressing the nuns of Soissons with the names of Jerome's patroness and correspondent Paula and her daughter.[10] As in the case of the correspondence between 'Paul' and 'Antony', there was no confusion about the identity of the author and his recipients. It seems likely that Alcuin provided Radbert with at least some appropriate examples of name-giving, both in the practice he had stimulated, and through his writings. It is perhaps no coincidence that both used the expression *praesag(i)um*, foreboding or portent, for the way in which a name would shape a person's behaviour or life.[11] Radbert used Alcuin's theological writings in *Cogitis me*, and drew upon his rhetorical expertise.[12]

Whether Wala identified himself in any way with his byname is unknown, but it is clear that for his monks, he went by the name of

[6] Garrison, 'Social World', p. 60.     [7] See above, p. 88.
[8] Garrison, 'Social World', pp. 67–8.
[9] *EA* I, prologue, p. 20: 'Quęso ne iuxta tui presagium nominis severius agas ...'.
[10] Ripberger, *Der Pseudo-Hieronymus-Brief IX*, p. 57.
[11] Alcuin, *Epistolae*, no. 113, p. 163: 'Praesagum tibi inposuere parentes ... '; *EA* I, prologue, p. 20.
[12] On Alcuin's work in Corbie, see Ganz, *Corbie*, pp. 43–5.

Arsenius during his lifetime. When in 831 Radbert dedicated the first version of his treatise on the Eucharist (*De corpore*) to Warin, then *magister* in Corvey, he referred to 'our Arsenius, whom these times of ours have turned into another Jeremiah'.[13] Wala might be compared to Jeremiah, or to Benedict of Nursia for that matter, but in this letter, Radbert addressed Warin by his monastic nickname of Placidius, Benedict's other pupil named in the *Dialogues*, while he identified himself, as he did in all his dedicatory letters, as Pascasius Radbertus.[14] The network of relationships within which such names had a meaning included the king and the court. When he re-dedicated *De corpore* to Charles the Bald, shortly after he had become abbot of Corbie in late 843 or early 844, Radbert called himself 'your humble and tiny Paschasius Radbertus, although abbot and deacon of Christ, the scum of all monks'.[15] In two verse dedications to Warin, the first letter of each line together formed the acrostic '*Radbertus levita*'.[16] Yet there were other instances in which he presented himself in a more functional manner; in the verse dedication to Charles, also of *De corpore*, he called himself *Radbertus abbas*, and this is how Lupus of Ferrières addressed him in the few letters sent towards the end of Radbert's abbacy. As I explained earlier, Lupus acted as a mediator for his 'dearest Abbot Radbert' at the court of Charles the Bald.[17] The more functional *Radbertus abbas* was used in the *privilegium* for Corbie granted at the synod of Paris in 846/7, which was probably drafted by Radbert himself.[18] As is to be expected, in a legal context nicknames were avoided, however significant they may have been in an epistolary setting. Neither Wala nor Adalhard was ever called 'Arsenius' or 'Antony' in charters, and the same holds true for mentions of these men in contemporary historiography or confraternity books.[19] Nicknames suggested the interconnectedness of those who used them, or at least a claim to such a relationship which could then be reciprocated or not. The latter may have been the case when Radbert dedicated *De corpore* to King Charles with his usual

---

[13] Paschasius Radbertus, *De corpore*, prologue, p. 3: ' ... quod Arsenius noster quem nostra nunc nobis saecula Hieremiam alterum tulerunt ... '.

[14] Paschasius Radbertus, *De corpore*, p. 3: 'Pascasius Radbertus Placidio suo salutem, dilectissimo filio et uice Christi praesidente, magistro monasticae disciplinae alternis successibus ueritatis condiscipulo.' On Placidius (or, rather, Placidus) as Benedict's pupil, see Gregory, *Dialogi* II, c. 5.2, p. 154 and n. 3 above.

[15] Paschasius Radbertus, *Epistolae*, no. 4, p. 135: ' ... humilis et exiguus Paschasius Radbertus, vester etsi indignus abbas ac levita Christi, monachorum omnium peripsema ... '.

[16] Paschasius Radbertus, *Carmina*, no. 2 and 3, pp. 51–2.

[17] Lupus, *Epistolae* no. 51 and 52, pp. 208–12; see above, pp. 65–8.

[18] See above, p. 57.

[19] See *MGH DD LdF* no. 226 (27 July 823 for Corvey), p. 561: 'Adalhardus abbas ... secum germane suo Uualone ... '.

self-designation as the 'Paschasius Radbertus, the greatest scum (*peripsima*) of all monks'.[20] On the other hand, this was how he presented himself in all his dedicatory epistles, be they to his friends or to his monarch. As a prolific author, he presented himself as Pascasius Radbertus, and he was known as such in the semi-public domain in which biblical commentary circulated, including the royal court. In other words, when he used Pascasius as his alter ego in the *Epitaphium*, it was not in order to hide his identity in high places.

The bynames discussed hitherto are potentially interactive, and therefore differ from the names given to the main protagonists of the second book and its narrative about the rebellions against Louis the Pious. These are best characterised as aliases: Justina (Judith), Justinian (Louis), Honorius (Lothar), Melanius (Pippin of Aquitaine), Gratian (Louis the German), Naso (Bernard of Septimania) and Phasur (Archbishop Ebo of Rheims). The older view used to be that Radbert used pseudonyms, not just for the political protagonists but also for himself and his fellow discussants, in order to hide the actual identities of those involved, and to shield himself from royal wrath.[21] This notion can be safely discarded, not least because, as we have just seen, there was nothing secret about the monastic names of Pascasius/Radbertus and Severus/Odilman. Furthermore, if modern historians are able to figure out who is who in the *Epitaphium*'s second book, so could Radbert's contemporaries. Up to a point, the 'political' aliases resemble the nicknames of monastic and court culture, such as Arsenius, Antony or Pascasius, in that they expressed moral qualities, and derived their meaning from a shared Latin literary tradition. Yet there is one obvious difference. Whereas the nicknames were used in epistolary and other communication, also by third parties, there is no sign that the aliases of the *Epitaphium*'s second book were ever used in any other text or context. Here, they were deployed not just to name, identify and characterise, but also, in some cases, to shame those involved. A naming practice that was usually aimed at strengthening bonds of friendship and solidarity within different groups of the Carolingian elite was now turned into a strategy for revealing moral depravity. To this end, Radbert adopted an exegetically inspired typology with which his intended audience was familiar.[22]

Although not intended for secrecy, the aliases may have provided some measure of discretion, avoiding the harsh and direct confrontation inherent in using proper names. More importantly, both the use of monastic

---

[20] See above, n. 15.
[21] A view established by Jean Mabillon and adopted by Ernst Dümmler in his introduction to his edition of the *Epitaphium*, p. 5.
[22] On these names as 'typological roles', see Booker, *Past Convictions*, pp. 45–8.

bynames for the discussants and the aliases for the political protagonists restricted the accessibility of the *Epitaphium* to a group of knowledgeable insiders. As I argued above, this was an exclusive readership, but it was not necessarily restricted to the monks of Corbie. By the mid-850s, in the realm of Charles the Bald, there surely were others, clerics and educated laymen, to whom the Christian and classical tradition resonated with meaning, and who could therefore grasp the significance of the aliases in the context of Radbert's narrative of the rebellions, and of his polemic against Wala's enemies. To those who had the appropriate frame of reference, bynames and aliases revealed the qualities of those designated. The name foretold the character of the bearer, and therefore helped to communicate the meaning of the narrative to the reader.

Although the majority of Radbert's aliases are in some way related to late antique imperial Christianity, they are deployed in a variety of ways. As we shall see, no close historical parallels or consistency should be expected: this was a loosely constructed 'world of Ambrose', which was nonetheless very much alive to the author and his intended readership. Radbert was nothing if not eclectic, and also chose some aliases from biblical and classical tradition (Phasur, Naso, Melanius). Insofar as he had an overall naming strategy, it depended on the pair Arsenius–Honorius, which is where I shall start this exploration.

## 2    Who is Who in the *Epitaphium Arsenii*?

### Honorius

Louis's eldest son and co-emperor Lothar was born in 795 and married in 821, so he was already a senior ruler with his own household when Wala/Arsenius, a generation older, became his chief adviser, deputy and right-hand man in the kingdom of Italy. According to the *Epitaphium*'s first book, Arsenius was 'tutor to the august Caesar beyond the Pennine Alps' and the 'regent of the kingdom and the emperor's teacher'.[23] As we have seen, Wala may have gained his byname as early as 814, when he left his prominent position at the palace and retreated to Corbie, but even if this is the case, his subsequent relationship with Lothar added specific connotations to his byname. When, in the 830s, the monks of Corbie referred to their abbot as 'our Arsenius', they associated him with the 'first' or 'earlier Arsenius' (*prior Arsenius*) who had reputedly tutored Theodosius'

---

[23] *EA* I, c. 25, p. 55: '... cum pedagogus esset augusti caesaris ultra Penninas Alpes ...'; *EA* I, c. 28, p. 58: '... procurator regni et magister imperatoris'.

two sons, Arcadius and Honorius.[24] The *Epitaphium*'s first book highlights the bond between the wise *magister* and his appreciative imperial pupil, yet it is only in the second book that Lothar is consistently referred to as Honorius, as part of a strategy of naming that hinges upon Wala's byname 'Arsenius'.

The historical Honorius (r. 393–423) was Theodosius' younger son, who was made co-emperor in 393. Two years later, after their father's death, he and his elder brother Arcadius divided the empire between them, leaving Honorius in charge of the Western part. Did it matter to Radbert's choice of this alias that during Honorius' reign the Western capital was moved to Ravenna (401) and that Rome was plundered in 410? It seems unlikely. Although Radbert was not uncritical of Lothar/Honorius, this is one of the aliases with generally positive connotations. It derives from Wala's byname and his close connection with Louis's eldest son, and from the fact that Lothar had been his father's legitimate co-emperor since 817, a point hammered home throughout the *Epitaphium*'s second book.[25] One of Radbert's key sources for the age of Ambrose was the *Historia ecclesiastica tripartita*, a translation and editorial selection from three fifth-century Greek histories by Socrates, Sozomen and Theodoret, made by Epiphanius and commissioned by Cassiodorus.[26] Honorius does not exactly play a prominent role in this text, but he is emphatically presented as Theodosius' co-emperor in the West,[27] and also as the one who, once he succeeded his father, put a stop to the spectacle of gladiators in Rome.[28] All this pales into insignificance, however, compared to the overwhelming presence of Theodosius I (r. 379–95) in this historical work. The Latin version retains the Greek historian Sozomen's dedication of his work to Theodosius II (r. 408–50). He was the grandson of the first Theodosius, and the nephew of the 'most righteous' Emperor Honorius I (*piissimus patruus tuus*). Still, it was his 'most delightful grandfather' (*iucundissimus avus tuus*) Theodosius who was the undisputed hero of the *Historia tripartita*.[29] This turns the absence of the name Theodosius in the *Epitaphium*'s second book into a resounding and meaningful silence.

---

[24] *EA* I, prologue, p. 20.    [25] *EA* II, c. 10, p. 74; c. 11, p. 77; c. 18, p. 89.

[26] St Petersburg, Lat. F v I 11; Jacob & Hanslik, *Die handschriftliche Überlieferung*, pp. 10–11. On the *Historia tripartita* in Corbie, see Ganz, *Corbie*, p. 143; Zechiel-Eckes, 'Ein Blick in Pseudo-Isidors Werkstatt'; on the ninth-century history of the work, see McKitterick, *History and Memory*, pp. 233–4; Scholten, 'Cassiodorus' *Historia tripartita*'.

[27] *Historia tripartita* IX, c. 45, p. 573.    [28] *Historia tripartita* X, c. 2, p. 582.

[29] *Historia tripartita* I, c. 1, p. 9.

*Justina – Gratian – Justinian*

The Empress Judith, Louis's second wife and Wala's nemesis, was called
'Justina', an alias that also invites an immediate comparison between
Wala and Ambrose. This alias, it should be noted, is introduced by
Radbert before any of the others, in a passage that underlines Louis's
total dependence on the empress in the months prior to the first rebellion.
There is no doubt as to why he chose this name for Judith, whom he
blamed for Wala's banishment from Louis's court. The Justina he had in
mind was the second wife of Emperor Valentinian I (364–75) who in 385/
6 had unleashed a relentless campaign against Bishop Ambrose of
Milan.[30] Justina's evil reputation originates with Ambrose himself, in
a letter that cites Elijah and John the Baptist as the victims of evil and
wilful women who dominated their husbands.[31] Subsequently, Justina
was vilified by Augustine in his *Confessions,* by Paulinus in his fifth-
century *Life of Ambrose* and, last but not least, by Rufinus in his continuation to Eusebius' *Historia ecclesiastica.*[32] While the Arian Justina assailed
the bishop of Milan with all her might, 'armed with the spirit of Jezebel,
Ambrose stood firm, filled with the power and grace of Elijah'.[33] It is likely
that Radbert had all of these texts at his disposal, but this was certainly the
case with the *Historia tripartita.* Here, Justina also figures as Ambrose's
persecutor, just as Judith had been Wala's implacable enemy. To begin
with, aspersion is cast on her marriage, for Valentinian issued a law
allowing him to have two wives, so that he could retain his first spouse
Severa while marrying Justina.[34] Then she is depicted as an Arian who did
not dare to harm her orthodox opponents while Valentinian I was still
alive but, when he died. came to Milan with her young son Valentinian,
made emperor at age four, to take up residence and pester Ambrose. She
ordered him exiled, but Ambrose flatly refused to go, daring the empress
to kill him first. Standing firmly behind their bishop, the people of Milan
refused to collaborate with Justina's evil designs.[35]

This alias also suited Judith because of Justina's dominance over her
young son Valentinian II. His weakness and subservience are stressed in
the *Historia tripartita,* but even more so by Rufinus: Valentinian, driven to

[30] On the historical context, see McLynn, *Ambrose,* pp. 170–1; Liebeschuetz, *Ambrose of Milan,* pp. 124–36.
[31] Ambrose, *Epistolae,* 76 [20].12, 18; transl. Liebeschuetz, *Ambrose of Milan,* pp. 160–73.
[32] Augustine, *Confessiones* IX, c. 7.15; Paulinus, *Vita Ambrosii* 13.1; Rufinus, *Historia ecclesiastica* XI, c. 15, pp. 1020–1. On Rufinus' own input into his translation of Eusebius, and his continuation, see Humphries, 'Rufinus's Eusebius', with references to previous literature.
[33] Rufinus, *Historia ecclesiastica* XI, c. 15, transl. Amidon, p. 75.
[34] *Historia tripartita* VIII, c. 11, p. 483–4.
[35] *Historia tripartita* IX, cc. 20–1, pp. 527–30.

fury by his mother's lies, dispatches armed men to drag Ambrose from his sanctuary and send him into exile. But soon the tables are turned, and Justina and her son have to take flight, and suffer the exile she had planned for the bishop and his supporters.[36] It was the saviour Theodosius the Great who, in both ecclesiastical histories, managed to contain Justina and restore the hapless Valentinian II to his realm: another reason not to ascribe this alias to Louis the Pious. 'Valentinian the Younger' might have been appropriate for Charles the Bald, but as we shall see, this monarch remained unnamed in all possible respects.

With Louis the German's alias, 'Gratianus', Radbert remained within an eclectic and associative framework of late antique imperial Christianity. The Emperor Gratian (r. 367–83), the eldest son of Valentinian I, was Justina's stepson, and had won military victories east of the Rhine. This name seems to have been chosen in relation to Justina, but was there more to it? Ambrose's work turned Gratian, murdered in 383 by the rebel Maximus, into the exemplary emperor who upheld Nicene Christianity, and supported the removal of the Victory Altar from the Senate in Rome.[37] It is difficult to make out how much of this guided Radbert's choice of this particular name, for the role of Louis's third son in the *Epitaphium* is positive, but minimal. Kept against his will by his father at a sinful court dominated by Justina and Naso, Gratian/ Louis reported what went on there to the outside world and decided, together with his brother Melanius/Pippin, that this could no longer be tolerated.[38] The two brothers supported the first rebellion, and once it had failed, Justina was adamant that they be kept apart from Arsenius, for she feared lest either of these kings should seek him out as an advisor, which would mean the exile's return to the political arena.[39] Yet, however minor his role in Radbert's narrative, the choice of alias is interesting, for it confirms that the genealogy of the late Roman emperors did not concern our author when he chose his aliases. Choosing 'Gratian' for Louis the German underlined his position as Justina's stepson, as well as his kingdom east of the Rhine.

This leaves the alias that is the least transparent of all, even though it is clear that it designates Louis the Pious himself: 'Justinianus'. I once took this to be a conflation of Emperor Justinian the Great (r. 527–65) with his unsuccessful namesake Justinian II (r. 681–711), on the assumption that the use of this byname for Louis was entirely negative.[40] I now think differently, and rather doubt whether the second Justinian played much

---

[36] Rufinus, *Historia ecclesiastica* X,I c. 15–16, transl. Amidon, pp. 75–6.
[37] McLynn, *Ambrose*, pp. 151–6.    [38] *EA* II, c. 9, p. 72.    [39] *EA* II, c. 14, p. 80.
[40] De Jong, *Penitential State*, p. 109; Booker, *Past Convictions*, p. 47.

of a role at all. In Paul the Deacon's *Historia Langobardorum*, he is portrayed as a violent ruler, maiming and killing his enemies, and asking the pope to intercede for his sins, but then disobeying him.[41] Whether Radbert knew this text is a moot point, but he must have been familiar with the *Liber Pontificalis*. Here, one encounters Justinian II in a doctrinal conflict with Pope Sergius I,[42] but also as the 'Christian August, crown on head', who prostrated himself and kissed the feet of Pope Constantine I before the latter performed Mass; the emperor then took communion and asked forgiveness for his sins, renewing all the church's privileges.[43] In the *Liber Pontificalis*, Justinian II was a Christian and orthodox emperor, and the news of his assassination was reason for mourning in Rome.[44]

This makes Justinian II an unlikely source of inspiration for a derogatory alias, but there are other reasons why it is doubtful whether he would have represented Louis the Pious as depicted in the *Epitaphium*. Although flawed and dangerously misled, Radbert's Louis is not an intrinsically depraved emperor. As the narrator Pascasius has one bishop exclaim in the heat of the first rebellion, if only this ruler could have rid himself of the deception in which others had enveloped him, he would have recovered himself and been the peerless emperor (*optimus imperator*) again that he had always been until then.[45] Despite his obstinacy and hardness of heart, and his sinful departure from God's law of love, this emperor remains a victim, bewitched and deceived by the wiles of a woman.[46] In modern historiography, Radbert is on record as one of Louis's fiercest opponents, and yet there were definite limits to his criticism of the emperor. Together with countless and nameless evil counsellors, Bernard and Judith bore most of the brunt of his polemical onslaught. As I shall demonstrate in the next chapter, Radbert was critical of Lothar's sudden takeover in the autumn of 833, and he was definitely uneasy about the public penance imposed on Louis.[47] Throughout the polemical second book, he refers to Louis time and again as *Augustus* or, less frequently, as Caesar, or '*piissimus Caesar*'.[48] All this makes it more likely that his alias was inspired by the first Justinian,

---

[41] Paul the Deacon, *Historia Langobardorum* VI, c. 31, ed. Bethmann and Waitz, p. 15.
[42] *Liber Pontificalis* 86.6, pp. 372–3 (Life of Sergius); transl. Davis, *Book of Pontiffs, Ancient Biograpies*, p. 86.
[43] *Liber Pontificalis* 90.6, p. 391 (Life of Constantine); transl. Davis, *Book of Pontiffs, Ancient Biograpies*, p. 93.
[44] *Liber Pontificalis* 90.8, p. 391 (Life of Constantine); transl. Davis, *Book of Pontiffs, Ancient Biographies*, p. 94.
[45] *EA* II, c. 9, pp. 72–3.     [46] *EA* II, c. 17, p. 88.     [47] See below, pp. 173–6.
[48] In the second book alone, Louis is called Augustus forty-nine times, Caesar ten times; for 'piissimus Caesar', see *EA* II, c. 9, p. 73.

the Christian emperor who was the successor of the great Constantine and Theodosius.[49]

If Radbert knew Paul the Deacon's *History of the Lombards*, he will have encountered Justinian as a victorious general, a celebrated lawgiver and admirable builder of the Hagia Sophia. In the fallout of the Three Chapters controversy, Justinian is portrayed as a ruler who interfered heavily with dogmatic issues and imposed his imperial decrees on matters that should have been decided on by churchmen.[50] Still, it is not clear how much of this determined his ninth-century image in the West, and the same holds true of Justinian as an emperor who high-handedly took charge of monasticism; this theme has been explored recently and thoroughly, but on the basis of Greek source material.[51] Did Radbert associate the name 'Justinian' with an imperial oppressor of monasteries, and did he assign it to Louis with this in mind? I have not been able to find any evidence for this in Latin sources. On the contrary, Justinian may have gained a reputation for orthodoxy through his *Edictum pro recta fide* of 551, also a result of the Three Chapters controversy. It circulated in Radbert's lifetime, together with other texts that counted as orthodox because they adhered to the Chalcedonian definition of Christ. This potentially debatable imperial edict thus gained the rare distinction of being disseminated in the West together with impeccably canonical texts.[52]

Meanwhile, it would be a mistake to put this particular alias on a par with more frequently used ones, such as Honorius or Justina. Louis is called Justinian only twice, in the context of a crucial episode: namely, the emperor's reneging on the solemn promises he made during the assembly of Compiègne in May 830. Having declared his eternal gratitude to those who saved him from Naso's clutches, Louis promised to restore the old order, with Lothar back in place as co-emperor. Soon it was not Lothar but Judith, however, who returned to her rightful place at the palace.[53] It is at this point that Louis is called Justinian, first as the one who in 817 had solemnly made Lothar co-emperor, but who had then ousted him from this rightful position, and then as the emperor who had been untruthful during the assembly of May 830. What he promised 'did not come from the heart and mind of Justinian', as Radbert expressed it. Goaded by his wife and taking the loyal rebellion as an attempt to

---

[49] Odilbert, *Ad Karolum magnum responsum*, MGH Capit. I, 126, p. 247.
[50] On this Christological controversy, see Sotinel, 'Emperors and Popes in the Sixth Century'; Chazelle & Cubitt (eds.), *The Crisis of Oikoumene*.
[51] Hasse-Ungeheuer, *Mönchtum*.
[52] Schieffer, 'Zur Überlieferung', p. 301; see also Gray, 'Legacy', pp. 234–5.
[53] On the contestation of this in various sources, see De Jong, 'Exegesis for an Empress'.

dishonour rather than to save him, he changed his mind and decided to punish the loyal rebels and his eldest son. 'In the meantime, he concealed the wound that was deep in his heart', which would eventually lead to the breaking up of a united imperial rule.[54]

The emperor's broken promises after the assembly at Compiègne in 830 constitute a turning point in the narrative of the rebellions. This was what Radbert blamed Louis for above all else, and the instigator of it all was Justina: invariably, Louis yielded to 'his wife's promptings'. One reason to choose the alias Justinian, and to use it at precisely this point in the *Epitaphium*'s second book, is to emphasise Louis's utter dependence on Judith. He was Justinian because he was 'of Justina', who had been introduced not long before:

> He did not accept anyone else in good faith except for whom Justina chose, and could not listen to or love or agree with, insofar as such feelings still had any strength, any except those whom she commended to him for fidelity, and, what is even more ominous, as they say, he could not want anything except for what she wanted.[55]

The message is that Judith/Justina controlled Louis's ability to attract faithful followers, and therefore his independence and effectiveness as a ruler. In view of this, I wonder whether Radbert's image of the Emperor Justinian I was also informed by the allegedly dominant Theodora. If so, this would make this alias even more appropriate. There is one text that could have provided him with much information on this topic, namely the mid-ninth-century Corbie copy of the *Collectio Sangermanensis*, which included the *Breviarium* of Liberatus of Carthage, another sixth-century author who covered the Christological controversies, including Justinian's part in them.[56] Liberatus' portrait of emperors in general, and that of Justinian in particular, was also favourable when it came to their direct interference in doctrinal strife, which was deemed entirely legitimate. If emperors made mistakes in this respect, Liberatus blames their advisors.[57] There is no way in which this author could have contributed to an image of Louis's unwarranted meddling in internal dogmatic affairs, but Liberatus does offer potential grist to the mill of those opposing queenly power. The *Breviarium* is scathing about the way in which Theodora, another second wife, manipulated Justinian and intrigued behind his back in the volatile ecclesiastical politics of the time. This

---

[54] *EA* II, c. 10, p. 74.

[55] *EA* II, c. 9, p. 72 (Pascasius): 'Non enim alium in fide recipiebat, nisi quem Justina vellet: neque alium aut audire, aut diligere valebat, aut assentire, quousque ista viguerunt, nisi quem illa ei in fide commendabat: et, quod prodigiosius est, ut aiunt, nec aliud velle, praeter quae ipsa vellet.'

[56] Patzold, 'Spurensuche', pp. 227–32.    [57] Leppin, 'Das Bild der Kaiser', pp. 161–2.

was precisely what Judith's enemies castigated her for: her close ties with bishops.[58] Her friendship with Ebo of Rheims was only one case in point; there were others awaiting Pope Gregory at the Rotfeld in 833: treacherous bishops who should have been loyal to their pontiff, but instead were in Justina's camp.[59] Like the Justinian of the *Breviarium*, Louis was a well-intentioned Christian emperor who erred primarily because of the wiles of his youthful and enterprising empress. Theodora and Judith were second wives who possessed the dangerous sexual allure of youth, and deployed this in politics, bishops not excluded.

If all this makes sense, then why not use Theodora as a name in the first place? The answer must be that Justina as Ambrose's tormenter was one of the key aliases; together with the connection Honorius–Arsenius, this determined other names. Louis becomes Justinian only once Judith's alias is already in place, and the emperor's utter dependency on his second wife has been sufficiently established. More importantly, Justinian and Honorius enter upon the scene together, in the same passage about Lothar coming from Italy to join the rebels in May 830. In the context of the arrival of the 'August Emperor Honorius', Radbert reminds his readers that 'previously Justinian had, with universal will and consent, made him a joint partner with himself in the imperial rule and the successor to the entire kingdom'.[60] To name Louis 'Justinian' meant emphatically *not* adorning him with the honorific alias of 'Theodosius'. This would have been an obvious choice, firstly because Theodosius the Great was Honorius' father, who made the latter his co-emperor before his death, and secondly because Louis's public penances in 822 and 833 evoked the celebrated atonement of Theodosius at Ambrose's behest. Radbert pointedly avoided this, however, for reasons that are not difficult to understand. While the Astronomer emphatically compares Louis's public atonement in Attigny in 822 to Theodosius' penance of 391, Radbert in his *Vita Adalhardi* mocks the insincerity of this gesture: those who had eyes could observe the emperor's unwillingness.[61] This very insincerity was the issue once more with the promises made at the assembly of Compiègne – the point at which Radbert names Louis 'Justinian'. This was an imperial yet more ambivalent alias, which called to mind both

---

[58] Agobard of Lyon, *Liber Apologeticus* I, c. 5, p. 311. De Jong, 'Exegesis for an Empress' and 'Bride Shows'; on the accusations against Judith, see now also Dohmen, *Ursache*, pp. 115–80.

[59] *EA* II, c. 16, p. 84.

[60] *EA* II, c. 10, p. 74 (Pascasius): 'Caesar Augustus Honorius ab Italis evocatus venisset, eoquod consortem imperii Justinianus sibi olim et successorem totius monarchiae cum voluntate et consensu omnium eum fecerat ... '.

[61] Astronomer, c. 35, p. 482; *VA*, c. 51, cols. 1534D–1535A; De Jong, *Penitential State*, pp. 122–31.

the emperor's subservience to Justina, and the absence of a true
Theodosius. Through the alias of Justina, and the withholding of the
honorific name 'Theodosius' from Louis, Ambrose remains an unspoken
yet constant presence in the second book. Wala's *and* Radbert's fearless-
ness in speaking truth to power is highlighted by the figure of Jeremiah,
but also by the implicit evocation of Ambrose of Milan, who stood firm
against his sinful emperor.

### *Phasur – Melanius – Naso*

With 'Phasur' as the alias for Ebo of Rheims, Radbert turned to the Old
Testament, and to his presentation of Wala as a latter-day Jeremiah.
Remarkably, this is Radbert's only biblical alias. Phassur, as he is called
in Latin Scripture, was Jeremiah's jailer, who would himself be carried off
to Babylon and die as an exile.[62] As archbishop of Rheims, Ebo had been
the ecclesiastical authority responsible for Wala's banishment from the
court in 831, only to end up as an exile himself from the see of Rheims, in
the aftermath of the second rebellion.[63] In the *Epitaphium*, Phasur is one
of Justina's leading allies, present when Pope Gregory IV goes to meet the
emperor in the Alsace in June 833. The pope is cold-shouldered by Louis,
at the empress's behest.[64] Indeed, Ebo remained loyal to the imperial
couple until the very last, when, on the Field of Lies, Louis's troops had
defected massively to Lothar and his two rebellious brothers.[65] By the
850s, when the second book was written, this alias had gained some
additional layers of meaning. Not only had Ebo become the scapegoat
of the rebellion of 833, but all his subsequent attempts to return to the see
of Rheims had proven unsuccessful. Having ended up as bishop of
Hildesheim by 847, Ebo died in 851, an exile as the biblical Phassur
had once been.[66] With hindsight, Radbert was no doubt implying that
banishment was Ebo's just deserts for his maltreatment of
Wala/Jeremiah.[67]

Whereas historians have been slow to identify Radbert's Phasur as
Ebo,[68] there has been no doubt that, by 'Melanius', which means

---

[62] Jer. 20:2: ' . . . et percussit Phassur Hieremiam prophetam et misit eum in nervum quod
erat in porta Beniamin superiori in domo Domini.'
[63] For a recent overview of Ebo's career, see Booker, 'Ebbo's *fama ambigua*'.
[64] *EA II*, c. 16, p. 84.    [65] De Jong, *Penitential State*, pp. 109–10.
[66] Goetting, *Das Bistum Hildesheim*, pp. 71–9; Patzold, *Episcopus*, pp. 322–5.
[67] Booker, 'Ebbo's *fama ambigua*', pp. 238–9.
[68] I thought I was the first to have spotted this (De Jong, *Penitential State*, pp. 109–10), but
as Booker has pointed out, Heinrich Gottlob Erhard Paulus had already reached this
conclusion in 1833. His suggestion was forgotten amidst much other speculation; see
Booker, 'Ebbo's *fama ambigua*', pp. 238–9, with the various identifications of Phassur
listed in n. 114.

'black' or 'swarthy' in Greek, Pippin of Aquitaine was designated. In this case, however, the problem is finding out whether Radbert had a specific Melanius in mind for Louis's second son, and if so, which one. Admittedly, I get no further than highly tentative suggestions. I once entertained the notion that, through his Breton connection, Pippin was associated with the saintly sixth-century bishop Melanius of Rennes,[69] but to name a king after this bishop seems far-fetched. Could it be that Melanius was a misspelling of Menelaus, the younger brother of Agamemnon, who dashed off to Troy to rescue Helen from Paris's embraces? If this is the case, the connection with Pippin of Aquitaine, the younger brother who took the lead in cleansing the palace in 830, seems less tenuous than the one with a sixth-century Breton bishop. As Kıvılcım Yavuz has shown, Trojan narratives were a formidable presence in Carolingian libraries, be it through Servius' commentary on the *Aeneid* or through the *Trojan History* of Dares of Phrygia, or the *Historia de origine Francorum* ascribed to the same author.[70] Servius was known in Corbie, and to this we can add Ovid's *Epistulae Heroidum*.[71] These feature Menelaus, the king of Sparta and husband to Helen of Troy, whom we have already encountered at the beginning of the *Epitaphium*, where Radbert compares himself to the painter Zeuxis, attempting to capture Helen's beauty.[72] Menelaus sought his revenge on Paris, Priam and Troy: a theme that, at a pinch, might just fit Pippin of Aquitaine/Melanius, who did not experience the immoral court dominated by Judith and Bernard. Corbie's library had a manuscript, dated by Bernard Bischoff to the middle or third quarter of the ninth century (BnF lat. 8242) that contained both the *Epistulae Heroidum* and the *Amores*.[73] This is as far as I have got so far; hopefully others will do better.

'Naso', for the despicable Bernard, was inspired by our author's knowledge of the abundant Latin pagan literature present in Corbie's library, and his awareness of the personal history of the poet Publius Ovidius Naso.[74] 'Alas for that wretched day, which was followed by a worse night, though none is more unhappy than the day on which the accursed Naso was recalled from Spain . . .'.[75] This is how Radbert introduces Bernard,

---

[69] De Jong, *Penitential State*, p. 109.
[70] See Yavuz, 'Late Antique Accounts of the Trojan War'.
[71] Ganz, *Corbie*, p. 61 (Servius was the most intensively copied classical author in Corbie).
[72] Menelaus figures in Ovid, *Heroides* 5, 8 and 16; for the painter Zeuxis, see *EA* I, prologue, pp. 18–19; see above, pp. 75–6.
[73] McKie, 'Ovid's *Amores*'; Ganz, *Corbie*, p. 152; Bischoff, *Katalog* III, no. 4536, p. 141.
[74] Ganz, *Corbie*, pp. 81–102 and *passim*.
[75] *EA* II, c. 6, p. 67. On Ovid's exile: Gaertner, *Writing Exile*; Thibault, *The Mystery of Ovid's Exile*.

Wala's arch-enemy, whom he named after Ovid. At Charlemagne's court, 'Naso' had been an affectionate and honorific nickname for the poet Modoin, the friend of Theodulf and, since 815, bishop of Autun.[76] For reasons still hotly debated, Ovid was exiled to the Black Sea by Augustus. Ninth-century poets such as Ermoldus Nigellus and Walahfrid Strabo admired Ovid's poetry, and Corbie's library possessed his letters from exile in Pontus as well as the love poetry he wrote there.[77] However, it is not with admiration that Radbert bestowed the alias 'Naso' on Bernard. There was a tradition that associated the poet's banishment with immorality and, more specifically, with adultery, which explains Radbert's choice. Less than half a year after Louis made Bernard his chamberlain, rumours that he enjoyed sexual relations with the Empress Judith ran rife, and because Bernard was the emperor's godson, this amounted to nothing less than incest.[78] Effectively banished from Louis's court in 831, and switching sides with great regularity, in 832 he joined forces with the still rebellious Pippin of Aquitaine (d. 838).[79] Influence in Aquitaine was the card he also played in 842, when he supported the attempt of the young Pippin II to reclaim his inheritance from Charles the Bald. Bernard was executed in February 844 on Charles' orders.[80]

### Just Themselves: Ermengard and Charles the Bald

Finally, two royal protagonists should be noted who did not receive an alias, but whose presence in the second book may offer some clues about Radbert's political allegiances at the time of writing. First, there is *Ermingardis regina,* the wife of Emperor Lothar, who not only relayed (*referente*) the news of Arsenius' death at Bobbio to Corbie, but also organised the commemoration thereof in the monasteries of the kingdom of Italy. Furthermore, she passed on a reliable written report in order to publicise further a miracle connected with the abbot's demise that had been witnessed by two nuns in her royal monastery, San Salvatore–Santa Giulia in Brescia.[81] Radbert's use of the empress's own name signals that

---

[76] Having replaced Agobard as archbishop of Lyon in 835, Modoin was accused by Florus of neglecting the clergy of Lyon; see Zechiel-Eckes, 'Florus' Polemik gegen Modoin'. It is likely that Radbert sided with Florus on this, so Modoin/Naso may have gained some negative connotations over time.

[77] BnF lat. 8242; Ganz, *Corbie*, p. 152, with references to the relevant literature. For some helpful bibliography on Ovid's exile, see also Breternitz, 'Ludwig der Fromme', pp. 188–9, n. 6.

[78] De Jong, *Penitential State*, p. 195; Thegan, c. 36, p. 222.

[79] Astronomer, c. 47, pp. 468–70; Nelson, *Charles the Bald*, pp. 89–91.

[80] *Annals of St Bertin*, s.a. 844; Nelson, *Charles the Bald*, pp. 139–40.

[81] *EA* II, c. 24, p. 97.

his narrative has now moved on beyond the two rebellions against Louis. Only in the part of the *Epitaphium* dealing with these rebellions, shaped by judicial rhetoric, are the aliases for the political protagonists used. They are part of a polemical defence against Wala's accusers – and, I suspect, also against Radbert's own enemies. Ermengard surfaces in a very different context: namely, that of Wala's death and commemoration, at the point where the confabulating monks return to the theme of grief and self-consolation with which the *Epitaphium* started off. This empress had clearly been an eminent and influential friend of Corbie, which is unsurprising given Adalhard's and Wala's close ties with Lothar I. Was Lothar I (d. 855) still alive when Radbert completed his *Epitaphium*, or had his son Lothar II already succeeded him in the northern part of his realm? Whatever the case, this elaborate mention of Ermengard's friendship for Wala and his bereaved community shows that the old ties between Arsenius and Honorius were still worth recalling.

The most intriguing monarch mentioned without an alias, however, is Charles the Bald, who remains nameless throughout the entire *Epitaphium*. Occasionally he is referred to as 'the king', generally with negative implications. This is just one of the more moderate examples: 'Although the king made a good start with these matters [reform], in the end they [the monasteries] have been pervaded by spreading worldly evils'.[82] The reasons for the *Epitaphium*'s vilification of Judith, Charles the Bald's mother, should also be considered as they relate to the 850s. The empress had certainly been Wala's political opponent, and blaming a Jezebel-like woman rather than the emperor himself was par for the course,[83] but does this explain why, two decades later, Bernard and the empress were still being held responsible for all the evils that had befallen the realm? Hardly. This raises questions about the contemporary context of the 850s, in which Radbert turned Judith into a vicious Justina. This was quite an exceptional thing to do in a kingdom in which, at Attigny in 854, Charles the Bald's faithful men swore an oath of fidelity (*sacramentum fidelitatis*) to 'Charles, son of Louis and Judith',[84] and in which Charles's ruler portrait in the Codex Aureus of St Emmeram (Munich, Bayerische Staatsbibliothek Clm 14000, fol. XXX), usually dated c. 870, was adorned with a poem of 869 by John Scottus Eriugena, who celebrates Judith, 'of illustrious descent' (*de claro sanguine*), having given birth to Charles.[85] In this world, in which Judith was remembered with veneration, Radbert penned his second book, depicting her as the main source of

---

[82] *EA* II, c. 4, p. 65.    [83] Nelson, 'Queens as Jezebels'.
[84] *MGH Capit.* II, no. 261, p. 278, ll. 19–20.
[85] Johannes Scottus Eriugena, *Carmina*, App. 10, p. 128, l. 7. In line 6, Louis is depicted as a lawgiver; this he had in common with Justinian the Great.

all the evils that had befallen the kingdom. What better way to get back at his reigning monarch, her son, who had made him abbot of Corbie and then deposed him? Unlike all other protagonists in this polemical narrative, Charles the Bald remains nameless. Radbert's silence where Charles is concerned is almost deafening.

*Part III*

# Politics

# 7    Radbert and the Rebellions

## 1    The Loyal Palace Revolt (830–831)

### Familiarity Lost

The only reason Wala and his fellow rebels had acted against Louis was because they had wanted to save the emperor, and so they did, unselfishly risking their lives. Rather than receiving Louis's thanks, they were unjustly punished and sent into ignominious exile.[1] This, in short, is the crux of Radbert's account of the first rebellion, which concentrates above all on the perfidy of Bernard/Naso, and on the urgent need to remove him from power. The chamberlain had not just overturned the order of the palace, and thereby of the entire realm, but had threatened the lives of the emperor and his elder sons. As soon as Naso was in power, he had undermined the two pillars of the political order: namely, the loyalty of the *populus* and the obligations created by family ties. Pursuing only his own gain and interests, Naso lusted after power for its own sake, resorting to adultery, plunder, sorcery and, if need be, murder.[2] Turn all these vices into their positive opposites, and the image of Wala emerges: the epitome of *fides*, prudence, public-spiritedness and selflessness. Although lambasting Naso certainly helped to highlight Arsenius' virtues, and thereby support his defence, one gets a sense of a more than literary anger still simmering a decade after Bernard's death.[3]

The second book's narrative proceeds in chronological order, but with some telling omissions. It was clearly aimed at an audience that did not need to be told how to get from one stage to the next. Directly after the long opening section on Wala's admonition to Louis, Lothar and their counsellors in the winter of 828/9, the account proceeds to Bernard's

---

[1] *EA* II, c. 9, p. 73.
[2] On the accusations of witchcraft against Gerberga, Bernard's sister, see De Jong, *Penitential State*, pp. 51, 200–1.
[3] For my interpretation of Radbert's invective against Bernard I have profited greatly from Flower, *Emperors and Bishops*.

appointment in August 829. The reforming councils of June 829, including the one in Paris, are mentioned in passing, and with considerable disdain: 'they' had only organised these gatherings to keep the king happy.[4] Bernard's takeover of the court is painted in apocalyptic hues:

> Alas for that day that brought virtually never-ending darkness and danger to this world, that rent into pieces and divided the peaceful and united empire, violated ties of brotherhood, tore kinsmen apart, begat hatreds everywhere, scattered fellow citizens, exiled faith, destroyed charity, violated churches, and corrupted everything! This is why civil wars happen on a daily basis, so to speak, and wars more than civil. For this reason, there are invasions of heathens and enemies on all sides; for this reason, the whole people is cut down, and countless villages and cities are put to the torch. Alas for that wretched day, which was followed by a worse night, though none is more unhappy than the day on which the accursed Naso was recalled from Spain, that fornicator who abandoned everything honourable [to which he had been appointed] and stupidly plunged himself into every filthy sty. Accordingly, when he arrived, like a wild boar, he turned the palace upside down, put an end to counsel, and destroyed all the laws of reason. All the counsellors, [of things] human and divine, he expelled and humiliated. He occupied the marriage bed and seditiously took over everything so that his plots became even more apparent.[5]

This is how Radbert introduces the perfidious Naso: from the perspective of a dismal present, the root cause of which was Bernard's being favoured over Wala. Above all, he focuses on Naso's disordering of the palace. On the one hand, *palatium* refers to the entire court, in the sense of the entourage of the royal family, including the lay magnates and prelates who formed the inner circle of counsellors; they are referred to as the *rectores et primi palatii*, while those with a specific office are called *officiales palatii*. This is a fairly wide constituency. On the other hand, the palace is also presented as a closed and inaccessible location, where scandalous practices could remain hidden from the outside world, unless insiders

---

[4] *EA* II, c. 4, p. 65.

[5] *EA* II, c. 7, p. 67: 'O dies illa, quae pęne aeternas huic orbi tenebras attulit et discrimina, quae pacatum imperium et unitum conscidit particulatim ac divisit, germanitates violavit consanguineos dirempsit, inimicitias ubique procreavit, et concives dispersit, fidem exterminavit, charitatem delevit, ecclesias quoque violavit et omnia corrupit! Unde quotidie civilia surgunt bella, ut ita loquar, et plusquam civilia. Exercitus totius patriae pęne huc illucque perimitur: provinciae, pagi, et urbes passim depopulantur. Si qui residui sunt, sine viribus ubique aut fugiunt, aut caeduntur gladiis. Hinc undique paganorum et hostium incursiones, hinc quod omne vulgus conciditur, villae, civitates innumere cremantur. Heu misera dies, quam infelicior nox sequitur! sed nulla infelicior illa, quando sceleratus Naso vocatus est ab Spaniis, amisarius ille, qui cuncta reliquit honesta, in quibus erat ordinatus; et immersit se fatuus ad omnia cęni volutabra. Siquidem ut advenit, ac si ferus aper evertit palatium, destruxit consilium, dissipavit omnia rationis iura; consules omnes, divinos, humanosque expulit, et attrivit; thorum occupavit, atque factiose, ita ut insidię viderentur, manifestius omnia pervasit ... '.

divulged these sordid secrets. The once honourable palace had become a theatre,[6] 'a brothel where fornication held sway and an adulterer ruled, where crimes were piled up upon one another, where every type of evil deed and sorcery of magicians could be found, so much as never could have been believed still to have existed in the world'.[7] These goings-on remained hidden for a while, but then rumours began to seep out. The shocking news was brought to Wala in Corbie by some worried courtiers, who urged him to come to the rescue. Radbert goes to considerable lengths to explain how word about these by definition secret sins first got out, and then became reliable common knowledge, for only a real *scandalum*, a sin that had scandalised both God and human society, could justify a collective and corrective action of the kind undertaken by the rebels in the spring of 830.[8]

The *palatium* that emerges from Radbert's prose is nameless and without any indication of a specific location. There may have been the implicit assumption that this was Aachen, for this is where Louis had hitherto mostly resided, though by no means exclusively, in the months between Bernard's appointment and the outbreak of the first revolt.[9] The palace in Aachen, moreover, played a central role in both rebellions, especially as the scene of Judith's reinstatements in 831 and 834.[10] All the same, it is unlikely that Radbert's notion of the sacred palace (*sacrum palatium*) from which the loyal rebels expelled the evildoers was restricted to this one palace, however important it had become.[11] He is referrring to the imperial court in general, wherever its residence, but depicts it as delineated by strict boundaries, not unlike a monastery. Arsenius did not act until he knew precisely what was going on 'inside' (*intus*), and one of his most reliable informants was Gratian, Louis's third son, who allegedly fled from the palace to the rebels, and related 'everything he had learned when he was detained on the inside'.[12] This opposition between inside and outside was part of Radbert's monastic experience, but there is also

---

[6] *EA* II, c. 8, p. 68: ' ... eo quod esset theatrum, honestatis olim, palatium factum ... '.

[7] *EA* II, c. 8, p. 69: 'Fit palatium prostibulum, ubi moechia dominatur et adulter regnat, coacervantur crimina, requiruntur nefanda et sortilega maleficiorum omnium genera, quanta nunquam credidi in saeculo remansisse ... '.

[8] On the meaning of *scandalum*, see De Jong, *Penitential State*, pp. 232–3, 237–9; De Jong, 'Power and Humility'.

[9] Louis remained in Worms until September and then travelled via Treburt (*MGH DD LdF* no. 283, 14 October 829) to Frankfurt, where he hunted; by 11 November he was back in Aachen; see *ARF* s.a. 829 and *AB* s.a. 830.

[10] De Jong, *Penitential State*, pp. 210–11; *AB* s.a. 831; *AMP* s.a. 830, pp. 97–8.

[11] *EA* II, c. 9, p. 72: ' ... vel alii quamplures malignis instituti artibus, a sacro pellerentur palatio ... '.

[12] *EA* II, c. 9, p. 72: ' ... ad quos cum fugisset, narravit omnia, quae intus detentus resciverat.'

the sense of the court as a place that was utterly unapproachable for anyone except the inner circle that enjoyed royal favour.

Central to the attack on Bernard is the idea that he monopolised access to the emperor and empress, and kept away one-time members of that inner circle. Not only did Naso oust all the current counsellors, be they bishops or laymen, by cunning and deceit; he also got Louis to exclude all those once raised at the court by himself or his father 'from secret deliberation, from consultation, from familiarity and counsel, from the loyalty of fidelity, from honours, and from all the fellowship of their earlier life'.[13] The chamberlain is labelled as an upstart who rode roughshod over all the longstanding ties that had been forged since youth, when adolescent aristocrats lived in the royal household and were trained for their future roles as royal representatives: counts, bishops, abbots, *missi* and whatever other 'ministries' they were to occupy. These *nutriti* formed a formidable old boys' network indeed, and as Louis's baptismal son, Bernard/Naso had enjoyed this kind of close association with the ruler from childhood onwards. In 824 he had even married his wife Dhuoda at the palace in Aachen, surely a privilege granted only to a happy few.[14] Radbert's portrayal of his nemesis as a parvenu merely shows how effective an upbringing at the palace was thought to be by himself and his audience: it would create connections that would bridge generations and last a lifetime, not just amongst the aristocratic youngsters in question, but also between them and older and more powerful courtiers and, above all, with the ruler himself. In the *Epitaphium*'s first book, the young Wala figures as a model *nutritus* at Charlemagne's court. Forging useful ties with senior courtiers, he proved his mettle in any test his ruler set him, while preserving the humility that singled him out as a true leader.[15]

The accusation of having excluded someone as illustrious as Wala from the court where he had grown up was explosive ammunition. The key word is *familiaritas,* a term that was used for the protection extended by Carolingian rulers to monasteries;[16] here, however, it refers to the privileged proximity to the ruler that was based on having lived in the royal household. This was what Naso allegedly withheld from his peers, and it triggered the first revolt. But there was more. As Radbert has it, Bernard 'tore kinsmen apart', and this also held true for himself and Wala. In an

---

[13] *EA* II, c. 9, p. 71: '... ut omnes repelleret, quos aut ipse, aut magnus pater eius imperator nutrierat a secreto, a colloquio, a familiaritate et consilio, a fidei fide, ab honoribus, et ab omni consortio prioris vitae.'

[14] Dhuoda, *Liber manualis*, p. 48; Nelson, 'Dhuoda', p. 118.

[15] A point made extensively in *EA* I, c. 6, pp. 28–9. On youths in the Carolingian palace, see Innes, 'A Place of Discipline'. See above, pp. 25–8.

[16] Niermeyer, *Lexicon Minus,* s.v. 'familiaritas', 1; De Jong, 'Familiarity Lost'.

aside that has been largely overlooked, it transpires that Wala had formerly been married to the sister of Bernard's father, William of Gellone, rather than to Bernard's sister, as has been thought hitherto. Given the age difference between the two adversaries, this makes much more sense.[17] It also explains why Wala had to move cautiously, once the scandal in the palace began to break. He first tried to reason with the new chamberlain, whom he had known since the latter's youth, but Bernard was pig-headed and refused to listen to the older and wiser man. Radbert makes the most of their age difference, for in all other ways, these adversaries were perfect equals.

He even spoke faithfully to that seditious beast, with all of the deference of kinship (*amicitia*), for that man's father and he had previously been the closest of kinsmen. And not without reason, because in the past he [A.] had taken the sister of this man [i.e. of Bernard's father, *ipsius*] as his wife, the daughter of a most noble and magnificent man. Hence, from the cradle, he [A.] had, like a father, surrounded him [B.] in all respects with conscientious affection, care and solicitude, even more than if he had been his [real] father.[18]

Not heeding Arsenius' paternal advice was only one of Bernard's sins against the societal and natural order. This also gives an idea of the havoc his appointment as chamberlain wrought among older courtiers such as Wala. Once he had been Bernard's mentor and educator, but now he was obliged to defer to this junior. In the diatribes against him, the chamberlain's age did matter: he was the younger man, full of ambition and virility, who had seduced the young empress married to an older husband. Although it was Agobard who in his polemical treatises of 833 made the most of Judith's lascivious youth, Radbert's dark intimations about her hold over Louis, and the immoral court that was like a theatre or a brothel, speak volumes as well.[19] The dark arts were fed by the sexual power of both Justina and Naso.[20]

---

[17] My interpretation that the sister who married Wala was William of Gellone's and not his son Bernard's has been accepted by Depreux, 'Der karolingischer Hof'', pp. 21–2, and, albeit implicitly, also by Dohmen, *Die Ursache*, p. 148; *pace* Dohmen, Wala's bride must remain nameless. Justin Lake and I will translate this passage accordingly.

[18] *EA* II, c. 8, p. 69: 'Nam et belluę factiosissimę quia prius ei pater eius et ipse amicissimi fuerant, affatus est fideliter cum omni amicitiarum obsequio. Nec immerito igitur, eo quod olim sibi sororem ipsius, filiam nobilissimi viri et magnificentissimi duxerat. Unde ab incunabulis quasi pater circa eum in omnibus pium gerebat affectum, curam ac sollicitudinem, plus etiam quam si pater esset.'

[19] The theatre and the brothel are connected by Isidore, *Etymologiae* XVIII, c. 42, 2: 'Idem vero theatrum, idem et prostibulum, eo quod post ludos exactos meretrices ibi prostrarentur.'

[20] For a more extensive discussion, see De Jong, *Penitential State*, pp. 185–213, with references to older literature.

Although Radbert depicted them as absolute opposites, there are intriguing similarities between Bernard and Wala, and not just because both had risen to a desirable but all too dangerous position. By serving, formally or informally, as the head of the royal household, or the top man at the court, Frankish magnates laid themselves open to accusations of barring other members of the elite from access to the ruler. This could eventually lead to murder, as had been the case with the *maior domus* Ebroin (d. 681).[21] The removal of Count Matfrid of Orléans in 828, together with Lothar's father-in-law Hugh of Tours, was less violent, but it was another case of men who had become too powerful. They were accused of cowardice and disloyalty and, in Matfrid's case, of being a 'wall' who stood between the emperor and his faithful men.[22]

In Bernard's relatively well-documented case, it becomes clear that things went beyond the general pattern of the head of the royal household being attacked for barring access to the ruler. Although Radbert was the most vociferous, all major ninth-century historians loathed Bernard, regardless of their stance in the rebellions. As Philippe Depreux has pointed out, they had their reasons. This was not just the second man in the realm (*secundus in imperio*); he also held the office of *camerarius*, which gave him control of the royal treasury. On top of all this, he was Louis's godson, which made for an unprecedented combination of political roles. Whether his reliance on kinsmen was a sign of Louis's weakness and inability to connect with the aristocracy is a moot point; this may also be a symptom of an imperial and therefore more dynastic approach to rulership. Yet Depreux is right in perceiving Bernard as an exceptional case, and something of a novelty. Through baptismal sponsorship, as Louis's godson, he was a member of the imperial family, *and* he stemmed from the highest echelon of the aristocracy that was related to the ruling dynasty. By blood, he was not connected quite as closely to Louis as Wala was, but given that the latter married a sister of William of Gellone, Bernard's father, the two adversaries operated at the same level. To add insult to injury, in 829 Louis commended his youngest son Charles to Bernard, even though Lothar was Charles' godfather.[23] Along with Bernard's becoming second only to the emperor, and thereby effectively displacing the *consors imperii*, this constituted a terrible affront to Lothar, and an unprecedented concentration of resources of power in the hands of one man.

---

[21] On the portrayal of Ebroin in seventh- and eighth-century sources, see De Jong, 'Monastic Prisoners', pp. 318–23.
[22] Depreux, 'Matfrid'; De Jong, *Penitential State*, pp. 148–57, 251–2.
[23] Nithard I, c. 3, p. 10.

There were yet more reasons why Bernard posed an exceptional threat: unlike the clerical leadership of the court he had driven away, the new chamberlain was capable of having legitimate offspring. So was Wala, before he was tonsured in 814, which brings to mind the Astronomer's dark intimations about what Wala was up to during Louis's precarious succession: 'For Wala, who held the highest place with Emperor Charles, was especially feared in case he might lay some sinister plot against the emperor'.[24] During the brief transition period after Charlemagne's death, Wala was very much like Bernard: a royal kinsman with ambition. By 830, however, when Bernard was brought down, the requirements for what constituted a valid royal marriage had become more strict, and the one and only empress's alleged adultery had become an effective weapon in this struggle for power.[25] Whatever Wala's own plans and designs may have been at the time, as the leading lay magnate at Charlemagne's later court, and the first of the non-clerical signatories of Charlemagne's will, he remained a threat to the new emperor and his sons until his entry into Corbie neutralised the danger. Eventually, Wala's withdrawal from the world opened the way to his renewed prominence at the court, first as Lothar's second in command in Italy, and then as one of Louis's and Lothar's most prominent courtiers in Aachen. In neither of these roles did he present a challenge to the ruling dynasty, unlike Bernard, who elbowed him out. Radbert's entire invective is geared towards showing that Naso was intent on replacing not just Lothar, but also the senior emperor himself. Having invaded the imperial marriage bed, he had slowly poisoned Louis, leading him to an inevitable death, like a lamb to slaughter. Had the loyal Arsenius not intervened, this would only have been the beginning:

Such is the faithlessness of Arsenius, as those people falsely believe who fail to recognise that, through his wise counsel, he prevented a tyrant from carrying out his plans to kill the emperor, extinguish all of his offspring, and take to himself his wife, whom he had faithlessly corrupted. If he had been allowed to do so, he would have usurped the imperial office together with her, and either killed or evilly subjected to the yoke of oppression all the great men of the land, or else he would have taken himself to Spain with her. This is the reason why Arsenius put himself in danger and freed everyone from the evil of such wickedness.[26]

---

[24] Astronomer, c. 21, p. 346.    [25] De Jong, *Penitential State*, pp. 186–95.

[26] *EA* II, c. 10, p. 73 (Pascasius): 'Talis quippe est infidelitas Arsenii, falso ut opinantur, quibus non est precognitum, quod suo sapienti consilio tyrannum prevenerit, ne perficeret quae moliebatur, ut perimeret augustum, prolemque eius omnem exstingueret, et uxorem, quam infideliter coinquinaverat, acciperet. Cum qua, si cederetur, imperium pervaderet, et omnes seniores terrae aut interficeret, aut male subiugaret oppressos; sin alias, ad Hispaniam cum ipsa se transponeret. Propterea ergo dedit se periculo Arsenius, et liberavit omnes a tanti sceleris malo.'

This is what Louis had risked by making Bernard 'second only after himself in ruling the empire', as Nithard expressed it, or a 'bulwark' against his enemies, in the Astronomer's terms.[27] The main thrust of Radbert's diatribe was Naso's evil plan to take over the *imperium* by marrying Judith and producing heirs of his own. This was not a realistic prospect at all, but that was not the point of these accusations. The Astronomer, with the turbulent events of 830–3 at the centre of his narrative and at the back of his mind, knew all about the dangers that an untonsured Wala might have posed to Louis upon the latter's accession. The Astronomer never called Wala 'second only after the emperor' or anything of the sort, for this would have been too much honour for a man for whom he had little liking, but Radbert did, in the first book of his *Epitaphium*. Discussing the young Arsenius at the court of Charlemagne, the narrator Pascasius explains to his fellow monks that their abbot's career had been nothing short of stellar, for he was appointed 'steward over the whole household by the emperor, second only to the emperor himself, such that you would think another Joseph was wielding the sceptre of the realm'. Then follows a catalogue of qualities which, according to Radbert, singled out real leadership at this elevated level: dispensing equitable justice without ever taking any bribes, a total lack of self-interest, an abundance of foresight and prudence, and a constant and energetic striving for what was right.[28]

Radbert's portrait of Wala's early precociousness is reminiscent of all those saints whose virtues were already obvious in childhood and adolescence. As a young man, Arsenius had served Charlemagne as an envoy and commanded armies on his behalf. Other sources indicate that Wala's rise at the court dates only to the last decade of this emperor's reign, so Radbert seems to have projected this later prominence onto an earlier period.[29] Yet I also wonder whether, in the first book, Wala as Joseph already invites a comparison with Bernard. Although portrayed as opposites, a paragon of virtue and a villain, in many respects these two men were similar. Stemming from the same aristocratic echelon, and closely connected by a variety of ties to the ruling dynasty, both became 'second only to the emperor himself' while they were still lay magnates. At different stages, therefore, they each posed a potential threat to Louis the Pious.

---

[27] Nithard, c. 3, p. 10; Astronomer c. 43, p. 434: ' ... quasi quoddam propugnaculum'.
[28] *EA* I, c. 6, p. 29.
[29] Weinrich, *Wala*, pp. 18–19; Depreux, *Prosopographie*, pp. 390–1. The *Translatio S. Viti*, p. 40, takes a similar approach, claiming that Wala had great power in Charlemagne's reign, and was 'more venerable than all who were part of the palace'.

In yet another way, the *Epitaphium*'s narrative suggests a connection between Wala and Bernard. With the hindsight of two decades, Wala was blamed for all the misery that had happened meanwhile. As one of the confabulating monks remarks, all those who do not know better say that he was the instigator of the evils that had hit the realm ever since this rebellion.[30] Radbert, in his guise as the narrator Pascasius, counters this allegation with his furious attack on Bernard. By the 850s, all and sundry agreed on his depravity, so it could safely be used to shore up Wala's reputation. The interesting question is, however, why it was still important, two decades later, to clear Arsenius' name: 'By Hercules, even today many people are mistaken when it comes to him and declare what is good to be evil, and the evil that everyone was decrying at the time to be good. From this evil there arose countless others, and even more frightful evils continue to spring up every day.'[31]

### Compiègne 830

The lamentation just cited is part of Radbert's account of an assembly held in Compiègne in May 830, with Lothar in charge.[32] He had travelled north from Italy, joined the rebels, and was now all set to reclaim his previous status as co-emperor. Although this gathering has been briefly discussed in the previous chapter, as the context in which Radbert called Louis 'Justinian', it deserves some extra attention here, for it is one of the highlights of the *Epitaphium*'s narrative of the first rebellion. Glossed over or ignored as the assembly was by all authors favourable to Louis, Radbert made the most of it. Here Louis had publicly promised to Lothar, and to his two elder brothers and their followers who attended the assembly, to return to the *status quo ante*. The situation before Bernard's appointment would be restored: Lothar would be co-emperor once more, while Judith would enter a nunnery and do penance there for her sins.

The narrator Pascasius' elaborate account starts with a disclaimer: yes, he was present at the assembly and indeed, much criticism was levelled at the emperor. This he omits, however, pleading a bad memory, only to embark on a detailed story of the solemn promises made by Louis which were subsequently broken.[33] These are emphasised by the narrator's prevarication, which in fact reveals the pivotal nature of this part of his account: the rebels were right and Louis had admitted this in public.

---

[30] *EA* II, c. 9, p. 71.
[31] *EA* II, c. 10, p. 74 (Pascasius): 'Hinc hercule est, quod adhuc hodie plures in eo errant, et dicunt bonum malum, et malum quod omnes tunc detrectabant, bonum. Ex quo sane malo innumera creverunt, et quotidie atrociora crescunt mala.'
[32] Astronomer, c. 45, p. 460.    [33] *EA* II, c. 10, p. 73.

At the heart of Radbert's justification of the first rebellion is the constant participation and consent of the *populus*. Together with the 'people', that is, the lay and ecclesiastical *fideles* and their own followers, in Compiègne in May 830 the emperor gave thanks to God for having been saved, even though 'he concealed something else in his heart'. Radbert used invented direct speech on Louis's part as a way to specify the promises in question:

'You', he said, 'have done things of a kind no people has ever been observed to have done before, because I too have before admitted and committed deeds of a kind that no king before me has been found to have done. And therefore', he said, 'thanks [are due] to the almighty God, who brought such a threatening evil to such a peaceful end. Surely, I promise that from now on I will do nothing of the sort, [and] nothing without your counsel. That is to say, the imperial rule by me, as it was once ordained in unanimity with you and constituted,[34] I decree and wish to remain in this way. As regards this [issue] (*huic*) of the woman of whom you have judged that the revenge against her is mine: according to the laws of the whole community, as you requested, I grant her life, on condition, however, that from now on she wear the sacred veil and do penance'.[35]

Although the *Epitaphium* is the only extant source to highlight these assurances so extensively, they are also referred to in the episcopal document drafted to justify Louis's public penance of 833: this warned the emperor not to dissemble and do anything deceitful, as he had done earlier, 'in the presence of the whole Church, in the palace of Compiègne', denouncing the 'craftiness of a duplicitous heart'.[36] That Louis indeed went along with the rebels in May 830 but then backtracked also transpires from the ensuing fury and resentment, most eloquently expressed in the polemics produced in 833 by Agobard of Lyon. By rejecting the veil imposed on her three years before and returning to the imperial bedchamber, Judith had committed apostasy.[37]

This is one of Radbert's main charges as well, but another and equally important one is Justinian's essential lack of trustworthiness. The emperor, who until then might still have been redeemed, now

---

[34] The verb *constituere* is a key word in the so-called *Ordinatio imperii* (817), *MGH Capit.* II, no. 136, pp. 270–1 (which would have been better called *Constitutio regni*).

[35] *EA* II, c. 10, p. 73: 'Vos enim, inquit, fecistis, qualia nunquam populus unquam fecisse cernitur, quia et ego prior admisi et feci, qualia nullus ante me rex fecisse invenitur. Et ideo, inquit, gratias omnipotenti Deo, qui tam imminens malum ad tam pacificum deduxit exitum. Porro deinceps nihil tale, nihil sine vestro consilio me acturum ulterius profiteor. Imperium namque a me, ut olim ordinatum est una vobiscum, et constitutum, ita manere decerno et volo. Feminę quoque huic, quam adiudicastis, quia mea est in illa ultio, iuxta communes leges, sicut deposcitis, vitam concedo, ita tamen ut sub sacro velamine deinceps degeat, et poenitentiam gerat'.

[36] *Relatio episcoporum* (833), p. 53, ll. 38–44; transl. De Jong, *Penitential State*, p. 274; for a new edition, see Booker, 'Public penance'.

[37] Agobard, *Liber Apologeticus* I; De Jong, *Penitential State*, pp. 195–6, 203–4.

showed a total lack of dependability, in stark contrast to the unwavering fidelity of those who had just managed to save him. Radbert has Louis pronounce the rebels' own defence of their actions, as part of a solemn and public declaration of his eternal gratitude, but the reader is warned that Louis's words did not match his intentions: he 'hid things in his heart', and what he promised 'came neither from his heart, nor from his mind'.[38] When Louis went back on his promises, his heart played a role once more: 'meanwhile, the much hardened wound in his heart had been covered'.[39] The heart was the location of wounding remorse, but also of the sincerity of *fides*, and in Louis's case it had been damaged. *Fides*, with meanings ranging from loyalty and fidelity to trust and faith, runs like a thread through the entire second book, but it is particularly important in the context of the first rebellion and its justification. Judith was not just blamed for having used her female wiles, but for having urged and flattered the emperor away from 'true fidelity and justice' (*fides et iustitia*). In contrast to Arsenius' consistent truthfulness and staunch loyalty to his emperor, there was Louis/Justinian, who wavered and deceived.

The assembly of May 830 is central to Radbert's defence of Arsenius, for this was his abbot's finest hour: his enemies had been brought low, the entire *populus* had sworn fidelity to Lothar, and 'the Fury's brother' (Bernard's brother Heribert) was sentenced to death by the *consors imperii*, now totally in charge. As Radbert remembered wistfully, perhaps with an undertone of reflected glory: 'at the time everyone praised him [Arsenius] as if he were the liberator of all, and they sang their songs of praise everywhere.'[40] In October 830, however, at an assembly in Nijmegen where Louis had gathered his loyal followers from the eastern parts of his realm, 'Abbot Wala was ordered to go back to the monastery of Corbie and to keep to the monastic life there', as the Astronomer expressed it.[41] Culminating in a brief diatribe about Louis's change of heart in the face of Wala's attempts to save his emperor, people and fatherland, at the risk of losing his own life, Radbert's account then moves directly to the loyal rebels' expulsion and exile, without any formal accusation or due process of law. 'All the rights of the law – both divine and human – were rescinded.

---

[38] *EA* II, c. 10, p. 74: 'Sed quia cuncta quae fiebant, non errant ex corde Iustiniani neque ex animo ... '.
[39] *EA* II, c. 10, p. 74: 'Tegitur interdum vulnus in corde valde defixum ... '.
[40] *EA*, c. 10, p. 74: 'Tunc tamen eum quasi liberatorem omnium omnes magnificabant, et extollebant ubique laudibus ... '.
[41] Astronomer, c. 45, pp. 460–2.

This utter deception was concealed, as it were, under the cloak of fidelity and the royal will.'[42]

## 2    Exile (831–833)

There is no doubt that Radbert was mortified about his abbot's exile, and did his utmost to alleviate the disrepute that this had brought on his beloved Arsenius and Corbie, but also on himself. His two means to accomplish this are somewhat contradictory. On the one hand, his unjustified exile turned Arsenius into a martyr, of which Radbert made the most, with the literary aid of inaccessible caves and faraway islands. On the other, he was adamant that his abbot's reputation remained unimpaired. Banishment made Arsenius even more loved throughout the realm, and wherever he travelled in his exile, he was universally acclaimed by the locals. The message is that Arsenius was still much in demand as a counsellor, and constantly moved from one location to the next, to ensure that none of Louis's three elder sons would get the chance to engage him as their personal counsellor –something they would of course be tempted to do. This was what Justina wanted to avoid above all else, so onwards he went, driven away whenever there was a danger that he might gain a foothold in one kingdom or the next. For fear that Arsenius would liaise with Honorius, he was moved from his cave in the mountains to Noirmoutier, whither his brother Antony had been banished after Louis's accession in 814. In this 'most distant place on earth' he lived in total isolation, like John on Patmos, seeing only what was divine.[43]

Understandably, Wala's itinerary puzzled his biographer Lorenz Weinrich, who found it difficult to pinpoint any of these locations. From the 'high cave' Arsenius supposedly could see the Lake of Geneva and the Pennine Alps.[44] Was it the castle of Chillon, or the monastery of St-Maurice d'Agaune?[45] The latter is unlikely, for St-Maurice was and still is located in a deep valley and does not command such wide vistas. For other reasons as well it would be best to let go of such precise geography, as Radbert did himself throughout his account of Wala's exile. The *Epitaphium* is the only source for his abbot's alleged sojourn in Noirmoutier, and for the lofty 'cave' in Burgundy. What mattered most

[42] *EA* II, c. 10, p. 74: 'Rescinduntur ergo eo in facto paulo post iura legum omnia, divina scilicet et humana. Occultabatur autem nimia fraus, quasi sub fidei scemate et voluntate regia.'
[43] *EA* II, c. 11, p. 77: ' ... si quomodo cum beato Ioanne solummodo quae divina sunt cernat ... '.
[44] *EA* II, c. 12, p. 78.    [45] Weinrich, *Wala*, p. 76.

to Radbert, apart from the wildness and inaccessibility of these places, and Adalhard's lingering presence in Noirmoutier, was to get across that Arsenius, wherever he was exiled, continued to be a magnet for the powerful.[46] Even the strictest custody proved insufficient, for he was still so much in demand as an influential counsellor that each time there was the risk that one of Louis's sons would turn to him for advice. While he was in Noirmoutier, it was Pippin of Aquitaine/Melanius who was a candidate for aid and counsel from Arsenius, so the latter 'was harshly liberated from exile and attentively conveyed, like sweet-smelling incense, through the middle of Gaul to Germania'.[47] Arriving at a nameless monastery, he was not allowed to stay for long there either, 'lest in those parts he would engage Gratian in his counsel or colloquy'.[48]

For all we know, Wala was indeed moved through the empire like a man 'venerated for his merits and feared because of his counsels', who might attract a royal admirer wherever he went.[49] Yet what we are dealing with is a literary salvage operation to recover Wala's severely damaged reputation, and it was his banishment from Louis's court that had done the damage. It had not only impaired Wala's standing among his peers, the royal counsellors with access to the emperor, but had also affected Corbie's collective reputation, upon which Radbert's own sense of worth largely depended.[50] With every literary strategy at his disposal, he therefore attempts to turn this ignominious fall from royal grace into its opposite. In fact, Arsenius had relished his high cave and his island isolation, and did not want to be liberated from this eremitical freedom rooted in biblical and monastic tradition. Wherever he went, he carried his fatherland with him, for he was known and loved everywhere, and cherished all the more because of his innocence.[51] Kings turned to him as they always had, and Arsenius' journey from Noirmoutier to Germania was like a royal progress: wherever he went, a chorus of monks time and again received him with joy, and although this was meant to be a disgraceful journey (*inhoneste*), he was honoured (*honestatur*) by an escort of bishops and abbots.[52] The entire narrative of Arsenius' exile is

---

[46] *EA* II, c. 13, p. 79.
[47] *EA* II, c. 13, p. 80: ' ... relevatur cum iniuria exsilio, et deportatur officiosissime, quasi incensum odoriferum, per medias Gallias ad Germaniam.'
[48] *EA* II, c. 14, p. 81: ' ... ne forte Gratiano illis in partibus misceretur consilio vel colloquio ... '.
[49] *EA* II, c. 13, p. 80: ' ... quia venerabatur meritis, et timebatur consiliis ... '.
[50] See also the stimulating discussion in Stofferahn, 'New Majesty'; I am less inclined, however, to stress *lèse-majesté* as a major aspect of Radbert's treatment of exile.
[51] *EA* II, c. 13, p. 80: 'Ipse vero semper ubique secum patriam ferebat: quia ubique notus, ubique dilectus, ubique ab omnibus quanto innocentior, tanto carius amabatur.'
[52] *EA* II, c. 13, p. 80.

aimed at showing that despite his exile, his reputation was unimpaired. He was with God, so therefore he was in his fatherland. What relevance did banishment have in this case?[53] This point is made by Teofrastus, the frank speaker of the second book, but Pascasius, the narrator, then drives it home:

> It is just as you say, and for this reason it is not he who should be called an exile, but rather those who forced him into exile. For no matter where they were, these men were exiled from themselves, from understanding, and from counsel, when through their crimes they handed their fatherland over to what amounted to an exile from its citizens and its most responsible leaders. For what does the name of exile signify in and of itself? At the very least, a punishment implying disaster and disgrace. When, therefore, is it disgraceful? Truth be told, when it is a punishment for sin. This is also the view men take when, as in this case, it is the punishment of someone unjustly condemned. For in this case he did not bear the name of exile because of his own sin, but because of an unjust decree enacted through the just workings of God.[54]

Throughout his elaborate depiction of Arsenius' exile, Radbert tries to turn the tables on Arsenius' enemies: they themselves were the ones who had been banished. His ingenious defence of his abbot reveals the depth to which the once glorious Wala had fallen in the estimation of his peers, and the extent to which this still affected Corbie and its one-time abbot Radbert in the mid-850s.

Against this background, I return to one of the most intriguing passages of the *Epitaphium*'s second book. Angels were not the only ones to tread in Arsenius' high cave with a view of the Lake of Geneva and the Italian Alps. By his own admission, his disciple Radbert visited him there as well, on a journey undertaken at Louis's behest, to deal with ecclesiastical property and monastic business. As Radbert relates, there was not just a joyful reunion with his beloved Arsenius, but also a tempting proposal for reconciliation with Louis.[55] Arsenius flatly refused, pointing out to his pupil that he was as innocent as Radbert himself, so why not fight for justice? Yet his disciple pressed on, claiming that together with Arsenius' supporters, he would be able to engineer not only a pardon, but even greater *honores* and imperial favour than he had enjoyed before. Arsenius

[53] *EA* II, c. 11, p. 77.
[54] *EA* II, c. 11, p. 78: 'Ita est ut asseris, et ideo non exsulem eum appellare licet, sed eos qui eum exsulare cogebant; quoniam ipsi in quocunque loco essent, exsulabantur a se, a sensu, a consilio, cum omnem patriam civibus et optimis curis simillimam exsilio suis sceleribus reddebant. Quid est enim exsul ipsum per se nomen? calamitatis utique poena et turpitudinis. Quando igitur est turpe? Revera, cum est poena peccati. Opinio est etiam hominum, sicuti huic, cum est poena iniuste damnati. Alias autem hic non in peccato suo nomen tulit exsilii, sed decreto iniusto iuste Deo agente.'
[55] *EA* II, c. 10, p.75.

replied with a scathing diatribe, warning about the dangers of delivering a spurious confession of guilt against himself, and abandoning truth and fidelity: he would run the risk of a divine judgement, and incur far harsher punishment than what he received at present. A confused Radbert had to admit that Arsenius' moral conviction (*conscientia*) was completely oriented towards God and the public weal: he pursued not his own interests, but only those of Christ.

Telling the truth about Arsenius required invented speech, not an accurately remembered conversation. Radbert deliberately positions himself within the narrative as the one making an offer that was both immoral and grandiose. As Arsenius asked him, do you think you have all these people in your power? Ultimately this rebounds on Louis, however, who is said to have gone along with this reprehensible scheme. This amounted to something like reconciliation by mutual confession, which is not at all implausible, but impossible to verify. It is beyond any doubt that Radbert aimed to convince his audience that his beloved abbot had been wrongly accused of infidelity, so any admission of guilt would be a false confession, inviting divine wrath. Furthermore, the great man was uncompromisingly truthful and loyal to God, and could not be lured by the promises of earthly riches.

Apart from this, other messages too are communicated, such as that Radbert himself was as innocent as his abbot and perhaps even more so, for he could move about freely, while Arsenius had been exiled. Sent on imperial business by Louis, Radbert had the kind of proximity to the emperor that enabled him to act as a mediator, and he wants his reader to be aware of his status. Yet in the final analysis, this anecdote helps to sustain the overarching narrative: namely, that Arsenius' banishment was not a shameful affair that detracted from his reputation. The key argument is that this particular exile did not result in the loss of honour that was usually caused by the use of force and coercion.[56] On the contrary, like Jeremiah, Wala had chosen exile himself, because he could only tell the truth and adhere to it. Initially confused, Pascasius realises this and learns his lesson. How mistaken had he been to offer the indomitable Wala a prospect of more *honores*, and expect him to accept! Instead, his master *chose* to remain alienated from Louis, turning the exilers into the exiled. That this defence was still needed in the 850s shows how much losing access to the court must have hurt Wala, Radbert and their illustrious monastery, Corbie, not only at the time it happened but also in the longer term.

---

[56] On this distinction, see De Jong, 'Monastic Prisoners'.

## 3      The Reluctant Rebellion (833–834)

### Apostolic Authority

Sometime late in 832 or early in 833, Wala returned to Corbie, no longer an abbot, and stripped of all the other offices and lands (*honores*) with which Louis had favoured him.[57] Was Radbert, who depicted himself as the third party in a *consortium* with Adalhard and Wala,[58] in fact the one who assumed a kind of informal leadership? This would explain his close contacts with Louis, and the role of mediator in 831 with which he credited himself. For his monks of Corbie, the return of an Arsenius deprived of all formal authority was an occasion for joy mixed with profound sadness, but the one-time abbot himself behaved with impeccable humility, as was to be expected.

Against this background of Arsenius living as a simple monk in his own community, the narrative of the second rebellion unfolds. Finally, a reluctant Wala decided to join in, 'urged on by his own monks, summoned by the pope, implored by Louis's sons and entreated by the people and the prelates with whom he had once started this affair', that is, the first rebellion. The language used is that of formal encounters between the high and mighty, with frequent use of the expressions *advenire* and *obviam venire*: the royal and papal envoys 'came to' Wala, begging him to 'go towards' the pontiff – that is, give him a proper reception. Ultimately swayed by the greatness of papal authority and physical threats on the part of the royal sons, he gave in. Radbert makes it clear that he had no choice whatsoever. The rebellious brothers would not take no for an answer. 'If he had refused this, the *augusti* would have ordered him to be abducted by force, albeit with all [due] honour and reverence.'[59]

Meanwhile in Corbie, the monks feared that they themselves would become part of the conflict, and that their *claustrum* would be desecrated by the presence of soldiers. The entire community was terrified, but Wala dug his heels in and refused to collaborate. A public reading of a papal *bulla* and more pressure from the sons had already gone a long way towards convincing him, as had a divine miracle that smoothed the passage north from Italy, through the Pennine Alps. His own monks exhorted him 'for the sake of the peace, to obey God's highest pontiff, even if it entailed dying alongside him, "For great is the authority by which you are called," we said. "And great are the necessity and the

---

[57] *EA* II, c. 14, p. 81.    [58] *EA* I, c. 15, p. 43.
[59] *EA* II, c. 14, p. 81: 'Quod si nollet, iusserunt augusti vi eum abducere, cum omni tamen honore et reverentia.'

justice for the sake of which you are summoned."'[60] In other words, Wala had no choice, and went with the backing of his community. When all is said and done, Radbert's defence of Wala's participation in the second rebellion rests primarily on his obligation to obey apostolic authority. Unlike the pope, the rebellious sons had to use threats of coercion, however respectful, and their intentions are presented as suspect from the beginning, because they reeked of selfishness: 'after all, at first we did not know what they [the sons] wanted for themselves.'[61] On the one hand, given Wala's close ties with Italy, Rome and the papacy, we may safely assume that, by the spring of 833, Radbert and his abbot welcomed the intervention of Gregory IV, as did Agobard of Lyon at the time.[62] On the other hand, Radbert's emphasis on the pontiff's central role may also reflect a subsequent development, observed with hindsight: namely, the growing involvement of successive popes in contentious issues north of the Alps, not of their own volition, but because of increasing appeals to Rome. Although this became even more marked in the decades after Radbert's death, it is already visible in sources from the 850s.[63] Whether this can be partly explained by the influence of the so-called Pseudo-Isidorian forgeries, and whether Radbert was indeed involved in their creation, will be discussed in the next chapter. With the exception of one brief mention of the ordination of Pope Eugenius II in 824, in which Wala was instrumental, the first book never breathes a word about the bishop of Rome, even though it covers the great man's years in Italy.[64] By contrast, it is the 'highest pontiff' who dominates Radbert's account of the second revolt, while the rebellious sons gradually sink into a quagmire of selfishness.

### Law on the Field of Lies

Most of the *Epitaphium*'s account of the rebellion of 833 is situated on or near the so-called 'Field of Lies', the Rotfeld in Alsace, where Louis and his three elder sons established opposing camps, to confront each other. Here, the old emperor's followers went over to the other side, flocking to Lothar like chicks seeking shelter under a hen's wings.[65] That this was a divine judgement, provoked by Louis's refusal to accept mediation from

---

[60] *EA* c. 14, p. 81: ' ... coepimus exortari eum, ut obediret pro pace summo Dei pontifici, etiamsi eum mori cum eo contingeret, quoniam multa est, inquimus, auctoritas, qua vocaris, multa etiam necessitas et iustitia, pro qua vocaris ... '.
[61] *EA* II, c. 14, p. 81: 'Nos tamen primum nesciebamus, quid sibi vellent.'
[62] Agobard, *De privilegio apostolicae sedis*, c. 5, p. 305.
[63] Noble, 'Pope Nicholas I'; De Jong, 'Hincmar, Priests and Pseudo-Isidore'.
[64] *EA* I, c. 28, p. 58.      [65] *EA* II, c. 18, p. 89.

the pope, is at the heart of the narrative. It opens with Wala and Radbert travelling from Corbie to the Alsace, amidst ambushes and troop movements, 'with dread and trembling', and courageously risking their lives. What with Justina wielding the sceptre once more, in all aspects of one-headed imperial rule (*monarchia*), the twosome could only travel in secret and hope for the best.[66] When they reached the rebel camp, they received a warm welcome from 'the kings, the magnates and the people'. They then presented themselves to an anxious and distraught Gregory IV. Having come from Rome as part of Lothar's entourage, he had intended to mediate between the father and his sons, but had soon discovered that this would be very hard indeed, not least because the emperor and his advisors considered the pope far from impartial. This was never expressed by either of the parties, however. The issue contested in the Astronomer's *Life of Louis* as well as in the *Epitaphium* is whether Gregory's sudden appearance was a breach of etiquette, which in turn justified Louis's refusal to receive him with the full pomp and splendour required by a papal visit.[67] The Astronomer thinks that Gregory had come without any formal invitation on the emperor's part, to meddle in affairs that were none of his business, while Radbert professes himself shocked by the pope's having been rejected and threatened by the emperor and his men. Even bishops had sworn to resist the rebellious sons and their followers, and they 'conspired, under oath –oh grief! – that they should depose the pope (*apostolicus*), because he had come uninvited'.[68]

This is the context in which Phasur/Ebo is mentioned, as a prominent member of Justina's faction, still loyal to the empress and Louis to the very last, when the defection of the emperor's men left him no other option but to side with Lothar, and to preside over Louis's penance and *de facto* deposition.[69] As Radbert explains, by way of encouragement and support to an astounded and frightened pontiff, Arsenius and Pascasius gave Gregory documents from which it transpired that he had every right: 'some writings confirmed by the authority of the holy fathers and of his predecessors, on the basis of which nobody could contradict that his was the power, or rather, God's and the Apostle Peter's, and his the authority to go and send out to all peoples (*gentes*) . . .'[70] As we shall see in the next chapter, this passage plays a key role in recent discussions about the origin and date of the Pseudo-Isidorian Decretals. Regardless, it is part of Radbert's spirited defence of the papacy in general, and of his justification

---

[66] *EA* II, c. 15, pp. 83–4.    [67] Discussed in De Jong, *Penitential State*, pp. 214–24.
[68] *EA* II, c. 16, p. 84: ' . . . insuper consiliabantur firmantes, proh dolor! quod eundem apostolicum, quia non vocatus venerat, deponere deberent.'
[69] De Jong, *Penitential State*, pp. 253–4.    [70] Acts 15:17 and 22.

of this particular pope's unasked-for mediation between Louis and his rebellious sons.[71]

Tensions mounted. As Radbert has the outspoken monk Teofrastus exclaim at this point, in one of his many frank asides: 'What kind of Augustus do we think this was, what kind of a Justina, who by her nod turned everything upside down; what kind of leaders, when there were prelates of the sort that, just like those in human affairs, rebelled likewise in divine matters!'[72] Interestingly, bishops as rebels are virtually absent from the *Epitaphium*'s account of the first revolt, in which Arsenius and the *populus* take centre stage. In the narrative of the events of 833, however, prelates are moved to the forefront. They are blamed for preventing peace and rejecting their pontiff, as the 'pseudo-prophets of yore' who agitated the people with their horns.[73] No justice was to be had, said Teofrastus, because all fought each other, and everyone struggled amongst themselves.

This complaint then allows the narrator Pascasius to shift the emphasis to the topic of law. He expounds on the many different laws (*leges*) and customs of various peoples, and the three kinds of law (*lex*) that provide the ultimate and stable standard for justice: God's law (*lex dei*), as well as the law of the fatherland (*lex patriae*) and the law of nature (*lex naturae*).[74] Citing St Paul's precepts that children should obey their parents[75] and fathers should not provoke their children to anger,[76] Radbert creates a judicial context for a narrative that leads up to the divine judgement inflicted on the emperor. This effect is further enhanced by one of the more intriguing parts of the second book, 'the *capitula* ... which the august father sent to his sons in the manner of a complaint (*querela*) to notify them of his claims'.[77] This introduces a list of six brief and blunt charges levelled by Louis against his rebellious sons, each followed by their elaborate and courteous refutation. Although the brothers responded in unison, Honorius was their mouthpiece, for he bore the brunt of the accusations. The term *capitula* should here be understood to mean 'points of indictment', demanding a legal

---

[71] *EA* II, c. 16, p. 84; De Jong, 'Paschasius Radbertus and Pseudo-Isidore'; see below, pp. 199–205.
[72] *EA* II, c. 16, p. 84: 'Qualem putamus augustum tunc fuisse, qualemve Justinam, quae suo tunc cuncta vertebat nutu; qualesque principes, quando tales inventi sunt praesules Christi, ut sicut illi in humana, ita et ipsi consurgerent in divina!'
[73] *EA* II, c. 16, p. 85; see Ezek. 34:21'; Eccles. 5:11.   [74] *EA* II, c. 17, p. 85.
[75] Eph. 6:1.   [76] Eph. 6:4.
[77] *EA* II, c. 16, p. 85: 'Tamen ut elucescant quae proposui, commemoranda sunt capitula, quae augustus pater quasi pro querela filiis direxit, ut enuntiaret quid contra requireret.' This refers to the satisfaction or admission of guilt Louis demanded from his sons; *requirere contra* means to bring legal action. For the entire *querela*, see *EA* II, c. 16, pp. 85–8; also the brief discussion in De Jong, 'For God, King and Country', pp. 111–12.

and public defence.[78] It is not unthinkable that the emperor did call his sons to account in a formal manner, or that this presentation of accusations in the form of *capitula* to be answered was part of the judicial procedure of assemblies. We know very little about the way in which such public trials were conducted, but lists of brief accusations sent in advance by a plaintiff, followed during the session by the elaborate refutations of those accused, seem a likely scenario. Radbert presents the exchange between father and sons as a dynamic altercation, with Louis's complaints being carried to the sons by messengers.[79] He makes it clear that the insertion of the *capitula* serves to clarify his narrative, and concludes: 'This was their alternating altercation, this their mutual dispute (*querela*), this the case (*propositio*) of the father and the refutation (*responsio*) of the sons.'[80] Both *altercatio* and *querela* are part of contemporary judicial terminology, and a *propositio* could refer to a legal statement or case,[81] but the conceptual pair of *propositio* and *responsio* also belongs to the domain of scholarly disputation. Alcuin's dialectical writings were part of monastic learning, and it seems likely that these were also a source of inspiration for this highly crafted verbal exchange.[82]

Its main purpose is to show that Louis's complaints against his sons in general, and against Honorius in particular, were unfounded. They had not been disobedient sons or disloyal *fideles*; Lothar had not excluded his father from the defence of the Holy See, prevented the pope's access to Louis, forced his brothers to side with him or accepted his father's vassals (*vasalli*) when they came to him and retained them.[83] These were the grievances against Lothar (and Wala) that still rankled two decades later, and which needed to be addressed. Their refutation gives Radbert an excellent opportunity to elaborate on the lofty intentions of Lothar and his two brothers, and to depict them as loyal rebels who intended the very best for their father. It is Radbert's forensic rhetoric that is striking here, and his carefully constructed and cumulative judgement of Louis's transgressions. First, there is his stubborn refusal to receive Gregory IV with due honour, followed by the pope's stern rebuttal: 'Therefore, emperor, if you receive us and the peace of Christ in a worthy manner, let this give

---

[78] Niermeyer, *Lexicon Minus*, s.v. *capitulum*, 6.

[79] *EA* II, c. 16, p. 87: 'Mandavit namque gloriosus cęsar rursus … '.

[80] *EA* II, c. 17, p. 88: 'Haec siquidem est alterna altercatio, hae quęrelę ad invicem: haec propositio paterna, et responsio filiorum.'

[81] Cf. Lewis & Short, s.v. *propositio*, IV: a statement of a question of law, a case submitted for legal opinion.

[82] For a recent overview, see Rädler-Bohn, 'Re-dating Alcuin's *De dialectica*'.

[83] Given the response, these are not lowly dependents but *vasalli regis*, the equivalent of *fideles regis*.

peace to you and also your kingdom; if not, the peace of Christ will return to us, as you read in the Gospel, and be with us.'[84] Teofrastus' indictment of this refusal is loud and clear, and once more connects the past rebellions with the authorial present; we are now suffering from the consequences of Louis's blind obstinacy and his wife's evil coaxing:

Woe, how great was then the bewitching and blinding of the mind that so deceived a man of such greatness, amidst so many tribulations and dangers, amongst so many scandals[85] that he could never be recalled nor be healed by any counsel from sacred Scripture! He seemed to meditate daily on God's law; how far had he withdrawn from the law of true love by his hardened heart. Otherwise he would never have provoked his sons so obstinately to anger, against God's commandment . . . [86]

This sinful and blinkered emperor was about to be struck by a divine judgement, and in this, Gregory IV also played a key role. On the very night after the day that the pontiff gave up and decided to return to Rome, 'without success, without honour, and without reward for such a great effort', all of Louis's men, from high to low, went over to Lothar, without any persuasion. In the morning, their tents were simply pitched on the other side. Miraculously, all the ties that had bound them to Caesar and his Justina until the day before had been suddenly dissolved: paternal authority, the counsel of magnates and bishops, and solemn oaths taken. For Radbert, this sudden dissolution of a divinely sanctioned order constituted a judgement of God, but only when it had been authenticated by apostolic authority. Accordingly, on that morning the miracle of Louis's sudden desertion was reported to Gregory IV, and a cleric from his retinue appropriately burst out in psalmody, singing 'the hand of the Lord has wrought strength.'[87] Then the pontiff and those present 'judged that the so illustrious and glorious imperial rule (*imperium*) fell from the father's hand, so that the August Honorius, who was the heir and had already been made and created *consors* by his father and by all, would relieve him of it and receive it himself'.[88] In other words, in Radbert's

---

[84] *EA* II, c. 17, p. 88: 'Idcirco, imperator, si nos et pacem Christi digne susceperis, requiescet in vobis ipsa, nec non in regno vestro: sin autem pax Christi ad nos revertetur, uti legistis in evangelio, et nobiscum erit.' (Luke 10:6).

[85] For the meaning of *scandalum* (public and notorious crime, offensive to God), see De Jong, 'Power and Humility', pp. 36–9; *Penitential State*, pp. 151–2, 237–9.

[86] *EA* II, c. 17, p. 88: 'Heu, quae et qualis tunc fuit fascinatio et mentis obcecatio, quae talem et tantum virum, inter tot tentationes et pericula, inter tot scandala sic decepit, ut nunquam revocari potuerit, neque ullis mederi scripturarum sanctarum consiliis! Qui cotidie visus est meditari in lege Dei, et tam longe a lege verae dilectionis indurato corde recessit. Alioquin filios nunquam tam pertinaciter contra mandatum ad iracundiam provocasset . . . '.

[87] Ps. 117:16.

[88] *EA* II, c. 18, p. 89: 'Tunc ab eodem sancto viro, et ab omnibus qui convenerant, adiudicatum est, quia imperium tam praeclarum et gloriosum de manu patris ceciderat,

version, all this had been decided there and then, as soon as Louis had been deserted by his *fideles*. There is no mention of the assembly in October 833 in Soissons, where the arguments for imposing a public penance on Louis were mustered. The emperor had lost the right to rule because of a divine judgement that had been declared genuine by the highest possible authority in these matters, the Roman pontiff. Juridical language still abounds: Louis lost his *imperium* by the verdict of 'this holy man' (Gregory IV) and all those gathered with him, who had witnessed the miracle.

## 4     Failure and Flight (834–836)

On the Field of Lies, together with the pope, Lothar still occupies the moral high ground of the *Epitaphium*, but then, suddenly, Radbert's tone changes. As he points out, Honorius agreed to accept the sole rule of the entire empire (*totius monarchiam imperii*) because 'everyone' declared that, in any case, they would elect him unanimously, for he would provide them with the best protection. So the new emperor accepted their offer, but, as Radbert comments, he took his father with him 'on the basis of a verdict unknown to me'.[89] The author then re-introduces himself into his own narrative, questioning Arsenius about this sudden takeover of Louis's sole rule (*monarchia*) by a son who had been made co-emperor from a position of trust and fidelity (*in fide*). It seemed a bad thing, he maintained to his master, that something so accidental should have such immediate and grave consequences, without any major counsel or a more careful deliberation. Arsenius did not mince his words. They had completed their task, he said, counselling peace to everyone, and trying to contain the war between father and sons that was about to break out. We succeeded, he told Radbert, but now, we are no longer heard. Those who had been afraid that their rebellion would be avenged are only after their own interests, and the others, who had advised the emperor to act against his sons, are merely fearful of their impending loss. As Arsenius wryly reminds his companion, only a few had in mind what belonged to God, and was in the common interest.[90]

This lament is about being excluded from the corridors of power, but it also reveals a Radbert who explicitly distanced himself from the consequences of the rebellion of 833. These two themes are developed in a long and fiery diatribe against bad royal counsellors, voiced by Adeodatus, the

ut augustus Honorius, qui heres erat, etiam consors factus et procreatus a patre et ab omnibus, eum relevaret, et acciperet.'
[89] *EA* II, c. 18, p. 89: ' ... nescio quo iudicio patrem ducens secum ... '.
[90] *EA* II, c. 18, p. 89.

monk who remains a discussant throughout the two books of the *Epitaphium*. What were these men but birds of prey, intent as they were on gaining benefices (*honores*) for themselves and plundering others? They should have taken care of the *respublica* and the stability of the realm, and given straightforward advice to their ruler, but instead, they went for universal destruction or the total dominance of the victor. As I shall argue in the next chapter, this impassioned speech addresses the present (*hodie*) of the 850s in which 'the *respublica* is tending to get ever worse, and is collapsing', and Radbert was banished from the corridors of power. My focus here is on his trenchant criticism of Louis *and* Lothar; in fact, it is the latter's failure to live up to God's demands that dominates Adeodatus' denunciation. Because he was not established on the throne in a prudent manner and did not rule as a victor with God, because he did not fully restore the peace and allowed self-interest to run rife, with him in control the realm perished once more and returned to a ruinous state. 'Neither of them [Louis and Lothar] walked before God sincerely.'[91] In a secret meeting with Lothar, his inner circle of magnates divided up the empire, riding roughshod over the rights of kinsmen, nobles, well-deserving *fideles* and religious communities.

As soon as this had been completed, Arsenius arrived. And they, in a state of confusion, because they were accessories, presented to him the proposed shares of the division[92] [to see] if there would be anything that might displease him. And he responded, perceptive as he was: 'All has been disposed well, except that you have left God nothing that is His by rights, and what you have ordained does not please good men.' Having answered them in this way, he became increasingly saddened, overwhelmed by the cupidity of the blind, for he found a hearing with hardly anybody.[93]

Adeodatus claims that the situation became even more perilous when Louis was restored and Lothar expelled, but Pascasius disagrees: this was not a case of expulsion. Moreover, Lothar did not act foolishly; he only deprived his father of power and went along with the bishops who imposed a penance on him because the 'universal senate and the people' – that is, the assembly of 833 in Compiègne – had made him do so.

[91] *EA* II, c. 19, p. 90.
[92] *Sortes distributionis*: the implicit suggestion may be that the division has been done by unchristian casting of lots (*sortilegia*). But see Niermeyer, *Lexicon Minus*, for more businesslike meanings of *sors* in the context of divisions of heritage.
[93] *EA* II, c. 19, p. 90: 'Quod cum subito factum esset, supervenit Arsenius. At illi confusi, quia conscii, obtulerunt ei distributionis sortes, si quidpiam esset quod displicere potuisset. Tum ille, ut erat sagax in responsis: "Totum, inquit, bene dispositum est, nisi quod Deo sui juris nihil reliquistis, neque quod bonis placeat ordinastis." Quibus ita inlatis, magis magisque contristari coepit, quoniam pene in nullo iam audiebatur, cecorum cupiditate superatus.'

During that autumn, when matters got out of hand, Honorius had not acted of his own volition, and this is how Lothar apparently felt himself by the late 840s, when, in a letter to Pope Leo IV, he referred to 'the time of unhappy discord between us and our father, which, at the instigation of the devil and his satellites, lasted for some time'.[94] Radbert's comments with hindsight are equally interesting: Adeodatus' attack on Lothar and Pascasius' repartee expresses the author's deep ambivalence about the second revolt and its aftermath. Apart from apostolic authority, the only justification for Wala's and his own involvement was that they had tried to mediate between father and son, in the spirit of Gregory IV and to the best of their ability.

Remarkably, Radbert's attempt to exonerate Lothar is his only direct reference to the emperor's public penance of 833. For the rest, Louis's atonement is only alluded to, and the same goes for the events that followed, in rapid succession: first there was Louis's reinstatement on 2 February 834 in St-Denis and Lothar's flight, then the latter's resistance and vicious attack on Chalon-sur-Saône during that summer, and finally his submission to his father in August at Blois.[95] Shortly thereafter, the eldest son left for Italy 'with those men who preferred to follow him'.[96] In the *Epitaphium*, this particular phase of the second rebellion is covered only obliquely, in a passionate speech by the narrator, Pascasius, interspersed with phrases and expressions taken from Job 12:13–25, where an exuberant Job bears witness to God's omnipotence. Wala entrusted everything to God's judgement, Pascasius claimed, lest something even more infamous should happen between Louis and Lothar. This greater infamy was parricide: the son might kill the father, or vice versa.[97] Both were groping in the dark and swaying like drunkards, and only God could put an end to this (Job 12:25). In this extraordinary peroration, biblical language is used effectively to allude to these troubling events, while divine agency is stressed throughout. I give just one example, in which I do not use any standard English version of the Bible, but translate the relevant scriptural passages with ninth-century political terminology in mind. Eventually, Arsenius eventually managed to bring about a reconciliation between father and son,

---

[94] *Epistolae selectae Leonis*, no. 46, *MGH Epp.* V = Karol. aevi III, p. 610; see De Jong, *Penitential State*, pp. 260–1.
[95] De Jong, 'Hraban Maur as Mediator'.
[96] *AB* s.a. 834, p. 26; transl. Nelson, *Annals of St Bertin*, p. 31.
[97] *EA* II, c. 20, p. 91: '... ne forte parricidium proveniret, fecit suo sancto consilio, augustus filius relicto patre rursus in solio imperii ... '.

... in a way that gave all to understand that the only almighty king would be He Himself *who brought counsellors to a foolish end, and judges to stupidity;*[98] *and He also loosens the belt of office of kings and girds their loins with a cord,*[99] which we clearly saw happen. But because neither of them completely sought God in a worthy way, their successes were turned into alternating ones, and the people was scourged, so all would understand that this was God Himself who *leads away infamous bishops and supplants magnates.*[100] In any case, never would there have been such great vexation and confusion[101] on all, had it not been because of their sins. *For the advice of truth-tellers was replaced,*[102] and the *wisdom of venerable elders was rejected.*[103]

In a veiled discourse infused with the language of the Book of Job, Radbert alludes to the actions that made up the failure of the second rebellion. Voluntary power-sharing between the two emperors as demanded in 830 by the rebels would have been acceptable, as would an old emperor graciously acknowledging his eldest son's seniority after a divine judgement, but not this episcopal imposition of a public penance on Louis in order to secure his deposition, and the ensuing violent conflict between father and son. In the *Epitaphium*, the details of this sorry episode are left unsaid, or at best hinted at. They were painful, not least because Wala's loyalty to Lothar was not entirely shared by his devoted Radbert. Whether he already had his doubts at the time of the events narrated, in 833–4, is a moot point. All we know is how he felt with hindsight, two decades later. He then depicted his Arsenius as a man who was on nobody's side but God's, and who decisively extricated himself from the political fracas, including the claims of both father and son. Of course, the great man was much in demand. 'With me as a witness', the narrator Pascasius relates, Louis and Lothar competed for Arsenius' favour and loyalty, but he would have none of either and took himself off to Italy.[104]

Despite Radbert's rueful conclusion that Wala's influence was continuously waning, he credits his master with having brought about

---

[98] Job 12:17–18.
[99] Which reflects on Louis's penance; the cord of the penitential/monastic garb versus the *cingulum militiae.*
[100] Job 12:19.   [101] Ps. 43:16; Isa. 19:28.   [102] Job 12:20.
[103] *EA* II, c. 20, p. 91 (Pascasius): '... ita ut daretur omnibus intelligi quod ipse sit rex solus omnipotens, *qui adducit consiliarios in stultum finem, et iudices in stuporem ; balteum quoque regum dissolvit, et praecingit fune renes eorum,* quod huic sane contigisse vidimus. Sed quia neutra pars eorum ex toto digne Deum requisierat, vicissim alternis successibus commutantur, et flagellatur populus, ut intelligant omnes quod ipse sit Deus, qui ad*ducit sacerdotes inglorios, et optimates supplantat.* Alioquin nunquam, nisi eorum ex culpis, tanta esset vexatio et confusio omnium. *Commuta*tum namque erat labium veracium, et ablata doctrina senum.' For further comments on Radbert's use of the Book of Job in the *Epitaphium,* see De Jong, 'Jeremiah, Job, Terence'.
[104] *EA* II, c. 20, p. 92.

Lothar's submission to Louis, and also with the fact 'that the father with all who wished to be with him would remain in charge of imperial rule'.[105] Whether Wala was indeed instrumental in all this is not the issue here. With hindsight, Radbert did not identify himself unreservedly with Lothar's cause. On the contrary, Wala's departure for Italy, surely as one of the magnates who followed the co-emperor, to whom they had been loyal throughout, is portrayed as a decision on Wala's part that was disconnected from Lothar, as is his gaining the abbacy of Bobbio – surely a benefice and office granted by Lothar. As we have seen with regard to Wala's exile, the fact that he made his own choices, rather than being forced into anything, is part and parcel of Radbert's defence of the great man's reputation, but his stress on Wala's very own decision to flee for Italy is something of a contradiction in terms. This is only partly resolved by comparing Arsenius with Columbanus, driven out of Francia by Queen Brunhild, as an able abbot who kept robbers far from Bobbio. By this stage, Lothar has disappeared from the narrative, only to make a brief re-entry through his wife Ermengard, who acted as a go-between for Corbie when Wala died. From Italy, she informed the monastery that its abbot had been carried to heaven by angels; she was also the one who established the commemorative prayer for Wala in the kingdom of Italy, beginning with her own convent of San Salvatore–Santa Giulia in Brescia.[106] Radbert's warm reference to Ermengard's staunch friendship for Corbie indicates that some long-term loyalties did survive the upheaval of two rebellions. Ermengard, daughter of Count Hugh of Tours, was Lothar's wife for a full thirty years, from 821 until her death in 851. No doubt she got to know Wala well in 822–5, when he was Lothar's second in command.

Some of the pain and grievances caused among his monks by Wala's choice of Bobbio over Corbie is expressed by Teofrastus' pointed remark that it would perhaps have been more monastic (*religiosus*) of Arsenius to remain in his own community.[107] In reply, Pascasius can do no better than to stress the similarity with Columbanus' actions. Both had to flee south, for their own safety. It would have been impossible for the great man to stay in his own monastery, Corbie, or flourish as an abbot there, Pascasius claims, answering Teofrastus' doubts, and perhaps also is own. Arsenius no longer belonged in this world where spurning secular honours and choosing religious life was viewed as

---

[105] *EA* II, c. 20, p. 91: ' ... fecit ut filius patri deferret, et cum suo exercitu inlęsus abiret; ac pater cum his qui cum eo vellent, in imperio remaneret ... '.
[106] *EA* III, c. 24, pp. 96–7.    [107] *EA* II, c. 21, p. 92.

faintheartedness.[108] Looking back over two decades, Radbert saw the emergence of a world in which a man of Wala's calibre would not have survived. From this perspective of emphatic hindsight, Radbert's wider view of religious, social and political order needs to be assessed. This is the topic of the two next and final chapters of this book.

---

[108] *EA* II, c. 21, p. 92 (Pascasius): '... inter quos, honores contemnere saeculi pro religione, ignavia putatur'.

# 8    For God, King and Country

## 1    Political Vocabulary in the *Epitaphium*: The Second Book

Whereas the *Epitaphium*'s first book is laced with the language of Terence, and punctuated by explicit or implicit references to classical authors, this is no longer the case in the second book. Biblical citations prevail, and instead of playful borrowing of Terence's idiom, Radbert speaks with the ponderous voice of Job.[1] Even though there is little explicit citation, however, his thorough reading of classical authors did also leave a clear imprint on the later second book. His terminology with regard to the world of politics is a case in point. To give just a few examples: the inner circle of Louis's counsellors is called the senate (*senatus*) and its members the *senatores*, while *patria* (fatherland) can refer not just to a region, but also to the entire Frankish polity. In this sense, *patria* is combined with *cives* ('citizens'). The latter functions as the equivalent of *populus*, either in the broader sense ('the Christian people'), or to refer to the free and active members of a political community, such as the constituency of an assembly. Another instance is Radbert's deliberate use of *officium* for 'office', as in 'let the emperor and king be bound to his office, and let him undertake nothing foreign to it.'[2] This is the preferred expression, in place of 'ministry' (*ministerium*), the term that dominated ninth-century discussions on the royal and episcopal office and its responsibilities. Other key concepts from the *Epitaphium*, such as *fides*, *respublica* or *honestas*, were central to contemporary Carolingian political discourse, but here too, the author's classical learning had some impact. As an avid reader of Cicero, Radbert must have encountered these three terms in the *De officiis*, and it seems likely that this

---

[1] See above, p. 175.
[2] *EA* II, c. 2, p. 62: 'Ut sit imperator et rex suo mancipatus officio, nec aliena gerat ... '. Even though I do not agree with his conclusions, a good overview of the use of *ministerium* is given by Busch, *Vom Amtswalten zum Königsdienst*, pp. 79–108.

particular work, at least in part, inspired his preference for *officium* over *ministerium*.

One pitfall that should be avoided is equating Radbert's classicising vocabulary with an attempt to emphasise the secularity of the political domain; another is the related assumption that the meaning of classical terms remained unchanged when read in a new and different context, and could therefore be relied upon to provide a terminology considered properly political because devoid of clerical or religious overtones. In Radbert's narrative, God is the ultimate judge of any human action or thought, in a way that entirely transcends modern distinctions between the religious and political spheres. What I here call his political vocabulary, for want of a better expression, refers to a polity perceived as an all-encompassing *ecclesia*, of which the *respublica*, together with the churches, was a constituent part, with a leadership that consisted of churchmen and laymen. This means that distinguishing between political and religious discourse is always problematic, even if it needs to be done in order to identify the distinctions made in ninth-century discourse. In the *Epitaphium*, as in other political thought formulated in the age of Louis the Pious, the entire leadership is answerable to God, but they have different 'ministries' or functions. Between these, there is a substantial overlap, so it makes little sense to view 'Church' and 'State' as opposites. Nonetheless, the distinction between the secular and ecclesiastical domains remains relevant, for this underpinned the model of binary cooperation and synergy.[3] Within the ninth-century discourse about the relation between these two spheres, Radbert's voice in the *Epitaphium*'s second book is more articulate than most.

This interconnectedness of religion and politics poses challenges to any translator of this text. Should *respublica* be rendered as 'state' or 'commonwealth', or as a more restricted notion, denoting a public domain consisting of landed wealth controlled by the king? What does Radbert mean when he refers to the 'republic of the churches'(*respublica ecclesiarum*)?[4] Even more difficult is the concept of *fides*, which is central to both books of the *Epitaphium*, but especially to the second, in which Wala's alleged infidelity to Louis the Pious is refuted at great length. In the process, Radbert makes the most of all the possible connotations of *fides*, and of the fact that the same word was used for loyalty to God, the emperor and all lords to whom others had been sworn.

---

[3] I have reflected on this in '*Sacrum palatium*', '*Ecclesia* and the Early Medieval Polity' and 'The State of the Church'; see now also Patzold, '"Einheit" versus "Fraktionierung"'.
[4] *EA* II, c. 6, p. 67: '... res publica et ecclesiarum pauperrima est ... '.

This chapter derives its title from these converging and at times conflicting loyalties that are at the very heart of the *Epitaphium*. The rest of
this section offers a preliminary exploration of the second book's political
vocabulary and its possible sources of inspiration, classical and otherwise.
Thereafter, Radbert's rich and complex discussion of *fides* and *respublica*
respectively are given a separate and more in-depth treatment, not least
because this sheds further light on two other important issues broached in
earlier chapters: namely, the dating of the second book and its rhetorical
strategies. I then address the issue of 'Radbert as Pseudo-Isidore'.
Recently, far-reaching claims about Radbert's role in these (in)famous
forgeries have been made, with the *Epitaphium* often put in the role of
crown witness. Although I have expressed my doubts about this elsewhere, I shall briefly revisit my arguments in the light of the present state
of the debate on Pseudo-Isidore, but only insofar as this illuminates
Radbert's political ideology.

## 2    *Officium, cives* and *senatores*

Radbert's great admiration for 'Tullius, the king of Latin eloquence'[5] also
extended to other works by Cicero. *Laelius de amiticia*, the *Tusculan
Disputations* and *Cato Maior de senectute* are cited in the later books
(V–XII) of his commentary on Matthew, written after he had stepped
down as abbot of Corbie.[6] Possibly he became acquainted with these texts
only at a later stage of his life, but this is not the case with *De officiis*, which
also appears in the first section of Radbert's exegesis on Matthew, which
he completed in 831.[7] His references to Cicero are reminiscent of his use
of Terence: expressions, phrases and partial sentences are integrated into
his main discourse, and literal citations are rare. Of course, explicit
citations are not the only indicator of an author's prior reading.
Although Radbert's commentary on Lamentations does not cite
Cicero's rhetorical work, it does offer an interpretation of the structure
of this biblical book 'according to the law of the orators'.[8] Furthermore,
there is the borrowing of certain expressions or turns of phrase, which can

---

[5] *VA*, c. 20, col. 1518C; see above, p. 73.

[6] *In Matthaeum* V, p. 462, ll. 90–3; p. 469, ll. 215–23 (*Cato Maior de senectute* 28 and 26);
IX, p. 932, ll. 4–5 (*Cato Maior de senectute* 2); VIII, p. 797, l. 19 (*Laelius de amicitia* 96; XII,
p. 1391, ll. 4047–8 (*Tusc. Disp.* I. 9); Paschasius Radbertus, *Expositio in Lamentationes* III,
p. 201, ll. 1722–3 (*Tusc. Disp.* I.52).

[7] On the two parts, see Beda Paulus, introduction to *In Matthaeum*, viii-ix. Cicero, *De officiis*
I.5 = *In Matthaeum* III, pp. 259–60, ll. 827–9 (*De officiis*, I.5); XI, p. 1149, ll. 5–14 (*De
officiis* III.1). On the gradual extension of Radbert's reading as apparent from his commentary on Matthew, see Ganz, *Corbie*, pp. 82–3.

[8] Paschasius Radbertus, *Expositio in Lamentationes* V, prologue, p. 310, ll. 4–6.

be difficult to spot, or the use of certain classical or late antique concepts. The latter, however, had attained new layers of meaning by the time Carolingian authors encountered them in their original sources. *Officium* is an interesting case in point. The modern English translation of Cicero's title *De officiis* is *On Duties*: it is about what those aspiring to a role in public life should strive for: namely, *honestas* (the honourable) and whatever was *utile* (useful, effective).[9] *Utilitas* could not thrive, however, without *honestas*, and the four virtues on which it was based: wisdom, justice, temperance, and magnanimity.[10] Another key characteristic of the man with *honestas* was that he had *fides*: that is, he was trustworthy and could be relied on.[11] Cicero's *officium* is the duty of whoever operates in the public arena, not an office bestowed by God on the ruler and/or his leadership. It is in this latter sense, as the equivalent of *ministerium*, that it figures most often in the *Epitaphium*: in this sense, the 'office' of the king occurs occasionally in episcopal admonitions from the 820s onwards,[12] although, compared with *ministerium*, this usage remains rare. Jonas of Orléans uses it once in his *Admonition* to Pippin of Aquitaine,[13] but 'ministry' abounds in his more extensive treatise on kingship, known as *De institutione regia*.[14]

What induced Radbert to opt for the royal *officium* where contemporaries mostly preferred *ministerium*? Was it because *officium* tended to be used more often in a monastic context, or in an ecclesiastical one, with reference to abbots and bishops? Perhaps; given that Radbert was familiar with two works entitled *De officiis*, however, Cicero's and Ambrose's, it seems likely that these did influence his terminology. The question then is, did Radbert read Cicero's *De officiis* through the prism of Ambrose's *De officiis*, which was also available at Corbie and cited in the pre-831 part of his commentary on Matthew?[15] This possibility cannot be discounted, of course, but the same holds true for the possibility of the direct influence

---

[9] Dyck, *Commentary*, pp. 491–4 on the overlap between *honestum* et *utile*; Dyck also points out (pp. 4–8 and 124–5) that *officium* in Cicero's day and age had a broader meaning than 'duty' as an ethically required act, and is best translated as 'appropriate action'.
[10] The cardinal virtues (*prudentia, iustitia, fortitudo* and *temperantia*) figure in *EA* II, c. 7, p. 68 as the opposite of Bernard's twisted values; see Mähl, *Quadriga virtutum*, and Kempshall, 'Virtues of Rhetoric', on their use by Alcuin.
[11] Powell (ed.), *Cicero the Philosopher*, pp. 1–35.
[12] *MGH Capit I*, no. 178, c. 8, p. 367: ' ... quia perfectio ministerii vestri maxime in huiuscemodi consistit officio. Erit enim precium ad omnes iudices huic officio puriores atque meliores.' *MGH Capit*. II, no. 196, c. 1, p. 48, l. 9: ' ... testimonia regio nomini et officio convenientia; see also the Synod of Aachen (836), *MGH Conc*. II, no. 56, c. 6, p. 717–8.
[13] Jonas, *Admonitio*, p. 194, l. 164: ' ... pro officio vobis a Deo commisso ... '.
[14] See especially Jonas, *De institutione regia*, c. 4 ('Quid sit proprie ministerium regis'), pp. 198–202.
[15] Paschasius Radbertus, *In Matthaeum* III, pp. 259–60, ll. 827–9.

of Cicero's *De officiis*. As far as I can see now, for Radbert's conceptualisation of the Frankish political order, Cicero's version may have been more attractive than Ambrose's. Cicero's moral agenda operates in a public domain, for the public interest. Ambrose, on the other hand, aims to replace Cicero's dominant moral model for public service, reorients the twin concepts of *honestas* and *utile* towards the duties of the church and its ministers, and turns away from the *respublica*. He is interested in the *ecclesia*, and in the duties of the clergy.[16] In the fourth century, the state was a given, but the church demanded greater dedication from its ministers. As Ambrose puts it, if there are rules for those who serve the state, how much more should we who serve the church exert ourselves to act in a way that pleases God?[17] The church is the all-important institution in Ambrose's *De officiis*, and it is perceived as distinct from the secular state.

By the time Radbert addressed the political realities and ideals of his day and age, Ambrose's vision of the church as an alternative to the state had become an alien concept. In the *Epitaphium*'s second book, Radbert has much to say about the *ecclesiae*, plural – the 'churches', by which he means monastic and episcopal religious communities – and very little about the *ecclesia*. By now, *ecclesia* (singular) had become a way of referring to the entire Frankish polity, which encompassed these 'churches' as well as a *respublica*, so this Carolingian model differed fundamentally from the one envisaged in Ambrose's *De officiis*. Furthermore, the church father's focus on clerical offices was not very helpful either in a polemical treatise intent on legitimising Wala's exploits. These had been accomplished very much in a public arena that took him away from his monastery, a point of criticism Radbert allows the monk Adeodatus to voice in no uncertain terms. If Arsenius was such a champion of humility, how could he speak up so forcefully and resolutely in the senate, in the presence of the emperors and his most prominent counsellors, prelates as well as senators?[18] The answer is that, although humble, Arsenius also availed himself of frank speech, for the good of the commonwealth.

For those who reflected on the Carolingian political order, Cicero's view on public men and their duties was better to think with than Ambrose's version, which saw the church as an alternative to the *saeculum*, and therefore focused on a code of conduct that served clerical authority. This meant reframing Cicero's core concepts of *honestas/utile*

---

[16] See the excellent introduction by Ivor Davidson to his edition and translation of Ambrose, *De officiis*, especially pp. 45–64.
[17] Ambrose, *De officiis*, I, c. 37.186, p. 226.    [18] *EA* II, c. 5, p. 65.

in terms of salvation and ascetism: something that was by no means foreign to the *Epitaphium*. And yet, the virtues with which Wala is credited, such as *gravitas*, constancy and moderation, and which together made up his reputation as a leading figure, were not clerical ones by definition; in fact, they were quite close to Cicero's eminently political and public *honestas*.[19] Whereas Ambrose is concerned with the collective standing of the clergy and the church, Radbert's notion of *honestas* refers to the public honour and integrity of the entire Carolingian polity, with the palace as its epicentre.[20] Transcending the divide between secular and clerical leadership, Wala embodied the shared virtues and ideals of the Carolingian governing elite: his withdrawal from the world had made him the most monastic of monks,[21] yet he managed to retain the charisma of a magnate and military leader.

Cicero was certainly not the only source for Radbert's political vocabulary; notions such as *respublica*, *senatores* or *cives* were present in postclassical texts as well, and did not disappear along with the West-Roman empire.[22] Radbert's access to those of Cicero's works present in Corbie's library, though, rhetorical and otherwise, exposed him to an unusually high dose of this terminology, which is apparent in the way he conceptualised his own political world. As we have seen with regard to *officium*, this entailed a shift in meaning. The plural *officia* retained its general sense of duties, including Ciceronian public duties,[23] and had also gained new connotations associated with monastic prayer. But in the singular, *officium* came to denote the functions or offices characteristic of the Carolingian political orders, notably the 'ministries' of the king or emperor and abbots,[24] but also, occasionally, those of bishops and counts.[25] The responsibilities of an *officium* could be transposed from the political sphere into other areas. When Radbert writes about Arsenius having assumed 'the duty (*officium*) of Jeremiah, with his steely visage and

---

[19] *EA* II, c. 13, p. 80.
[20] Turned into its opposite by Bernard: *EA* II, c. 7, p. 67: 'amisarius ille, qui cuncta reliquit honesta, in quibus est ordinatus'; *EA* II, c. 8, p. 68: 'eo quod esset theatrum, honestatis olim, palatium factum ... '; *EA* II, c. 9, p. 71: ' ... honesta omnia obscenis permiscuit, et religiosa vanis ... '.
[21] *EA* I, c. 9, p. 36: 'Erat enim monachus.'
[22] Another example of the use of classical terminology for contemporary political institutions is the *Polipticum* of Atto of Vercelli (885–961); Vignodelli, 'Politics, Prophecy and Satire'.
[23] *EA* II, c. 1, p. 62 (Pascasius).
[24] *EA* I, c. 15, p. 43; *EA* II, c. 15, p. 81: ' ... quia hinc mesti, quod suo privabatur officio ... ' (the abbatial office).
[25] *EA* II, c. 10: ' ... inter quos etiam Arsenius noster rapitur, pontificum tamen officio, iubente augusto, ac si cum honore ingenti, exsiliatur'. *EA* II, c. 2: 'Certum quippe quod secundum singulorum officia requirendus est ordo disciplinae, et status reipublicae.'

fierce determination',[26] a contemporary reader of the *Epitaphium* might also associate this with Jeremiah's 'office' or 'ministry' as a prophet in God's service.

Whereas *officium* had a broad range of connotations, Radbert's use of *senatus* and *senatores* is quite specific: these expressions refer to the inner circle of the ruler's advisers. Giving frank and constructive advice (*consilium*) was their core duty. Occasionally, one encounters the more common term 'counsellors' in the *Epitaphium* as well: as abbot of Corbie, Arsenius became counsellor of the entire empire (*consiliarius totius imperii*).[27] But the preferred terms in the *Epitaphium*'s second book are *senatores* and *consules*.[28] These were the men who should have 'watched out for the fatherland', but became robbers who sold the dignity of their office.[29] There is a tendency to distinguish the senators from the ecclesiastical counsellors (*praesules*): more often than not, the 'senate' is associated with the lay advisers, as when Radbert differentiates between the *praesules Christi* on the one hand and the *senatus totius imperii* on the other.[30] Interestingly, in his commentary on Matthew, Radbert presents Joseph of Arimathea's requesting the return of Jesus' body (Matt. 27:58) as the petition of an honourable man, which would be all the more successful because he was 'a senator of the Jews and a Decurion of the republic'.[31] The author's own experience helped to shape his exegesis: holding an office created familiarity with the powers that were, and would render one's petition more effective.

*Cives*, 'citizens', is a central concept in Cicero's work, and *De officiis* is no exception. The notion of Roman citizenship may well have impinged on Radbert's understanding of the term, which for him denotes the entire Christian Frankish polity. *Populus* is the more usual expression in Carolingian sources, and one encounters it in the *Epitaphium* as well: for example, in the context of God's punishment of the people.[32] More often, however, *populus* refers specifically to the faithful men (*fideles*) of the ruler, including the wider constituency of military men who participated in the dramatic assemblies of the 830s, and who were in danger of

---

[26] *EA* I, prologue, p. 20: ' ... interdum autem, ut prelibatum est, officio Heremie fronte adamantino acrius insistens fungebatur.'
[27] *EA* II, c. 15, p. 82. See also *EA* II, c. 21, p. 91: ' ... qui adducit consiliarios in stultum finem, et iudices in stuporem'.
[28] *EA* II, c. 5, p. 65.
[29] *EA* II, c. 6, p. 66 (Adeodatus): ' ... non consules, non provisores patriae fuerunt ... Unde non consules sed mercatores et venditores tantę dignitatis ... '.
[30] *EA* II, c. 9, p. 72 (Pascasius).
[31] *In Matthaeum* XII, p. 1405, ll. 4488–93: 'Qui cum esset ut ita dicam senator Iudeorum ac decurio rei publicae facilius impetrare potuit quod petebat.'
[32] *EA* II, c. 1, p. 61 (Pascasius).

perjury because of having had to take sides in the conflict between Lothar and Louis.[33] By contrast, *cives* tends to be a more inclusive notion, which often appears in combination with *patria*.[34] Like *populus, patria* is an expression carrying a more restricted meaning in Carolingian usage: namely, that of an often ethnically defined region or part of the realm. Saxony was Wala's *patria*, and the Saxons his countrymen.[35] Already in the first book, though, Radbert makes it clear that his conception of *patria* and *cives* owes much to his classical reading. As Pascasius, the narrator, asks the youngest member of his monastic confabulation:

> Or are you unaware, Adeodatus, that a good man puts the interests of his fatherland and countrymen before himself? You know also that Scipio and the other men of that era endured hatred and mortal dangers of all kinds in return for the great benefits to their fatherland and the abundant rewards of the virtues.[36]

This is not the celestial *patria* that looms so large in Radbert's commentary on Matthew, but an earthly one, just as the *cives* of the *Epitaphium* denote an earthly polity. It is likely, though, that some of the eschatological inflections would have resonated here as well.

## 3      What Wala Believed In

Together with *populus* in the inclusive sense of the term, *patria* and *cives* are an integral part of the series of mantra-like pronouncements on Wala's ideals and intentions. These deserve some extra scrutiny in this particular context. They provide an invaluable insight into Radbert's political vocabulary, and it is mostly the narrator Pascasius, Radbert's persona in the *Epitaphium*, who delivers these statements. Here is just one example out of at least twelve such proclamations, all of them in the second book:

> It is true, brother, that he beheld the innumerable and immense evils that were arising every day, but he could not foresee what was going to happen. These he wanted to counter and resist, as much as he had it in him, for the sake of fidelity to the realm and the king, for the love of his fatherland and people, for the religious

---

[33] *EA* II, c. 10, p. 76 (Pascasius).

[34] Ambrose, *De officiis* II, par 70, p. 122, l. 16. In Ambrose's *De officiis* the *cives* are hardly mentioned, but when they do occur, it is in connection with 'the fatherland': to restore citizens to their *patria* is a gesture of generosity (*liberalitas*).

[35] *EA* I, c. 13, p. 42 (Pascasius): 'Unde ut erat iste amore fervens circa Deum et circa religionem sanctam, circa propinquos sui generis et patriam ... '; *EA* I, c. 16, p. 46 (Pascasius).

[36] *EA* I, c. 1, p. 22: 'An ignoras, Adeodate, quod vir bonus non plus sibi quam patriae consulit et civibus? Scipionem quoque nosti, et reliquos eiusdem saeculi viros, qui pro maximis patriae ac plurimis virtutum beneficiis odia tulerunt, et varia mortis discrimina'.

life of the churches and the salvation of the inhabitants, all of which were more precious to him than his own life.[37]

Such declarations of 'what Wala stood for' are indebted to classical rhetoric and the stylistic device called *repetitio*. It is explained in the fourth book of *Ad Herennium*,[38] which was in Corbie's library, but Radbert could also have encountered a rather splendid example in his main literary model, Ambrose's funeral oration for his brother Satyrus.[39] In these formulaic pronouncements, Radbert integrates a more classical repertoire with the Carolingian administrative terminology of capitularies, conciliar acts and royal donation charters,[40] in which the *status* or *stabilitas* of the realm was a fixture: Wala acted *pro statu regni, pro salute populi, pro stabilitate ecclesiarum*.[41] These are not lofty yet impractical goals that would appeal only to the monks of Corbie, but the core values of the Carolingian leadership in its entirety. Their repetition is all the more effective because they combine authoritative expressions from different literary traditions, but are also anchored in a contemporary political discourse. On the one hand, Radbert was clearly inspired by his reading of the classics: in Cicero's work, the well-being of the citizens (*salus civium*) is a recurrent concern, along with its equivalent, the *salus populi*. On the other hand, for the Carolingians *salus* also meant salvation, and the fact that the *cives* are at times paired with the *ecclesiae*, the religious communities who ensured salvation by their prayer, should be taken into account. In another of these repetitions of Wala's ideals, we find that he was *pro salute populi et salvatione patriae*, which associates earthly well-being with heavenly salvation.[42]

Most of these refrains hinge on the repetition of the word *pro*, and connect Wala's love (*amor/dilectio*) with the objects thereof: his love for

---

[37] *EA* II, c. 8, p. 68 (Pascasius): 'Verum, frater, quia videbat mala quae quotidie surgebant innumera et immensa, sed prenoscere non valuit quae futura erant. Quibus, quantum ex se fuit, obviare voluit, et resistere pro fide regni et regis, pro amore patriae ac populi, pro religione ecclesiarum et salute civium, quę omnia cariora illi erant, quam sua vita'. Other examples: *EA* II, c. 5, p. 66 (2x); c. 8, pp. 69 and 70; c. 9, pp. 71 and 72; c. 10, pp. 73, 75, 76; c. 10, p. 78; c. 14, p. 81 (2x). For further discussion, see De Jong, 'For God, King and Country'.

[38] *Ad Herennium* IV, xiii, pp. 274–6; Paris, BnF lat. 7714; Ganz, *Corbie*, pp. 51, 79, 151; Bisschoff, *Katalog* III, p. 133.

[39] Ambrose, *De excessu fratris* II, c. 7, p. 255: 'Deforme est enim eos, qui *pro* fide, *pro* religione, *pro* patria, *pro* aequitate iudicii atque intentione virtutis obvium morti debeant pectus offerre ... '.

[40] On these documents, see now Davis, *Charlemagne's Practice of Empire*.

[41] De Jong, 'For God, King and Country', pp. 109–11.

[42] *EA* II, c. 11, p. 78 (Pascasius): ' ... pro fide, pro vita caesaris, pro filiis et imperio, pro salute populi et salvatione patriae, pro iustitia et legibus augustorum, pro stabilitate et unitate regni ... '.

the fatherland and the people (*patria et populus*), the realm and the king (*regnum et rex*) and the churches (*ecclesiae*).[43] The other key sentiment is fidelity (*fides*): to the realm and the king, to Christ and to the emperor.[44] Although *fides imperatoris* occurs only once, in the discussion of the rebellion of 830 and Wala's ensuing exile it is underlined that he acted 'out of fidelity, for the life of Caesar, for the sons and the empire'. Also frequently mentioned are the permanence/stability (*status/stabilitas*) of both the kingdom/empire[45] and the *salus* (prosperity/salvation) of the *populus, cives, patria* or *ecclesiae*.[46] As the second book proceeds, however, there are also inversions, where *contra* becomes the key proposition; given the more general background of the positive pronouncements, these are all the more striking. Whereas Wala fought against evil, Louis acted against all the moral imperatives shared by the author and the readers he sought to persuade:

But lest the adversary of evil should prevail with his counsel *against* the plots of wicked men, *against* the shameless deeds of the unjust, and indeed *against* Augustus himself, who fought *against* the sons, *against* imperial rule (*imperium*), *against* the fatherland, *against* the salvation of the people, as became clear every day – by might, honours, scheming, by whatever method possible [and] by a multitude of soldiers – he was banished, thrown out, exiled, and stuck away, as you say, in the highest cave; so that he would not be able to give any salutary counsel anymore to any mortal being, by which he could have prevented evil purposes.[47]

Be it negatively or positively, the repetitive hammering home of Wala's principles appeals to the values of Radbert's contemporaries, the members of the Carolingian elite. It provides a web of social signs aimed at catching the readers, sufficiently general to serve as a repertoire for identification (who could be against love or fidelity?) but specific enough

---

[43] *EA* II, c. 5, p. 66; c. 8, p. 68 (pro dilectione/amore patriae et populi).
[44] *EA* II c. 5, p. 77 ('ab amore ecclesiarum et fide imperatoris'); c. 8, p. 68; c. 9, p. 71 ('pro fide regni et regis').
[45] *EA* II, c. 5, p. 68: 'Propter quae nunquam, quia futura praeviderat, dubitavit sententiam pro statu regni, pro salute populi, pro stabilitate ecclesiarum, et religione pacis dignam dicere etsi quibuslibet displicuisset'; c. 8, p. 68; c. 9, p. 71; c. 11, p. 78; c. 15, p. 82 (Teofrastus).
[46] *EA* II, c. 5, p. 68; c. 14, p. 81: 'Ostendebatur coram auctoritas, et legebatur, summi pontificis, pro pace, pro reconciliatione patris et filiorum, principum et seniorum, pro statu ecclesiarum, pro adunatione populi et salvatione totius imperii.'
[47] *EA* II, c. 10, p. 77 (Adeodatus): 'Sed ne prevaleret consilio *contra* insidias malignantium oppugnator malorum, *contra* improbitates iniquorum, immo *contra* ipsumque augustum, qui *contra* filios, *contra* imperium, *contra* patriam, *contra* salutem populi, ut manifestum est quotidie potestate, honoribus, ingenio, arte qua poterat, armis, multitudine militum decertabat; expellitur, deicitur, exsilio mancipatur, religatur, ut asseris, altissima in specu; ne ulli mortalium iam ultra consilium salutis porrigere posset, quod voluntati pessimę obviare posset.'

to remind his select audience of their own duties and commitments amidst the political turbulence they were living through.

## 4    *Fides*

*Fides* is such a central concept in the *Epitaphium* that it deserves separate consideration. The key accusation against which Radbert defended his abbot was that Wala had been unfaithful to his emperor, Louis the Pious. Although occasionally the word *infidelitas* is used, the overwhelming number of references are to the term *fides*. Had Wala lived up to this obligation, or had he been found wanting? That was the central question. In Carolingian political and religious discourse, *fides* looms large, with a wide range of connotations. On the one hand, the legacy of classical and patristic Latin texts continued to shape ninth-century understandings of this notion. At one end of the spectrum, there was *fides* in the sense of trust and good faith: a fundamental principle of Roman forensic and commercial law that had been extended to social obligations, such as the relations between clients and patrons. On the other hand, there was the Christian version of *fides* deployed in the Vulgate and by the church fathers: *fides* as belief and trust in Christ and the teachings of the Christian church.[48] Yet the *patres* also retained *fides* in its traditional legal meaning. As Ambrose concludes, commenting on the Prophet Elisha striking the Syrian army with blindness: 'So, it is quite clear that good faith *and* justice need to be respected even in war, and there can be nothing seemly about any situation in which good faith is violated.[49] For fourth-century Christian authors, the social implications of *fides* as 'good faith' helped to articulate relations of trust and belief in the religious sphere, and vice versa; something happened in the Carolingian world, in which royal charters could be addressed to *fideles dei et nostri/imperatoris*.[50]

Historians have long seen *fides* as an essentially Germanic feature of what used to be called the barbarian successor kingdoms, on the assumption that loyalty to one's lord entirely replaced the apparatus of the Roman state. It has become increasingly clear, however, that early medieval interpretations of *fides* and its obligations were in fact shaped by late Roman traditions, and also that the sudden transition from Roman statehood to a stateless post-Roman West is mostly a modern projection.[51] On the basis of this treacherous historiographical legacy,

[48] Flierman, *Saxon Identities*, pp. 100–02.
[49] Ambrose, *De officiis* I, c. 29, par. 140, pp. 198–9: 'Liquet igitur etiam in bello fidem et iustitiam servari oportere nec illud decorum esse posse si violetur fides.'
[50] Esders, '"Faithful Believers"'; Flierman, *Saxon Identities*, p. 103.
[51] Esders, '"Faithful Believers"' provides the best access to these issues; see also the volumes produced by the European Science programme on the Transformation of the

translating the *Epitaphium*'s frequent usage of *fides* into English poses some problems. Unlike the German, which distinguishes between 'Glaube' (belief) and 'Treue' (fidelity), the English 'faith' covers both aspects: the 'faithful' denotes those who believe in God as well as the emperor's faithful men (*fideles*). All the same, nowadays 'faith' tends to be associated with religious belief, while terms such as 'fidelity' or 'loyalty' are more often used in a secular context, especially with regard to social bonds or ties of mutual dependence. The challenge of translating the *Epitaphium* lies in the close connection forged in the text between *fides* in the divine and the human spheres: Radbert makes the most of the fact that there is only one word for both (namely, *fides*), while also making it clear that these are by no means identical categories. Expressing this in English by translating *fides Christi* as 'faith in Christ' and *fides regis* as 'fidelity to the king' is not a satisfactory option, but neither is rendering almost all instances of *fides* as 'faith', even though its modern meaning covers both religious and non-religious senses, and *fides regis* could be rendered as 'keeping faith with the king'. This dilemma presents itself early on in the first book, where Radbert reflects at length on the nature of *fides*. With St Paul's Letter to the Romans as his point of departure, he explores the limits of fidelity to one's earthly lord, and of oaths sworn for this purpose, and thereby prepares the ground for what would become the main theme of the second book: Wala's fidelity towards his emperor had been of a much higher level than the loyalty dictated by human oaths, for he had obeyed God's commands and saved Louis's life. Elaborating on St Paul's maxim that the faith (*fides*) of Christians is brought to fruition by love (*dilectio*) (Gal. 5:6), Radbert warns that *fides* should never mean following a terrestrial lord's will if it goes against God's precepts:

Otherwise, if faith required doing anything asked of you, and you were obliged to carry out whatever you had promised, then Herod and his henchmen would be innocent of any crime, since he was bound by an oath.[52] For this reason, you must first take care not to make a profession of faith rashly. Then, if you have sworn an oath, deviate from it sooner than proceed on to greater evils. For we have no obligation, says the Apostle, 'but to love one another'.[53] Let each person, therefore, discharge the obligations required of him, and in discharging them let him owe the faith that works through love. For otherwise faith is not faith, because it does not come from the love for God and one's neighbor, but is rather an earthly and bestial oath and a snare of the devil. No one, therefore, keeps his faith well in cases where there is disdain for God and disregard for the salvation of one's neighbour in the next life.[54]

Roman World; see Wood, 'Report'; Airlie, Pohl & Reimitz (eds.), *Staat im Frühmittelalter*; Pohl and Wieser (eds.), *Frühmittelalterliche Staat*.
[52] Matt. 14:6–11.    [53] Rom. 13:8.
[54] *EA* I, c. 3, pp. 24–5 (Pascasius): 'Alioquin Herodes ille, eiusque complices, quia iuramento erat astrictus, alieni a crimine, si fides praescriberet quodcunque velle, et quod

In the course of the narrative of the rebellions, an ever closer link is created between Wala's *fides Christi* and his equally unwavering fidelity towards Louis and his sons. This is not just a matter of the latter being infused with religious connotations; conversely, connotations derived from earthly loyalty help to shape the notion of human commitment to God or Christ. When Wala, reluctant to intervene in the dismal situation in the palace in 830, was accused of 'not being faithful to God and His Holy Church', this resembles the fidelity which great men owed their lords and rulers.[55]

In the *Epitaphium*'s first book, *fides* also refers to the faith and trust placed by the bereaved monks in their much-maligned abbot. As the young monk Adeodatus offers, displaying his school learning: did you know Cato's dictum, 'little trust is to be assigned to what many are saying'? After all, even the apostles had doubted when they encountered the risen Christ, lest their faith should be reckless.[56] The argument still revolves around *fides*, but the focus is similar to that of Radbert's treatise 'On Faith, Hope and Charity' (*De fide, spe et caritate*): namely, that men should have trust in an invisible God: 'faith is the substance of things to be hoped for, the evidence of things that are not seen' (Heb. 11:1).[57] It is our lack of faith (*infidelitas*) which has caused the saints to issue warnings by means of miracles, the monk Teofrastus warns at the beginning of the second book. As St Paul wrote (1 Cor. 14:22), such signs are not given to the faithful, but to the faithless who stumble in the dark, waiting for the true light that is Christ.[58]

Towards the very end of the second book, when Radbert embarks on the narrative of Wala's death, he returns to this theme of *fides* as trust and belief in a merciful God: death should not be lamented, for it offers hope of resurrection and a better life.[59] And yet, for the most part, the second book is about Arsenius' alleged infidelity to his emperor. As Radbert remarks scathingly, this consisted of nothing less than saving Louis

---

promiseris adimplendum. Unde prius cavendum, ne quid fide pollicearis incautus: deinde si voveris, ne ad peiora provenias declina. Nihil enim debeamus, ait apostolus, nisi ut invicem diligamus. Idcirco quisque quod debet solvendo adimpleat, et implendo debeat, fidem videlicet, quae per dilectionem operatur. Alias autem, fides non est fides, quia non est dilectione Dei et proximi, sed terrena obiuratio animalis et diabolica devinctio. Nemo igitur bene servat fidem, ubi contemnitur Deus, et negligitur futurae vitae proximi salus.'

[55] *EA* II, c. 8, p. 70: ' ... quod non esset Deo fidelis et sanctae ipsius ecclesiae ... '. A fundamental discussion of Carolingian oaths, with references to older literature, is offered by Esders, '"Faithful Believers"'.

[56] *EA* I, c. 7, p. 31; *Disticha Catonis*, I, 13.2, p. 46: ... *rara fides ideo est, qui multi multa locuntur*; see also II, 20.2, p. 122.

[57] Paschasius Radbertus, *De fide, spe et caritate* I, c. 3, pp. 14–16.    [58] *EA* II, c. 1, p. 62.

[59] *EA* II, c. 22, p. 93.

from Bernard's evil designs and restoring him to the throne at Compiègne in 830, while 'all the people faithfully submitted to him with even greater fidelity (if this were possible) than before'.[60] Once the first revolt had run its course, those who had taken part, and done so only for the sake of fidelity (*pro fide*), were rewarded by rejection and exile. With regard to the second revolt of 833, *fides* once more divided the good from the bad, but here Wala's fidelity is less of an issue. Already discredited, his interventions on and around the Field of Lies seem to have been undertaken on his own initiative – the reflex of an old courtier who could not shake the habit of serving his ruler by his good faith and counsel (*fides et consilium*).[61] Furthermore, Radbert is eager to convey that Arsenius was his own man, and not blindly following Lothar. With regard to 833 and its aftermath, the obedient loyalty of Lothar and his rebellious brothers to their father takes centre stage. This point is driven home in the so-called *querela* between Louis and his sons, a judicial altercation already discussed in the previous chapter.[62] It is an 'invented' verbal exchange, which nonetheless offers a vivid insight into the political vocabulary and values of the 850s, when competing kings vied for each other's *vasalli* (vassals). Radbert has the sons defend themselves against the accusation that they had not only broken their own oath of allegiance to their father, but had also persuaded Louis's vassals to follow suit: this is the culmination of a series of brief and blunt allegations on Louis's part. Eloquently, Honorius/Lothar voices the sense of rejection of those who had been ousted from the inner circle of the palace in 830 and the years thereafter. Radbert also turns Lothar into the guardian of the traditional ideals of *fides*, and of the high moral ground his father had undermined:

And then, finally; 'You have,' he [Louis] says, 'also received our vassals without just cause and you have retained them.'
  Honorius: 'Your Blessedness should know it is not as it seems; in fact, when they themselves had been dispersed or been put to flight or detained in custody or exile, they took refuge with us and with that blessed prelate [Pope Gregory IV], so that he would intercede with Your Most Serene Clemency for them, lest those who stood up for fidelity to you and to justice should be unjustly condemned [and] lest the deceit and treachery of the most wicked should prevail. This I have always heard in your sacred council, and in the senate of most illustrious men, this I have always observed in your deeds, this I have learned from you, this we read in the deeds of the ancients: that strong and most pre-eminent and well-deserving men should be honoured and covered in glorious fame, rather than driven away: they who with foresight prevented the onslaught and intrigues of evil men, who by

---

[60] *EA* II, c. 10, p. 73: '... et subditur ei omnis populus in fide amplius fidelis, si posset fieri, quam prius.'
[61] *EA* II, c. 15, p. 82.  [62] See above, pp. 169–70.

fidelity, who by constancy, who by greatness of mind and counsel also resisted the effronteries of the plotters, that is, of those men who by their fickleness and perniciousness have, with complete unscrupulousness, defiled your imperial rule. Those who uncovered them and put them to flight should be honoured and glorified, rather than be accused by most pestilent men, for they themselves have been brought up from early on in your discipline, have been taught by your counsel, raised to high rank by your authority; and, made illustrious by benefices (*honores*), they have always been the first and most distinguished of the palace. Therefore we have deemed it right to lead them back to your most merciful pity and to exhibit them to your gaze: and thus we ought not to give offence if we restore and reconcile to your advantage those whom the treachery of the seditious has ruined.'[63]

The very values Louis taught his eldest son are thrown back in his face, including the ruler's obligation to honour and reward those who remained faithful to him. It was the emperor's own lack of faith and unreliability vis-à-vis his own inner circle in 830, and Wala in particular, that had landed the emperor into the deep trouble of the next revolt. Lothar had done nothing but attempt to rescue his father from his predicament, offering him papal mediation and a renewal of the fidelity of those who had expressed this earlier by rebellion. Louis's faithful men had done something unheard of: they rose up against the ruler *on his behalf*.[64] This, in a nutshell, is Radbert's view of the first rebellion.

---

[63] *EA* II, c. 17, p. 87 (Pascasius): 'Tunc ad ultimum: "Vassallos quoque, inquit, nostros indebite recepisti, et eos tecum retines." Honorius: "Non itaque, sciat beatitudo vestra, ita est, sed cum essent et ipsi dispersi, fugati, aut in custodiis et exsiliis detenti, fecerunt ad nos, et ad istum beatum antistitem confugium, quatinus pro illis apud vestram serenissimam clementiam intercedat, ne iniuste damnentur, qui pro fide vestra et iustitia exstiterunt, ne fraus praevaleret et dolus scelestissimorum. Hoc semper audivi in vestro sacro concilio, et in clarissimorum senatu virorum, hoc semper in vestris recognovi factis, hoc a vobis audivi, hoc legimus in gestis antiquorum, fortes viros et clarissimos, ac bene meritos honorari magis debere, et gloria illustrari quam depelli; qui pravorum hominum impetus et conatus provide represserunt; qui auctoritate, qui fide, qui constantia, qui magnitudine animi et consiliis insidiantium audaciae restiterunt: eorum scilicet hominum, qui levitate sua et pernitiae vestrum cum omni improbitate foedaverunt imperium. Quos quia isti detexerunt et fugarunt, honorandi essent et glorificandi potius quam a pestilentissimis viris criminandi, quia et ipsi primum vestris sunt enutriti disciplinis, vestrisque edocti consiliis, vestra sublimati dignitate, et inlustrati honoribus, semper habiti sunt primi et eximii palatii. Unde censuimus eos reducere ad vestram misericordissimam pietatem, vestrisque representare aspectibus: et ideo non debemus offensam contrahere, si quos fraus factiosorum perdidit, vestris restituimus et reconciliamur profectibus."'

[64] *EA* II, c. 9, p. 73 (Adeodatus): 'A saeculo huiusmodi res gesta, quantum video, non legitur, ut pro principe contra principem ... '.

5     ***Respublica* and the Churches**

The notion of *respublica* is absent from the *Epitaphium*'s first book, composed in the years directly after Wala's death in 836. It surfaces at the very
beginning of the second book, in a narrative that opens with the intrepid
Arsenius addressing the emperor and his inner circle of magnates and
churchmen on the moral dangers of using ecclesiastical wealth for the
military needs of the realm. Given the general chronology of the
*Epitaphium*, the setting seems to be the palace in Aachen during the winter
of 828/9, where Louis and Lothar had gathered with their inner circle
(*senatores et proceres terrae*) to discuss the many disasters that had recently
hit the realm. From Radbert's account it transpires that Wala attended
a series of meetings at the palace in the course of that winter.
The participants resolved to find out how God had been offended and
might be placated (*placitum*), and to report on this 'at the next assembly'.
This was not one of the big reform synods that met in Paris and other
places across the realm in June 829, but another, smaller gathering.
Arsenius rose to the occasion: armed with a short document (*schedula*)
by way of an aide-memoire for himself, he returned to the court. He
explained, like another Jeremiah, 'in the presence of the emperor and of
the leaders of all the churches and the senators', why divine punishment
was inflicted on the realm: the boundaries between the different orders
and their spheres of competence had become blurred, and rulers had
availed themselves of the landed wealth of 'the churches' in order to
reward their military men.[65]
    In this context, *respublica* is presented by Radbert as one of the two
major spheres within the *ecclesia* that should have remained distinct, but
which had recently become disordered because of a blurring of boundaries. It is the domain of the king and his lay magnates, and is defined not
in contradistinction to 'the Church,' but as connected with, yet different
from the 'churches' plural (*ecclesiae*). The *ecclesia Christi*, which encom-
passes all domains and orders, is occasionally mentioned in the second
book,[66] but the great majority of Radbert's well over forty uses of the word
refer to 'the churches': religious communities, monastic and otherwise,
with landed resources that were being put to military use, at the service of
the *respublica*. Protecting the landed wealth of 'the churches' is one of
Radbert's central concerns in his second book, so it is no coincidence that
it is precisely in this context that he articulates the nature of the Frankish

---

[65] *EA* II, c. 1, p. 61 (Pascasius).
[66] Notably in *EA* II, c. 2, p. 62 (Pascasius); *EA* II, c. 8, p. 68 (Pascasius); *EA* II, c. 8, p. 70
    (Pascasius); *EA* II, c. 10, p. 76 (Adeodatus); *EA* II, c. 16, p. 85 (Teofrastus); *EA* II, c. 17,
    p. 86 (Pascasius); *EA* II, c. 17, p. 88 (Pascasius).

polity. The polity and the orders within it constituted an *ecclesia* writ large, with ecclesiastical and secular leadership collaborating as distinct entities. The king both straddled and transcended this divide. It was his duty (*ministerium*) to protect and further God's cult, but in no way should he interfere directly with what went on 'inside' (*intus*) – that is, the way in which divine worship operated – nor with the landed property that enabled this operation. In this balancing act, says Radbert, citing Solomon (Wisd. 6:26), rests the stability of the entire kingdom. If the king involves himself more than necessary in divine affairs, this stability will be disturbed. In order to get this message across, Radbert makes liberal use of direct speech:

'By the way,' he [Arsenius] asked, 'do you know the orders that make up the church of Christ? For it is beyond doubt that the order of religious life (*ordo disciplinae*) and the state of the realm (*status respublicae*) should be investigated according to the responsibilities (*officia*) of each. Hence, we must first consider what is internal and divine, and then what is external and human, because without doubt the state of the church as a whole is governed through these two orders. So let the emperor and king be bound to his office, and let him undertake nothing foreign to it, but rather those things that fall within the sphere of his responsibilities; and let him not neglect these things, because the Lord will call him to account for all of this. Let the bishop, however, and the ministers of the churches have particular responsibility for what belongs to God. Let the king, moreover, appoint such rulers in the realm as the Lord in his Law commands be diligently sought out, men in whom and for whom he may rest secure because he knows them to be righteous and suited to rule over the holy people of God, not those who support him for their own gain, but who hate avarice and love God and righteousness, whose task it is, in short, always to establish what is righteous and just and to correct what has become corrupted. For otherwise, O king, if you do not preserve what has been ordained, then worse torment awaits you,[67] and, through you, all will meet a single death, if God turns away. You must see to it, therefore, that you neglect nothing, because on you alone, according to Solomon, rests the stability of the whole kingdom.[68] But do not involve yourself in divine affairs more than is fitting.[69]

---

[67] Wisd. 6:9: 'Fortioribus autem fortior instat cruciatio.'

[68] Wisd. 6:26: 'Multitudo autem sapientium sanitas est orbis terrarum, et rex sapiens populi stabilimentum est.'

[69] *EA* II, c. 2, p. 62 (Pascasius): 'Interea nostis, inquit, quibus ordinibus Christi constat ecclesia? Certum quippe quod singulorum officia requirendus est ordo disciplinę et status reipublicę. Unde primum considerari oportet intus divina, tum exterius humana, quia procul dubio his duobus totius ecclesiae status administratur ordinibus: ut sit imperator et rex suo mancipatus officio, nec aliena gerat, sed ea quae sui iuris competunt propria, neque pretermittat ea, quia pro his omnibus adducet eum Dominus in iudicio: episcopus vero et ministri ecclesiarum, specialius quae Dei sunt, agant. Deinde rex rectores in regno tales constituat, quales eos Dominus diligenter in lege perquirere iubet, et in quibus rex et pro quibus securus maneat, quos utique probos ad regendum populum sanctum Dei et idoneos cognoscat, non secundum proprios libitus qui ei faveant, sed qui avaritiam

Arsenius' admonition reveals a world in which monasteries such as Corbie put up a fight against a ruler who generously bestowed ecclesiastical offices and wealth on others as they pleased, despite the fact that such estates (*res*) had been consecrated to God and his churches, for the benefit of his poor and his servants. Was this indeed what Wala argued in the winter of 828/9? Or is Radbert using his master as a mouthpiece to address a contentious issue that arose only in the 840s and 850s?[70] In 823, Agobard of Lyon seems to have argued for earlier origins for such criticism, for (allegedly) the archbishop called it a serious sin for property dedicated to churches to end up in the hands of laymen, including those of the king.[71] I have my doubts about this interpretation. Indeed, Agobard was fiercely opposed to laymen helping themselves to gifts offered to the altar, yet he emphatically exculpated Louis, claiming that it was not the lord emperor, who 'had done this', but his predecessors.[72] Even if we assume that Agobard was being polite, it does not make him an ideal witness for Louis's alleged despoiling of church property. More importantly, however, during Louis's reign, kings and emperors were not ranked as *laicales*, the expression used by Agobard. His oft-cited remarks should therefore be read as a statement about the ruler's responsibility to prevent lay usurpation of 'sacred wealth' (*res sacras*). In this duty, Agobard maintained, Louis had not failed. To turn the emperor into a layman would go against all thinking current in the 820s and even 830. Surely churchmen and laymen had their separate competencies, but as the guarantor of this distinction, the ruler transcended these various orders.

Despite Louis's generally positive reputation as a protector of church property, Radbert has Arsenius fulminate against the emperor for granting the *honores* of the churches (that is, offices and their land and income) to his followers, and of pillaging goods that had been given to God. In the case of Arsenius' speeches, there is every reason to suppose that Wala was

oderint, et Deum ac iustitiam diligent, cuius profecto officium est, semper quae recta et iusta sunt disponere, et quae depravata corrigere. Alioquin tu, rex, nisi servaveris quod preceptum est, fortior tibi cruciatus instat, et omnibus in te, si avertatur Deus, unus interitus. Ideo providendum nihil negligas: quia in te uno, secundum Salomonem totius stabilimentum est regni; in divinis autem ne ultra te ingeras quam expedit.' See De Jong, 'The Two Republics'.

[70] Breternitz, 'Ludwig der Fromme'; De Jong, 'Paschasius Radbertus and Pseudo-Isidore', pp. 158–63; 'Familiarity Lost'; differently, Esders & Patzold, 'From Justinian to Louis', pp. 389–403.

[71] Esders and Patzold, 'From Justinian to Louis', p. 401; also, Ganz, 'Ideology of Sharing', pp. 25–7.

[72] Agobard, *De dispensatione*, c. 4, p. 123: 'Sed quoniam quod de sacris rebus in laicales usus inlicite translatis dicimus, non fecit iste dominus imperator, sed precessores eius ...'. See Breternitz, 'Ludwig der Fromme', pp. 198–200.

a prominent presence during the deliberations of the winter of 828/9, and he may well have prepared a document (*schedula*) as a reminder to himself, as Radbert claims. The literary rendering of Wala's addresses themselves, however, set in direct speech, was the domain of *inventio*, a rhetorical practice in which Radbert was thoroughly versed.[73] Veracity was not a matter of faithfully recording his master's precise words, but of remaining true to the great man's ideas and principles, with the full liberty, and even the duty, to embellish and expand. In such texts it is only to be expected that contemporary concerns help to shape the contents, and the various instances of this in the *Epitaphium*'s second book are no exception. They are summarised in the bitter conclusion drawn by the outspoken monk Teofrastus: 'I do not know which one of our rulers might be saved, for whom nothing is quite as delightful as the robbing of churches, and nothing quite so gratifying, as it has been written: Stolen waters are sweeter, and hidden bread is more pleasant.'[74]

These barbed remarks fit the fierce debates that raged in the early 840s in the kingdom of Charles the Bald about the integrity of ecclesiastical property in general and monastic wealth in particular; the Council of Ver (844) is the most radical case in point, but there are others as well. As Franz Felten has shown, it was in the 840s, and not before, that the phenomenon of the lay abbot was first articulated and then attacked.[75] As Felten also saw clearly, Arsenius' speeches, in which he berates the emperor for generously handing out the *honores ecclesiarum* to his followers, relate to the 850s, when the second book was written, and the same holds true for Radbert's army of clerics at the palace, generally called *capellani*, who were not subject to the canonical authority of a bishop, nor to the regular discipline of an abbot.[76] Such hybrid figures had been a presence at the court of Charlemagne and Louis, but by the time the former's grandson Charles ruled, they had started to give offence.

This is only one example of Radbert explaining the evils of the present by identifying their origins in a sinful past. From the outset, hindsight is the perspective of the second book. This hodiecentric perspective is reinforced in all possible ways, including by the introduction of a new interlocutor, Teofrastus. As his fellow monk Adeodatus claims, the newcomer's bold comments ('all rulers are robbers') would once have put the confabulating monks at risk, because he is unable to restrain his speech.

---

[73] See above, pp. 73–6.

[74] *EA* II, c. 2, p. 63: ' . . . nescio principium nostrorum quis salvus esse possit, quibus nihil tam dulcia sint, quam predia ecclesiarum, nihilque tam suavia, sicut scriptum est: *Panis absconditus suavior est, et aquę furtive dulciores*' (Prov. 9:17).

[75] Felten, 'Laienäbte', pp. 408–16.    [76] Felten, *Äbte und Laienäbte*, pp. 294–5.

This is then Teofrastus' cue to present himself as a deeply serious discussant (no more jesting!) who is ready to speak openly about the evils of the present, 'so that they might serve as a warning for correction, if not for us, then at least for future generations'. This then leads up to Arsenius speaking truth to power like a true Jeremiah. Arsenius' addresses are phrased as a retrospective prophecy, voicing the author's own concerns and warnings. Radbert constantly moves back and forth between then and now: as he explains, already in Wala's time many monasteries were held as benefices by laymen, but now those ruled by their own (monastic) order are rare.[77] What matters is Radbert's perception of present abuses and their past origins, and his efforts to convince his audience that when Arsenius had been alive, he had fought these to the hilt.

The very terminology of Arsenius' speeches indicates a contemporary context. Why are there so many references to 'the king' (*rex*) in a text that otherwise tends to refer to Louis the Pious as *Augustus* or *Caesar*? Arsenius points his accusing finger at 'our king' who 'has helped himself to many of the resources of churches for his own needs and those of his men'[78] against the well-known anathemas of the holy fathers. Is it a coincidence that in this most direct attack he addresses a *rex*, rather than an emperor? Certainly Louis was both an emperor and a king, but Arsenius' admonitions suggest that Radbert deliberately is mentioning both roles, in order to include the rulers of his own day and age. 'Let the emperor and king be bound to his office' (*ut sit imperator et rex suo mancipatus officio*) can be taken as a more general statement that also addressed the ruler with whom Radbert himself had to deal: Charles the Bald.

The frequency of *rex* in this early part of the second book does suggest that Radbert had not just Louis in his sights, but also his son Charles. Surely he is referring to Charles, rather than to his father, in an aside explaining that 'the king' had made a good start with regard to protecting monasteries against grasping laymen, but that in due course these communities had succumbed to this evil after all.[79] Initially, the young king had made substantial concessions with regard to the integrity of the ecclesiastical property, but once he found his feet, he began to make more substantial claims on monastic wealth. Charles was confronted with a vociferous and self-confident episcopate that would not take this lying down, but by 845 he was no longer prepared to back down himself, which yielded a different discourse. The *rex* addressed by Arsenius had

---

[77] *EA* II, c. 4, p. 65; Breternitz, 'Ludwig der Fromme', p. 204.
[78] *EA* II, c. 3, p. 64: 'Ecce rex noster, ut saepe ostensum est, de facultatibus ecclesiarum multa in suis suorumque praesumit usibus, sanctorum autem patrum anathemata multa sunt nimis divina auctoritate prolata ... '.
[79] *EA* II, c. 5, p. 66 (Pascasius).

'helped himself' to the gifts of God, and was therefore as sinful as his rapacious followers. Thus the king had become one of those whom Radbert called the *saeculares*, the secular men, rather than transcending the divide, like the Solomon he should have been. According to Radbert, Arsenius attempted to broker a compromise:

If, as you say, therefore, the *respublica* cannot survive without the aid of the property of the churches, then with the greatest reverence and Christian devotion a method and an orderly system must be devised to see if what you and yours take from the churches is for the purpose of protection rather than rapine, lest this presumption go so far as to bring with it the maledictions and curse of the holy fathers. Moreover, if something must be rendered up for military use, let these saintly bishops present it as such, and in all cases let it take place in such a reasonable way that they themselves are not compelled to flutter across to worldly things and to devote themselves irreligiously to the worldly pomp which they have abjured, since, according to the Apostle, as I have said, 'no man who serves God entangles himself in worldly business' (2 Tim. 2:4).[80]

All this fits the 840s better than the 820s. Casting the bishops in the role of protectors and middlemen was precisely what Abbot Radbert of Corbie requested and received from the synod gathered in Paris in 846/7, which granted him a *privilegium*, underwritten by all, that safeguarded Corbie's property against the encroachment of 'our sons and lords', the rulers of the earth.[81]

Radbert's conception of the *respublica* was further articulated in the course of a confrontation that was first of all about the control of material resources (*res*), whether those of ecclesiastical communities (the *res ecclesiarum*) or those directly available to the public purse (the *respublica*). It should be clear by now that this Carolingian public domain, also evident in other narrative sources of the period, did have explicitly trans-personal features, without conforming to any modern Weberian notion of the state.[82] Like Radbert, his fellow authors who commented on Carolingian politics admired public men, public offices and public-spiritedness, and expressed their disdain for anyone chasing gains that

[80] *EA* II, c. 3, pp. 64–5 (Pascasius): 'Idcirco, ut dicitis, si respublica sine suffragio rerum ecclesiarum subsistere non valet, quaerendus est modus et ordo cum summa reverentia et religione Christianitatis: si quid vos, vestrique ab ecclesiis ob defensionem magis, quam ad rapinam accipere debeatis, ne cum maledictionibus et exsecratione sanctorum patrum itatenus praesumatur. Porro isti sancti pontifices, si quid ad usus militię exhibendum est, sic exhibeant, et sic fiat rationabiliter in quibuslibet rebus, ne ipsi cogantur ad sęcularia transvolare, et pompis saeculi quibus abrenuntiaverunt, irreligiosus deservire, quia iuxta apostolum, ut dixi, *nemo militans Deo implicat se negotiis saecularibus.*'
[81] See above, pp. 63–4.    [82] De Jong, 'The Two Republics'.

could be qualified as *privata*.[83] With this hierarchy of values in mind, a good translation for *respublica* might be 'commonwealth', but it should be kept in mind that Radbert's focus is as much on *res* as on *publica*. The ruler defends the entire *ecclesia*, which includes the *respublica* and the churches, and if the resources of the public or royal domain are depleted, he has the right to turn to the *res ecclesiarum* for the common good. What we encounter here is something paradoxical in Carolingian immunities. Radbert goes out on a limb to convince his audience that, unlike the *respublica*, ecclesiastical wealth should not be directly available to rulers, yet, at the same time, monasteries protected by royal immunities did have the duty to support the *respublica* with their landed wealth. If this system was to work, a delicate balance needed to be maintained. By the 840s, in the case of Corbie, this balance had clearly become disturbed, so in 846/7 Abbot Radbert called upon the bishops gathered in Paris to come to the rescue. None of this was an alternative to royal protection; it was presented as a reinforcement thereof, even if with hindsight we can see it was a counterweight. If the state was to survive, it would have to take all the support from the churches it could get.

## 6    Radbert as Pseudo-Isidore?

The *Epitaphium Arsenii* has long been treasure trove for purported facts concerning the rebellions against Louis and the 'reformers' that drove them. This time-honoured view received a new lease of life in recent publications on the so-called Pseudo-Isidorian forgeries. In the year 2000, Klaus Zechiel-Eckes identified Corbie as the 'workshop' in which the celebrated forgery originated, and Radbert, the monastery's top scholar, as the genius who was likely behind it.[84] According to this eminent scholar of canon law, it had been Louis's suppression of the rebellion of 833, and the emperor's subsequent cracking down on the episcopate, that had triggered this elaborate forgery. At its heart are the False Decretals, a collection of early papal letters offering procedural law that protected bishops from accusations by their archbishops and emperors, and allowed them to appeal to Rome.[85] Zechiel-Eckes' novel perspective almost entirely replaced the older consensus, namely that the so-called False

---

[83] Nelson, 'The Problematic in the Private'; De Jong & Renswoude, 'Introduction'; De Jong, 'The Two Republics'.

[84] The two key articles are Zechiel-Eckes, 'Ein Blick in Pseudo-Isidors Werkstatt' and 'Auf Pseudoisidors Spur'; the most complete recent discussion of ongoing research is offered by Ubl & Ziemann (eds.), *Fälschung als Mittel der Politik?*.

[85] For a succinct overview of the components of Pseudo-Isidore and recent research on how they are connected, see Knibbs, 'Ebo', pp. 145–7; on the ninth-century manuscript tradition, see Patzold, *Gefälschtes Recht*.

Decretals had originated after 847 in the archdiocese of Rheims, under the aegis of clerics who withstood the might of its formidable archbishop, Hincmar. Some scholars have had reservations, however.[86] Why would a monastic community have produced a collection of false decretals that tried to defend bishops against judicial arbitrariness on the part of their archbishops? Had Louis's reprisals against the bishops who imposed a public penance on him really been so harsh? It seemed that Ebo of Rheims had become the scapegoat for his rebellious colleagues; some went with Lothar to Italy in 834, but most continued as if nothing had happened.

After Zechiel-Eckes' untimely death in 2010, the research he had inspired moved ahead at full speed, and in two interconnected directions. Firstly, much debate followed as to which group of manuscripts represents the beginnings of Pseudo-Isidore's enterprise. Given that the oldest manuscripts containing the Decretals date to the 860s, the entire argumentation is based on content and context, rather than on palaeographical criteria. For example, Zechiel-Eckes thought a particular group of manuscripts (A2) was the oldest, for they did not contain strictures against auxiliary bishops (*chorepiscopi*): since these came in for criticism only in the 840s, A2 must have originated at an earlier stage.[87] Secondly, the date of Pseudo-Isidore's earliest core has steadily moved backwards. Whereas Zechiel-Eckes still saw the council of Aachen (836) as the *terminus post quem* of the False Decretals, Gerhard Schmitz has now detected Pseudo-Isidorian ideas in the acts of the council of Paris (829).[88]

In works published during his lifetime, Zechiel-Eckes was reluctant to use the *Epitaphium*'s second book as evidence for his own dating of Pseudo-Isidore, but a lecture published posthumously in 2011 is less careful.[89] Meanwhile, most scholars have enthusiastically accepted his suggestion that Radbert was somehow behind these forgeries. His narrative about Wala and himself meeting with Pope Gregory IV and presenting the pontiff with authoritative 'writings' (*conscripta*) that confirmed papal authority has been taken as proof of their deep involvement in the Pseudo-Isdiorian project, as well as for the early genesis of the False Decretals.[90] This view is also expressed in quite a few of the papers presented at a conference in 2013 that paid tribute to Zechiel-Eckes

[86] Fuhrmann, 'Stand', pp. 227–62; Patzold, *Episcopus*, pp. 221–6; De Jong, *Penitential State*, pp. 262–3; De Jong, 'Paschasius Radbertus and Pseudo-Isidore'.
[87] Zechiel-Eckes, 'Eine "unbeugsame" Exterminator?'.
[88] Schmitz, 'Die Synode von Aachen (836) und Pseudo-Isidor', pp. 341–2.
[89] Zechiel-Eckes, 'Falschung als Mittel politischer Auseinandersetzung'.
[90] Fried, *Donation*, pp. 93, 101–3; Knibbs, 'Pseudo-Isidore on the Field of Lies'; Ubl, *Inzestverbot*, pp. 323–5.

and his work.[91] The appearance of the proceedings more or less coincided with the publication of an article by myself which argued that the *Epitaphium*'s second book should be treated primarily as a text of the 850s, and therefore cannot be used in support of an early date for Pseudo-Isidore; furthermore, it contains no conceptions that can be called Pseudo-Isidorian in the sense generally accepted in current scholarship: namely, with the determining thrust of providing judicial precedents aimed at protecting bishops against their metropolitans and rulers.

To a considerable extent, this consensus, established by Emil Seckel and expanded upon by Horst Fuhrmann, still holds. As so often in early medieval history, there is a nineteenth-century background. Against heated accusations in the 1870s that Pseudo-Isidore was an evil instrument of papal claims to infallibility, leading scholars argued that this forgery had not so much boosted the might of the papacy as supported the position of Carolingian bishops. These forged decretals provided procedural law that made accusing and convicting bishops very difficult, if not practically impossible. In short, it was all about bishops, and this is the view to which most authors of recent publications still subscribe. Indeed, at present there is a tendency to see any texts underpinning episcopal authority, such as the *Relatio episcoporum* of 833 that legitimated Louis's public penance, as 'Pseudo-Isidorian'.[92] Clara Harder has challenged this consensus: she argues that Pseudo-Isidore's boost to papal authority was much more than a mere by-product of its episcopal agenda, and that the best and earliest evidence should be looked for in the Pseudo-Isidorian *Chalcedon Excerpts*, which are silent on bishops but all the more eloquent on popes.[93] Here, papal authority is expanded at the expense of imperial might, and the protection of bishops is of no interest whatsoever. In Harder's view, these *Excerpts* precede the False Decretals, and therefore provide a precious glimpse of the core issues that guided the original design of the entire forgery. The most important of these was the enhancement of the position of the pope, not shielding bishops from judicial trouble.[94] In this respect, Harder steers a different course, but otherwise, like most of the contributors to the 2015 volume for Zechiel-Eckes, she is in search of an ever earlier date for what is still seen as a cunning

---

[91] Ubl & Ziemann (eds.), *Fälschung als Mittel der Politik?*, published in 2015; De Jong, 'Paschasius Radbertus and Pseudo-Isidore' appeared in 2014; I sent a copy of my paper to the editors of the volume, but for most authors this came too late to take on board.
[92] Heinen, 'Pseudoisidor', p. 121.    [93] Harder, 'Der Papst', pp. 179–81.
[94] Harder, 'Der Papst', pp. 182–3.

forgery. In this 'whodunnit' Radbert is the most likely suspect, with his *Epitaphium* as the undisputed crown witness.[95]

There is never a dull moment in such research. A very recent article by Eric Knibbs steers a radically different course, taking us back to the earlier orthodoxy that 'Pseudo-Isidore as we now know it', that is, the complete collection of forgeries with the False Decretals at its heart, originated between 845 and 852/7,[96] in reaction to the plight of Ebo of Rheims – not just his trial in 835, but also his much-contested appointment as bishop of Hildesheim in 845; Pseudo-Isidore's focus on facilitating the transfer of bishops from one see to another has led Knibbs to opt for this new *terminus post quem*. In a surprising departure from his earlier certainty that, on the Field of Lies in 833, Wala and Radbert presented Gregory IV with an early version of the False Decretals,[97] Knibbs now dismisses this possibility out of hand. On further consideration, there appears to be no evidence that Radbert and the Pseudo-Isidorians did any more than use the same library (Corbie), and no clear connections between their respective agendas have yet been found. Moreover, in the late 840s, when there were practical efforts in the Rheims province to spread the False Decretals, 'the abbot of Corbie seems distant from Pseudo-Isidore's activities'.[98]

There has indeed been no convincing identification of Radbert as the mastermind behind an early version of the False Decretals, and unsurprisingly so, not just because the *Epitaphium*'s second book is not of much use in this respect, but also because some other problems remain unresolved. To begin with, the discovery that Corbie's library was used as an important resource for the creation of the False Decretals does not mean that this was also the place of production. And then there is the growing disagreement about the nature and limits of what can be classified as 'Pseudo-Isidore'. Is it specifically procedural law, purportedly from early papal Rome, but entirely in favour of bishops? This has been the traditional view that is still widely accepted, but as I just noted, there is also a more inclusive concept of the collection as part of a broader movement that boosted the position of bishops in more general ways, as well as enhancing papal authority. Those who rose to the occasion, in Corbie and elsewhere, scrupulously mined the *Historia Tripartita* and the *Liber*

---

[95] The most outspoken representative of this tendency is Heinen, 'Pseudoisidor', e.g. p. 98, with Radbert as the accused ('Hauptbeschuldigte'), in this case of forgery.

[96] Fuhrmann, *Einfluss und Verbreitung*, pp. 200–19: the first possible use is in Hincmar's *Second episcopal statute* (1 October 852); the first certain use is in his *Collectio de raptoribus* (857). On Hincmar and the spreading of Pseudo-Isidorian ideas to the lower ranks of the clergy, see De Jong, 'Hincmar, Priests and Pseudo-Isidore'.

[97] Knibbs, 'Pseudo-Isidore on the Field of Lies'.    [98] Knibbs, 'Ebo', p. 181.

*Pontificalis* in order to create an image of the earliest popes that would be recognisable to their contemporaries, and they also inserted their own most pressing contemporary concerns. What these 'forged' decretals have in common with collections of genuine letters and *canones* is their association with ancient papal Rome and the authority of St Peter and his successors, of which the forgers made an in-depth study. As Zechiel-Eckes discovered, the Corbie copy of the *Historia Tripartita* of Cassiodorus/Epiphanes was systematically excerpted by whoever put together an early version of the False Decretals, and this remains an important and enduring discovery. The ongoing search for the one and only mastermind behind this enterprise, however, owes too much to the late nineteenth-century origins of Pseudo-Isidorian research, and the then prevailing view that the forgery had been perfidious Rome's early bid for papal supremacy. This ideological strife turned the 'author' of this complicated mixture of genuine and invented canon law into a culprit who needed to be unmasked, but it also created a conflation between modern conceptions of forgery and early medieval notions of *inventio/* discovery: if the earliest papal letters were lacking, they needed to be 'found', for the sake of truth. In recent decades, much has been published on the cultural context of medieval forgery, but this has left research on Pseudo-Isidore strangely untouched.[99]

This is not the place to elaborate on these considerations. Instead, I shall briefly revisit the key text from the *Epitaphium* that has been most often invoked as proof of Radbert's, or even Wala's, authorship of Pseudo-Isidore, along with some other recent arguments to this effect. None of these stands up to scrutiny. First, we return to Radbert's narrative about his dangerous voyage to Lothar's camp near Colmar. There, Wala and he encountered a despondent pontiff who had just been threatened with deposition by the bishops loyal to Louis. The twosome then presented the pope with written proof of his own authority:

We therefore gave him many writings confirmed by the authority of the holy fathers and his predecessors, on the basis of which nobody could contradict that his was the power, or rather, God's and the Apostle Peter's, and his the authority to go to and adjudicate all peoples,[100] for the fidelity to Christ and the peace of the churches, for the preaching of the Gospel and the proclamation of the truth, and that in him rested all the exalted authority and living power of the blessed Peter, by whom all mankind ought to be judged, so that he himself should be judged by nobody. He accepted gratefully and took much courage from these writings.[101]

---

[99] To begin with, see the five volumes of *Fälschungen im Mittelalter*.
[100] Acts 15:17 and 22.
[101] *EA* II, c. 16, p. 84 (Pascasius): 'Quibus auditis, pontifex plurimum mirabatur, ac verebatur. Unde et ei dedimus nonnulla sanctorum patrum auctoritate firmata,

This is yet another instance of Radbert using his favourite repetition (*pro ... pro*), this time to underline what papal authority was *for*. Whether this is a reference to some set of forged decretals or not remains a moot point. It has been pointed out that this exalted view of St Peter's successor was already elaborated in sixth-century forgeries that, three centuries later, had become entirely canonical texts.[102]

Taking this passage at face value, furthermore, means ignoring the entire context of the second book, which is one of emphatic hindsight well after the events narrated. It is at this level of interpretation that the second book begins to yield interesting information, but then different questions need to be asked. Why, for instance, did Radbert bother to write about these 'writings' (*conscripta*) offered to Gregory? Was it because he wished to lend credibility to versions of the Pseudo-Isidorian decretals that had surely started to circulate by the mid-850s, if not earlier? Might his reference to the *schedula* brought by Wala to the crisis meeting of the winter 828/9 in Aachen also be a bid to legitimise the great man's interventions, which were shown to be not just any attempts to throw his illustrious weight around, but manifestations of the real authority that is based on canonical texts? It is this way of thinking that prevails in the *Epitaphium*'s second book, and it should give us pause for thought, for it reveals much about the fertile ground onto which Pseudo-Isidore fell, from the 850s onwards. It also exposes something about the nature of the entire enterprise: both the *Epitaphium* and the False Decretals belong to a world in which authority and canonicity was created with reference to an ancient and venerable textual tradition. Radbert was not 'forgery-happy' when he wrote a treatise on Mary (*Cogitis me*) for his beloved nuns of Nôtre-Dame in Soissons, in the persona of Jerome writing to Eustochium and Paula.[103] Such borrowed authorial identities had nothing to do with what is now understood as forgery: they were a way of adding to one's own authority and honouring one's patristic models as well as one's audience, who were of course fully aware of this elegant ruse. At an earlier stage of his research, Zechiel-Eckes came up with a more fruitful perspective on Radbert's use of aliases, pointing out that these mostly derived from Christian late antiquity and therefore were in line

---

predecessorumque suorum conscripta, quibus nullus contradicere possit quod eius esset potestas, immo Dei et beati Petri apostoli, suaque auctoritas, ire, mittere ad omnes gentes pro fide Christi et pace ecclesiarum, pro predicatione evangelii et assertione veritatis, et in eo esset omnis auctoritas beati Petri excellens et potestas viva, a quo oporteret universos iudicari, ita ut ipse a nemine iudicandus esset. Quibus profecto scriptis, gratanter accepit, et valde confortatus est.'

[102] Fuhrmann, *Einfluss und Verbreitung* II, pp. 241–2, n. 13; Firey, 'Canon Law Studies', pp. 23–8.

[103] Zechiel-Eckes, 'Falschung'.

with the False Decretals' main thrust: the construction of a well-researched body of decretals that filled a real lacuna, in a Frankish world that had become ever more oriented towards canonicity bearing the stamp of Roman authority.

As for the second book of the *Epitaphium*, this can be put to a more productive use when it is treated primarily as a source for the 850s. Was Radbert's portrayal of Wala and himself handing canonical writings to Gregory IV a way to legitimise the production of such pro-papal *conscripta* in Corbie? This is much less far-fetched than the notion of a set of false decretals being presented to the pope in 833. The unexpected papal visit created shock and upheaval at the time, but it also helped to focus the minds of the opposition against Louis the Pious on Rome, as their best ally in the local competition for authority and canonicity. In his second book, Radbert is an exponent of the view that Pope Gregory IV could have saved the day in 833, had Louis accepted his mediation, but he also adapts Matthew's Gospel to grant the power of the keys to all the bishops: 'whatever these holy bishops will bind on earth, shall also be bound in heaven'.[104] This was in line with the daring *Relatio* of 833 that defended the public penance that the bishops imposed on their emperor. It is entirely possible that Radbert already had this view at the time, and that he was part of the strongly pro-papal faction to which Agobard also belonged, and which most probably produced the letter ascribed to Gregory IV that lambasted the Frankish episcopate for its miserable reception of their pontiff in 833.[105] But there is no way to be sure about this. What we do know is that in the mid-850s, when Radbert wrote his second book, he thought that there was nothing contradictory in standing up for papal and episcopal authority at the same time.

---

[104] *EA* II, c. 3, p. 64: 'Quod si secundum sententiam veritatis, quaecunque ligaverint isti sancti pontifices super terram ligata erunt et in coelis, timendi sunt tot anathematismi sanctorum patrum qui leguntur pro talibus prolati in sacris canonibus ... '. Cf. Matt. 16:19: ' ... et tibi dabo claves regni caelorum et quodcumque ligaveris super terram erit ligatum in caelis et quodcumque solveris super terram erit solutum in caelis.'

[105] Agobard, *Epistolae*, no. 17, pp. 228–32; Scherer, *Pontifikat Gregors IV.*, pp. 170–83; De Jong, 'Paschasius Radbertus and Pseudo-Isidore', pp. 165–6; Van Renswoude, 'Licence to Speak', pp. 337–50.

# 9    The World They Had Lost

## 1    Losing the Right Way

The *Epitaphium's* second book belongs to a small but significant group of texts produced after the death of Louis the Pious in June 840, and, more particularly, during and after the ensuing struggle for succession. The authors in question reflected on this political turmoil and its causes. Deploring the loss of an older world they perceived as more stable, they articulated the contemporary values of public service in a highly personal and idiosyncratic way. This is one of the reasons why each of these texts survives only in one or a few manuscripts. Another is that they were never meant for a large audience in the first place. These were narratives and reflections written by and for members of the highest echelon of the Carolingian elite, some of whom were related to the ruling dynasty by blood or marriage.

Two of these authors are well known: Nithard wrote his *Histories* between the spring of 841 and the middle of 843, roughly in the period when Dhuoda composed a *Liber manualis* (handbook) for her son William.[1] But there are other, shorter testimonies penned by those who, directly or indirectly, had been affected by the shocking battle of Fontenoy in 841 and the ensuing events. On 25 June 841, the 'huge carnage'[2] took place that had been avoided in 833 on the Field of Lies. In a moving poetic lament, Angilbert, a follower of Lothar, grieves for the fallen in the battle of Fontenoy, 'the name the peasants give to the spring and village/ where Frankish blood was shed in slaughter and destruction'.[3] A letter by an indignant aristocrat, possibly the very Adalhard 'the Seneschal' so much maligned by Nithard, assured the Empress Ermengard that he had in no way stirred up discord between her husband Lothar and his brothers, and expressed his best intentions as well as his fervent fidelity.[4] Florus of Lyon,

---

[1] Nelson, 'Search for Peace', pp. 98–9.    [2] Nithard III, c. 1, p. 86.
[3] Angilbert, *Versus de bella quae fuit acta Fontaneto, MGH Poet. lat.* II, pp. 138–9; transl. Godman, *Poetry*, no. 39, pp. 262–4.
[4] *Epistolae variorum* no. 27, *MGH Epp.* V = Karol. aevi III, pp. 343–5.

Archbishop Agobard's gifted disciple, also wrote a long poem deploring the fate of a great Frankish realm that had now lost the name and distinction of empire (*imperium*), while the once united kingdom (*regnum*) had fallen to three lots; there was not one emperor (*induperator*) but only kinglets, and fragments of kingdoms replaced a realm. For Florus, the terrible vision of the prophet Amos with all its unfolding disasters had become a daily reality.[5]

These authors have been the object of some highly inspiring scholarly scrutiny, above all from Jinty Nelson and Stuart Airlie.[6] It is now time to bring the *Epitaphium* into the equation, and especially its second book. This chapter offers some comparisons, with a focus on Nithard and Dhuoda, and with a deliberate helicopter view. Originating in the mid-to late 850s, Radbert's narrative about Wala and the rebellions of 830–3 represents a relatively late contribution to comments on the politics of the mid-ninth century, yet it is a valuable witness to the years of upheaval after the treaty of Verdun in 843. Radbert became abbot of Corbie shortly afterwards, in a political world that remained utterly unstable, with three rulers constantly jostling for position. As had been the case with Nithard, the dynamics generated by three fiercely competitive rulers brought him personal misfortune, and it shows in his work.

There are other, more mainstream ninth-century historical narratives that will now and then surface here, such as the Astronomer's *Life of Louis*.[7] It is generally agreed that this major biography and first in-depth assessment of the rebellions of the 830s was written in the autumn and winter of 840/1, when there was still hope of Lothar and Charles the Bald working together.[8] This author covers much of the same ground as Radbert does in his second book, but with a very different outlook: this was a champion of Louis the Pious, and someone close to Louis's loyal half-brother Drogo of Metz.[9] In what follows, however, Nithard, Dhuoda and Radbert will take pride of place.

---

[5] Florus of Lyon, *Carmina* no. 28, *MGH Poet. lat.* II, pp. 559–64; transl. Godman, *Poetry*, no. 40, pp. 265–73. On Dhuoda, Angilbert, Florus and Nithard and their connection with the debacle of Fontenoy (841), see recently Romig, *Be a Perfect Man*, pp. 98–117, from the perspective of questioning *caritas* in troubled times.

[6] On Nithard: Nelson, 'Public *Histories*'; Airlie, 'The World'; Nelson, 'Dhuoda', 'Dhuoda on Dreams'; Le Jan, 'Dhuoda ou l'opportunité du discours féminin'. For the political context of these two authors and others discussed in this chapter, I have gratefully relied on Nelson, 'Search for Peace'.

[7] For a brief survey of the relevant 'ninth-century narratives', see De Jong, *Penitential State*, pp. 59–111.

[8] Tremp, 'Überlieferung', pp. 128–56, at p. 138; Nelson, 'Search for Peace', p. 101.

[9] For two recent assessments of the Astronomer, see Romig, 'In Praise of the Too-Clement Emperor'; Ganz, 'The Astronomer's *Life of Louis the Pious*'. See also Booker, *Past Convictions*, pp. 34–9; De Jong, *Penitential State*, pp. 79–89.

At first glance, these seem to be disparate texts: the 'lay' status of the first two authors tends to be emphasised, as opposed to Radbert's monastic outlook. Wealthy monastic establishments such as Corbie, however, favoured first by Merovingian rulers and then by their Carolingian successors, helped to sustain the foundations of the Carolingian state, and to be an abbot or abbess was a public office (*ministerium*). All three of these authors, moreover, belonged to an elite culture dominated by the imperial/royal court and its monastic dependencies, and steeped in biblical knowledge. This is more evident in Dhuoda's *Liber manualis* than in Nithard's increasingly grim history of fraternal warfare, but when the latter decides to lash out against Charles, at the very end of his fourth book, he musters a formidable amount of biblical reserves. Like his contemporaries Dhuoda and Radbert, Nithard was perfectly capable of adapting Scripture to his authorial requirements.[10]

As for the parallels, as I already mentioned, our three central texts had an extremely limited manuscript transmission.[11] Were they in fact the tip of an iceberg of lively communication about the state of the realm, as Airlie has suggested? I think so, for the ninth century is a period of political scandal that could spread like wildfire, and then turn into the kind of *scandalum* that could be expiated only by public penance.[12] The more lowly hangers-on of the major players were indispensable in getting the rumours going;[13] they heard about the conflicting views held by their masters, including the ones defended by Radbert and Nithard. Yet these authors' personal reflections on turbulent times were infused with an ethos that was 'rigorously elitist',[14] intended for insiders from the highest political echelon, and therefore not meant to be circulated widely.[15] Furthermore, they were produced by and for those who operated within a public arena dominated by the royal court. Nithard and Radbert figured as political actors in their own works, and to a large extent, this also holds true of Dhuoda. As a woman, she did not hold a public *honor* in the sense of an office bestowed by the ruler, but she was married to a man who had been one of the most prominent office-holders in the realm: Bernard of Septimania, Louis's godson, who was

---

[10] De Jong, *Penitential State*, p. 102.
[11] On Nithard: Booker, 'An Early Humanist Edition'; Riché (ed.), Dhuoda, *Manuel*, pp. 45–50. See the comments of Nelson on such ninth-century *pièces d'occasion*, including the *Epitaphium* and Hincmar's *De ordine palatii*, in 'Public Histories', pp. 226–7.
[12] De Jong, *Penitential State*, p. 228–41; Airlie, 'Private Bodies'.
[13] On ninth-century rumour: Dutton, *Charlemagne's Mustache*, pp. 129–50.
[14] Noble, 'Secular Sanctity', p. 31.
[15] Airlie, 'The World', p. 59; another example is the treatise discussed and edited in Finsterwalder, 'Eine parteipolitische Kundgebung'; for a discussion and translation of this text, see Dutton, *Charlemagne's Mustache*, pp. 146–7, 191–3.

chamberlain in 829–30, and who figures as the arch-villain in the
*Epitaphium*'s second book. Whatever its other purposes may have been,
Dhuoda's *Liber manualis* aimed to prepare her eldest son for similar public
duty. Accordingly, the way in which these authors introduce themselves
and their personal concerns into their narratives is closely connected to
their discourse about the court, and to their own position within a public
domain governed by the ruler.

Last but not least, this threesome shares an intense preoccupation with
*fides*, including all the ramifications outlined in the previous chapter.
Paramount among these is fidelity to God and the ruler, but *fides* in the
sense of trustworthiness was also a key element of the honour and reputation of those who counted themselves among the *senatores* or *consiliarii*, as
Radbert calls them. The membership of this elevated echelon of men who
had the ear of the ruler depended not just on royal favour, but also on
being successful in the constant competition for *familiaritas*: that is, access
to the court and the courtiers who dominated this volatile configuration.
Accusations of infidelity went a long way towards tarnishing someone's
good name with the ruling family as well as with one's most important
peers.

## 2    *Familiaritas*: Dhuoda, Nithard, Radbert

Reflecting on history-writing at the courts of Louis the Pious and Charles
the Bald, and on Nithard's work in particular, Nelson notes that the latter
presented himself as one of Charles's closest counsellors (*participes secre-
torum*), and then observes that ninth-century history was not written for
private purposes, 'but to advance a cause – and at the same time,
a career – in public life'.[16] History-writing was a way in which the learned
participated in giving counsel, and an important aspect of their duty to
speak truth to power. This is an important point to keep in mind, for it
also explains why criticism of the ruler could be sharp yet still
constructive.[17] All the same, there were limits to what could be said
directly to or about a king or queen. Those who were usually the target
of unmitigated critique, or even invective, were the top-level royal counsellors. Their failure in the 830s to assist their emperor is a recurrent

---

[16] Nelson, 'History-writing', p. 438. Airlie, 'The World', has a similar approach. A recent
article instead emphasises on Nithard's offended honour as a son from an illegitimate
union, and seems to be setting the clock backwards: Polanichka and Cilley, 'The very
personal history'.

[17] Nelson, 'History-writing'; De Jong, *Penitential State*, pp. 112–47. The 'art of safe criticism' is central to Van Renswoude, 'Licence to Speak', and to her forthcoming book,
*Rhetoric of Free Speech*.

theme in the *Epitaphium*'s second book. The monk Adeodatus comments that they were robbers who pursued their own interests, not percipient leaders of the fatherland. Their depravity was such 'that they were incapable of understanding or perceiving the dignity of being a counsellor, the illustriousness of this rank, and the importance of this office, or of taking charge and maintaining it'. Because of their selfish scheming and betrayal, they were not counsellors, but peddlers and merchants who created upheaval in the churches. Refusing to listen to Arsenius and his reprimands, they ignored the truth and embraced error and confusion. 'This is why, up to the present day, none of the rulers can show the *respublica* the ways towards justice.'[18]

For all this, Bernard was to blame, and one of Radbert's key passages spells out what Wala and his allies stood to lose when they lost their central role at Louis's court in August 829. Resorting to omens and divination, rather than to proper counsel, Bernard

... had so deluded the most sacred emperor through his impostures that the latter drove away all those whom he or his worthy father the emperor had nurtured from secret deliberation, from consultation, from intimate association (*familiaritas*) and counsel, from the loyalty of fidelity, from *honores*, and from all the fellowship of their earlier life.[19]

This was the world that Wala had lost – and Radbert as well, by proxy – but note that the ensuing palace rebellion was legitimated by a general appeal to the public weal and the ideals underpinning the stability of the *respublica*. With hindsight, this may seem obvious, but at the time it was a novelty. The question remains: should this be dated to the 830s themselves, or to two decades later? I would opt for the latter.

The 'familiarity' enjoyed by those with access to the court also becomes evident from the regular appearance of the same protagonists in different texts, albeit with varying assessments. The condemnation of Bernard of Septimania is remarkably consistent, with the exception of Dhuoda's *Liber manualis*, in which he is a revered husband, deserving of loyalty. Otherwise, Bernard figures in all contemporary writing as the epitome of fickleness and infidelity. In Radbert's second book, Bernard's perfidy, which is tersely commented on by the Astronomer and Nithard, is expanded into the full-blown portrait of someone who overturned the interconnected order of the palace and the realm. That the former

---

[18] *EA* II, c. 6, p. 66: 'Inde est quod adhuc hodie nemo principum explicare potest reipublicç vias at iustitiam.'

[19] *EA* II, c. 9, p. 71 (Pascasius): ' ... eo quod sacratissimum augustum sic haberet suis delusum praestigiis, ut omnes repelleret, quos aut ipse, aut magnus pater eius imperator nutrierat a secreto, a colloquio, a familiaritate et consilio, a fidei fide, ab honoribus, et ab omni consortio prioris vitae.'

chamberlain remained everyone's favourite villain in the 840s and 850s was largely the result of his being 'second only after the emperor' in 829 and 830: a dangerous position to be in, even if it was only for a few years. Wala himself had risen to this height and was remembered keenly as a threat to dynastic stability by the Astronomer in his narrative of Louis's succession in 814. In a similar vein, Nithard wrote about the redoubtable Adalbert of Metz, a count promoted to be duke, whose voice was so authoritative (*prudens*) among Lothar's counsellors that nobody dared to contradict him, with dire consequences.[20] And then there was Adalhard 'the Seneschal', whose niece married Charles the Bald – according to Nithard, because he had been given a free hand by Louis the Pious in misappropriating public resources – so the young king had to reckon with Adalhard if he wanted to get his followers on his side. For reasons Nelson has clarified, Adalhard became a threat to Nithard's interests, which is why he casts a shadow over the fourth and last book of the *Histories*.[21]

It is not entirely certain that this particular Adalhard is indeed the one who replied to a stern warning from the Empress Ermengard, Lothar's wife, not to stoke up the fires of discord among the royal brothers; she also reminded him of his obligation of fidelity to her husband, the legitimate successor.[22] Whatever the case, this letter, which survives in only one manuscript, was written by a magnate who subscribed to the same values as Nithard did. To be accused of undermining the stability of the state through a wavering fidelity towards one's royal lord meant a loss of honour and reputation among one's peers, and the public view of the empress mattered deeply.

From all these documents from the 840s and 850s a set of principles emerges, to which the political elite needed to subscribe in order to belong to the inner circle of the royal court. This was more than lip service: the authors, who were also courtiers, and in some cases also political actors, express pride in their proximity to the palace.[23] This is one of the reasons why Ermoldus Nigellus relates how Pippin of Aquitaine gently mocked him for being a cleric, unaccustomed to handling a sword. 'You'd better stick to writing!'[24] Banter with royal sons or magnates singled out the true insider, as Radbert knew very well.[25] When it comes to an author who identifies himself as a courtier in his own work, the Astronomer provides

---

[20] Nithard II, c. 7, p. 68.    [21] Nelson, Public *Histories*', pp. 222–4, 232–3.
[22] See above, n. 4; Nelson, 'Search for Peace', pp. 102–3.
[23] For more expressions of connectedness with the palace, even at a distance, see Airlie, 'Palace of Memory'.
[24] Ermoldus Nigellus, *Carmen*, ll. 2016–19; De Jong, *Penitential State*, p. 90.
[25] See above, pp. 72–3.

a celebrated case in point, through the anecdote that earned him the modern nickname 'the Astronomer'. Summoned to the roof of the palace at Aachen, and in the daunting presence of the emperor, he had to shed light on the meaning of a comet that had been observed in the year 837. The courtier dithered, so it was only Louis himself who, allegedly, said out loud what this portent really meant: a major change in the realm and the death of a ruler.[26] This is a story with multiple meanings, but one of them is surely that the author is presenting himself as a man of the palace, and sufficiently close to the emperor to be consulted on this weighty matter.

In such narratives, personal experience and public reputation are mutually enhancing. In Radbert's first book, there are some self-referential passages which show a similar pride in serving the emperor, for example, when sent on important and delicate missions. As we have seen, he elaborates on his shock and grief upon learning about Wala's exile, in the refectory of a monastery in Cologne, during a journey on which he had been sent by *Augustus*.[27] Why mention that he was on imperial business? Because this needed to be impressed on his readership, who would appreciate the trust Louis put in his Radbert. In another key passage just mentioned, he travelled to the palace in 826 to argue that Wala should succeed Adalhard as abbot of Corbie, and had to engage in a battle of wits with some magnates. Presumably, they served as inter-mediaries, for Radbert did not get an audience with Louis, but his hope that his repartee may have been relayed to the emperor himself speaks volumes about the awe in which he then held an emperor that he would later criticise severely in the *Epitaphium*'s second book.[28] And even here, where he makes clear that Louis was incapable of recognising a good and faithful counsellor if he stumbled over one, Radbert still portrays himself as delegated by the emperor to negotiate with Wala.[29] That he then depicts his master as rejecting all these imperial advances does not detract from his need to inform his readers that it fell to him, Radbert, to serve as an intermediary between his intransigent abbot and an emperor who was by then eager to compromise. In the central part of the second book, which covers the two rebellions, Radbert was there in the thick of it, firmly and faithfully at the side of his abbot, but this also brought him close to the imperial father and his rebellious sons, and the intractable mess they had created. It was important that his audience know that, like Arsenius, he, Radbert, had been on the side of the forces of public order. It was not just

---

[26] Astronomer, c. 58, p. 522: ' ... mutationem regni et mortem principis ... '. On Carolingian kings and their stars, see Dutton, *Charlemagne's Mustache*, pp. 93–127.
[27] *EA* I, c. 8, p. 33 (Pascasius).    [28] *EA* I, c. 11, p. 39.    [29] *EA* II, c. 10, pp. 74–5.

the mantra-like pronouncements of Arsenius' beliefs that had to get this
message across, but also the glimpses he gave his readers of himself as an
able and trusted emissary of Wala and Louis, even though they turned out
to be the rock and the hard place that he got caught between.

## 3    The Public Domain

These authors and their audiences were insiders at the court, a position
that was insecure at best, but highly prized, so it is no surprise that they
made much of their proximity to the ruler. By dismissing them as 'courtiers', however, we risk taking for granted their extraordinary statements
of what it meant to belong to the Carolingian leadership, both as a context
for their works and as expressions of shared values at this exalted political
level. These are the values of men (and one woman) who operated to
a greater or lesser extent in a public arena.[30] This is also what Dhuoda
refers to when she devotes a brief chapter to William's life in the *respublica*.
It was his mother's express desire that William, once he reached man-
hood, should arrange his household lawfully (*utiliter*), according to
a legitimate hierarchy, and that he should conduct all his actions in the
*respublica* loyally and in an orderly manner.[31] This is a public domain
defined by the king and those who serve him; in the same sentence
Dhuoda alludes to one of King David's right-hand men, who was 'like
the most tender little worm of the wood'. A well-informed reader could
add the rest of this biblical text: this mild-mannered hero, the little worm,
had killed 800 men in one fell swoop.[32] Dhuoda's most frequently used
term for the general weal, both religious and political, is *utilitas* (with its
derivatives), which appears in the passage just discussed. To organise
one's household (*domus*) *utiliter* was more than 'useful' or 'practical'.[33]
In the case of the royal household, it meant managing an ordered

---

[30] Nelson, 'The Problematic in the Private'; De Jong & Van Renswoude, 'Introduction',
pp. 11–14; De Jong, 'For God, King and Country', 'The Two Republics'. Two publications relevant to this topic I saw too late to take into account: Leyser, 'Introduction', and
Wickham, 'Consensus and Assemblies'.
[31] Dhuoda, *Liber manualis* X, c. 3, p. 348: 'Volo enim et ortor ut cum, auxiliante deo, ad
perfectum perueneris tempus, domum tuam per legitimos gradus utiliter disponas, et, ut
scriptum est de quodam uiro, uelut tenerrimus ligni uermiculus, in re publica cuncta
ordinabili cursu fidenter perage.'
[32] 2 Kgs (=2 Sam.) 23:8.
[33] Dhuoda, *Liber manualis* III, c. 4, p. 150: 'Tu ergo, fili Wilhelme, ex illorum progenie
ortus, seniori ut praedixi tuo sis uerax, uigil, utilisque atque praecipuus; et in omni
negotio utilitatis regiae potestati, in quantum tibi deus dederit uires, intus forisque
prudentius te exhiberi satage'. On the theme of the interdependence between the royal
*domus* and the polity, see Nelson, 'Kingship and Empire', and Airlie, 'Private Bodies and
the Body Politic.'

microcosm that not just reflected but also safeguarded the peace of the polity. This kind of *domus*, modelled on a peaceful palace, is elaborated on by Jonas of Orleans for the benefit of Count Matfrid,[34] and it was also the ideal aristocratic household Dhuoda evoked in her *Liber manualis*. Even if his parents failed, William might learn to live up to this ideal in the place where it originated: the royal household.

In Nithard's view, the so-called seneschal Adalhard had 'thoroughly destroyed the commonwealth' by handing out public resources to whomever requested such favours.[35] In the letter that Adalhard may or may not have written in response to the Empress Ermengard's admonition, one encounters a man who is as principled as Nithard in his obligations to his ruler and the common weal. Sides might change, but the ethos of public service remained in place. This can be observed in Radbert's second book, as well as in the last section of Nithard's work, written at a point in his life when his position within Charles' inner circle was becoming more insecure. To view him as an author indulging in autobiography is misleading, for this evokes a modern notion: the uncovering of one's private and innermost feelings to share them with a wider audience.[36] Nithard qualifies his aside about his parentage as something he is touching on briefly, before returning to the course of historical events.[37] What he manages to do in these few sentences, however, is establish his credentials as someone with a full right to criticise his royal cousin Charles the Bald, through a shared grandfather, a mother proudly named, and a saintly father. At this point in his life and work, Nithard needed to remind his readership of his illustrious parentage, and of the firm commitment to the public cause that went with this impressive ancestry. It is no coincidence that Nithard praises Charlemagne's reign with the two keywords of Ciceronian public duty: in all respects, his imperial rule (*imperium*) had been 'honourable and beneficial' (*honestum et utile*).[38]

This is also how Radbert portrays Wala: as the defender of public order par excellence, precisely because he came from a royal lineage (*regalis prosapia*).[39] Most of this comes in the second book, which was written after the author himself had lost his abbacy, and therefore had forfeited his position in the political arena. His vicious indictment of Wala's enemies as royal counsellors turned robbers fits a state with immense

---

[34] Jonas, *De institutione laicali*; Stone, *Morality*, pp. 38–40, with reference to older literature.
[35] Nithard IV, c. 6, p. 142. On *respublica* in Nithard, see Depreux, 'Nithard'.
[36] Here I disagree with Polanichka & Cilley, 'The Very Personal History'.
[37] Nithard IV, c. 5: 'His paucis de origine mea delibatis, ad historiae seriem redire libet.'
[38] Nithard I, c. 1, p. 4; Dyck, *Commentary*, pp. 29–36.
[39] *EA* I, c. 12, p. 41 (Severus on Adalhard's and Wala's royal ancestry); see also *EA* I, c. 7, p. 31 (Pascasius compares Wala to King David).

patronage powers that extended throughout almost the entire realm.[40] Within this public domain controlled by the ruler, aristocratic fortunes were amassed, while reputations were made and broken when measured by a yardstick of public-spiritedness.[41]

## 4    *Fides* Once More

Already in his *Life of Adalhard*, in or shortly after 826, Radbert had accused Louis of insincerity when he publicly confessed his sins in Attigny in 822.[42] Likewise, the *Epitaphium*'s narrative about the emperor's empty promises made in Compiègne in 830 underlines 'the obscuring of a great deception, as if under the cloak of fidelity and the royal will'.[43] Louis's heart was hardened, and within it, the wound of duplicity festered. The emperor got as good as he gave, for once he had rejected those who tried to save him, there were no great men in his entourage who gave him counsel 'from their heart or soul, but [only] by assenting [to his wishes] and [offering] adulation for favours'.[44] In Radbert's final analysis, neither Louis nor Lothar had walked sincerely (*sinceriter*) before God. This was why, two decades later, when he wrote his second book, secret wounds remained branded on the hearts of the rulers and many of their men, and the *respublica* was in a state of collapse.[45]

Not walking sincerely before God is a biblical allusion,[46] but it is also part of a typically Carolingian discourse on the emptiness of solemn gestures and pronouncements informed by deception. Just as penitence would be efficacious only if the sinner had a contrite heart and genuine tears, a *sacramentum* of fidelity would turn into an 'animal oath' if there was dissimulation rather than genuine *fides*.[47] That these norms were shared by the upper levels of the aristocracy, and those aspiring to belong to this echelon, is clear from the way in which they

---

[40] Wickham, *Inheritance of Rome*, pp. 391–2.
[41] Astronomer, c. 6, pp. 302–3; Nelson, 'The Problematic in the Private'; De Jong & Van Renswoude, 'Introduction'.
[42] *Vita Adalhardi*, c. 51, cols. 1534D–1535A; De Jong, *Penitential State*, pp. 126–7.
[43] *EA* II, c. 10, p. 74: 'Occultabatur autem nimia fraus, quasi sub fidei schemate et voluntate regia.'
[44] *EA* II, c. 16, p. 85: ' ... neque principi consilia ex corde aut ex animo dabant: sed assentando et adulando pro favoribus ... '.
[45] *EA* II, c. 19, p. 90: 'Sicque alternatim dum neuter eorum sinceriter coram Deum incedit, labefactum adhuc hodie iacet et divisum. Manet quoque obscurum odium inter fratres, atque in pectoribus insitum vulnus penitus, et inustum animis hominum amplissimorum: pro quibus indesinenter ad peius tendit respublica, et collabitur.'
[46] Tobit 3:5: 'Et nunc Domine, magna iudicia tua, quia non egimus secundum praecepta tua, et non ambulavimus sinceriter coram te.'
[47] *EA* I, c. 3, pp. 24–5.

could be used to discredit political opponents. *Fides* as articulated by the authors of the texts discussed in this chapter is reminiscent of the later ethos of knighthood, but the crucial difference is that ninth-century notions of fidelity were still oriented towards the ruler and the *respublica*.[48] Dhuoda writes of the 'madness of infidelity' (*infidelitatis vesania*) which might arise in her son's heart, and of the shameful reputation incurred by those who acted in such a despicable manner towards their royal lord.[49]

William's commendation of Charles the Bald and his life at the court served multiple political purposes. It was a gesture of goodwill on the part of Bernard that might yield him short-term benefits, but in the long run it could also give Charles more control over this still dangerous magnate. Judging by the universal disparagement levelled at him by his contemporaries, Bernard may have been a somewhat extreme case, but this mutual benefit was the very essence of the practice of *commendatio*.[50] Accordingly, Dhuoda prepares her son not for an existence as a hostage but for life as a magnate and royal counsellor, and devotes her best powers of persuasion to the responsibilities that this entails.[51] As in Radbert's *Epitaphium*, it is the combination of loyalty and veracity that makes the ideal counsellor, which is why truth-telling outsiders should prevail over insiders who just dispense flattery.[52] In fact, to denounce one's peers as flatterers was another potent accusation. Dhuoda finds a pertinent example in the Book of Esther, a biblical text that confronted the Carolingian elite with a world close to their own, full of palace intrigues.[53] Briefly: the scheming royal adviser Haman, the quintessential insider and sycophant, meets with a dire fate, while Esther's uncle, the outsider Mordecai, ends up taking his place, thanks to Queen Esther's judiciously woven hold over her royal husband Ahasuerus.

To say that for Dhuoda, Radbert and Nithard *fides* to God and one's ruler was a key value is stating the obvious. Their stance does not represent some overblown rhetoric, detached from reality, with which Carolingian authors have so often been credited, but was formed in a longstanding practice of gaining status and authority through loyalty

[48] Nelson, 'Ninth-century Knighthood', on comparisons between Carolingian royal service and later knighthood.
[49] Dhuoda, *Liber manualis* III, c. 4, p. 150.
[50] Pezé, 'Compétition'; Innes, 'A Place of Discipline'.
[51] Dhuoda, *Liber manualis* III, cc. 5–7, pp. 152–64, on the art of counsel-giving that William should learn.
[52] Van Renswoude, 'Licence to Speak', pp. 180–6, 260–80; Stone, *Masculinity*, pp. 142–6.
[53] Dhuoda, *Liber manualis* III, c. 7, pp. 162–4. On Carolingian exegesis of Esther, see De Jong, 'Bride Shows' and 'Exegesis for an Empress'.

to the ruler.[54] The tenaciousness of such ties of fidelity becomes particularly visible in texts from the years of rebellion in the 830s, and even more
so in the 840s, when, as Florus of Lyon expressed it, 'the united realm had
succumbed to a threefold division', and choices had to be made between
competing royal lords.[55] This is the kind of so-called rhetoric that highlights *fides* as an ideal, and the anguish it might cause if, in practice,
difficult choices had to be made in a world governed by three rulers.

This dilemma was a core element in the self-representation of the
authors discussed here, but it could also be a formidable literary weapon
to wield against one's enemies. Reputations were built or broken by
showing that one's hero had the *fides* it took to exert real leadership,
while the protagonists of the other party lacked the essential qualities.
In the Astronomer's *Life of Louis*, the fickle royal sons, unable to conduct
themselves properly in public, face an imperial father who quietly but
resolutely sticks to the rules of royal comportment.[56] This image is
inverted in the *Epitaphium*'s second book, where Louis has become
unreliable to the point of impetuousness, and gets lectured by his sons
on what it means to adhere to the basic principles of fidelity, which also
required loyalty on the part of the ruler.[57] In a similar vein, there are
repeated references to Wala's 'constancy' (*constantia*), and to how he
admonished the great and the good *constanter*, according to Jeremiah's
example.[58] This signals to the reader that this was a royal counsellor at his
very best: someone ready to remind all present of his unwavering adherence to what should have been a shared position, and who was unafraid to
speak truth to power. Its opposite was 'childlike counsel'. As the reply to
the Empress Ermengard's admonition had it, it was their heeding this
*consilium puerile* that had created the discord between the three royal
brothers in the first place; alas, perhaps they could be recalled to concord
only by the efforts of wise outsiders and the strong enemies that gathered
around the realm.[59] This was a pointed attack by the respondent on his
peers, and also an instance of an almost universal stereotype: it is never

---

[54] Airlie, '*Semper fideles?*'; Nelson, 'Ninth-century Knighthood'; Esders, '"Faithful
believers"'.
[55] Godman, *Poetry*, no. 40, p. 268: 'Et regnum unitum concidit sorte triformi.'
On competition over fidelity, see Pezé, 'Compétition', pp. 143–58.
[56] Astronomer, c. 48. p. 473. De Jong, 'Admonition and Criticism', pp. 324–6.
[57] *EA* II, c. 7, p. 87.
[58] *EA* II, c. 2, p. 62 (Pascasius), p. 63 (Adeodatus); c. 5, p. 65 (Adeodatus), p. 66
(Pascasius); c. 8, p. 70 (Adeodatus); c. 9, p. 72 (Pascasius); c. 13, p. 80 (Teofrastus);
c. 17, p. 87 (Pascasius/Honorius); and c. 18, p. 89 (Pascasius). On the connection
between *constantia* and frank speech, see Van Renswoude, 'Licence to Speak', pp. 50,
56–9, 86–8, 109–14.
[59] *Epp. Var.* no. 27, *MGH Epp.* V = Karol. Aevi III, p. 344; Nelson, 'Search for Peace',
pp. 102–3; Pezé, 'Compétition', p. 155.

the ruler who has failed, always his advisers. Radbert blames them for the revolt of 833 as well as for its failure: it was because of their audacity and bad counsel 'that Caesar Augustus did these things against his sons'.[60]

Speaking one's mind at inconvenient moments, risking royal anger, was an integral part of *fides*, and of the duty of the royal counsellor.[61] When severe criticism was levelled, however, high birth and Carolingian connections were also an asset. Radbert did not possess these qualities by birth, but portrays himself as closely associated with his much-lamented abbot, who did. Through Wala's dire warnings to Louis and Lothar, Radbert could speak unpalatable truths to contemporary rulers, and, I suspect, to Charles the Bald in particular. Both he and Nithard were masters at drawing the line between 'us and them' using the idea of (in) fidelity. In the *Histories*, Charles's men are faithful, as they should be, while Lothar's followers are not.[62] In Radbert's second book, the counsellors who replaced Wala had their eyes on their own *honores*, rather than on the interests of the *respublica*.[63] But both authors went further, deploying *fides* or the lack thereof as a key category in the characterisation of their protagonists. Bernard of Septimania is an obvious case in point, the 'fall guy' for every author involved. In the *Histories*, he is introduced as Louis's chamberlain who abused the resources of the state,[64] and then a more elaborate portrait is drawn, almost entirely in terms of Bernard's infidelity. At Bourges in January 841 he left Charles in the lurch, as had been his habit elsewhere. Bernard fled when the king came after him on a punitive expedition, leaving his men to bear the brunt of the king's wrath. Made more humble (*humilior effectus*), Bernard then submitted himself after all, claiming that he used to be faithful and wished to be so once more; Charles was persuaded to believe him (*credulus effectus*).[65] Clearly, the king's credulity could only spell more trouble ahead, and indeed, Bernard failed to come to his aid during a campaign against Pippin of Aquitaine. When he learned that Charles had been victorious, Bernard sent the king his own son William to commend himself to the king, provided the latter would return the lands in Burgundy that Bernard had once held as a benefice.[66] For Radbert, all the political instability created by Bernard's dominance, and his criminal dispensing of benefits and favours, were 'the fruit of infidelity and discord'.[67]

---

[60] *EA* II, c. 18, p. 89: ' ... quorum audacia vel consiliis talia caesar augustus contra filios gessit ... '.

[61] De Jong, *Penitential State*, pp. 112–22.    [62] Nelson, 'Search for Peace', p. 106.

[63] *EA* II, c. 19, p. 89–90.    [64] Nithard I, c. 3, p. 10.    [65] Nithard II, c. 5, pp. 50–2.

[66] Nithard III, c. 2, pp. 82–4.

[67] *EA* II, c. 7, p. 68: 'Movebatur enim iam vertigo totius imperii, ne ullus acquireret potentiam, ne ullus honorem, ne ullus facultates, sine scelere, aut sine aliorum damnationis dispendio. Iste quippe fructus est infidelitatis et discordiae.'

*Fides* Once More

219

In Radbert's second book, Bernard serves as the perfidious counterpart to Wala's ideal counsellor; in Nithard's narrative, he is a secondary villain. As Airlie puts it, this author only really draws blood in his portrait of Lothar.[68] He embodies a lack of *fides* in all of its possible ramifications. This is clear from the very beginning of the *Histories*, where Lothar is presented as the son who consistently undermined his father's reign. Having confirmed with an oath the decision that his young half-brother Charles would receive part of the realm, he came to regret it, and resorted to secret machinations to undo what his father had decided.[69] Throughout his account of the rebellions of the 830s, Nithard refrains from putting his authorial knife into Louis. Lothar is another matter altogether, for his conduct after the revolt of 830 is only one case in point, and he himself condemned to death those who had been on his side; pointedly, he is not credited with their subsequent pardon and exile.[70] Among these exiles was Wala, who, together with Helisachar, Matfrid and others fallen from grace, 'compelled Lothar to take possession of the *respublica*'.[71] In other words, Wala was blamed also for the second rebellion. As for its aftermath, Nithard highlights Louis's readiness to make peace with his eldest son: the emperor did not want to take military action, but sent emissaries summoning him to his court.[72] By contrast, Lothar and his men, swollen with pride because of the military successes of the summer of 834, aimed for a third rebellion, but the Franks, who already repented of having abandoned their emperor twice and judging it shameful to do so again, turned their back on these instigations to defection.[73]

Just in case anyone might still think that Louis was the main target of Nithard's ire,[74] there is his depiction of Lothar's humble submission to his father in 839 at an assembly in Worms, where Louis treated his son with the utmost clemency, going out of his way to accommodate Lothar in the division of his realm; but because of Lothar's ignorance of territory, he made nothing of this opportunity.[75] Nonetheless, the father dismissed his son and sent him back to Italy, enriched by a pardon and the riches of the realm. He even reminded Lothar of how many times he had sworn oaths, how often he had gone back on these, how often he, Louis, had pardoned him, enjoining him not to go back on what he had publicly promised.[76]

Nithard's Lothar is reminiscent of Radbert's Louis: a ruler who could not recognise or reward true fidelity. But at least the *Epitaphium* largely

[68] Airlie, 'The World', p. 67.  [69] Nithard I, c. 3, p. 8.  [70] Nithard I, c. 3, p. 12.
[71] Nithard I, c. 4, p. 14: '... Lodharium ut rem publicam invadat compellunt ...'.
[72] Nithard I, c. 4, p. 8.  [73] Nithard I, c. 5, p. 22.
[74] For a recent example, see Polanichka & Cilley, 'The Very Personal History'.
[75] On this division, see Nelson, *Charles the Bald*, pp. 100–1.  [76] Nithard I, c. 5, p. 30–2.

exonerates Louis through the magic worked on him by Bernard and Judith and their accomplices. This is not the case with Nithard's Lothar, who remains faithless and devious throughout all four books of the *Histories*. As may be expected from the source of the celebrated Strasbourg Oaths, such *sacramenta* play a central part in Nithard's narrative. There are no fewer than twenty of them, proposed, taken or violated, with Charles and Lothar as the two most active oath-swearers. Predictably, the first consistently honours his *fides*, while Lothar reneges on all his promises.[77]

Nithard is not the only author to charge Lothar with swearing oaths lightly, or compelling others to do so. According to the *Annals of St Bertin*, the rebellious eldest son even forced nuns to take oaths to himself,[78] and in the aftermath of the second revolt, Radbert has Wala stand up to Lothar's pressure to make him swear fidelity.[79] In 833, Louis the Pious was accused of making men take or break oaths and thereby endangering their souls.[80] Such claims were part and parcel of the political debate in the 830s and 840s, but there is more to it. When Louis admonished his son Lothar in 839 that he should stop reneging on his oaths, he did so, according to Nithard, 'from his pious entrails': that is, with his innermost and sincere conviction.[81] Nithard's portrait of Lothar is not just that of an oath-breaker but also of a ruler who deviously manipulated the principles of *fides* in order to persuade others who still believed in its binding constraints. This image of Lothar, evoked in Nithard's run-up to the battle of Fontenoy, has a counterpart in Radbert's story of the faithful men who were so earnest in their *fides* that they could not see Bernard drawing them into a well of evil. As Radbert explains, as an exile in his high cave Arsenius worried deeply about the fate of these well-intentioned men, and he grieved for the fact that it was precisely those who were innocently faithful, without any ulterior motive, who were oppressed and dishonoured, and handed over to exile, imprisonment and various harassments.[82]

Radbert's passionate defence of his former abbot and himself goes much further than systematically disproving Wala's alleged infidelity to

---

[77] Lo Monaco, 'Swearing', p. 117, with a survey of the relevant text in n. 25.
[78] *Annals of St Bertin*, s.a. 841, transl. Nelson, p. 52.    [79] *EA* II, c. 20, p. 92.
[80] *Relatio episcoporum* (833), pp. 54–5; for a new edition, see Booker, 'A New Prologue'; for my translation, see De Jong, *Penitential State*, p. 276.
[81] Nithard I, c. 7, p. 32: ' ... in memoriam reducens ac piis visceribus monens contestabatur, ne saltem id, quod tunc novissime peregerant, coramque cunctis ita se velle confirmaverat, frustrari quolibet modo permittat.'
[82] *EA* II, c. 11: 'Dolebat quod boni et optimi oppugnabantur; viri innocentissimi, et fideles quique premebantur et exhonorabantur, tradebanturque exsiliis, carceribus, et diversis iniuriarum fatigiis.'

his emperor. Arsenius is portrayed a leader who was deeply committed to the stability of the state in the broadest sense of the word, which included the religious communities that sustained this stability by their prayer. And although there was much personal resentment behind Nithard's attack on the ever more powerful Adalhard, he discredits his adversary first and foremost as a man who did not have the public interest at heart when he served Charles's father. Using public resources for his own gain, Adalhard had utterly destroyed the *respublica*.[83] The latter's own view was that he had done nothing of the sort: he had pursued his own *iustitia*: that is, his fully justified claims to lands that had been granted to him.[84] Regardless of one's particular allegiance or political position, the reputations of the great and good depended on the way they had fulfilled their obligations to God, king and country. To be found lacking in *fides* by one's peers was tantamount to embracing self-serving greed and the ensuing annihilation of the resources on which the state depended.

## 5    *Unitas, dignitas, concordia*

Finally, Radbert's ideas about unity and division of the Carolingian empire merit further scrutiny, if only because Wala and Agobard of Lyon have been treated as the most prominent members of the *Reichseinheitspartei* in 829 and 830. For this, the *Epitaphium*'s second book is the crown witness, although it represents the ideas Radbert expressed only towards the end of his life. The persistence of this paradigm owes much to Germany's difficulties of state formation in the nineteenth and twentieth centuries, and the consequent preoccupation of its historians with the history of the 'Reich'. Meanwhile, international scholarship largely ignored this topic.[85] It was up to a younger generation of German historians to offer a pertinent critique of the so-called *Reichseinheitspartei* that had supposedly instigated the 'loyal palace rebellion' of 830. As Steffen Patzold has shown, these twin notions were built on shaky foundations, including an anachronistic interpretation of ninth-century political terminology. Only rarely did *imperium* designate a territorially defined 'empire', and its *unitas* was not so much a territorial unity as a unanimity of the rulers and the Frankish leadership.[86] More recently, Patzold has argued that there was no contradiction between

[83] Nithard IV, c. 6, pp. 142–4.
[84] I follow the interpretation of this aspect of the letter given by Nelson, 'Search for Peace', pp. 102–3.
[85] De Jong, 'The Two Rebellions'.
[86] Patzold, 'Eine "loyale Palastrebellion"'; Pohl, 'Creating Cultural Resources'. For a recent example of a more traditional approach, see Hindrichs, 'Zwischen Reichseinheit und adeligen Machtegoismen'.

a *regnum* that could be divided among sons on the one hand, and an *ecclesia* that should be unified by a divinely approved concord on the other. Both concepts represented a religiously defined vision of community, and both existed side by side, without any of the dichotomies between church and state or religion and politics that have hampered modern historiography.[87]

In retrospect, it is difficult to understand how Agobard and Wala (or rather Radbert) could become the main champions of a unity of empire conceived in territorial terms. Modern editions of a letter written in 829 by Agobard to Louis the Pious bear the title *De divisione imperii*.[88] On closer inspection, however, this epistle goes without title in the ninth-century manuscript of Agobard's work, and is not a warning to the emperor to refrain from dividing his empire. Instead, the archbishop refers to a document known by another modern title as the *Ordinatio imperii*, in which the succession arrangements made by Louis in 817 had been recorded. Without mentioning any of the protagonists by name, and choosing his words carefully, Agobard explains that the younger sons were to receive parts of the realm, but in order that 'there would be one *regnum*, not three, you [i.e. Louis] have elevated him over them, him whom you have made a participant in your name'.[89] Lothar, who since 817 had shared the imperial name with his father, was to take precedence over his two younger brothers. Reminding the emperor that these decisions had been reached with the greatest solemnity, seeking divine approval, and that the agreement, subscribed by all, had been sent to Rome for papal confirmation, Agobard added that Louis had then ordered everyone to swear that they would follow and uphold this election and division.[90]

This is the only mention in Agobard's letter of a *divisio*, and it concerns the *regnum*, not the *imperium*. More importantly, the rest of the text is about the dangers attendant on those who had sworn to this succession arrangement and now were compelled by their own emperor to commit perjury. Agobard's opening address sets the tone, for it consists of deft word play on *fides* in the double meaning of faith and fidelity, and underlines the point that as a Christian, Louis himself was one of the faithful, even though everyone owed fidelity to this 'most eminent *fidelis*, to whom the government of the *respublica* had been

---

[87] Patzold, '"Einheit" versus "Fraktionierung"'.

[88] Agobard, *De divisione imperii*; BnF lat. 2853, fols. 187r–190r.

[89] Agobard, *De divisione imperii*, c. 4, p. 248, ll. 21–3: 'Ceteris filiis vestris designastis partes regni vestri, sed ut unum regnum esset, non tria, pretulistis eum illis, quem participem nominis vestri fecistis.'

[90] Agobard, *De divisione imperii*, c. 4, p. 248, ll. 25–7: '... ac deinde iurare omnes iussistis, ut talem electionem cuncti sequentur et servarent.'

entrusted'.[91] Nonetheless, Agobard's admonition to Louis has served as one of the prime witnesses for those historians who have envisaged a clerical 'party for the unity of the empire' that in the years 829–33 strove to uphold the *Ordinatio imperii* of 817, in the face of indigenous Frankish traditions of dividing kingdoms as a patrimony among legitimate sons.[92]

The second book of the *Epitaphium* explicitly addresses the key 'political' concepts that have so much vexed modern historians: *regnum* and *imperium*. Radbert uses this terminology in a flexible but above all associative manner. This is particularly evident in his repeated enumerations of the ideals to which Arsenius was committed.[93] On the one hand, expressions such as *regnum* and *imperium* are distinguished and articulated, but on the other, they are closely associated. Something similar can be found in the Astronomer's biography, where Louis is said to have taken care of affairs that were 'ecclesiastical as well as public' (*tam ecclesiastica quamque publica*).[94] This is not a contradistinction but a pairing of two distinct concepts that creates a close and complementary connection. The same holds true for the juxtaposition of *regnum* and *imperium* as the objects of Arsenius' devotion and loyalty. In Radbert's discourse, these two terms are by no means mutually exclusive. On the contrary, there was a considerable overlap, and both *regnum* and *imperium* could be associated with the benefits of unity and the perils of division.[95] Arsenius stood firm for the 'unity of this glorious and most Christian *regnum*' and, in the next sentence, he defends to the hilt the 'unity and dignity of the entire *imperium*'.[96]

*Regnum* in the *Epitaphium* has more territorial connotations, while *imperium* is often better translated as the 'imperial rule' shared by Louis and his eldest son. There is also a frequent use of the genitive *totius imperii*,

[91] Agobard, *De divisione imperii*, c. 1, p. 247, ll. 3–6: 'Cum unusquisque fidelis omni fidelis fidei sinceritatem debeat, dubium non est, quod precipue fideli praelato, cui res publica ad gubernandam conmissa est, fides servanda est ab omnibus, qui divine dispositione fideliter subiecti sunt ... '.
[92] This historiography is summarised and discussed by Patzold, 'Eine "loyale Palastrebellion"'; for an interpretation of the *Epitaphium Arsenii* from this perspective, see Wehlen, *Geschichtsschreibung*, pp. 105–30.
[93] See above, pp. 185–7.
[94] Astronomer, c. 61, p. 536; this phenomenon is further discussed in De Jong, 'The Two Republics'.
[95] *EA* II, c. 7, p. 67 (Pascasius, on Bernard's rise to power): 'O dies illa, quae pene aeternas huic orbi tenebras attulit et discrimina, quae pacatum imperium et unitum conscidit particulatim ac divisit ... ; *EA* II, c. 11, p. 78 (Pascasius): ' ... pro stabilitate et unitate regni, pacisque concordia, pro depulsione vitiorum et abominationum ... '.
[96] *EA* II, c. 10, p. 76 (Pascasius): 'Voluit enim sui consilii vigilantia providere, tam gloriosum regnum et christianissimum ne divideretur in partes ... Voluit ut unitas et dignitas totius imperii maneret ob defensionem patriae et ecclesiarum liberationem, ob integritatem rerum, et dispensationem facultatum ecclesiarum ... '.

which underlines the inclusiveness of the notion of empire.[97] Another term associated by Radbert with indivisible imperial rule is *monarchia*, perhaps best translated as 'supreme leadership by one emperor'. In 817, Louis had made Lothar his 'successor to the entire monarchy', (*successor totius monarchiae*), that is, the one-headed rule of the entire realm, and it was this that should not be divided, according to Arsenius. *Imperium* and *monarchia* tend to be used as synonyms for exercise of authority by one senior emperor, rather than as a reference to a territorial notion of empire.[98]

The passages most focused on political unity and division, with strong religious connotations, occur in the context of Radbert's indictment of self-interested counsellors. A particularly eloquent example is voiced by the monk Adeodatus, who delivers a scathing diatribe on the divisive and even ruinous results of the rebellion of 833. Having likened those who replaced Wala to birds of prey (*milvi*), Radbert continues to attack these so-called counsellors where it hurt most in the eyes of his readers: they had lacked the foresight and withheld the counsel on which the *respublica* and the stability of the entire empire (*status totius imperii*) depended. Because of their negligence, the realm was divided and destroyed, and remained so to the present day.[99] Radbert's lament over this outcome, voiced by Adeodatus, ends with a conclusion that encapsulates his argument throughout the *Epitaphium*: Arsenius had devoted his earthly life to God, but the rulers he had to contend with had not, and they refused to heed his advice. 'Thus, according to the Word of Truth, from day to day *a kingdom divided shall be brought to desolation*[100]and be corrupted, because where there is no helmsman, the people come to grief.'[101] It is not the division of the *imperium* or *regnum* among legitimate heirs that is condemned, but the way in which both Louis and Lothar went about it, cutting through the social and religious fabric that held together the Frankish polity, and without

[97] *EA* II, c. 1, p. 61 (haec mala totius imperii); c. 7, p. 68 (vertigo totius imperii); c. 8, p. 69 (iura totius imperii); c. 8, p. 70 (subversionum totius imperii); c. 9, p. 72 (de totius imperii edixit subversione, senatus totius imperii); c. 10, p. 76 (unitas et dignitas totius imperii); c. 11, p. 78 (contumelia totius imperii); c. 14, p. 81 (pro adunatione populi et salvatione totius imperii; consiliarius totius imperii); c. 15, p. 82 (pro statu totius imperii); c. 17, p. 86 (consortem totius imperii); c. 19, pp. 89–90 (status totius imperii).

[98] *Monarchia* occurs thrice in *EA* II, c. 10, pp. 73–6; see also *EA* II, c. 16, p. 84 (totius monarchiae sceptra) and c. 19, p. 89 (omnem monarchiam; totius monarchiae imperii).

[99] *EA* II, c. 19, p. 89–90 (Adeodatus).

[100] Luke 11:17: 'ipse autem ut vidit cogitationes eorum dixit eis omne regnum in se ipsum divisum desolatur et domus supra domum cadet ... '.

[101] *EA* II, c. 19, p. 90 (Adeodatus): 'Idcirco iuxta veritatis sententiam, divisum regnum quotidie desolatur, et corrumpitur: quoniam ubi non est gubernator, populus corruit.'

the consensus of all those who had a stake in this commonwealth. This meant going against God's precepts by sowing discord and putting 'unity' in danger. Modern historians need to remember that in these debates, God is the heaviest ammunition that can be mustered, not because religion simply reinforces politics, but because divine approval is the ultimate point of reference in any ninth-century debate about politics.

Hence, the unity of the realm is associated, first and foremost, with the restoration of peace and concord, and is almost synonymous with unanimity. The loss of this, in a welter of discord and self-interest, spells the loss of collective dignity: a sentiment that is also central to Florus of Lyon's lament of 842/3 about the loss of the name and distinction of *imperium*, and an emperor's having been replaced by kinglets.[102] A kingdom divided against itself would suffer a grievous loss of reputation and honour in the eyes of outsiders, but the issue was not territorial division, it was the loss of an internal consensus that was generally understood as divinely sanctioned and humanly limited. In one of Radbert's eloquent onslaughts against counsellors who did not live up to their task, the monk Teofrastus marvels that 'for such a great empire, for such a great dignity, of the kingdom and the churches' no strong-minded prelates and magnates could be found to safeguard the stability of the entire empire and the common weal.[103] The semantic field of *dignitas* includes authority, rank and honour, but also the (landed) wealth that sustained it – a meaning that resonates especially in Radbert's references to the *dignitas ecclesiarum*.[104] The estates and rights of religious communities would fall prey to 'domestic robbery' in a realm governed by discord, but they would also suffer the loss of honour and dignity that ensued from being plundered with impunity, and this in turn reflected on the rulers who were supposed to guarantee the stability of prayer. The fact that Radbert in 846 felt the need to have a synodal privilege to confirm his monastery's exceptional number of royal privileges of immunity

---

[102] Godman, *Poetry*, p. 268, ll. 73–7.

[103] *EA* II, c. 15, p. 82: 'Mirabar nimium, et mirantur plurimi quid esset, quod pro tanto imperio, pro tanta dignitate regni et ecclesiarum, nequaquam satis multi praesules vel senatores forti et magno animo invenirentur, qui auderent se et salutem suam in discrimen offerre pro statu totius imperii, pro communi salute'.

[104] *EA* II, c. 3, p. 64: 'Hinc igitur tunc omnes coeperunt, maxime ecclesiastici viri, quaerere et contradicere, quomodo aliter dignitas et honor ecclesiarum stare potuisset, ac si decreta sanctorum patrum non legissent; *EA* II, c. 15, p. 82: '... vel cum bonis omnibus tunc temporis dignitatem regiam, et ecclesiarum, afflictam et dejectam, vel constupratam reerexerint, et a latrocinio domestico liberaverint ... '.

speaks volumes in this respect. This was all about Corbie's honour, and about its abbot's duty to preserve it.[105]

In this type of discourse, the *ecclesia* (singular) was an alternative and inclusive way to denote the Carolingian polity, because it transcended the ethnic distinctions that defined the Frankish *regnum*, and was therefore more in agreement with the notion of an expanding Christian empire that included many peoples (*gentes*).[106] Yet the *Epitaphium*'s second book is not the most convincing source to cite in this context. As I have argued in my discussion of Wala's speeches in the previous chapter, Radbert's *ecclesia* comprised an ecclesiastical and a secular order, and it included the *respublica* proper: that is, the royal and therefore public domain, as well as the plural *ecclesiae*, of which Radbert maintained that they were like a public domain (*quasi respublica*). These two entities were interconnected, but separate. As we have seen, these 'churches', in the sense of religious communities and their rights and properties, are much more prominent in Radbert's discourse than 'the Church' as it still looms large in modern historiography. Despite his emphatic qualification of the empire as a totality, he did not think in terms of an all-encompassing *sancta ecclesia* that might serve as an alternative model for the political community. *Ecclesia* and *imperium* are most closely associated in Radbert's view that Lothar, once he had become emperor, had become the protector of the bishop of Rome, and therefore had the right and duty to defend the pontiff, just like his father.[107] By the mid-850s, this was hardly a revolutionary view. Radbert's *ecclesia Christi* is best characterised as the total sum of all those devoting their lives to the worship of God: the vast network of churches, communities of prayer that, together with the people and the *respublica*, had been entrusted to an emperor who failed to live up to high expectations.[108]

In the political turmoil of the decades after Louis's death in 840, the unity of the Frankish realm became more of an issue than it had ever been before. Three rulers fought for their share in their father's legacy, and remained frequently at loggerheads in the decades that followed. No wonder, then, that the clamour for unity became stronger and

---

[105] See above, pp. 57–64.

[106] De Jong, 'Empire as *ecclesia*'; Patzold, '"Einheit" versus "Fraktionierung"'.

[107] *EA* II, c. 17, p. 87 (Honorius/Lothar as speaker): 'Unde quia coram sancto altare, et coram sancto corpore beati Petri principis apostolorum, a summo pontifice, vestro ex consensu et voluntate, benedictionem, honorem et nomen suscepi imperialis officii, insuper diademata capitis et gladium ad defensionem ipsius ecclesiae et imperii vestri . . . '.

[108] *EA* II, c. 17, p. 88.

more articulate. This was not a yearning for territorial unity, which had clearly been lost, but for unity of purpose, dignity in the eyes of outsiders, and internal consensus and concord. All these ideals were projected onto the recent past, when Charlemagne had reigned and Louis had not yet been challenged. The *Epitaphium*'s second book is a precious witness to this process.

# Conclusion

My aim has been to get an inside view of Radbert's turbulent and rapidly changing world, from the vantage point of just one of this author's many works: his *Epitaphium Arsenii*. This funeral oration for Abbot Wala consists of two books that were written at two different stages of Radbert's life and career. The first book dates to the years immediately after Wala's death in 836 and, I suspect, before the demise of Louis the Pious in 840. The second was added some two decades later, in the mid- to late 850s, at a time when Radbert had been compelled to step down as abbot of Corbie after a tenure of approximately seven years. Some monks of Corbie affectionately called Wala 'our Arsenius', but others felt let down by this controversial abbot. He got involved in the two revolts against Louis in 830 and 833, and then in 834 Wala followed the rebellious eldest son Lothar to Italy, to become abbot of Bobbio, leaving Corbie in the lurch. In the aftermath of all this, Wala's name remained tainted, and Radbert rushed to the defence of his master, not least because his own position was affected. This is the crux of this funeral oration: it was about restoring the two interconnected reputations of the author and his mentor. The distance in time between the two books lends an extraordinary dynamism to the *Epitaphium*, but this emerges only from the contents of the text itself. The only extant manuscript from Corbie was copied not long after the completion of the second book (Paris, BnF lat. 13909). It is a carefully corrected copy that looks as if it was prepared to be inspected by discerning eyes outside the monastery.

Or should we conclude from this one surviving manuscript that Radbert wrote only for internal consumption: that is, for his own religious community? On the basis of the contents of the *Epitaphium*, I have come to a different assessment. This is not to say, however, that this sophisticated debate between three monastic discussion partners was meant for a large audience. Radbert's ambitious literary strategies, as well as the bynames and aliases he chose for his protagonists, excluded those who were not familiar with the Latin classics, or with the legacy of late imperial

Christianity I have referred to as 'the world of Ambrose'. It was not just learned churchmen who had access to this tradition, however, but also members of the Carolingian lay elite. The *Epitaphium*, and especially its second book, is best compared with Nithard's *Histories* and Dhuoda's *Liber manualis*, works by two contemporary authors who addressed the vicissitudes and dilemmas of the Carolingian *respublica* in the 840s. Their work is discussed in the last chapter of this book. Like Radbert, they wrote from a personal perspective, and their works never enjoyed a wide dissemination, and yet there is nothing 'private' about their approach. All three belonged to a court-connected elite that judged its peers by a common yardstick of public service, and it was for the benefit of these peers, in the first place, that they expressed their views of an ideal polity and their own role therein.

This also holds true of the *Epitaphium*'s so-called 'monastic' first book. It features Wala/Arsenius as a novice at Charlemagne's court and as the old emperor's second in command who led victorious armies into battle; then, once he had been tonsured and entered Corbie in 814, Wala became the informal head of the community, until he succeeded his brother Adalhard as abbot in 826. The account of the brothers' harmonious cooperation is also a portrait of two conflicting ideals of monastic leadership. Wala's vigorous asceticism gets much attention, but so does his charisma in the outside world: this was a natural leader, who could manage an assembly of unruly Saxons like the best of them. By contrast, the old and humble Adalhard, formally the abbot, went unnoticed at such public gatherings, and quietly retreated to the monastery, accompanied by Radbert, who also felt more at home in the cloister. Of course this is a simplified image, for throughout his career, Adalhard had never been a stranger to the palace. In fact, Radbert portrays two different aspects of the role of abbots, and, to some extent, of abbesses as well. They constantly had to balance their ascetic authority within their communities with their manifold duties in the world outside, not least those in the corridors of royal power. The tension between these two sides of the abbacy is a key issue in the *Epitaphium*'s first book, and, given the vital importance of Corbie and other large religious establishments to the exercise of Carolingian royal power, such problems are no less 'political' than those concerning loyalty and rebellion discussed in the second book.

The entire *Epitaphium* is pervaded by the values Radbert shared with other members of the Frankish leadership, regardless of whether they were allies or enemies. Nonetheless, the articulate way in which the second book voices the dilemmas of loyalty (*fides*) to God and one's ruler is typical for the years after Louis's death in 840. Here, the comparison with Nithard and Dhuoda is most pertinent, for their work also bears the imprint of the first real crisis of the Carolingian empire, as opposed to the prelude of the early 830s, when bloodshed within the Frankish elite had still been avoided. Inevitably, the struggle for succession that broke out in 841 led to a further reflection on the nature of political division and unity. It also produced the first explicit discussions of the *unitas imperii*, an expression best translated as the 'unanimity of imperial rule', rather than as the 'unity of the empire' in a modern territorial sense of the word. In his discussion of this and other key notions, such as *respublica* and *fides*, Radbert relies on his classical and late antique reading, but in the context of his own world, the terminology he derived from Cicero or Ambrose gained a new and different meaning. The same is true of his more general understanding of the Carolingian polity. Rather than opposing a secular state to a monolithic Church, Radbert envisages an archipelago of religious communities, monastic and otherwise. This plurality of 'churches' (*ecclesiae*) functioned like an alternative public domain, closely connected with, and yet separate from, the public domain proper, the *respublica* to which the ruler had direct rather than indirect access. The distinction between these two republics was above all a matter of who controlled their landed wealth. Hence, the *Epitaphium*'s discussion of *respublica* concentrates on the extent to which the ruler could use monastic estates to raise troops or reward followers. In other words, the *res* component was as important as that of the 'public', and this fits Radbert's own fierce defence of the integrity of Corbie's property in the years 843–49/53, when he was this community's abbot and joined the bishops in their fight to contain an ambitious ruler, Charles the Bald. This king is never explicitly mentioned or criticised in the *Epitaphium*'s polemical second book, yet his presence is palpable.

Radbert's vision of the better world that had disappeared in a welter of discord focused not just on Charlemagne's blessed government, but also on Louis's once happy rule, that had lasted until Bernard of Septimania took over the palace in 829. The years before had been Wala's heyday, when royal counsellors understood their duties and stood up to their rulers, rather than pursuing private gain like robbers. Although this line of attack was Radbert's way of getting back at the competition, it also shows that the principles he bewailed as lost were alive and well, and very much a part of the dismal present he loudly lamented. Both in the 830s and mid-850s, when he wrote the two books of his *Epitaphium*, he had incurred royal disfavour, like his subject Wala/Arsenius, who had been exiled repeatedly from the court. Identifying with the exiled Wala and with Jeremiah enabled Radbert to position himself as an outsider, also in the rhetorical sense of the word. In the second book, as ex-abbot, he could deliver the kind of frank criticism that he would never have been able to voice had he still been in office. His outsider status was more than a mere literary strategy aimed at improving his own position, which continued to be bound up with Wala's reputation. The two tight spots out of which Radbert attempted to extricate himself, first after Wala's death and then when he lost the abbacy of Corbie, were no figment of his literary imagination.

When all is said and done, the *Epitaphium* is a text shaped by the realities of two intertwined and turbulent lives, in which author and subject were themselves part of the story. But it was a story that deeply mattered, even years afterwards when the second book was added, and not just to a few learned monks in Corbie who happened to enjoy Terence's comedies. This passionate attempt to restore Wala's damaged character was addressed to an elite audience whose opinion could make or break such reputations, including Radbert's own. Separating the real Wala from his disciple's narrative has never been my purpose. On the contrary, I set my sights on Radbert's fascinating vision of his recent past, for which he was writing an epitaph, as much as he was for Wala/Arsenius, his beloved master. This was an author who habitually presented himself in his prefaces as the greatest scum of all the monks, but who also fervently hoped that his witty remarks would be reported to the Emperor Louis the Pious himself. This suggests a complex and interesting personality, but since we know next to nothing about the man himself, I have allowed myself very little speculation, even though I suspect that the intransigence with which he credits his intrepid Arsenius was in fact his own obstinacy. If at times I did not manage to resist Radbert's persistence, or his formidable powers of persuasion, so be it: this was what the author intended. I hope that others may build on the outcome of my years of close engagement with the *Epitaphium Arsenii*, or simply enjoy getting to know the territory, as I have.

# Bibliography

## Primary Sources

Adalhard of Corbie, *Statuta seu Brevia*, ed. J. Semmler, *Corpus consuetudinum monasticarum* 1 (Siegburg, 1963), pp. 365–422.

Agobard of Lyon, *Opera omnia*, ed. L. van Acker, CCCM 52 (Turnhout, 1981).

*De dispensatione ecclesiasticarum rerum*, ed. L, van Acker, *Opera omnia*, pp. 121–42.

*De divisione imperii*, ed. L, van Acker, *Opera omnia*, pp. 247–50.

*De privilegio apostolicae sedis*, ed. L. van Acker, *Opera omnia*, pp. 301–6.

*Epistolae*, ed. E. Dümmler, *MGH Epp.* V = Karol. aevi III, pp. 150–239.

*Liber Apologeticus I, II*, ed. L, van Acker, *Opera omnia*, pp. 307–12, 313–9.

Alcuin, *Disputatio de rhetorica et virtutibus*, ed. and transl. W.S. Howell (Princeton, 1941).

*Epistolae*, ed. E. Dümmler, *MGH Epp.* IV = Karol. aevi II (Berlin, 1895), pp. 18–481.

Amalarius of Metz, *Prologus antiphonarii a se compositi*, ed. J.M. Hanssens, *Amalarii episcopi opera liturgica omnia I: Introductio – opera minora*. Studi e testi 138 (Vatican City, 1948), pp. 361–3.

Ambrose of Milan, *De bono mortis*, ed. W.T. Wiesner, *S. Ambrosii De bono mortis: A Revised Text with an Introduction, Translation, and Commentary*. Patristic Studies 100 (Washington DC, 1970).

*De excessu fratris Satyri*, ed. O. Faller, CSEL 73 (Vienna, 1955), pp. 207–325; transl. H. de Romestin, E. de Romestin and H.T.F. Duckworth, *On the Death of Satyrus*, in P. Schaff and H. Wace (eds.), *Nicene and Post-Nicene Fathers*, Second Series, Vol. 10 (Buffalo NY, 1896). Revised and edited K. Knight, http://www.newadvent.org/fathers/3403.htm.

*De fide*, ed. O. Faller, CSEL 78 (Vienna, 1962).

*De obitu Theodosii*, ed. O. Faller, CSEL 73, pp. 369–401; transl. J.H.W.G. Liebeschuetz, *Ambrose of Milan, Political Letters and Speeches*, pp. 174–203;

*De obitu Valentiniani*, ed. O. Faller, CSEL 73, pp. 327–67; transl. J.H.W.G. Liebeschuetz, *Ambrose of Milan, Political Letters and Speeches*, pp. 358–99.

*De officiis*, ed. I.J. Davidson, 2 vols. (Oxford, 2001).

Angilbert, *Versus de bella quae fuit acta Fontaneto*, ed. E. Dümmler, *MGH Poet. lat.* II, pp. 138–9; transl. P. Godman, Poetry, no. 39, pp. 262–4.

*Annales Bertiniani*, ed. R. Rau, Quellen zur karolingsche Reichsgeschichte 2 (Darmstadt, 1972), pp. 13–287; trans. J.L. Nelson, *The Annals of St-Bertin*. Ninth-Century Histories 1 (Manchester, 1991).

*Annales Fuldenses*, ed. G.H. Pertz and F. Kurze, *MGH SRG* 7 (Hanover, 1891); transl. T. Reuter, *The Annals of Fulda*. Ninth-Century Histories 2 (Manchester, 1992).

*Annales Iuvavenses maiores*, ed. H. Bresslau, *MGH SS* XXX/2, pp. 732–40.

Augustine of Hippo, Confessionum in libri tredecim, ed. L. Verheijen, CCSL 27 (Turnhout, 1981).

*De doctrina christiana*, ed. and transl. R.P.H. Green. Oxford Early Christian Texts (Oxford, 1995).

*De magistro*, ed. K.-D. Daur, CCSL 29 (Turnhout, 1970), pp. 157–203.

*Enarrationes in psalmos*, ed. E. Dekkers and J. Fraipont, CCSL 38–40 (Turnhout, 1956).

*Biblia sacra iuxta vulgatam versionem*, ed. R. Weber (Darmstadt, ⁴1994).

Boethius, *De consolatione philosophiae*, ed. and transl. H.F. Stewart, E.K. Rand and S.J. Tester, *Boethius, The Theological Treatises*. LCL 74 (Cambridge MA, 1974).

Cicero, *Brutus. Orator*, ed. G.L. Hendrickson, transl. H.M. Hubbell, LCL 342 (Cambridge MA, 1939).

*De inventione*, ed. J. Henderson, transl. H.M. Hubbell, LCL 386 (Cambridge MA, 1949), pp. 1–345.

*De officiis*, ed. M. Winterbottom (Oxford, 1994); transl. M.T. Griffin and E.M. Atkins, *Cicero, On Duties* (Cambridge, 1991).

*De optimo genere oratorum*, ed. J. Henderson, transl. H.M. Hubbell, LCL 386 (Cambridge MA, 1949), p. 355–74.

*De oratore*, books 1–2, ed. H. Rackham, transl. E.W. Sutton, LCL 348–49 (Cambridge MA, 1949).

*Topica*, ed. G. L. Hendrickson, transl. H.M. Hubbell, LCL 386 (Cambridge MA, 1949, repr. 2006), pp. 382–458.

Dhuoda, *Liber manualis*, ed. P. Riché, *Manuel pour mon fils*. SC 225bis (Paris, 1991).

*Disticha Catonis*, ed. M. Boas and H.J. Botschuyver (Amsterdam, 1952).

Einhard, *Epistolae*, ed. K. Hampe, *MGH Epistolae Karolini aevi* III (Berlin, 1899), pp. 105–49; transl. P.E. Dutton, *Charlemagne's Courtier* (Peterborough ON, 1998).

*Translatio SS Petri et Marcellini*, ed. G. Waitz and W. Wattenbach, *MGH SS* XV (Hanover, 1888).

*Vita Karoli magni*, ed. O. Holder-Egger, *MGH SRG* 25, 6ᵗʰ edn. (Hanover and Leipzig, 1911).

Ekkehard IV of St Gall, *Casus S. Galli*, ed. H. Haefele, AQ 10 (Darmstadt, 1980).

Engelmodus, *Carmina*, ed. L. Traube, *MGH Poet. lat.* III, 1 (Berlin, 1896), pp. 62–6.

Ermoldus Nigellus, *In honorem Hludowici christianissimi caesaris augusti. Ermold le Noir. Poème sur Louis le Pieux et épitres au roi Pépin*, ed. and transl. E. Faral (Paris, 1964).

Florus of Lyon, *Carmina* no. 28, ed. E. Dümmler, *MGH Poet. lat.* II, pp. 559–64; transl. P. Godman, Poetry, no. 40, pp. 265–73.

Gregory the Great, *Dialogi*, ed. A. de Vogüé and P. Antin, *Grégoire Le Grand, Dialogues*, SC 251, 260 and 265 (Paris, 1978–80).

Hrabanus Maurus, *Epistolae*, ed. E. Dümmler, MGH *Epp.* V = Karol. aevi III (Berlin, 1899), pp. 379–533.

*Commentaria in libros II Paralipomenon, PL* 110, cols. 279–540.

Isidore of Seville, *Etymologiae sive origines,* ed. W.M. Lindsay, 2 vols. (Oxford, 2011).

Jerome, *Adversus Iovinianum, PL* 23, cols. 211–338.

*Altercatio Luceferiani et Orthodoxi, PL* 23, cols. 155–92.

*Dialogus aduersus Pelagianos,* ed. C. Moreschini, CCSL 80 (Turnhout, 1990); *PL* 23, cols. 517–618.

*Epistolae,* ed. I. Hilberg, 3 vols., CSEL 54–6 (Vienna, 1910–1918).

*Hebraicae quaestiones in libro Geneseos. Liber interpretationis hebraicorum nominum,* ed. P. de Lagarde, G. Morin and M. Adriaen, CCSL 72 (Turnhout, 1959).

*Vita Pauli,* ed. P. Leclerc, E. M. Morales and A. de Vogüé, *Trois vies de moines: Paul, Malchus, Hilarion,* SC 508 (Paris, 2007), pp. 144–82.

Johannes Scottus Eriugena, *Carmina,* ed. M.W. Herren. Scriptores Latini Hiberniae 12 (Dublin, 1993).

Jonas of Bobbio, *Vita Columbani, MGH SRM* IV (Hanover and Leipzig, 1902), pp. 61–152; trans. A. O'Hara and I. Wood, *Jonas of Bobbio, Life of Columbanus, Life of John of Réomé, and Life of Vedast.* Translated Texts for Historians 64 (Liverpool, 2017).

Jonas of Orléans, *Admonitio ad Pippinum regem,* ed. and transl. A. Dubreucq, Jonas d'Orléans, *Le métier du roi,* SC 407 (Paris, 1995), pp. 148–70.

*De institutione laicali, PL* 106, cols. 121–278.

*De institutione regia,* ed. and transl. A. Dubreucq, Jonas d'Orléans, *Le métier du roi.* SC 407 (Paris, 1995), pp. 172–284.

*Liber Pontificalis,* ed. L. Duchesne, *Le Liber Pontificalis: texte, introduction et commentaire,* 2 vols., (Paris, 1886–9; transl. R. Davis, rev. edn. (Liverpool, 2000); *The Lives of the Eighth-Century Popes (Liber Pontificalis)* (Liverpool, 1992); The Lives of the Ninth-Century Popes (Liverpool, 1995).

Lupus, *Epistolae,* ed. and transl. L. Levillain, *Loup de Ferrières, Correspondance,* 2 vols. (Paris, 1927 and 1935); transl. G.W. Regenos, *The Letters of Lupus of Ferrières* (The Hague, 1966).

*Menander Rhetor,* ed. and transl. D.A. Russell and N.G. Wilson (Oxford, 1981).

*Notitia fundationis monasterii Corbeiensis* II, ed. O. Holder-Egger, *MGH SS* XV/2, pp. 1043–5.

Notker, *Gesta Karoli magni imperatoris,* ed. H.F. Haefele, *MGH SRG* n.s. 12 (Berlin, 1959); transl. D. Ganz, *Einhard and Notker the Stammerer: Two Lives of Charlemagne* (London, 2008).

Paschasius Radbertus, *Carmina,* ed. L. Traube, *MGH Poet. lat.* III (Hanover, 1896), pp. 45–53.

*De assumptione Sanctae Mariae virginis,* E.A. Matter and A. Ripberger, CCCM 56 C (Turnhout, 1985).

*De benedictionibus patriarcharum Jacob et Moysi,* ed. B. Paulus, CCCM 96 (Turnhout, 1993).

*De corpore et sanguine Domini; cum appendice Epistola ad Fredugardum,* ed. B. Paulus, CCCM 16 (Turnhout, 1969).

*De fide, spe et caritate,* ed. B. Paulus, CCCM 97 (Turnhout, 1990),

*De partu virginis,* ed. E.A. Matter and A. Ripberger, CCCM 56 C (Turnhout, 1985).

*Epistola beati Hieronymi ad Paulam et Eustochium de assumptione sanctae Mariae virginis*, ed. A. Ripberger, *Der Pseudo-Hieronymus-Brief IX "Cogitis me". Ein erster Marianischer Traktat des Mittelalters von Paschasius Radbertus.* Spicilegium Friburgense 9 (Freiburg, 1962), pp. 49–113.

*Epistolae*, ed. E. Dümmler, *MGH Epp.* VI = Karol. aevi IV, (Berlin, 1925), pp. 132–49.

*Expositio in lamentationes Hieremiae libri quinque*, ed. B. Paulus, CCCM 85 (Turnhout, 1988).

*Expositio in Matheo libri XII*, ed. B. Paulus, 3 vols., CCCM 56–56A–56B (Turnhout, 1984).

*Expositio in psalmum XLIV*, ed. B. Paulus, CCCM 94 (Turnhout, 1991).

*Passio Rufini et Valerii, PL* 120, cols. 1489–1508.

Paul the Deacon, *Historia Langobardarum*, ed. L. Bethmann and G. Waitz, *MGH SRL* (Hanover, 1878), pp. 12–187.

*Privilege of the Synod of Paris (846/7) for Corbie*, ed. W. Hartmann, *MHG Conc.* III, pp. 140–9.

Quintilian, *Institutionis oratoriae libri duodecim*, ed. M. Winterbottom (Oxford, 1970).

Regino of Prüm, *Chronicon*, ed. F. Kurze, *MGH SRG* 50 (Hannover, 1890); transl. S. MacLean, *History and Politics in Late Carolingian and Ottonian Europe. The Chronicle of Regino of Prüm and Adalbert of Magdeburg.* Manchester Medieval Sources Series (Manchester and New York NY, 2009).

*Regula Benedicti*, ed. and transl. B. Venarde. Dumbarton Oaks Latin Library 6 (Cambridge MA, 2011).

*Rhetorica ad Herennium*, transl. H. Caplan, LCL 403 (Cambridge MA, 1954).

Rufinus, *Historia ecclesiastica*, E. Schwartz and T. Mommsen, 2nd edition by F. Winkelmann, *Eusebius, Werke II.1–3, Die Kirchengeschichte. Die griechischen christlichen Schriftsteller der ersten Jahrhunderte*, NF 6.1–3 (Berlin, 1999); transl. P.R. Amidon, *Rufinus of Aquileia: History of the Church.* Fathers of the Church 133 (Washington DC, 2016); partly transl. P.R. Amidon, *The Church History of Rufinus of Aquileia: Books 10 and 11* (Oxford, 1997).

Sulpicius Severus, *Gallus*, ed. J. Fontaine and N. Dupré, *Sulpice Sévère, Gallus. Dialogues sur les "vertus" de saint Martin*, SC 510 (Paris, 2006).

Terence, *Comedies*, ed. and transl. J. Barsby, 2 vols., LCL 22–3 (Cambridge MA, 2001).

*Translatio S. Viti martyris*, ed. and transl. I. Schmale-Ott. Übertragung des hl. Martyrers Vitus. Veröffentlichungen der historischen Kommision für Westfalen 41 (Münster, 1979).

*Vita Paschasii Radberti*, ed. O. Holder-Egger, *MGH SS* XV/1, pp. 452–4.

Wala of Corbie, *Breve memorationis Walae abbatis a. 834/36 Bobbiensi monasterio datum*, ed. J. Semmler, CCM I (Sigmaringen, 1963), pp. 420–2.

## Secondary Sources

Adkin, N., 'Terence's Eunuchus and Jerome', *Rheinisches Museum für Philologie*, n.s. 137 (1994), 187–95.

Airlie, S., 'The Aristocracy in the Service of the State in the Carolingian Period',
in S. Airlie, W. Pohl and H. Reimitz (eds.), *Staat*, pp. 93–112; repr. in
S. Airlie, *Power and its Problems* V.
'I, Agobard, Unworthy Bishop', in R. Corradini et al. (eds.), *Ego Trouble*,
pp. 175–84.
'The Palace of Memory: The Carolingian Court as Political Centre', in S. Rees
Jones, R. Marks and A. Minnis (eds.), *Courts and Regions in Medieval Europe*
(York, 2000), pp. 1–20; repr. in S. Airlie, *Power and its Problems*.
*Power and its Problems in Carolingian Europe*. Variorum Collected Studies Series
(Farnham, 2012).
'Private Bodies and the Body Politic in the Divorce Case of Lothar II', *Past and
Present* 161 (1998), 3–38; repr. in S. Airlie, *Power and its Problems*.
'*Semper fideles*? Loyauté envers les Carolingiens comme constituant de
l'identité aristocratique', in R. Le Jan (ed.), *La royauté et les élites dans
l'Europe carolingienne (début du IXe siècle aux environs de 920)* (Lille, 1997),
pp. 129–43; repr. in S. Airlie, *Power and its Problems*.
'Towards a Carolingian Aristocracy', in M. Becher and J. Jarnut (eds.),
*Dynastiewechsel*, pp. 109–27; repr. in S. Airlie, *Power and its Problems*.
'The World, the Text and the Carolingian. Aristocratic and Masculine
Identities in Nithard's *Histories*', in P. Wormald and J.L. Nelson (eds.), *Lay
Intellectuals*, pp. 51–77; repr. in S. Airlie, *Power and its Problems*.
Airlie, S., W. Pohl and H. Reimitz (eds.), *Staat im frühen Mittelalter, Forschungen
zur Geschichte des Mittelalters* 11 (Vienna, 2006).
Amory, F., 'Whited Sepulchres: The Semantic History of Hypocrisy to the High
Middle Ages', *Recherches de théologie ancienne et médiévale* 53 (1986), 5–36.
Angenendt, A., *Monachi peregrini. Studien zu Primin und den monastischen
Vorstellungen des frühen Mittelalters*. Münstersche Mittelalterschiften 6
(München, 1972).
Appleby, D, 'Beautiful on the Cross, Beautiful in his Torments: The Place of the
Body in the Thought of Paschasius Radbertus', *Traditio* 60 (2005), 1–46.
Aris, M.-A., 'Paschasius Radbertus', *Lexikon des Mittelalters* 6, cols. 1754–5.
Barbier, J. and L. Morelle, 'Le diplôme de fondation de l'abbaye de Corbie (657/
661): contexte, enjeux et modalités d'une falsification', *Revue du Nord* 391-2
(2011), 613–54.
Batlle, C., *Die Adhortationes sanctorum patrum (Verba seniorum) im lateinischen
Mittelalter. Überlieferung, Fortleben und Wirkung*. Beiträge zur Geschichte des
alten Mönchtums und des Benediktinerordens 31 (Münster, 1972).
Bayless, M., 'Alcuin's *Disputatio Pippini* and the Early Medieval Riddle
Tradition', in G. Halsall (ed.), *Humour, History and Politics in Late Antiquity
and the Early Middle Ages* (Cambridge, 2002), pp. 157–78.
Becher, M. and J. Jarnut (eds.), *Der Dynastiewechsel von 751. Vorgeschichte,
Legitimationsstrategien und Erinnerung* (Münster, 2004).
Bertrand, P., Die Evagriusübersetzung der Vita Antonii: Rezeption,
Überlieferung, Edition. Unter besonderer Berücksichtigung der Vitas
Patrum-Tradition. Unpublished PhD thesis, Utrecht University (2005).
https://dspace.library.uu.nl/bitstream/handle/1874/7821/full.pdf.

Berschin, W., *Biographie und Epochenstil im lateinischen Mittelalter*, 5 vols., Quellen und Untersuchungen zur lateinischen Philologie des Mittelalters 8–10; 12/1–2; 15 (Heidelberg, 1986–2004).

'Epitaphium als biographische Form', in W. Berschin, J. Gómes Pallarès and J.M. Gásques (eds.), *Mittellateinische Biographie und Epik/Biografia latina medieval y epigrafia* (Heidelberg, 2005), pp. 47–54.

Biermann, M, *Die Leichenreden des Ambrosius von Mailand. Rhetorik, Predigt, Politik* (Stuttgart, 1995).

Bischoff, B., 'Hadoardus and the Manuscripts of Classical Authors from Corbie', in S. Prete (ed.), *Didascaliae. Studies in Honor of Anselm M. Albareda* (New York, 1961), pp. 39–57; revised German version in B. Bischoff, *Mittelalterliche Studien*, 3 vols., pp. 49–6.

*Mittelalterliche Studien*, 3 vols. (Stuttgart, 1966–88).

*Die südostdeutschen Schreibschulen und Bibliotheken in der Karolingerzeit II: Die vorwiegend Österreichischen Diozesen* (Wiesbaden, 1980).

Bischoff, B., with B. Ebersperger, *Katalog der Festländischen Handschriften des neunten Jahrhunderts (mit Ausnahme der wisigotischen)*, 3 vols. (Wiesbaden, 1998–2014).

Bishop, T.A.M., 'The Script of Corbie, a Criterion', in *Varia codicologica: Essays Presented to G.I. Lieftinck I* (Amsterdam, 1972), pp. 9–16.

Booker, C.M., 'An Early Humanist Edition of Nithard's *De dissensionibus filiorum Ludovici Pii*', *Revue d'histoire des textes* 5 (2010), 231–58.

'The False Decretals and Ebbo's *fama ambigua*. A Verdict Revisited', in K. Ubl and D. Ziemann (eds.), *Fälschung als Mittel der Politik?*, pp. 207–42.

'Hypocrisy, Performativity and the Carolingian Pursuit of Truth', *EME* 26 (2019), 174–202.

'A New Prologue of Walahfrid Strabo', *Viator* 36 (2005), 93–105.

*Past Convictions. The Penance of Louis of Pious and the Decline of the Carolingians* (Philadelphia, 2009).

'The Public Penance of Louis the Pious: A New Edition of the *Episcoporum de poenitentia, quam Hludowicus imperator professus est, relatio Compendiensis* (833)', *Viator* 39 (2008), 1–19.

Boshof, E., *Erzbischof Agobard von Lyon. Leben und Werk* (Cologne, 1969).

'Traditio Romana und Papstschutz im 9. Jahrhundert. Untersuchungen zur vorcluniazensischen libertas', in E. Boshof and H. Wolter (eds.), *Rechtsgeschichtlich-Diplomatische Studien zu frühmittelalterlichen Papsturkunden*. Studien und Vorarbeiten zur Germania Pontifica 6 (Cologne and Vienna, 1976), pp. 1–100.

Breternitz, P., 'Ludwig der Fromme und die Entfremdung von Kirchengut. Beobachtungen zum Epitaphium Arsenii', in K. Ubl and D. Ziemann (eds.), *Fälschung als Mittel der Politik?*, pp. 187–206.

Brown, W., M. Costambeys, M. Innes and A.J. Kosto (eds.), *Documentary Culture and the Laity in the Early Middle Ages* (Cambridge, 2013).

Brühl, C., *Studien zu den merowingischen Königsurkunden*, ed. T. Kölzer (Köln/Wien, 1998), pp. 226–59.

Brunhölzl, F., *Histoire de la littérature latine I/2. L'époque carolingienne* (Turnhout, 1991).

Bullough, D., *Alcuin: Achievement and Reputation. Being Part of the Ford Lectures Delivered in Oxford in Hilary Term 1980* (Leiden, Boston, 2004).

Busch, J.W., *Vom Amtswalten zum Königsdienst. Beobachtungen zur 'Staatssprache' des Frühmittalters am Beispiel des Wortes* administratio. MGH Studien und Texte 42 (Hanover, 2007).

Cabaniss, A. (intr. and transl.), *Charlemagne's Cousins. Contemporary Lives of Adalhard and Wala* (Syracuse NY, 1967).

Cain, A. (ed. and transl.), *Jerome's Epitaph on Paula: A Commentary on the Epitaphium Sanctae Paulae* (Oxford, 2013).

'Jerome's "Epitaphium Paulae": Hagiography, Pilgrimage and the Cult of Saint Paula', *Journal of Early Christian Studies* 18 (2010), 105–39.

'Terence in Late Antiquity', in A. Augoustakis & A. Traill (eds.), *A Companion to Terence. Blackwell Companions to the Ancient World* (Oxford, 2013), pp. 380–96.

'Two Allusions to Terence, *Eunuchus* 579 in Jerome', *The Classical Quarterly* 63 (2013), 407–21.

'Vox clamantis in deserto. Rhetoric, Reproach and the Forging of Ascetic Authority in Jerome's Letters from the Syrian Desert', *Journal of Theological Studies* 57 (2006), 500–25.

Calvet-Marcadé, G., 'L'abbé spoliateur de biens monastiques (France du Nord, IXe siècle)', in P. Depreux, F. Bougard and R. Le Jan (eds.), *Compétition et sacré au haut Moyen Âge: entre médiation et exclusion*. Collection Haut Moyen Âge 21 (Turnhout, 2015), pp. 313–27.

Les clercs carolingiens et la défense des terres d'Eglise (Francie du Nord, ixe siècle). Unpublished PhD thesis, Pantheon-Sorbonne University, Paris (2012).

Cameron, A., *Dialoguing in Late Antiquity* (Cambridge MA and London, 2014).

Cameron, M., 'Augustine and Scripture', in M. Vessey (ed.), *Companion to Augustine*, pp. 200–14.

Chazelle, C., *The Crucified God in the Carolingian Era: Theology and Art of Christ's Passion* (Cambridge, 2001).

Chazelle, C., and C. Cubitt (eds.), *The Crisis of the Oikoumene: The Three Chapters and the Failed Quest for Unity in the Sixth-Century Mediterranean*. Studies in the Early Middle Ages 14 (Turnhout, 2007).

Cizek, A., 'Der "Charakterismos" in der Vita Adalhardi des Radbert von Corbie', *Rhetorica. A Journal of the History of Rhetoric* 7 (1989),185–204.

Clark, G., 'Can We Talk? Augustine and the Possibility of Dialogue', in S. Goldhill (ed.), *End of Dialogue*, pp. 117–34.

Contreni, J. J., 'Carolingian Biblical Culture' in G. van Riel, C. Steel and J. McEvoy (eds.), *Johannes Scottus Eriugena: The Bible and Hermeneutics* (Leuven, 1996), pp. 1–23.

'The Patristic Legacy to c. 1000', in R. Marsden and E. Ann Matter (eds.), *The New Cambridge History of the Bible, II: From 600 to 1450* (Cambridge, 2012), pp. 505–35.

Cooper, K. and M. Dal Santo, 'Boethius, Gregory the Great and the Christian "Afterlife" of Classical Dialogue', in S. Goldhill, *End of Dialogue*, pp. 172–89.

Corradini, R., 'Pieces of a Puzzle: Time and History in Walahfrid's *Vademecum*', *EME* 22 (2014), 476–91.

Corradini, R., M. Gillis, R. McKitterick and I. van Renswoude (eds.), *Ego Trouble. Authors and their Identities in the Early Middle Ages*. Forschungen zur Geschichte des Mittelalters 15 (Vienna, 2010).

Dal Santo, M., *Debating the Saints' Cults in the Age of Gregory the Great* (Oxford, 2012).

Davis, J.R., *Charlemagne's Practice of Empire* (Cambridge, 2015).

Davis, J.R. and M. McCormick (eds.), *The Long Morning of Medieval Europe. New Directions in Early Medieval Studies* (Aldershot, 2008).

Delogu, P., 'Lombard and Carolingian Italy', in R. McKitterick (ed.), *NCMH* II, pp. 290–319.

Denoel, C. 'Antoine de Caulaincourt (1482–1536/40?), Official de l'abbaye Saint-Pierre de Corbie, historien et possesseur de livres', *Scriptorium* 64 (2010), 81–94 and plates 1–8.

Depreux, P., 'Le comte Matfrid d'Orléans (av. 815–836)', *Bibliothèque de l'Ecole des Chartes* 152 (1994), 332–74.

'Der karolingische Hof als Institution und Personenverband', *Le Corti nell'Alto Medioevo* I, Settimane 62 (Spoleto, 2015), 137–64.

'Nithard et la *Res Publica*: un regard critique sur le règne de Louis le Pieux', *Médiévales* 22–23 (1992), pp. 149–61.

'The Penance of Attigny (822) and the Leadership of the Bishops in Amending Frankish Society', in R. Meens et al. (eds.), *Religious Franks*, pp. 370–85.

*Prosopographie de l'entourage de Louis le Pieux (781–840)*. Instrumenta 1 (Sigmaringen, 1997).

Diem, A., 'The Carolingians and the *Regula Benedicti*', in R. Meens et al. (eds.), *Religious Franks*, pp. 243–61.

*Das monastische Experiment. Die Rolle der Keuschheit bei der Entstehung des westlichen Klosterwesens*. Vita regularis 24 (Münster, 2005).

Dohmen, L., '... everterit palatium, destruxit consilium ... Konflikte im und um dem Rat des Herrschers am Beispiel der Auseinandersetzungen am Hof Ludwigs den Frommen (830/31)', in A. Plassmann and M. Becher (eds.), *Streit am Hof in frühen Mittelalter* (Göttingen, 2011), pp. 285–316.

*Die Ursache alles Übels. Untersuchungen zu den Unzuchtsvorwürfen gegen die Gemahlinnen der Karolinger*. Mittelalter-Forschungen 53 (Ostfildern, 2017).

Dutton, P.E., *Charlemagne's Courtier. The Complete Einhard* (Peterborough ON, 1998).

*Charlemagne's Mustache and Other Cultural Clusters of a Dark Age* (New York NY, 2004).

'The Identification of Persons in Frankish Europe', *EME* 26 (2018), 132–73.

*The Politics of Dreaming in the Carolingian Empire* (London and Lincoln NB, 1994).

Duval, Y.-M., 'Formes profanes et formes bibliques dans les oraisons funèbres de Saint Ambroise', in M. Furhmann (ed.), *Christianisme et formes littéraires de l'Antiquité tardive en Occident*. Entretiens sur l'antiquité classique 23 (Genève, 1977), pp. 235–91.

Dyck, A.R., *A Commentary on Cicero's De Officiis* (Ann Arbor MI, 1996).

Erskine, A., 'Cicero and the Expression of Grief', in S. Morton Braund and C. Gill (eds.), *The Passions in Roman Thought and Literature* (Cambridge, 1997), pp. 36–47.

Esders, S., '"Faithful Believers". Oaths of Allegiance in Post-Roman Societies as Evidence for Eastern and Western "Visions of Community"', in W. Pohl, C. Gantner and R. Payne (eds.), *Visions of Community*, pp. 357–74.

Esders, S. and S. Patzold, 'From Justinian to Louis the Pious: Inalienability of Church Property', in R. Meens et al. (eds.), *Religious Franks*, pp. 386–408.

Ewig, E., *Fälschungen im Mittelalter. Internationaler Kongress der Monumenta Germaniae Historica, München, 16.–19. September* 1986, 6 vols. (Hanover, 1988–1990).

'Das Privileg des Bischof Berthefrid von Amiens für Corbie von 664 und die Klosterpolitik der Königin Balthild', *Francia* 1 (1973), 62–114.

Felten, F.J., *Äbte und Laienäbte im Frankenreich: Studie zum Verhältnis von Staat und Kirche im früheren Mittelalter.* Monographien zur Geschichte des Mittelalters 20 (Stuttgart, 1980).

'Laienäbte in der Karolingerzeit. Ein Beitrag zum Problem der Adelsherrschaft über die Kirche', in A. Borst (ed.), *Mönchtum, Episkopat und Adel zur Gründungszeit des Klosters Reichenau.* Vorträge und Forschungen 20 (Sigmaringen, 1974), pp. 397–431.

Finsterwalder, P.W., 'Eine parteipolitische Kundgebung eines Anghänger Lothars I', *Neues Archiv der Gesellschaft für ältere deutsche Geschichtskunde* 47 (1928), 393–415.

Firey, A., 'Canon Law Studies at Corbie', in K. Ubl and D. Ziemann (eds.), *Fälschung als Mittel der Politik?*, pp. 19–79.

*A Contrite Heart. Prosecution and Redemption in the Carolingian Period.* Studies in Medieval and Reformation Traditions 145 (Leiden, 2009).

Flierman, R., *Saxon Identities, AD 150–900* (London, 2017).

Flower, R., *Emperors and Bishops in Late Roman Invective* (Cambridge, 2013).

Frank, K.S., 'Arsenios der Grosse. Vom Apophthegmata zum hagiographischen Tekst', in *Mémorial Dom Jean Gribomont (1920–1986)*, Studia Ephemeridis "Augustinianum" 27 (Rome, 1988), pp. 271–87.

Freire, J.G., *Commonitiones sanctorum patrum: Una nova colecção de apotegmas* (Coimbra, 1974).

'Traductions latines des *Apophthegmata Patrum*', in J. Ysebaert et al. (eds.), *Mélanges Christine Mohrmann. Nouveau recueil offert par ses anciens élèves* (Utrecht and Antwerp, 1973), pp. 164–71.

*A versão latino por Pascásio de Dume dos Apophthegmata patrum* (Coimbra, 1971).

Fried, J., *'Donation of Constantine' and 'Constitutum Constantini': The Misinterpretation of a Fiction and its Original Meaning.* Millennium Studies 3 (Boston, 2007).

'Elite und Ideologie oder die Nachfolgeordnung Karls des Grossen vom Jahre 813', in R. Le Jan (ed.), *La royauté*, pp. 71–109.

'Kanonistik und Mediëvistik. Neue Literatur zur Kirchenrecht, Inzest und zur Ehe Pippins von Italien', *HZ* 294 (2012), 115–41.

*Karl der Grosse. Gewalt und Glaube. Eine Biographie* (München, 2013).

'Ludwig der Fromme, das Papsttum und die frankische Kirche', in P. Godman and R. Collins, *Charlemagne's Heir*, pp. 231–73.

Fuhrmann, H., *Einfluss und Verbreitung der Pseudo-Isidorischen Fälschungen. Von ihrem Auftauchen bis in die neuere Zeit*, 3 vols. Schriften der *MGH* 24 (Stuttgart, 1972–4).
'Pseudoisidor und die Bibel', *DA* 55 (1999), 183–191.
'Stand, Aufgaben und Perspektiven der Pseudoisidorforschung', in *Fortschritt durch Fälschungen? Ursprung, Gestalt und Wirkungen der pseudoisidorischen Fälschungen*, ed. W. Hartmann and G. Schmitz, MGH Studien und Texte 31 (Hanover, 2002), pp. 227–67.
Gaertner, J.F. *Writing Exile. The Discourse of Displacement in Greco-Roman Antiquity and Beyond* (Leiden, 2007).
Gantner, C., R. McKitterick and S. Meeder (eds.), *The Resources of the Past in Early Medieval Europe* (Cambridge, 2015).
Ganz, D., 'The Astronomer's Life of Louis the Pious', in V.L. Garver and O.M. McPhelan (eds.), *Rome and Religion*, pp. 129–48.
*Corbie in the Carolingian Renaissance*. Beiheifte der Francia 21 (Sigmaringen, 1990).
*Einhard and Notker the Stammerer: Two Lives of Charlemagne. Translated with an Introduction and Notes by David Ganz* (London, 2008).
'Einhard's Charlemagne: The Characterization of Greatness', in J. Story (ed.), *Charlemagne, Empire and Society* (Manchester, 2005), pp. 38–51.
'Einhardus peccator', in P. Wormald and J.L. Nelson (eds.), *Lay Intellectuals*, pp. 37–50.
'The *Epitaphium Arsenii* and Opposition to Louis the Pious', in P. Godman and R. Collins (eds.), *Charlemagne's Heir*, pp. 537–50.
'Humour as History in Notker's *Gesta Karoli Magni*', in E.B. King, J.T. Schaefer and W.B. Wadley (eds.), *Monks, Nuns and Friars in Medieval Society* (Sewanee, 1989), pp. 171–83.
'The Ideology of Sharing: Apostolic Community and Ecclesiastical Property in the Early Middle Ages,' in W. Davies and P. Fouracre (eds.), *Property and Power in the Early Middle Ages* (Cambridge, 1995), pp. 17–30.
'The Preface to Einhard's "Vita Karoli"', in H. Schefers (ed.), *Einhard: Studien zu Leben und Werk* (Darmstadt, 1997), pp. 299–310.
'Theology and the Organization of Thought', in R. McKitterick (ed.), *NCMH* II, pp. 758–85.
Garrison, M., 'An Aspect of Alcuin: "Tuus Albinus" – Peevish Egotist? Or Parrhesiast?', in R. Corradini et al., *Ego Trouble*, pp. 137–52.
'The Bible and Alcuin's Interpretation of Current Events', *Peritia* 16 (2002) 68–84.
'The Franks as the New Israel? Education for an Identity from Pippin to Charlemagne', in Y. Hen and M. Innes (eds.), *The Uses of the Past*, pp. 114–61.
'*Praesagum nomen tibi*: The Significance of Name-wordplay in Alcuin's Letters to Arn', in M. Niederkorn-Bruck and A. Scharer, *Erzbischof Arn von Salzburg* (Wien, 2004), p. 107–27.
'The Social World of Alcuin: Nicknames at York and at the Carolingian Court', in L.A.J.R. Houwen and A.A. McDonald (eds.), *Alcuin of York. Scholar at the Carolingian Court*. Germania Latina 3 (Groningen, 1998), pp. 59–79.

Garver, V.L. and O.M. Phelan (eds.), *Rome and Religion in the Medieval World. Studies in Honor of Thomas Noble* (Farnham, 2014).

Gillis, M.B., *Heresy and Dissent in the Carolingian Empire: The Case of Gottschalk of Orbais* (Oxford, 2017).

Godman, P., *Poetry of the Carolingian Renaissance* (London, 1985).

Godman, P., and R. Collins, (eds.), *Charlemagne's Heir: New Perspectives on the Reign of Louis the Pious (814–840)* (Oxford, 1990).

Goetting, H., *Das Bistum Hildesheim: Die Hildesheimer Bischöfe von 815 bis 1221 (1227)*. Germania Sacra, n.s. 20/3 (Berlin and New York NY, 1984).

Goldberg, E.J., *Struggle for Empire. Kingship and Conflict under Louis the German, 817–876* (Ithaca NY, 2006).

Goldhill, S. (ed.), *The End of Dialogue in Antiquity* (Cambridge, 2009).

'Introduction: Why Don't Christians Do Dialogue?', in S. Goldhill (ed.), *End of Dialogue*, pp. 1–11.

Goosmann, E., 'Politics and Penance: Tranformations in the Carolingian Perception of the Conversion of Carloman (747)', in C. Gantner, R. McKitterick and S. Meeder (eds.), *Resources of the Past*, pp. 51–66.

Gravel, M., *Distances, rencontres, communications. Réaliser l'empire sous Charlemagne et Louis le Pieux*. Collection Haut Moyen Âge 15 (Turnhout, 2012).

'Judith écrit, Raban Maur répond: Premier échange d'une longue alliance', in J.-F. Cottier (ed.), *Ad libros! Mélanges d'études médiévales offerts à Denise Angers et Joseph-Claude Poulin* (Montreal QC, 2010), pp. 35–48.

Gray, P.T.R., 'The Legacy of Chalcedon: Christological Problems and Their Significance', in M. Maas (ed.), *The Cambridge Companion to the Age of Justinian* (Cambridge, 2005), pp. 215–38.

Grierson, P., 'Eudes Ier Évêque de Beauvais', *Le Moyen Age* 6 (1935), 161–98.

Gross, F., *Abbés, religieux et monastères dans le royaume de Charles le Chauve*. Unpublished PhD thesis, Paris IV-Sorbonne (2006).

Hack, A.T., *Das Empfangszeremoniell bei mittelalterlichen Kaiser-Papsttreffen: Forschungen zur Kaiser- und Papstgeschichte des Mittelalters*. Beihefte zu J.F. Böhmer, Regesta Imperii 18 (Cologne, 1999).

Hagendahl, H., *Augustine and the Latin Classics*, 2 vols. Studia Graeca et Latina Gotoburgensia 20 (Gothenburg,1967).

'Jerome and the Latin Classics', *Vigiliae Christianae* 28 (1974), 216–27.

*Latin Fathers and the Classics. A Study on the Apologists, Jerome and other Christian Writers.*(Gothenburg, 1958).

Hamilton, S., 'Review Article: Early Medieval Rulers and Their Modern Biographers', *EME* 9 (2000), 247–60.

Harder, C., 'Der Papst als Mittel zum Zweck? Zur Bedeutung des römischen Bischofs bei Pseudoisidor', in K. Ubl and D. Ziemann (eds.), *Fälschung als Mittel der Politik*, pp. 173–86.

*Pseudoisidor und das Papsttum. Funktion und Bedeutung des apostolischen Stuhls in den pseudoisidorischen Fälschungen*. Papsttum im mittelalterlichen Europa 2 (Cologne, Weimar and Vienna, 2014).

Harrison, T.P. and H.J. Leon, *The Pastoral Elegy. An Anthology* (Austin TX, 1939).

Hartmann, W., *Die Synoden der Karolingerzeit im Frankenreich und in Italien.* Konziliengeschichte Reihe A: Darstellungen (Paderborn, Munich, Vienna and Zürich, 1989).

Hasse-Ungeheuer, A., *Das Mönchtum in der Religionspolitik Kaiser Justinians I. Die Engel des Himmels und der Stellvertreter Gottes auf Erden* (Berlin and Boston, 2015).

Haubrichs, W., *Geschichte der deutschen Literatur von den Anfängen bis zum Beginn der Neuzeit, Band I: Von den Anfängen zum hohen Mittelalter. Teil I: Die Anfänge: Versuche volkssprachlichen Schriftlichkeit im frühen Mittelalter (ca. 700–1050/60)* (Tübingen, 1995).

Heath, M., *Menander. A Rhetor in Context* (Oxford, 2004).

Heinen, S., 'Peudoisidor auf dem Konzil von Aachen im Jahr 836', in K. Ubl and D. Ziemann (eds.), *Fälschung als Mittel der Politik?*, pp. 97–126.

Helbig, H. '*Fideles Dei et regis*: Zur Bedeutungsentwicklung von Glaube und Treue im hohen Mittelalter', *Archiv für Kulturgeschichte* 33 (1951), 275–306.

Hen, Y. and M. Innes (eds.), *The Uses of the Past in the Early Middle Ages* (Cambridge, 2000).

Heydemann, G., 'Relics and Texts: Hagiography and Authority in Ninth-century Francia', in P. Sarris, M. Del Santo and P. Booth, *An Age of Saints? Power, Conflict and Dissent in Early Medieval Christianity* (Leiden and Boston MA, 2011), pp. 187–204.

Hillner, J., *Prison, Punishment and Penance in Late Antiquity* (Cambridge, 2015).

Hindrichs, K., 'Zwischen Reichseinheit und adeligen Machtegoismen. Zu den Gründen des Aufstands von 830', *Concilium Medii Aevi* 13 (2010), 252–81.

Hlawitschka, E., 'Die Vorfahren Karls des Grossen', in W. Braunfels (ed.), *Karl der Große: Lebenswerk und Nachleben I: Persönlichkeit und Geschichte*, ed. H. Beumann (Düsseldorf, 1965), pp. 51–82.

Hoffmann, M., *Der Dialog bei den christlichen Schriftstellern der ersten vier Jahrhunderte* (Berlin, 1966).

Huelsenbeck, B., 'A Nexus of Manuscripts Copied at Corbie, ca 850–880: A Typology of Script-Style and Copying Procedure', *Segno e Testo* 11 (2013), 287–309.

Humfress, C., *Orthodoxy and the Courts in Late Antiquity* (Oxford, 2007).

Humphries, M., 'Rufinus's Eusebius: Translation, Continuation and Edition in the Latin Ecclesiastical History', *Journal of Early Christian Studies* 16 (2008), 143–64.

'Savage Humour: Christian Anti-Panegyric in Hilary of Poitiers' *Against Constantius*, in M. Whitby (ed.), *The Propaganda of Power. The Role of Panegyric in Late Antiquity* (Leiden, 1998), pp. 201–23.

Illmer, D. *Erziehung und Wissensvermittlung. Ein Beitrag zur Entstehungsgeschichte der Schule* (Kastellaun and Hunsrück, 1979).

Innes, M., 'Charlemagne's Will: Inheritance, Ideology and the Imperial Succession', *English Historical Review* 112 (1997), 833–55.

'A Place of Discipline: Carolingian Courts and Aristocratic Youths', in C. Cubitt (ed.), *Court Culture in the Early Middle Ages: The Proceedings of the First Alcuin Conference. Studies in the Early Middle Ages* 3 (2003), pp. 59–6.

'Practices of Property in the Carolingian Empire', in J.R. Davis and M. McCormick (eds.), *The Long Morning of Medieval Europe*, pp. 247–66.

Jacob, W. and R. Hanslik, *Die handschriftliche Überlieferung der sogenannten Historia Tripartita des Epiphanius-Cassiodor. Texte und Untersuchungen zur Geschichte der altchristlichen Literatur* 54 (Berlin, 1954).

Jeanjean, B., 'Le *Dialogus Attici et Critobuli* de Jérôme et la prédication pélagienne en Palestine entre 411 et 415', in A. Cain and J. Lössl (eds.), *Jerome of Stridon: His Life, Writings and Legacy* (Farnham, 2009), pp. 59–71.

Jong, M. de, 'Admonition and Criticism of the Ruler at the Court of Louis the Pious', in R. Le Jan, F. Bougard and R. McKitterick (eds.), *La culture du haut Moyen Âge. Une question des élites?* Collection Haut Moyen Âge 7 (Turnhout 2009), pp. 315–40.

'Becoming Jeremiah. Radbert on Wala, Himself and Others', in R. Corradini et al. (eds.), *Ego Trouble*, pp. 185–96.

'Bride Shows Revisited. Praise, Slander and Exegesis in the Reign of the Empress Judith', in L. Brubaker and J.M.H. Smith (eds.), *Gender in the Early Medieval World: East and West, 300-900* (Cambridge, 2004), pp. 257–77.

'Carolingian Monasticism: The Power of Prayer', in R. McKitterick (ed.), *NCMH* II, pp. 622–53.

'Carolingian Political Discourse and the Biblical Past – Hraban, Dhuoda, Radbert', in C. Gantner, R. McKitterick and S. Meeder (eds.), *Resources of the Past*, pp. 87–102.

'Charlemagne's Balcony: The Solarium in Ninth-century Narratives', in J.R. Davis and M. McCormick (eds.), *The Long Morning of Medieval Europe*, pp. 275–89.

'*Ecclesia* and the Early Medieval Polity', in S. Airlie, W. Pohl and H. Reimitz (eds.), *Staat*, pp. 113–32.

'Einhard, the Astronomer and Charlemagne's Daughters', in R. Grosse and M. Sot (eds.), *Charlemagne: les temps, les espaces, les hommes. Construction et déconstruction d'un règne.* Collection Haut Moyen 34 (Turnhout, 2018), pp. 556–65.

'The Empire as *ecclesia*: Hrabanus Maurus and Biblical *historia* for Rulers', in Y. Hen and M. Innes (eds.), *The Uses of the Past in the Early Middle Ages*, pp. 191–226.

'Exegesis for an Empress', in E. Cohen and M. de Jong (eds.), *Medieval Transformations: Texts, Power and Gifts in Context* (Leiden, 2001), pp. 69–100.

'Familiarity Lost: On the Context of the Second Book of the *Epitaphium Arsenii*', in M. Gravel and S. Kaschke (eds.), *Politische Theologie und Geschichte unter Ludwig dem Frommen/Histoire et théologie politiques sous Louis le Pieux, Relectio.* Karolingische Perspektiven – Perspectives carolingiennes – Carolingian Perspectives, 2 (Ostfildern, forthcoming).

'For God, King and Country: The Personal and the Public in the Epitaphium Arsenii', *EME* 25 (2017), 102–13.

'From scholastici to scioli. Alcuin and the Formation of an Intellectual Elite', in L.A.J.R. Houwen and A.A. McDonald (eds.), *Alcuin of York. Scholar at the Carolingian Court.* Germania Latina 3 (Groningen 1998), pp. 45–57.

'Growing Up in a Carolingian Monastery: Magister Hildemar and his Oblates', *Journal of Medieval History* 9 (1983), 99–128.

'"Heed That Saying of Terence". On the Use of Terence in Radbert's *Epitaphium Arsenii*', in M. Teeuwen and S. O'Sullivan (eds.), *Carolingian scholarship and Martianus Capella: Ninth-century Commentary Traditions on Martianus's De nuptiis in Context*. Cultural Encounters in Late Antiquity and the Middle Ages 12 (Turnhout, 2011), pp. 277–305.

'Hincmar, Priests and Pseudo-Isidore: The Case of Trising in Context', in R. Stone and C. West (eds.), *Hincmar of Rheims, Life and Work* (Manchester, 2015), pp. 268–88.

'Hraban Maur as Mediator: *De honore parentum* (Autumn 834)', in L. Jegou et al. (eds.), *Splendor reginae: passions, genre et famille – Mélanges en l'honneur de Régine Le Jan*. Collection Haut Moyen Âge 22 (Turnhout, 2015), pp. 49–58.

'*Imitatio morum:* The Cloister and Clerical Purity in the Carolingian World', in M. Frassetto (ed.), *Medieval Purity and Piety. Essays in Medieval Clerical Celibacy and Religious Reform* (New York NY and London,1998), pp.49–80.

*In Samuel's Image: Child Oblation in the Early Medieval West*. Studies in Intellectual History 12 (Leiden, 1996).

'Internal Cloisters: the Case of Ekkehard's Casus sancti Galli', in W. Pohl and H. Reimitz (eds.), *Grenzen und Differenz im frühen Mittelalter*. Forschungen zur Geschichte des Mittelalters 1 (Vienna, 2000), pp. 209–21.

'Jeremiah, Job, Terence and Paschasius Radbertus: Political Rhetoric and Biblical Authority in the *Epitaphium Arsenii*', in J. Nelson and D. Kempf (eds.), *Reading the Bible in the Middle Ages* (London, 2015), pp. 57–76, 209–15.

'Monastic Prisoners or Opting Out? Political Coercion and Honour in the Frankish Kingdoms', in M. de Jong, F. Theuws and C. van Rhijn (eds.), *Topographies of Power in the Early Middle Ages*, pp. 291–328.

'Old Law and New-found Power: Hrabanus Maurus and the Old Testament', in J.W. Drijvers and A.A. MacDonald (eds.), *Centres of Learning. Learning and Location in Pre-modern Europe and the Near East* (Leiden, New York NY and Cologne, 1995), pp. 161–76.

'Our Sons and Lords: On Kings, Bishops and Monastic Property in the Mid-ninth Century', in N.K. Yavuz and R. Broome, *Transforming the Early Medieval World. Studies in Honour of Ian N. Wood* (Leeds, forthcoming).

'Paschasius Radbertus and Pseudo-Isidore: The Evidence of the Epitaphium Arsenii', in V.R. Garver and O.M. Phelan (eds.), *Rome and Religion in the Medieval World*, pp. 149–78.

*The Penitential State. Authority and Atonement in the Age of Louis the Pious (814–840)* (Cambridge 2009).

'Power and Humility in Carolingian Society: The Public Penance of Louis the Pious', *EME* 1 (1992), 29–52.

'The Resources of the Past: Paschasius Radbertus and his *Epitaphium Arsenii*', in S. Dusil, G. Schwedler and R. Schwitter (eds.), *Exerpieren – Kompilieren – Tradieren. Transformationen des Wissens zwischen Spätantike und Frühmittelalter*. Millennium-Studien 64 (Berlin and Boston MA, 2017), pp. 131–51.

'*Sacrum palatium et ecclesia*: L'autorité religieuse royale sous les Carolingiens (790–840)', *Annales: Histoire, Sciences Sociales* 58 (2003), 1243–69.

'The State of the Church: *ecclesia* and Early Medieval State Formation', in W. Pohl and V. Wieser (eds.), *Der frühmittelalterliche Staat: Europäische Perspektive*. Forschungen zur Geschichte des Mittelalters 16 (Vienna, 2009), pp. 241–55.

'Transformations of Penance', in F. Theuws and J.L. Nelson (eds.), *Rituals of Power From Late Antiquity to the Early Middle Ages* (Leiden, 2000), pp. 185–224.

'The Two Republics: *ecclesia* and the Public Domain in the Carolingian World', in R. Balzaretti, J. Barrow and P Skinner (eds.), *Italy and Early Medieval Europe. Essays Presented to Chris Wickham* (Oxford, 2018), pp. 486–500.

'What was *Public* about Public Penance? *Paenitentia publica* and Justice in the Carolingian World', in *La giustizia nell'alto medioevo (secolo ix-xi)*. Settimane 44 (1997), pp. 863–904.

Jong, M. de, and I. van Renswoude, 'Introduction: Carolingian Cultures of Dialogue, Debate and Disputation, *EME* 25 (2017), 6–18.

Jong, M. de, F. Theuws and C. van Rhijn (eds.), *Topographies of Power in the Early Middle Ages*. The Transformation of the Roman World 6 (Leiden, 2001).

Kasten, B., *Adalhard von Corbie. Die Biographie eines karolingischen Politikers und Klostervorstehers*. Studia humaniora 3 (Düsseldorf, 1986).

Kelly, C., 'Political History: The Later Roman Empire', in M. Vessey (ed.), *Companion to Augustine*, pp. 11–23.

Kempshall, M., '*De Republica* 1.39 in Medieval and Renaissance Thought', in J.F.G. Powell and J.A. North (eds.), *Cicero's Republic* (London, 2001), pp. 99–135.

*Rhetoric and the Writing of History, 400–1500* (Oxford, 2011).

'The Virtues of Rhetoric: Alcuin's *Disputatio de rhetorica et virtutibus*', *Anglo-Saxon England* 37 (2008), 7–30.

Klopsch, P., 'Prosa und Vers in der mittellateinischer Literatur', *Mittellateinisches Jahrbuch* 3 (1966), 9–24.

Knibbs, E., 'Ebo of Reims, Pseudo-Isidore, and the Date of the False Decretals', *Speculum* 92 (2017), 145–83.

'Pseudo-Isidore in the A1 Recension', in K. Ubl and D. Ziemann (eds.), *Fälschung als Mittel der Politik?*, pp. 81–95.

'Pseudo-Isidore on the Field of Lies: 'Divinis praeceptis' (JE 2579) as an Authentic Decretal', *Bulletin of Medieval Canon Law*, n.s. 29(2011),1–34.

Knox, P.E., 'The *Heroides*: Elegiac Verses', in B. Weiden Bond (ed.), *Brill's Companion to Ovid* (Leiden, Boston MA and Cologne, 2002), pp. 117–40.

Kölzer, T., *Merowingerstudien*, 2 vols. MGH Studien und Texte 21 and 26 (Hanover, 1998/9).

Konecny, S. *Die Frauen des karolingischen Königshauses. Die politischen Bedeutung der Ehe und die Stellung der Frau in der frankischen Herrscherfamilie vom 7. bis zum 10. Jahrhundert* (Vienna, 1976).

Kosto, A., 'Hostages in the Carolingian World (714–840)', *EME* 11 (2002), 123–47. *Hostages in the Middle Ages* (Oxford, 2012).

Kottje, R., 'Busse oder Strafe? Zur "iustitia" in den "libri paenitentiales"', in *La giustizia nell'alto Medioevo (secoli V-VIII)* I, Settimane 42 (1995), pp. 443–68.

Kramer, R., '" . . . quia cor regi in manu Dei est": the Pharaoh in Carolingian Monastic Narratives', in P. Depreux, F. Bougard and R. Le Jan (eds.), *Compétition et sacré au haut Moyen Âge: entre médiation et exclusion.* Collection Haut Moyen Âge 21 (Turnhout, 2015), pp. 137–61.

Krüger, K.H., 'Zur Nachfolgereglung von 826 in den Klöstern Corbie und Corvey', in N. Kamp and J. Wollasch (eds.), *Tradition als historische Kraft. Interdisziplinäre Forschungen zur Geschichte des früheren Mittelalters* (Berlin and New York NY, 1982), pp. 181–96.

*Studien zur Corveyer Gründungsüberlieferung* (Münster, 2001).

Lake, J., 'Truth, Plausibility and the Virtues of Narrative at the Millennium', *Journal of Medieval History* 34 (2009), 221–38.

Lanéry, C. 'La tradition manuscrite de la *Passio Sebastiani* (Arnobe le Jeune), BHL 7532', *Revue d'Histoire des Textes* 7 (2012), 37–116.

Lausberg, H., *Handbuch der literarischen Rhetorik. Eine Grundlegung der Literaturwissenschaft* (Munich, 1973).

Le Jan, R., 'Dhuoda ou l'opportunité du discours féminin', in C. La Rocca (ed.), *Agire da donna: Modelli e pratiche di rappresentazione (secoli vi-x)*, Collection Haut Moyen Âge 3 (Turnhout, 2007), pp. 109–28.

(ed.), *La royauté et les élites dans l'Europe carolingienne (début du IXe siècle aux environs de 920)* (Lille, 1997).

Lepping, H., 'Das Bild der Kaiser bei Liberatus', *Zeitschrift für Antikes Christentum* 14 (2010), 149–65.

Levillain, L., 'De quelques lettres de Loup de Ferrières', *Le Moyen Age* 32 (1921), p. 193–217.

*Examen critique des chartes mérovingiennes et carolingiennes de l'abbaye de Corbie,* Mémoires et documents publiés par la Société de l'École des chartes 5 (Paris 1902).

Levine, Ph., 'Cicero and the Literary Dialogue', *The Classical Journal* 53 (1958), 146–151.

Leyser, C., *Authority and Asceticism from Augustine to Gregory the Great* (Oxford, 2000).

'From Maternal Kin to Jesus as Mother: Royal Genealogy and Marian Devotion in the Ninth-century West', in C. Leyser and L. Smith, *Motherhood, Religion, and Society in Medieval Europe, 400–1400: Essays Presented to Henrietta Leyser* (Burlington VT, 2012), pp. 21–39.

'Introduction: Making Early Medieval Societies', in C. Leyser (ed.), *Making Early Medieval Societies. Conflict and Belonging in the Latin West, 300–1200* (Cambridge, 2016), pp. 1–15.

Leyser, K., 'Early Medieval Canon Law and the Beginnings of Knighthood', in T. Reuter (ed.), *Communications and Power in Early Medieval Europe: The Carolingian and Ottonian Centuries* (London and Rio Grande, 1994), pp. 51–72; orig. in L. Fenske, W. Rösener and T. Zotz (eds.), *Festschrift für Josef Fleckenstein* (Sigmaringen, 1984), pp. 549–66.

Liebeschuetz, J.H.G.W., with C. Hill, transl. and intr., *Ambrose of Milan, Political Letters and Speeches.* Translated Texts for Historians 43 (Liverpool, 2005).

Lim, R., 'Christians, Dialogues and Patterns of Sociability in Late Antiquity', in S. Goldhill (ed.), *End of Dialogue*, pp. 151–72.

Lo Monaco, F., 'Swearing in Nithard's *Historiae*', in F. Lo Monaco & C. Villa (eds.), *I giuramenti di Strasburg: Testi e tradizione/The Strasbourg Oaths: Texts and Transmission*. Traditio et renovatio 3 (Florence, 2009), pp. 111–40.

Löwe, H, 'Geschichtsschreibung der ausgehenden Karolingerzeit', *DA* 23 (1967), 1–30.

Mabillon, J., *Prolegomena ad opera Paschasii Radberti*, PL 120, cols. 9–24.

MacKendrick, P., *The Philosophical Books of Cicero* (London, 1989).

MacLean, S., *History and Politics in Late Carolingian and Ottonian Europe. The Chronicle of Regino of Prüm and Adalbert of Magdeburg*. Manchester Medieval Sources Series (Manchester and New York NY, 2009).

Mähl, S., *Quadriga virtutum. Die Kardinaltugenden in der Geistesgeschichte der Karolingerzeit* (Cologne, 1969).

Matter, A.E., 'The Lamentations Commentaries of Hrabanus Maurus and Paschasius Radbertus', *Traditio* 38 (1982), 137–63.

Mayr-Harting, H., 'Two Abbots in Politics: Wala of Corbie and Bernard of Clairvaux', *Transactions of the Royal Historical Society*, 5th ser. 40 (1989), 217–37.

McKie, D.S., 'Ovid's Amores. The Prime Sources for the Text', *Classical Quarterly* n.s. 36 (1986), 219–38.

McKitterick, R., 'The Audience for Latin Historiography in the Early Middle Ages: Text Transmission and Manuscript Dissemination', in A. Scharer and G. Scheibelreiter (eds.), *Historiographie*, pp. 96–114.

(ed.), *Carolingian Culture. Emulation and Innovation* (Cambridge, 1994).

*The Carolingians and the Written Word* (Cambridge, 1989).

*Charlemagne. The Formation of a European Identity* (Cambridge, 2008).

(ed.), *The Early Middle Ages*, Short Oxford History of Europe (Oxford, 2001).

*History and Memory in the Carolingian World* (Cambridge, 2004).

'The Illusion of Royal Power in the Carolingian Annals', *The English Historical Review* 115 (2000), 1–20.

'Knowledge of Canon Law in the Frankish Kingdoms Before 789: The Manuscript Evidence', *Journal of Theological Studies* 36 (1985), 97–117.

(ed.), *The New Cambridge Medieval History II, c. 700-c. 900* (Cambridge, 1995).

'Nuns' scriptoria in England and Francia in the Eighth Century', *Francia* 19/1 (1992), 1–35.

'Perceptions of Justice in Western Europe in the Ninth and Tenth Centuries', in *La giustizia nell'alto Medioevo (secoli IX-XI)*, Settimane 44 (1997), pp. 1075–1102.

'Unity and Diversity in the Carolingian Church', in R. Swanson (ed.), *Unity and Diversity in the Christian Church*. Studies in Church History 32 (1996), pp. 59–82.

(ed.), *The Uses of Literacy in Early Medieval Europe* (Cambridge, 1990).

'Women and Literacy in the Early Middle Ages', in R. McKitterick, *Books, Scribes and Learning in the Frankish Kingdoms, 6th-9th Centuries*, XIII. Variorum Reprints (Aldershot, 1994).

'Zur Herstellung von Kapitularien: Die Arbeit des Leges-Skriptoriums', *MIÖG* 101 (1993), 3–16.

Meens, R., D. van Espelo, B. van den Hoven van Genderen, J. Raaijmakers, I. van Renswoude and C. van Rhijn (eds.), *Religious Franks. Religion and Power in the Frankish Kingdoms. Studies in Honour of Mayke de Jong* (Manchester, 2016).

Moos, P. von, *Consolatio. Studien zur mittellateinischer Trostliteratur über den Tod und zur Problem der christlichen Trauer*, 4 vols. Münstersche Mittelalter-Schriften 3 (Munich, 1971).

*'Öffentlich' und 'Privat' im Mittelalter. Zu einem Problem der historischen Begriffsbildung*. Schriften der philsophisch-historischen Klasse der Heidelberger Akademie der Wissenschaften 33, (Heidelberg, 2004).

Morelle, L., 'Le Diplôme original de Louis le Pieux et Lothair (825) pour l'abbaye de Corbie. À propos d'un document récemment mis en vente', *Bibliothèque de l'École des Chartes* 149 (1991), 405–20.

Nahmer, D. von der, 'Die Bibel im Adalhardsleben des Radberts von Corbie', *Studi Medievali*, Ser. 3, 23 (1982), 15–83.

Nelson, J.L., 'Aachen as a Place of Power', in M. de Jong, F. Theuws and C. van Rhijn (eds.), *Topographies*, pp. 17–42; repr. in J.L. Nelson, *Courts*, XIV.

'The Annals of St. Bertin', in J.L. Nelson, *Politics and Ritual*, pp. 173–94.

'Bertrada', in M. Becher and J. Jarnut (eds.), *Dynastiewechsel*, p. 93–108; repr. in J.L. Nelson, *Courts*, IX.

'Charlemagne and Empire', in J.R. Davis and M. McCormick (eds.), *The Long Morning of Medieval Europe*, pp. 223–34.

*Charles the Bald* (London, 1992).

*Courts, Elites and Gendered Power in the Early Middle Ages. Charlemagne and Others*. Variorum Reprints (Aldershot, 2007).

'Dhuoda', in P. Wormald and J.L. Nelson (eds.), *Lay Intellectuals*, pp. 106–20.

'Dhuoda on Dreams', in C. Leyser and L. Smith (eds.), *Motherhood, Religion and Society in Medieval Europe, 400–1400. Essays Presented to Henrietta Leyser* (Aldershot, 2011), pp. 41–52.

*The Frankish World, 750–900* (London and Rio Grande, 1996).

'History-writing at the Courts of Louis the Pious and Charles the Bald', in A. Scharer and G. Scheibelreiter, *Historiographie*, pp. 435–42.

'The Intellectual in Politics: Context, Content and Authorship of the Capitulary of Coulaines', in L. Smith and B. Ward (eds.), *Intellectual Life in the Middle Ages. Essays Presented to Margaret Gibson* (London, 1992), pp. 1–4 (repr. in J.L. Nelson, *The Frankish World*, pp. 155–68).

'Kings with Justice, Kings without Justice: An Early Medieval Paradox', in *La giustizia nell'alto Medioevo (secoli IX-XI)*, Settimane 44, pp. 797–825.

'Kingship and Empire in the Carolingian World', in R. McKitterick (ed.), *Carolingian Culture*, pp. 52–87.

'Kingship and Royal Government', in R. McKitterick (ed.), *NCMH* II, pp. 383–430.

'Literacy in Carolingian Government', in R. McKitterick (ed), *Uses of Literacy*, pp. 258–96.

'Making a Difference in Eighth-century Politics: The Daughters of Desiderius', in A.C. Murray (ed.), *After Rome's Fall. Narrators and Sources of Early Medieval History* (Toronto ON, Buffalo NY and London, 1998), pp. 171–90.

'Ninth-century Knighthood: The Evidence of Nithard', in C. Harper-Bill, C.J. Holdsworth and J.L. Nelson (eds.), *Studies in Medieval History Presented to R. Allen Brown* (Woodbridge, 1989) (repr. in J.L. Nelson, *The Frankish World*, pp. 75–98).

*Politics and Ritual in Early Medieval Europe* (London and Ronceverte WV, 1986).

'The Problematic in the Private', *Social History* 15 (1990), 355–64, repr. in J.L. Nelson, *Courts*, IV.

'Public *Histories* and Private History in the Work of Nithard', *Speculum* 60 (1985), pp. 251–93 (repr. in J.L. Nelson, *Politics and Ritual*, pp. 195–237).

'Queens as Jezebels: Brunhild and Balthild in Merovingian History', in D. Baker (ed.), *Medieval Women: Essays Dedicated and Presented to Professor Rosalind M.T. Hill* (Oxford, 1978), pp. 31–77; repr. in J.L. Nelson, *Politics and Ritual*, pp. 1–48.

'The Search for Peace at a Time of War: The Carolingian *Brüderkrieg*', in J. Fried (ed.), *Träger und Instrumentarien des Friedens im hohen und späten Mittelalters*. Vorträge und Forschungen vom Konstanzer Arbeitskreis für mittelalterliche Geschichte 43 (Sigmaringen, 1996). 87–114.

'Was Charlemagne's Court a Courtly Society'? in C. Cubitt (ed.), *Court Culture in the Early Middle Ages: The Proceedings of the First Alcuin Conference*. Studies in the Early Middle Ages 3 (Turnhout, 2003), pp. 39–57; repr. in J.L. Nelson, *Courts*, XI.

'Women at the Court of Charlemagne: A Case of Monstrous Regiment?', in J.C. Parsons (ed.), *Medieval Queenship* (New York, 1993), pp. 43-61; repr. in J.L. Nelson, *The Frankish World*, pp. 223–42.

Noble, T.F.X., *Charlemagne and Louis the Pious. Lives by Einhard, Notker, Ermoldus, Thegan and the Astronomer* (University Park, Pennsylvania, 2009).

'Pope Nicholas I and the Franks: Politics and Ecclesiology', in R. Meens et al. (eds.), *Religious Franks*, pp. 472–89.

*The Republic of St. Peter. The Birth of the Papal State*, 680–825 (Philadelphia PA, 1984).

'Secular Sanctity: Forging an Ethos for the Carolingian Nobility', in P. Wormald and J.L. Nelson (eds.), *Lay Intellectuals*, pp. 8–36.

Patzold, S., 'Die Bischöfe im karolingischen Staat. Praktisches Wissen über die politische Ordnung im Frankenreich des 9. Jahrhunderts', in S. Airlie, W. Pohl and H. Reimitz (eds.), *Staat*, pp. 133–62.

'Eine "loyale Palastrebellion" der "Reichseinheitspartei"? Zur "Divisio imperii" von 817 und zu den Ursachen des Aufstandes gegen Ludwig den Frommen im Jahre 830', *FmSt* 40 (2006), 43–77.

'Einhard's erste Leser: zu Kontext und Darstellungsabsicht der *Vita Karoli*', *Viator Multilingual* 42 (2011), 33–56.

'"Einheit" versus "Fraktionierung". Zur symbolischen und institutionellen Integration des Frankenreichs im 8./9. Jahrhundert', in W. Pohl, C. Gantner and R. Payne (eds.), *Visions of Community*, pp. 375–390.

*Episcopus. Wissen über Bischöfe im Frankenreich des späten 8. bis frühen 10. Jahrhunderts*. Mittelalterforschungen 25 (Ostfildern, 2008).

*Gefälschtes Recht aus dem Frühmittelalter. Untersuchungen zur Herstellung und Überlieferung der pseudoisidorischen Dekretalen* (Heidelberg, 2015).
'Konsens und Konkurrenz. Überlegungen zu einem aktuellen Forschungskonzept der Mediävistik', *FmSt* 41 (2007), 75–103.
'Spurensuche: Beobachtungen zur Rezeption des Liberatus in der Karolingerzeit und im Hochmittelalter', in *Zeitschrift für Antikes Christentum* 14 (2010), 226–49.
'Überlegungen zum Anlass für die Fälschung früher Paptbriefe im Kloster Corbie', in K. Ubl and D. Ziemann (eds.), *Fälschung als Mittel der Politik?*, pp. 153–72.
Peltier, H., *Pascase Radbert, Abbé de Corbie. Contribution à l'étude de la vie monastique et de la pensée chrétienne au temps carolingien* (Amiens, 1938).
Pezé, W., 'Compétition et fidélité à l'épreuve de la guerre de succession, 840–843', in R. Le Jan, G. Bührer-Thierry and S. Gasparri (eds.), *Compétition. Rivaliser, coopérer dans les sociétés du haut Moyen Âge (500–1100)*. Collection Haut Moyen Âge 31 (Turnhout, 2017), pp. 141–65.
*Le virus de l'erreur. La controverse carolingienne sur la double prédestination.* Collection Haut Moyen Âge 26 (Turnhout, 2017).
Philippart, G., 'Vitae patrum. Trois travaux récents sur d'anciennes traductions latines', *Analecta Bollandiana* 92 (1974), 353–65.
Philippart, G., with M. Trigalet, 'Latin Hagiography Before the Sixth Century: A Synoptic View', in J.R. Davis and M. McCormick (eds.), *The Long Morning of Medieval Europe*, pp. 111–29.
Pohl, W., 'Creating Cultural Resources for Carolingian Rule: Historians of the Christian Empire', in C. Gantner, R. McKitterick and S. Meeder (eds.), *Resources of the Past*, pp. 15–33.
'Introduction: Strategies of Identification. A Methodological Profile', in W. Pohl and G. Heydemann (eds.), *Strategies of Identification. Ethnicity and Religion in Early Medieval Europe* (Turnhout, 2013), pp. 1–64.
Pohl, W. and V. Wieser (eds.), *Der frühmittelalterliche Staat – Europäische Perspektive. Forschungen zur Geschichte des Mittelalters* 16 (Vienna, 2009).
Pohl, W., C. Gantner and R. Payne (eds.), *Visions of Community. Community in the Post-Roman World. The West, Byzantium and the Islamic World, 300–1100* (Farnham and Burlington VT, 2012).
Polanichka, D.M. and A. Cilley, 'The Very Personal History of Nithard: Family and Honour in the Carolingian World', *EME* 22 (2014), 171–200.
Powell, J.G.F. (ed.), *Cicero the Philosopher: Twelve Papers* (Oxford, 1995).
Quadlbauer, F., 'Die genera dicendi bis Plinius d. J.', *Wiener Studien* 71 (1955), 55–111.
Raaijmakers, J.E., 'I Claudius. Self-styling in Early Medieval Debate', *EME* 25 (2017), 70–84.
*The Making of the Monastic Community of Fulda, c. 744–c. 900* (Cambridge, 2012).
'Studying Jerome in a Carolingian Monastery', in M. Teeuwen and I. van Renswoude (eds.), *The Annotated Book in the Early Middle Ages. Practices of Reading and Writing.* Utrecht Studies in Medieval Literacy (Turnhout, 2017), pp. 621–46.
Rädler-Bohn, E., 'Re-dating Alcuin's *De dialectica*: Or, Did Alcuin Teach at Lorsch?', *Anglo-Saxon England* 45 (2016), 71–104.

Reimitz, H., *History, Frankish Identity and the Framing of Western Ethnicity, 550–850* (Cambridge, 2015).

Rembold, I., *Conquest and Christianisation. Saxony and the Carolingian World, 772–888* (Cambridge, 2017).

Renswoude, I. van, 'The Art of Disputation: Dialogue, Dialectic and Debate Around 800', *EME* 25 (2017), 38–53.

'The Censor's Rod. Textual Criticism, Judgement and Canon Formation in Late Antiquity and the Early Middle Ages', in M. Teeuwen and I. van Renswoude (eds.), *The Annotated Book*, pp. 555–96.

Licence to Speak. The Rhetoric of Free Speech in Late Antiquity and the Early Middle Ages. Unpublished PhD thesis, Utrecht University (2011).

*The Rhetoric of Free Speech in Late Antiquity and the Early Middle Ages* (Cambridge, forthcoming).

Richter, M., *Bobbio in the Early Middle Ages. The Abiding Legacy of Columbanus* (Dublin, 2008).

Ripberger, A., *Der Pseudo-Hieronymus-Brief IX "Cogitis me". Ein erster Marianischer Traktat des Mittelalters von Paschasius Radbertus.* Spicilegium Friburgense 9 (Freiburg, 1962).

Röckelein, H., *Reliquientranslationen in Sachsen im 9. Jahrhundert. Über Kommunikation, Mobilität und Öffentlichkeit im Frühmittelalter* (Stuttgart, 2002).

Romig, A.J., *Be a Perfect Man. Christian Masculinity and the Carolingian Aristocracy* (Philiadelphia, 2017).

'In Praise of the Too-clement Emperor: The Problem of Forgiveness in the Astronomer's *Vita Hludowici imperatoris, Speculum* 89 (2014), 382–409.

Rose, V., *Verzeichniss der Lateinischen Handschriften der Königlichen Bibliothek zu Berlin, I: Die Meermann-Handschriften des Sir Thomas Phillipps. Die Handschriften-Verzeichnisse der Königlichen Bibliothek zu Berlin* 12 (Berlin, 1994).

Sassier, Y., 'L'utilisation d'un concept romain aux temps carolingiens: la res publica au IXe et Xe siècles', *Médiévales* 15 (1988), pp. 17–29.

Satoshi, T., 'La personnalité historique d'Arsène le Grand', in O. Kano and J.-L. Lemaitre (eds.), *Entre texte et histoire. Études d'histoire médiévale offertes au professeur Shoichi Sato* (Paris, 2015), pp. 367–73.

Savigni, R., '"Sapientia divina" e "sapientia humana" in Rabano Mauro e Pascasio Radberto" in C. Leonardi (ed.), *Gli umanesimo medievali. Atti del II Congresso dell' Internationales Mittellateinerkomitee* (Florence, 1998), pp. 591–615.

Savon, H., 'La première oraison funèbre de saint Ambrose (*De excessu fratris* 1) et les deux sources de la consolation chrétienne', *Revue des Études Latines* 58 (1980), 370–402.

Scharer, A., and G. Scheibelreiter (eds.), *Historiographie im frühen Mittelalter.* Veröffentlichungen des Instituts für Österreichischen Geschichtsforschung 32 (Vienna and Munich, 1994).

Scherer, C., *Der Pontifikat Gregors IV. (827–844). Vorstellungen und Wahrnehmungen päpstlichen Handelns im 9. Jahrhundert. Päpste und Päpsttum* 42 (Stuttgart, 2013).

Schieffer, R., 'Zur lateinischen Überlieferung von Kaiser Justinians Edictum de recta fide', *Kleronomia* 3 (1971), 285–302.

Schmidt, P.L., 'Zur Typologie und Literarisierung des frühchristlichen latei-
nischen Dialog', in M. Furhmann (ed.), *Christianisme et formes littéraires de
l'Antiquité Tardive en Occident*, Entretiens sur l'Antiquité Classique 23
(Genève, 1977), pp. 101–80.
Schmitz, G., 'Die Synode von Aachen (836) und Pseudo-Isidor', in Ph. Depreux
and S. Esders (eds.), *Produktivität einer Krise. Die Regierungszeit Ludwigs des
Frommen (814–840) und die Transformation des karolingischen Imperiums*
(Ostfildern, 2018), pp. 329–42.
'Verfilzungen. Isidor und Benedikt', in K. Ubl and D. Ziemann (eds.),
*Fälschung als Mittel der Politik?*, pp. 127–51.
Scholten, D., 'Cassiodorus' *Historia tripartita* Before the Earliest Extant
Manuscripts', in C. Gantner, R. McKitterick and S. Meeder (eds.),
*Resources of the Past*, pp. 34–50.
Scourfield, J.H.D., *Consoling Heliodorus. A Commentary on Jerome* Letter 60
(Oxford, 1993).
Screen, E., 'The Importance of the Emperor: Lothar I and the Frankish Civil
War', *EME* 12.1 (2003), pp. 25–51.
'Remembering and Forgetting Lothar I', in E. Screen and C. West (eds.),
Writing the Early Medieval West, pp. 248–60.
Screen, E. and C. West (eds.), *Writing the Early Medieval West. Studies in Honour of
Rosamond McKitterick* (Cambridge, 2018).
Semmler, J., 'Corvey und Hereford in der benediktinischen Reformbewegung des
9. Jahrhunderts', *FmSt* 4 (1970), 289–319.
Sharrock, A., *Reading Roman Comedy: Poetics and Playfulness in Plautus and
Terence* (Cambridge, 2009).
Shuger, B.K., 'The Grand Style and the "genera dicendi" in Ancient Rhetoric',
*Traditio* 40 (1984), 1–42.
Silk, E.T., 'Boethius' Consolatio Philosophiae as a Sequel to Augustine's
Dialogues and Soliloquia', *Harvard Theological Review* 32 (1939), 19–39.
Smith, J.M.H., 'Old Saints, New Cults: Roman Relics in Carolingian Francia', in
J.M.H. Smith (ed.), *Early Medieval Rome and the Christian West: Essays in
Honour of Donald Bullough* (Leiden, 2000), pp. 317–39.
Sotinel, C. 'Emperors and Popes in the Sixth Century: The Western Wiew', in
M. Maas (ed.), *The Cambridge Companion to the Age of Justinian* (Cambridge,
2005), pp. 267–90.
Steckel, S., *Kulturen des Lehrens im Früh- und Hochmittelalter. Autorität,
Wissenskonzepte und Netzwerke von Gelehrten*. Norm und Struktur 38
(Cologne, Weimar and Vienna, 2011).
Stofferahn, S.S., 'A New Majesty: Paschasius Radbertus, Exile and the Master's
Honour, in D. Blanks, M. Frassetto and A. Livingstone (eds.), *Medieval
Monks and Their World: Ideas and Realities. Studies in Honour of Richard
Sullivan* (2006), pp. 49–69.
Stone, R., *Morality and Masculinity in Carolingian Europe* (Cambridge, 2012).
Teeuwen, M. and I. van Renswoude (eds.), *The Annotated Book in the Early Middle
Ages. Practices of Reading and Writing*. Utrecht Studies in Medieval Literacy
38 (Turnhout, 2017).
Thibault, J.C., *The Mystery of Ovid's Exile* (Cambridge, 1964).

Traube, L., 'Prooemium ad Paschasii Radberti Carmina', *MGH Poet. lat.* III, pp. 38–45.

Tremp, L., *Die Überlieferung der Vita Hludowici imperatoris des Astronomus.* MGH Studien und Texte 1 (Hanover, 1991).

Ubl, K., *Inzestverbot und Gesetzgebung: Die Konstruktion eines Verbrechens (300–1100)*, Millennium-Studien 20 (Berlin, 2008).

Ubl, K. and D. Ziemann (eds.), *Fälschung als Mittel der Politik? Pseuodoisidor im Licht der neuen Forschung. Gedenkschrift für Klaus Zechiel-Eckes.* MGH Studien und Texte 57 (Wiesbaden, 2015).

'Einführung', in K. Ubl and D. Ziemann (eds.), *Fälschung als Mittel der Politik?*, pp. 1–17.

Uhalde, K., *Expectations of Justice in the Age of Augustine* (Philadelphia, 2007).

Van Nuffelen, P., 'The End of Open Competition? Religious Disputation in Late Antiquity', in D. Engels and P. Van Nuffelen (eds.), *Religion and Competition in Antiquity* (Brussels, 2014), pp. 149–72.

Verhulst, A.E., and J. Semmler, 'Les statuts d'Adalhard de Corbie', *Le Moyen Âge. Revue d'histoire et de philologie* 68, 1962, pp. 91–123, 233–269.

Verri, C., 'L'arte di ritratto. La descrizione del santo nella Vita Adalhardi di Pascaso Radberto, in J. Elfassi, C. Lanéry and A.-M. Turcan-Verkerk (eds.), *Amicorum Societas. Mélanges offerts à François Dolbeau pour son 65e anniversaire.* Millennio Medievale 96; Strumenti e Studi 34 (Florence, 2013), pp. 635–56.

'Il libro primo dell'*Epitaphium Arsenii* di Pascasio Radberto', *Bulletino dell'Istituto Storico Italiano per il Medio Evo* 103 (2001/2), pp. 33–131.

Vessey, M., 'Augustine Among the Writers of the Church', in M. Vessey (ed.), *Companion to Augustine*, pp. 240–59.

(ed.), *A Companion to Augustine* (London, 2012).

Vignodelli, G., 'Politics, Prophecy and Satire: Atto of Vercelli's *Polipticum quod appellatur Perpendiculum*', *EME* 24 (2016), 209–35.

Villa, C., 'Cultura classica e tradizioni langobarde tra latino e volgari', in P. Chiesa (ed.), *Paolo Diacono, uno scrittore fra tradizione langobarda e rinnovamento carolingio. Atti del Convegno Internazionale di Studi, Cividale di Friuli-Udine, 6–9 maggio 1999* (Udine, 2000), pp. 575–600.

'Die Horazüberlieferung und die "Bibliothek Karls des Grossen": zum Werkverzeichnis der Handschrift Diez B. 66', *DA* 51 (1995), 29–52.

'Terence's Audience and Readership in the Ninth to Eleventh Centuries' in A.J. Turner and G. Torello-Hill (eds.), *Terence Between Late Antiquity and the Age of Printing: Illustration, Commentary, and Performance* (Leiden, 2015), pp. 239–50.

Vocino, G., 'Bishops in the Mirror: From Self-Representation to Episcopal Model. The Case of Eloquent Bishops Ambrose of Milan and Gregory the Great', in R. Meens et al. (eds.), *Religious Franks*, pp. 331–49.

Voss, B., *Der Dialog in der frühchristlichen Literatur* (Munich, 1970).

Ward, E., 'Agobard of Lyons and Paschasius Radbertus as Critics of the Empress Judith', *Studies in Church History* 27 (1990), 15–25.

'Caesar's Wife: The Career of the Empress Judith, 819–829', in P. Godman and R. Collins (eds.), *Charlemagne's Heir*, pp. 205–27.

Wehlen, W., *Geschichtsschreibung und Staatsauffassung im Zeitalter Ludwigs des Frommen.* Historische Studien 418 (Lübeck and Hamburg, 1970).

Weinrich, L., *Wala. Graf, Mönch und Rebell: Die Biographie eines Karolingers.* Historische Studien 386 (Lübeck, 1963).

Weisweiler, J., 'Unreliable Witness: Failings of the Narrative in Ammianus Marcellinus, in P. van Nuffelen and L. Van Hoof, *Literature and Society in the Fourth Century* AD. *Performing* Paideia, *Constructing the Present, Presenting the Self* (Leiden, 2015), pp. 103–33.

Wellhausen, A., *Die lateinische Übersetzung der Historia Lausiaca des Palladius. Textausgabe mit Einleitung.* Patristische Texte und Studien 51 (Berlin and Boston MA, 2003; repr. 2016).

Werner, K.-F., 'Hludowicus Augustus: Gouverner l'empire chrétien – idées et réalités', in P. Godman and R. Collins (eds.), *Charlemagne's Heir,* pp. 3–123.

Whelan, R., 'Surrogate Fathers: Imaginary Dialogue and Patristic Culture in Late Antiquity', *EME* 25 (2017), 19–37.

Whitby, M., 'The Church Historians and Chalcedon', in G. Marasco (ed.), *Greek and Roman Historiography in Late Antiquity. Fourth to Sixth Century A.D.* (Leiden and Boston MA, 2003), pp. 449–95.

*The Propaganda of Power: The Role of Panegyric in Late Antiquity.* Mnemosyne Supplementum 183 (Leiden, 1998).

Wickham, C., 'Consensus and Assemblies in the Romano-Germanic Kingdoms: A Comparative Approach', in V. Epp and C.H.F. Meyer (eds.), *Recht und Konsenz im frühen Mittelalter.* Vorträge und Forschungen 82 (Ostfildern, 2017), pp. 389–425.

*Framing the Early Middle Ages. Europe and the Mediterranean, 400–800* (Oxford, 2005).

*The Inheritance of Rome. A History of Europe from 400 to 1000* (London, 2009).

Wilmart, A., 'Le recueil latin des apophtegmes', *Revue Bénédictine* 34 (1922), 185–98.

Wood, I.N., 'Entrusting Western Europe to the Church, 400–750', *Transactions of the Royal Historical Society,* 6th ser., xxiii (2013), pp. 37–74.

'Report: The European Science Foundation's Programme on the Transformation of the Roman World and the Emergence of Early Medieval Europe', *EME* 6 (1997), 217–27.

*The Transformation of the Roman West* (Leeds, 2018).

Wormald, P. and J.L. Nelson (eds.), *Lay Intellectuals in the Carolingian World* (Cambridge, 2007).

Yarnold, E. 'De Benedictionibus Patriarcharum Jacob et Moysi; Instrumenta Lexicologica', *Journal of Theological Studies* 45 (1994), 368–9.

Yavuz, N.K. 'Late Antique Accounts of the Trojan War: A Comparative Look at the Manuscript Evidence', in *Le manuscrit, entre écriture et texte. Première partie. Pecia* 17 (Turnhout, 2016), pp. 149–170.

Zechiel-Eckes, K., 'Auf Pseudoisidors Spur. Oder: Versuch, einen dichten Schleier zu lüften', in W. Hartmann and G. Schmitz (eds.), *Fortschritt durch Fälschungen? Ursprung, Gestalt und Wirkungen der pseudoisidorischen Fälschungen.* MGH Studien und Texte 31 (Hanover, 2002), pp. 1–28.

'Ein Blick in Pseudo-Isidors Werkstatt. Studien zum Entstehungsprozess der falschen Dekretalen. Mit einen exemplarischen Editorischen Anhang', *Francia* 28/1 (2001), pp. 37–90.

'Eine "unbeugsame" Exterminator? Isidorus Mercator und der Kampf gegen das Chorepiskopat', in *Scientia veritatis. Festschrift für Hubert Mordek zum 65. Geburtstag*, ed. O. Münch and T. Zotz (Ostfildern, 2004), pp. 173–90.

'Falschung als Mittel politischer Auseinandersetzung. Ludwig der Fromme (814–840) und die Genese der pseudoisidorischen Dekretalen'. *Nordrhein-Westfälische Akademie der Wissenschaft und der Künste, Vorträge: Geisteswissenschaften* 428 (2011).

'Florus' Polemik gegen Modoin. Unbekannte Texte zum Konflikt zwischen dem Bischof von Autun und dem Lyoner Klerus in den dreißiger Jahren des 9. Jahrhunderts', *Francia* 25 (1998), 19–38.

*Florus von Lyon als Kirchenpolitiker und Publizist. Studien zur Persönlichkeit eines karolingischen "Intellektuellen" am Beispiel der Auseinandersetzung mit Amalarius (835–838) und des Prädestinationsstreits (851–855)* (Stuttgart, 1999).

'Verecundus oder Pseudoisidor? Zur Genese der Excerptiones de gestis Chalcedonensis concilii', in *DA* 50 (2000), 413–46.

'Zwei Arbeitshandschriften Pseudoisidors', *Francia* 27/1 (2000), 205–10.

# General Index

Aachen
  palace of 153, 154, 193
  *see also* assemblies and synods
Acts of St Sebastian 106
Adalbert of Metz, count and duke 211
Adalhard, abbot of Corbie and Corvey
  as Antony 23, 132–133
  as monk and abbot 24, 34, 52–6
  as truth-teller (*assertor veritatis*) 48,
    103–105
  conversion 21–24
  exile 28–29
  family connections 20
  *Statuta vel Brevia* (822) 49
  Truth-teller (*assertor veritatis*) 48,
    103–105
  *See also* Corvey, foundation of
  *See also* Radbert, *Vita Adalhardi*
  *See also* Wala, and Adalhard
Adalhard, 'the Seneschal' 206, 211, 221
Adeodatus 85, 86–87, 89–90, 110, 111,
  128, 172, 190, 224
Agius of Corvey 92
Agobard, archbishop of Lyons 30, 104, 167,
  195, 222
  *Libri apologetici* 128, 160
Airlie, Stuart 6, 207, 208, 219
Allabigus 88, 114–116, 118
Alcuin of York 27, 38, 75, 92, 102, 132–133
Amalarius of Metz 33–34
Ambrose, bishop of Milan 124, 127, 138
  *De excessu fratris Satyri* 1, 7, 81–84, 186
  *De bono mortis* 81
  *De obitu Theodosii*
  *De obitu Valentiniani* 76, 79, 81
  *De officiis* 182–183
Amos (prophet) 124
Angilbert, *see* Fontenoy, battle of
*Annales Bertiniani* 220
Antony, *see* Adalhard
*Apophthegmata patrum, see Verba seniorum*
Arcadius, emperor 32

Arsenius, courtier of Theodosius and desert
  monk 31–32, 136
  *see also* Wala
assemblies and synods
  Aachen (816–817) 34
  Attigny (822) 30, 104–105, 215
  Aachen (828/9) 126, 193, 204
  Paris (829) 193, 200
  Compiègne (830) 159–162, 215
  Compiègne (833) 173
  Nijmegen (830) 161
  Thionville (836) 41
  Germigny (843) 63
  Ver (844) 196
  Epernay (845) 61
  Paris (846/7) 57–58, 134
  Quierzy (849) 42
  Attigny 854 147
  Astronomer, *Vita Hludowici* 158, 168, 207,
    217, 223
    On Wala 25, 28, 46, 47, 157, 161
Arsenius, *see* Wala
Attigny, *see* assemblies and synods
Augustine of Hippo 92
  and Terence 97, 117
  *Confessiones* 138
  *De doctrina christiana* 73–74, 122–124
  *De magistro* 86
*Augustus/Caesar, see* Louis the Pious

Balthild, queen 59
Benedict III, pope 59
Benedict of Nursia 33, 75
  *Rule* of 34, 96
Bernard, father of Wala and Adhalhard 20
Bernard of Italy 24, 30
Bernard of Septimania 40, 130,
  210–211, 218
  as Naso 145–146, 151–153
  *See also Epitaphium Arsenii*
Bernarius, brother of Wala, monk of Lérins
  20, 27, 29

257